NOTES

- great descrepancy among peop[...] Some are willing to risk death or b[...] fferent.
. One woman who responded ve[...] [...]vid about it. Another, less intense, was.
. Seeking intimacy not the only issue ~~since sele~~
. Masculinity (Femininity poorly or not defined in classical literature

Sexuality, Intimacy, Power

RELATIONAL PERSPECTIVES BOOK SERIES

Volume 22

RELATIONAL PERSPECTIVES BOOK SERIES

LEWIS ARON AND ADRIENNE HARRIS
Series Editors

Sexuality, Intimacy, Power

Muriel Dimen

THE ANALYTIC PRESS

2003   Hillsdale, NJ   London

The chapters herein published previously appeared elsewhere and are reproduced here, edited and revised, with the permission of their publishers:
Chapter 1—The engagement between psychoanalysis and feminism: A report from the front. *Contemporary Psychoanalysis*, 33:527–548, 1997.
Chapter 2—The third step: Freud, the feminists, and postmodernism. *American Journal of Psychoanalysis*, 55:303–320, 1995.
Chapter 3—On "our nature": Prolegomenon to a relational theory of sexuality. In: *Disorienting Sexualities*, ed. T. Domenici & R. Lesser. New York: Routledge, pp. 129–152, 1995.
Chapter 4—The body as Rorschach. *Studies in Gender and Sexuality*, 1:9–39. 2000.
Chapter 5—Between lust and libido: Sex, psychoanalysis, and the moment. *Psychoanalytic Dialogues*, 9:415–440, 1999.
Chapter 6—Deconstructing difference: Gender, splitting, and transitional space. *Psychoanalytic Dialogues*, 1:337–354, 1991.
Chapter 7—Power, sexuality, and intimacy. In: *Gender/Body/Knowledge: Feminist Reconstructions of Being and Knowing, ed.* A. M. Jaggar & S. Bordo. New Brunswick, NJ: Rutgers University Press, pp. 34–51, 1989.
Chapter 8—In the zone of ambivalence: A feminist journal of competition. In: *Feminist Nightmares: Women at Odds*, ed. S. Weisser & J. Fleishner. New York: New York University Press, pp. 358–391, 1994.
Chapter 9—Perversion is us? Eight notes. *Psychoanalytic Dialogues*, 11:325–360, 2001.

Published by The Analytic Press, Inc.
101 West Street, Hillsdale, NJ 07642
www.analyticpress.com

Typeset in Galliard 11/13 by Laserset, New York and Florida.

Library of Congress Cataloging-in-Publication Data

Dimen, Muriel
    Sexuality, intimacy, power / Muriel Dimen
        p. cm.—(Relational perspectives book series; v. 22)
    Includes bibliographical references and index.
    ISBN 0-88163-368-2
    1. Feminist psychology.   2. Dualism..   I. Title. II. Series.
    BF201.4.D556.2003
    155.3—dc21

                                                                    2003041945

Printed in the United States of America
10 9 8 7 6 5 4 3 2 1

For TL, who saw it then and sees it now.

Acknowledgments

Thanks, first, to the late Steve Mitchell for comprehending this book and agreeing to include it in the Relational Perspectives series; to Lew Aron, for agreeing to pick up where Steve left off and for helping me to see what I could contribute to general debate; to Paul Stepansky, for going ahead with the publication as well as for his astute comments on the Prologue; and to Adrienne Harris, coeditor with Lew of this series, for her editorial suggestions and friendship. My gratitude goes also to Natalie Kampen, Tom Lewis, and Sue Shapiro, who generously read all or parts of the manuscript and always gave useful, no-punches-pulled advice, critiques, and support. I am indebted to Eleanor Starke Kobrin, of The Analytic Press, for her humor, as well as her time and attention in seeing this project through, and to Elizabeth Budd for her careful and respectful copyediting.

Table of Contents

Prologue
A Personal Journey from Dualism to Multiplicity

But to look back from the stony plain along the road which led one to that place is not at all the same thing as walking on the road; the perspective, to say the very least, changes only with the journey; only when the road has, all abruptly and treacherously, and with an absoluteness that permits no argument, turned or dropped or risen, is one able to see all that one could have seen from any other place.

—James Baldwin, *Go Tell It on the Mountain*

What's Going on in This Book

This book might have had two introductions. One would capsule the book's ideas; the other would depict their expression. Intimacy of form and content here is precisely the point, however. I want to tell you how this synergy came to be. I certainly didn't plan it, but it didn't just happen either.

As I look back on the essays, which are rewritten as chapters in this book, I notice a tension. Old ideas were seeking new expression. New concepts jumped out of, and begged for, new ways of putting things. Experiments in form led to experiments in thought. Old questions found new answers, and these led to new queries. This introduction traces that tandem evolution of

1

thought and expression; if all goes well, a map of not only this book but its life and times will materialize.

Curiously, I can date my writing, but not my ideas. I can pinpoint the years when the university monotone into which I'd been initiated began to loosen into many tongues. But the questions on my mind—about gender and sexuality, about body, mind, and society, about the problem of dualism—have been with me as long as I can remember having a formed intellectual life. These questions are laced by patterns only retrospectively decipherable. Whether formally or substantively, the essays could not have anticipated each other.

No book is an island. The only way I can tell you how this book came to be is to sketch the historical and personal context for the original essays. What Carr (1961) said about historians still holds:

> Since Marx and Freud wrote, the historian has no excuse to think of himself as a detached individual standing outside society and outside history. This is the age of self-consciousness: the historian can and should know what he is doing [p. 186].

Carr's words anticipated the self-reflexive method that would emerge 15 years later in disciplines ranging from literary criticism to history to social science. Even eight years later, Carol Hanisch (1969) was to write "The Personal Is Political."

Perhaps this is a moment to stop and illustrate the sort of quandary—in this case, the Woman Question—that led to my writing experiments. You will have noted, of course, Carr's gendered language: the historian is "himself," "he," male. Absent is the other part of the gender dualism: she. Carr (1961) wrote his extraordinary primer, *What Is History?*, just before the androcentrism of language would be noticed; his book preceded by only two years the publication of Betty Friedan's (1963) *The Feminine Mystique* and Juliet Mitchell's (1963) *Women's Estate*. You couldn't have expected him to have noted the taken-for-granted binary of gender. But, even if you want to be relativist about his time and place, what do you do with his masculinist language? Language, analysts know, matters a lot. What you say or don't say makes all the difference in the world. Yes, writing "he or she" is clumsy; using three words where one would seem to suffice is stylistically dubious. But if readers (not to mention writers) don't see themselves reflected in what they read (or write), they become disaffected and disoriented, and maybe they don't learn or think as well or as much as they or we might like.

Perhaps, then (it began to dawn on me in the transitional cultural space of the later 1970s), your writing has to change. One way to do that, I discovered (or, at least for myself, invented), is to incorporate disjuncture into your style, just like the disjuncture you are reading right now. Breaking the literary frame opens a transitional space, a third (Ogden, 1994, p. 1) that belongs to neither author nor reader, where new experiences or thoughts may coalesce. And one method of disjuncture is to shift from your topic and address the reader, as I am doing now. After you've shifted into a different gear and driven as far as you need, you can shift back. Like right now.

This Book, Its Project, and Its Methods

Substantively, this book takes up great chunks of topic—sexuality, intimacy, and power—and it does so from three muscular perspectives—psychoanalysis, feminism, and social theory. Formally, it speaks not one but several languages—scholarly, clinical, ethnographic, vernacular, and personal—this heteroglossia (Bakhtin, 1934–1935, p. 63; see also Holquist, 1981, p. 428; Massey, 1996) being, of course, its own paradoxically singular voice. This book is also poised between audiences, addressed most immediately to psychoanalysts but talking to feminist and social theorists, too. Several keys are therefore necessary: a preview of form and content, a snapshot of the book's intellectual and cultural history, and a sketch of my personal journey from dualism to multiplicity. Given this interdisciplinarity, any given reader may find some ideas new and others yesterday's news.

Unifying this book's diversity is its commitment to working through the problem of dualism. Philosophers, says feminist philosopher Naomi Scheman (personal communication, November 25, 2001), use the term dualism to denote the idea that "some part of the world is divided into two kinds of stuff." You might sum up this idea with the phrase "either–or." Descartes, for example, posited two incommensurable realms of existence, *res cogitans* and *res extensa* (Scheman; P. Stepansky, personal communication, October 11, 2001): either/or and never the twain shall meet. But dualism is also a problem that, according to Scheman (1993), sets the core modern epistemological task: to identify and then bridge gaps, such as those between mind and body, masculine and feminine, psyche and society, and so on. My approach to this task is deconstructive, my form of argument is dialectical, and my perspective is one of contingency (Rorty, 1989). Because none of the chapters in this volume elaborates my method of analysis in so many words, I want to limn it in this introductory space.

The effort to transcend the either/or appears in all three of the fields that I call my own. Explicitly and implicitly, it has been my project in the essays and books I have written or coedited over the last two decades in anthropology, feminism, and psychoanalysis. Whether thinking about the relation between analyst and patient, or individual and society; the oppositions of gender; the varieties of sexual desire; or the disciplinary divisions of biology, psychology, and social theory, I have been seeking methods that do not commit us to reductions or determinisms, which is where dualism is likely to lead.

You need something—a "both/and" beyond the "either/or"— to bridge the gaps. You need a third term, toward whose creation (or discovery)[1] I take two routes. One is conceptual. Three polarities, each pair potentially confronted by a third, circulate throughout this book: mind–body, body–culture, culture–mind. Each of the book's three sections names three terms (I: "The Story So Far: Psychoanalysis, Feminism, and Politics"; II: "Mind, Body, Culture: Psychoanalytic Studies;" III: "The Personal Is Political Is Theoretical: A Sampler"). The chapters, for their part, take up the problem directly. Can we generate a way to discuss how such binaries do or do not interpenetrate? Chapter 6, for example, uncouples and tracks the binaries orbiting in relation to the contrast masculine–feminine and to each other as well—self–other, preoedipal–oedipal, infancy–adulthood, autonomy–dependency, superiority–inferiority, heterosexuality–homosexuality. More

---

[1] Between creation and discovery lies a blurry borderland, not a clear boundary. In a nondualistic world, would the absolute distinction between them fade?

generally, this book implies that interdisciplinarity is crucial to escaping dualistic handcuffs. A dialectic operates: anthropology and Marxism (or social theory) meet psychoanalysis; psychoanalysis and Marxism meet feminism; feminism and psychoanalysis meet social theory; and so on.

But it is not only what you say that changes things. It's how you say it. The medium is the message, went Marshall McLuhan's subversive 1960s sound bite. Stylistic unconventionality seems to me a way to shake up settled ways of being and thinking. Take traditional scholarly narrative. For more than 20 years, I have been both using and transgressing it. Even though all chapters in the book voice their share of academese, most (excluding Chapters 2 and 6) also chat informally, their pages dotted with slang and profanity. Here, as author, I am trying to engage the reader in any way I can. I mean this heteroglossia to get to you so that there emerges between us a third space of significance. And, like Sándor Ferenczi (1911), who found that his use of obscenity enabled patients to retrieve dissociated memories, I hope my use of demotic speech will spark in you an idea or experience either forgotten or, perhaps, not known before. My experiments in voice also show up via form. Each of the chapters in Section III speaks in two dissonant voices (fiction–theory; journal entries–afterthoughts; notes–commentary). Their goal is to produce a third voice in the reader's response, be it consternation, a feeling of reward, or a dream.

Less visibly, this book contains a certain redundancy or repetition, a feature familiar from psychoanalytic practice but not from psychoanalytic theory. Psychotherapy, I am fond of telling my patients, is not linear. It does not go from A to Z. Rather, it zigzags from A to B to Q to N to S, to B to A to L to Y and B, and so on.[2] As Sigmund Freud (1914) instructed, the patient

---

[2] On other occasions, I also say that therapy resembles a spiral that, whether ascending or descending, passes through the same points over and over again, even as these are viewed or experienced from a different position. This metaphor does not quite suffice either, because it suggests a regular sequence of sites to be passed through. The metaphor of the spiral, by the way, applies to more than the self. "The shape our knowledge takes is, in Piaget's (1970) metaphor, not the broad based, but the inverted pyramid; in Sartre's (1959) image, our perception of the world is an ever-widening and ever-rising spiral" (Dimen, 1976).

remembers the repressed, repeats it in the analytic relationship, and works it through, over and over again, by analyzing it. The process is necessarily circular; linearity appears only in retrospect: "from a knowledge of the premises we could not have foretold the nature of the result" (Freud, 1920b, p. 167).

Theory, I suggest, entails repetition and reworking, too. As in a therapy, however, the repetitions are always repetitions with a difference. Variously and multiply, theories and theorists rework (or "redescribe," as Rorty [1989, p. 7 and *passim*] puts it) the grand questions they share, each coming to different if related answers.[3] Likewise, this book sets out varied ideas, concepts, and conceits and then reapproaches them from a different angle in varied contexts: if you don't get it the first time, you'll have another chance.

Psychoanalysis Confronts Dualism

Psychoanalysts are no strangers to dualism. How could they be? Scheman's enigma may spring from the feminist critique of sexual difference, but, rooted in Western thought, it crops up everywhere. Many polar pairs line the psychoanalytic landscape—sexuality and aggression, consciousness and unconsciousness, transference and countertransference, analyst and patient, abstinence and gratification, neutrality and participation, intrapsychic and interpersonal, fantasy and reality. Dualism is a problem that therapists know in their bones, that academics have explicitly or implicitly theorized since Descartes, and that analysts are now beginning to work through.

Dualism often shows up as deadlock in daily clinical life. How often, for example, analyst and patient find themselves at loggerheads over an interpretation of the patient's past or a criticism of the analyst or, as is common now, a point of difference that has arisen in an enactment (Leary, 1994; Renik, 1996). Caught in a belief that only one of them can be right, analyst and patient have to struggle, alone and together, to find or create a place

---

[3] Until a critical shift in ideas occurs as the production of new knowledge potentiates a new constellation (Kuhn, 1972).

where their contradictions can live together. How hit and miss, how contingent, how "you-had-to-be-there" are such extrications.

Dualism is deceptive. It looks like‾two, but behind the two there is really only one; dualism dissolves into monism. Let me pause again for a minute to illustrate what I mean, because the deconstruction of dualism on which I embark in this prologue can be quite a useful tool, which I invite clinicians to share with me (and perhaps nonclinical readers will find a different sort of enlightenment in the clinical example). Analyst and patient may, for example, hold opposing views. The patient, say, feels ready to end the analysis, but the analyst believes the work is not yet done. Who is right? At the moment of confrontation, each holds that only one view is correct. Some analysts don't find this deadlock a problem. Stay or leave, they might say. If, in contrast, the analyst believes that analysis entails a meeting of minds, not a duel-ism of minds, what is to be done?   +

That a power struggle pops up as dualism is no accident. Dualism's separate-but-equal masks a hierarchy: the one behind the two is always on top. In the "tables of opposites" that have been around since the pre-Socratics (Naomi Scheman, personal communication, November 25, 2001)—for example, male–female, light–dark, reason–emotion, mind–body, nature–culture—one term is always implicitly better or higher than the other. Hence the usual deconstructive reading: a binary always conceals a hierarchy. Feminist philosophers make this point with regard to sex and gender. Irigaray (1985) argues "that the purportedly two are really one, as in 'husband and wife are one and that one is the husband'" (Scheman, personal communication, November 25, 2001). This construction renders the male the generic human being and voids the female of meaning.   ‒

Dualism, in this view, is always a setup. Complementarity is avowed, while the fight to the death is denied. Confronted with a polarity, we regularly want to know which pole is true. Does sexuality underlie human happiness and misery? Or is aggression the psychoanalytic *fons et origo*? Does it all start in the preoedipal phase or in the oedipal? Is psychic reality to be found inside or outside the mind? Is the origin of character intrapsychic or interpersonal, psychological or social, social or biological? In the end, the debate implicit in dualism presumes that there can be only one correct solution to any problem; determinism inhabits dualism. The battle is always over which of the two poles is right. Either/or.

One contemporary way out of the tight dualistic spot is to replace the "either/or" with the "both/and": "both," in the sense of both terms of the dualism; "and," in the sense of the two together and also in the sense of neither. Let me pause again to continue the clinical illustration. Patient wants to terminate, analyst thinks not. But instead of a struggle to the death, you, the analyst, accept the possibility that both are right, decide nothing about termination, and then go on to explore the meanings, for your patient, for you, for your relationship, and for the treatment, of the deadlocked wishes. Maybe the patient terminates, maybe not. But hay is being made while the sun still shines, meaning is mined and created, and the analysis does its work.

Solutions like this do not keep kosher; purity is not their concern. Nor do they position the truth somewhere between the extremes. Rather, they insist that truth is to be found in many places; as Jacques Derrida's (cited in Flax, 1990, p. 200) deconstructionist soundbite has it, there is "'too much truth.'" The both/and insists on having it all. Both parts of the dualism hold, but neither is the final answer, and there will always be other poles; there's always room for more. Which pole is the right pole? It all depends on context.

Psychoanalysis has begun to embrace what Scheman (personal communication, November 25, 2001) calls this "complexity, ambiguity, ambivalence, impurity." For some time now, psychoanalysis has been at the crossroads where two conceptual roads meet: a one-person psychology and a two-person psychology (Greenberg and Mitchell, 1983; Ghent, 1989). Schematically, a one-person psychology belongs to the classical psychoanalytic tradition as articulated, codified, and promulgated by Freud. The psyche consists of structures within an individual mind that develop according to inherent processes and stages. The notion of a two-person psychology originates in two postclassical critiques of Freudian thought. In the 1950s, Harry Stack Sullivan, on the American side, and Ronald Fairbairn, on Scottish shores, separately created bodies of thought and practice—interpersonal psycho-analysis and object relations theory, respectively—with a similar premise: because the relationship between people is key to personality development, the individual mind is structured by and made of personifications, or representations, of the earliest relationships one has known (Greenberg and Mitchell, 1983; Ghent, 1989).

Figuratively, a crossroads is a turning point. When you reach it, you make a decision: you choose to go left, right, or straight ahead (or, I suppose, back). Often enough, however, a crossroads proves just the right place to set up shop or settle down. Many a rural market has grown into many a big city at just such a spot. Settlers are joined by newcomers, new ideas variegate the old, inventions follow by accident or design. Psychoanalysis, at the either–or crossroads of a one-person and a two-person psychology, has decided to stop where it is, at the site of intersubjectivity. Interesting questions now populate the growing community. Emmanuel Ghent (1989) in fact insists that it is in the tension of this meeting point—this "both/and"—that analysts now need to work and, if their writings are any evidence, others seem to agree.

The idea of intersubjectivity functions as a third, registering the veridicality of the two psychologies. Subjectivity is both intrapsychic and interpersonal. Intersubjective processes—those at once within the individual mind and between different minds—inform psychic structure, character, health, illness, and, by the same token, the analytic process (Ogden, 1994, pp. 62–64 and *passim*). The contemporary clinical quandary is how to work simultaneously with both psychologies. The current theoretical controversy is how to conceptualize and actualize this paradigm shift. The solutions to both, it is turning out, will be plural, to work and theorize contingently depending on the context in which that work will have to take place. From dualism to multiplicity.

Psychoanalysts have been approaching these questions differently, often building on Winnicott's paradigm-shifting use of paradox to hold the tension of opposites. Mitchell (1993), for example, reconfigures paradox as the ambiguity inherent to psychic and interpersonal process (p. 57). Ghent (1992) applies paradox to clinical issues: sometimes, he proposes, the only solution to paradox is another paradox. Analyst and patient need to be able to survive the tension of knowing that, for instance, each loves and hates the other all at once. Benjamin (1998a, p. 34) deploys paradox developmentally: the capacity to recognize, entertain, and live with paradox is central to postoedipal development, particularly in regard to the inclusion of both masculinity and femininity in psychic gender repertoire. Others have dreamed up new metaphors for paradox. Working principally with dissociative processes, Bromberg (1998) imagines "standing in the spaces" within and between minds. The analyst treats the patient's impaired capacity to transit between conflicting states of mind—for example, the needs for stability and growth (p. 5)—as well as between clashing subjectivities—for example, the patient and analyst, the patient and early objects of attachment and desire. Pizer (1998), for his part, views paradox as negotiated by "building bridges"— intrapsychic bridges between states of mind (e.g., love and hate) or identifications (e.g., male and female), and intersubjective bridges between selves, especially analyst and patient.

A busy crossroads indeed. Call it, with Aron (1996, p. 10), a "transitional theoretical space."

Transitional space is, as Winnicott (1953) formulates it, a liminal state. An

> intermediate area of experience, unchallenged in respect of its belonging to inner or external (shared) reality, it constitutes the greater part of the infant's experience and throughout life is retained in the intense experiencing that belongs to the arts and to religion and to imaginative living, and to creative scientific work [p. 97].

In transitional space, both/and, not either/or, rules. The site of illusion, it is a one-person/two-person space. It is simultaneously internal (intrapsychic) and external (interpersonal), although within it these distinctions are senseless. There, where the impossible is conceivable, play and creativity are guaranteed for child and adult alike. For the child, transitional space is where you both invent and discover your parents, where you love them and destroy them and they survive, where you cannot tell who started the game. By extension, then, transitional theoretical space allows one, two, many theories to bloom. Excess is not too much. This book, with its multiplicity of voices and disciplines, tries to contribute such a both/and space to psychoanalytic praxis, for the reader as well as the author, a transitional space in which, as in the consultation room, surprise may be invited (Stern, 1997).

These psychoanalytic efforts at both/and may be summed up as attempts to create a third, which is the theoretical juncture at which this book enters. As Benjamin (2001) puts it, "The question of how we get out of complementary twoness, which is the formal or structural pattern of all impasses, is where intersubjective theory finds its real challenge" (p. 3). The elaborations and extensions of paradox, for example, fall under the rubric "the third"; paradox stands as the third term to the two terms of dualism. Once there are three, you have a conversation of multiplicity, not dualism—the sort of conversation found in this book, where each of the nine chapters speaks in its own way about the same problems all the others take on. The sociologist Georg Simmel (1950) argued, in his early 20th-century treatise on the building blocks of social life, that there were three primary social units: the monad or individual, the dyad or couple, and the triad. But the entrance of the third changed everything, he thought, and all subsequent social units were variations on the first three.

Philosophers traditionally theorize the third through the dialectic, a both/and that locates polarities in dynamic contest, not in static standoff. Dialectical method, although not unfamiliar in contemporary psychoanalytic thought, is variously interpreted. Attending principally to technical matters, Hoffman (1998), for example, works his way out of dualism by means of what he calls "dialectical constructivism." Defining the dialectic as "interdependence and interweaving" (p. xxi), he shows, for example, that although interpretive and noninterpretive interactions may be contraries, they are not, in the end, contradictory. In fact, they have meaning only in relation to one another.[4] You don't know, for example, how a treatment or a life will turn out; it all depends. This mutual, interdependent signification of the two terms creates a state of contingency, which, under the more affective name of "uncertainty," is a routine tension of analytic work.

Another psychoanalytic approach to the dialectic emphasizes the tension of contradiction. In Thomas Ogden's (1994) view,[5] "Dialectics is a process in which opposing elements each create,

---

[4] Hoffman (1983) applies the same mode of thought to the analyst's visibility and invisibility, to subjectivity and objectivity, the intrapsychic and the interpersonal, transference and countertransference, authority and mutuality, repetition and new experience, hierarchical structure and egalitarian free-play.
[5] Ogden (1994) works from the classical Hegelian model as interpreted by Kojève (1969) (not Marx's, 1867) dialectical materialism).

preserve, and negate the other" (p. 14). Here polarities are active, creating, destroying, and preserving each other.[6] Neither a standoff between mortal enemies nor a tapestry, this complex dynamic puts each of the two terms in an "ever-changing relationship to the other" (p. 14). Their relationship is inventive and contingent: what happens to each term depends on what just happened to the other and to the (transitional) space between them.

The outcome of dialectics is unstable. Hoffman's interweaving goes on forever. For Ogden (1994), "Dialectical movement tends toward integrations that are never achieved. Each potential integration creates a new form of opposition characterized by its own distinct form of dialectical tension" (p. 14). Such movement toward unfinished integrations is "the analytic third," the experience, comprehension, and narration of the shifting nature of the analysand's and analyst's mutual creation and destruction of the other. Ogden persuasively claims, in fact, that psychoanalytic conceptions of the subject, as well as of technique, are fundamentally dialectical (p. 7): for example, consciousness and unconsciousness each serve as an empty set to the other; neither makes sense without the other's existence.

It's been some time since I have paused in this prologue to address the reader. But I want, as a way of taking a breath and summing up before starting up again, to observe how tricky it is to escape from dualism. Let us say that we are persuaded that old-fashioned, either/or thinking does not suit our analytic or interpretive purposes. What do we do? Dualistic thinking would incline us to junk it and plump for the both/and. But this would be the same old, same old: behind the two is the one. A moment's reflection reveals that you can't have one without the other: there must be an either/or, two terms, in order that there be a both/and, a third. And what that third will turn out to be is contingent on the interaction in the either/or.

The third is no answer. It's just a moment in a process in which new possibilities are generated (Rorty, 1989, p. 108). Creating

---

[6] Also note the similarity to Winnicott's (1953) characterization of the self and other in transitional space. which Ogden (1994) considers the first completely articulated "dialectical conception of the intersubjective constitution of the decentered human subject" in psychoanalysis (p. 59).

new tensions, it calls for new resolution, because it becomes an either/or to yet another term. Dialectics, viewed this way, is an ongoing process that in principle, as Ogden suggests, never stops, even if, at any given moment, closure seems to have been reached. In actuality, psychoanalyses end: the patient terminates, carrying the analysis away, one hopes, in an idiosyncratic, personal fashion. Whether, to anticipate a theme in the next section, one can say the same of the dialectics of social life, is another question, and the results are not in. In the dialectics of psychic life, however, going from the either/or to the both/and is a voyage made repeatedly. This book is one of those voyages.

This Book and Its Many Histories

The third, dialectics, contingency—these are the three categories by which I want to conceptualize the thinking and the writing that went into the making of this book. The essays on which this book draws span a baker's dozen of years, 1989–2001, but their immediate history goes back twice that and more, their diversity issuing from a variegated past. This book's roots in intimate, intellectual, and cultural history entwine (as in Section III's title, "The Personal Is Political Is Theoretical"). My embrace of new expressive modes took place in the course of my intellectual travels among disciplines, my private encounters with my inner and interpersonal life, and my engagements with cultural and political events and their attendant ideas—feminism, the movement against the Vietnam War, the sexual revolution, and all the rest of the countercultural bequests of the Civil Rights Movement.

Anthropology

Long before I came to the dualism of psychoanalysis and feminism (the central focus of Section I), I was an anthropologist. Unconsciously, I was already undertaking the task that, years later, Scheman would set. Anthropological understandings of the relation between the individual and culture, for example, left much to be desired. The constructions of Margaret Mead and her student Ruth Benedict, to name the two most famous culture and personality theorists, or of Erik Erikson, who, from psychoanalysis, influenced them, seemed too mechanistic. Either they were additive (Sampson, 1993)—on one hand, the personal, on the other, the cultural—or they were symmetrical and static—the pattern of the personality matched the pattern of the culture. I learned that I wanted a stance that was less balanced and certain, more suited to tension and contradiction. I wished to escape the dualism between the psychic and the cultural.

I can see now as I look back that I was hankering for a methodological concept that has come to me only in recent years: contingency. And the value I find in it is best described by Rorty (1989). By contingency, I mean nothing more or less complicated than "It all depends." But on what? The "on what," as I will be articulating in this segment, is found in many third places. Writing of "the contingency of selfhood," for example, Rorty says, "Anything from the sound of a word through the color of a leaf to the feel of a piece of skin can, as Freud showed us, serve to dramatize and crystallize a human being's sense of self-identity" (p. 37). It all depends on where you were when. He elaborated:

Any *seemingly* random constellation of . . . things can set the tone of a life. Any such constellation can set up an unconditional commandment to whose service a life may be devoted—a commandment no less unconditional because it may be intelligible to, at most, only one person [p. 37; italics added].

The key word in Rorty's statement is "seemingly." In language and community, as well as in selfhood, what appears on the face of it to be random may not be random at all. It all depends on how you see it. There are multiple vocabularies, Rorty argues, for describing the same reality. As James Baldwin put it in the epigraph I used for this introduction, "the perspective, to say the very least, changes only with the journey." Perspectivalism suggests that it is impossible "to hold all the sides of our life in a single vision, to describe them with a single vocabulary" (Rorty, 1989, p. xvi). Viewed from afar, from above, below, or after the fact, causalities, consistencies, and determinations may be found in individual lives, in language, in social life. The reasons for my intellectual and literary choices emerge only when the fog of the moment passes. But even as I understand that systematic forces contour my own and anyone's social life and psychic process, I remain impressed with the "it-could-have-been-otherwise-ness" of it all.

My nearly obsessive interest in the relation between the mental and the material had an intellectual and political source. I was, as a graduate student in anthropology, very influenced by Marxist theory and its understanding of the distribution of power, or "class analysis." One of Marxism's principal problematics, or unresolved tensions, lies classically in the question of where social forms and social change come from. Is it history (what anthropologists call culture)? Or is it the individual? With a revolutionary insight, Karl Marx (1867) dissolved this impasse between materialism—the forces of History—and idealism—the forces of Mind. Human beings make their own history, he said, but they do not make it under conditions of their own choosing. We author our own destiny, except it never turns out as we envision because we are cultural beings whose environment consists of forces that, creating us, exceed us.

The similarity of Marx's paradox to Freud's will not escape the reader. But whereas Freud located those forces in the unconscious, in the interior world, Marx situated them in the external world. We are born into a culture, or socioeconomic formation, in whose eye, as the structuralist Marxist Louis Althusser (1971) was to put it, we are always already a gleam. Given this contingency, Marx held, it becomes imperative, in order to create a just and good life for all, to recognize what these forces are. If you understand them correctly, you can grasp the evolutionary tiller and steer the human ship toward its destination, the classless society.

Here, of course, is the great divide between Hegel's (and hence Ogden's) dialectic and that of Marx. The meeting of historical materialism and dialectical materialism predicts human fate. If you see history as a dialectical series of power structures progressing toward self-dissolution through their internal contradictions, if you see the working class and the ruling class as thesis and antithesis, whose clash ultimately creates the classless society, then you believe that the working class is the sole guide to the good society. Whether this is the case is a matter for continued debate in the wake of Eastern European Communism's demise, as well as of the 20th century's social movements around race and sex (Amariglio, Resnick, and Wolff, 1988; Laclau, 1988; Mouffe, 1988).

Still, we are not done with the either–or of the mental and the material. Marx's perception of their contingent relation contains a fruitful tension to whose mining I am devoted and out of which many thirds crystallize. Consider, for example, the title of Section II, "Mind, Body, Culture," which represents three instances of that tension. In the venerable debate between determinism versus free will, the provisional nexus of the mental and the material constitutes a third position, a dialectical negotiation between the powers of abstract, impersonal history and the powers of the person. C. Wright Mills (1959) and Jean-Paul Sartre (1959) recognize this philosophical juggling act when they argue that accounts of human life should always sit at the join of biography and history. That the value of Marx's thought depends on determinism yielding to contingency is an irony that has also inspired recent post-Marxist thinking, including Michel Foucault's, to which I return later. It is also a tension embodied and addressable by feminism and, as I have indicated, psychoanalysis.

The tension of contingency is hard to hold, as clinicians know all too well. You diagnose your patient, you think you know what to do. Yet diagnoses are but incomplete descriptions. The idiosyncratic details of any given case force you to rethink the categories you bring to, and the theories you construct from, each (Wolstein, 1975), and you tire from having to do it over and over again with each new patient or with each new day. One wants formulas, truths that hold universally definitive explanations, a clear this or that, not a fuzzy both/and. One wants to lay the tension to rest. One tends, as psychoanalysts say, to split. Dialectics collapses into dualism, tension into resolution.

Simplification by way of splitting snags Marxian thought too. Consider, for example, another distinction, according to which society's material "base" is said to determine its "superstructure" of ideas, beliefs, and mental life. Now, those familiar with Marxism's subtleties know that this dualism, although not absent from the theory, is a caricature. Nevertheless, like many a Freudian *reductio ad absurdum*—sex as the root of all neurosis—it has served as a shorthand whose grip on thought needs loosening. According to base–superstructure determinism, for example, the class into which you are born governs your economic future and your psychic state. But how does one explain the many familiar exceptions to "vulgar determinism"? We all know people who have gained (or lost) wealth and power despite (or even because of) the deprivations of their origins. You may even find yourself among them. If material determinism were the answer to the conundrum of history, how could people rise up against the conditions immiserating them, as they have done over and over again? How could minds change? How could patients ever get better?

How do you answer these questions in a way that preserves the breathtaking tension of Marx's insight? This challenge, which the content and form of this book are in part dedicated to meeting, presented itself to me when I was in graduate school (1964–1970, although I suspect it had been haunting me way before that). I could not know then, before I made the journey, what I can now see: solving the problem of vulgar determinism would entail not only refiguring the relation between the material and the mental, but rethinking the mental itself. Instead of "class reductionism," more recent interpretations of Marxism propose a multiplicity of "subject positions"(Mouffe, 1988, p. 90). Race, gender, sexuality, and other categories now join class in "overdetermining" individual and social life (Amariglio et al., 1988); having multiple determinants, personal fate, for example, can be understood from a variety of perspectives.

But subject positions are discursive as well as economic in character, origin, and effect. "Not a mental act in the usual sense" (Laclau, 1988, p. 254), "discourse" designates the unending negotiation of meaning, in which material things—like the money that makes the economy go 'round—also play a part. This negotiation can and must happen because meaning itself is multiple: in the Lacanian view, "a certain cleft, a certain fissure, misrecognition characterizes the human condition as such (Zizek, 1989, p. 2). This discontinuity, even division, founding human subjectivity creates a window for personal and social change. Because one's subject positions have their material bases as well as their personal, cultural, and historical meanings, one may, given the right circumstances, rework the subject position that one enters at birth, whether it is based on class, ethnicity, sexuality, or whatever. Out of our own psychic decenteredness—when we dream, we are not the same being as when we are awake—and our own plural subject positions, we can make more than has been dreamt of in many philosophies. Multiple self-states is an idea used by many relational psychoanalysts in their clinical and theoretical practices (e.g., Bromberg, 1996).

But that's now. Way back then, I was a dedicated materialist: there were single causes and single effects, single (class-based) positions, single meanings, and single explanations. Scientific clarity and certainty were all. Happy to find anthropology in (what I did not yet know was) the sunset of positivism, I applauded its claim to scientific standing and believed fiercely that cultural data could be studied objectively and laws of human nature derived therefrom.

The late Marvin Harris's (1968) brilliant, brash empiricist theory of cultural materialism ruled the day at Columbia University, where I was studying. The economic, indeed, the ecological basis of any given culture, was held to determine its system of kinship, its ladders of power, its color preferences, its dreams. Like any instance of vulgar Marxism, this base-superstructure theory admitted of few nuances. Its flatfootedness was timely and compelling, considering the brute social problems—poverty and starvation—that preoccupied us then.

Inspired by the civil rights movement, the university ethos of the 1960s–70s held this truth to be self-evident: the theoretical was political. A dualism was collapsing: the 1950s Cold-War shibboleth of science's neutrality was crumbling as the antiwar movement brought its political commitments to light. Graduate students and junior faculty, recognizing that systems of knowledge and structures of power interfaced, were going to put this recognition to good use by making thought relevant to social problems. In anthropology, theory was to focus not on what people say, but on what they do; not on their ideas but on their actions; not on pure ideals, but on the vulgar verities, like the physical violence of war and the social violence of injustice, that Americans were prone to deny. The hypocrisy supporting injustice was one target, not only of Marxist anthropologists but of the Students for a Democratic Society and its graduate and junior faculty counterpart, the New University Conference. People say one thing—for example, they write constitutions that declare all to be equal—and then do another—they segregate lunch counters and classrooms, disenfranchise African Americans, redline neighborhoods. To get at the truth, then, cultural materialist anthropology would examine only one pole of the mind–matter binary. If you studied people's materiality, not their ideality—the economic, ecological, and political conditions of culture—you'd get the hard data required for not only truth but also justice.

Materialism was, however, about to meet its negation. Positivism was, as I have intimated, on its way out. Uncertainty was on the way in, a subversive subtext in my graduate training. The image of the anthropologist as scientist contained contradictions that not only cultural materialism but also anthropological methodology overlooked. In the 1940s, Abram Kardiner and others had articulated the ethnographer's role as that of a "participant observer." (Sullivan, founder of the interpersonal school, borrowed this idea to characterize the therapist's position and activity.) But, as I practiced being the ethnographic observer who also participates, I came to understand that scientific objectivity was impossible. I was a subjective being, and so were my informants. A scientistic posture, moreover, reduced my humanity and aggravated my sense of perpetrating injustice. I felt like a thief. To aggrandize my own position in the world's dominant nation-state, I was taking data from people in one of its client states. "That's why the girl can sit on her ass for a year," snapped one woman in the Greek village I studied, "she has American dollars."

Surely I wasn't a thief, just as surely as I wasn't a scientist. But what was I? Dialectics soon (although not soon enough for my field research) came to the rescue. Being an anthropologist was a dilemma, not a profession, thought one of my professors, the late and all but forgotten Robert Murphy (1971). Ethnography "is the dialectics of reducing people to objects while trying to achieve understanding of them and of converting ourselves into instruments while struggling to maintain our identities" (p. 11).[7] A postmodernist *avant la lettre*, Murphy saw dialectics as a method and "philosophy for a period of dissolution in which firm verities are replaced by shifting mirages, in which predictability from the perspective of past expectations has been lost, and in which skepticism has become a mode of perception and not just of evaluation" (p. 4). It therefore suits practices of uncertainty, which include, notably, both anthropology and psychoanalysis. One must, as a participant observer, engage the objects of one's study. But if you talk with them, you must listen to them, see from their perspective. By implication, you need to decipher what happens in the space between what they say and what they do. Maybe people

---

[7] Inspired as much by Lévi-Strauss (1949), Simmel (1950), and Freud (1930) as by Marx (1867), Murphy's prescience prefigured not only the conditions spawning postmodernism but also the psychoanalytic use of it in dialectical (Ogden, 1994; Hoffman, 1998) and hermeneutic (Stern, 1997) theories.

don't do what they say, but maybe sometimes they do and maybe they also know a lot about the ambiguity between saying and doing.

Psychoanalysis

Mind, in other words, matters. Enter psychoanalysis and feminism—together, strangely enough (at least in my own life). Even as I was struggling with the mind–matter debate, help was on the way in the form of two new interlocutors. It was 1968, that signifier for the many disjunctures in cultural and political life that were to mark the last quarter of the 20th century. I'd just returned from my doctoral field research, found the campus in dazzling upheaval, joined my first consciousness-raising group and, a couple of months later, went into psychoanalysis. The ironies are delicious. My first bill from my first analyst remains in use as a bookmark for de Beauvoir's (1949) *The Second Sex*, published 19 years earlier. If psychoanalysis punctuated feminism for me, feminism has returned the favor and then some (as Chapter 1 recounts; see also Buhle, 1998).

Psychoanalysis, the premier disciplinary encounter with mind, is "a demand placed on Marxism," said radical psychoanalyst and educator Joel Kovel (1979). He was addressing the Group for a Radical Human Science, or GRHS, a short-lived organization of progressive psychoanalysts and psychotherapists.[8] This speech gave words to our need for a materialism conversant with the inner life. So many of us were caught between a rock and a hard place, having cut our left-wing teeth on a Marxist view of the world, but having embraced psychoanalysis for personal as well as professional reasons. We did not want to relinquish either of our two precious praxes, but we saw no way out of the seeming opposition between them. We felt open to both ways of viewing the world and tackling its problems but did not know how to make each open to the other.

---

[8] To which I and several current colleagues—Donna Bassin, Jessica Benjamin, Carole Bloom, Ken Corbett, Ann d'Ercole, Luise Eichenbaum, Virginia Goldner, Adrienne Harris, Daniel Hill, David Lichtenstein, Donald Moss, Susie Orbach, the late Adria Schwartz, Andrew Tatarsky, and Lynne Zeavin—belonged.

We were trapped in the reigning dualism: either mind or matter. Those working in mental health-related fields were the last of the New Left professionals to form intellectual and activist groups, and for good reason. For example, URPE, the Union of Radical Political Economists, had coalesced in the 1960s to formulate and disseminate disciplinary critiques of the ivory tower's relation to power. But, in New York City, radical psychoanalysts and psychotherapists congregated only in 1979 to form GRHS (a contemporaneous and more successful organization is the ongoing Institute for Labor and Mental Health, founded in San Francisco by Michael Lerner). Psychoanalysis, not being taught in the academy, came to most of us relatively late in our careers.

Nor, as I knew to my personal discomfort, was psychoanalysis in good political odor: its conformism (its 1950s adaptationism lasted into the 1970s) and its sexism (then under feminist critique) disgraced it in left-wing and feminist circles. At the time, politics were so polarized that if you were on the couch, it was thought that you had abandoned the barricades. I dared confide my guilty psychoanalytic secret to only one member of my consciousness-raising group, believing in my resentful heart that all the hypocritical rest were secretly in therapy. The exploration of one's private troubles seemed a shameful, individualist diversion from the urgent, collective project of struggling against forces of oppression. And psychoanalysis had not yet been reconfigured in those object-relational or Lacanian terms that presently in fact permit its integration with social theory and political concerns.

Left-wing resistance to psychoanalysis contained, of course, another, more common fear. "We are bringing the plague," Freud is said to have said to Jung (Fairfield, Layton, and Stack, 2002, p. 1). Psychoanalysis spotlights so much that most of us, including (at least some of the time) psychoanalysts, do not really care to entertain. Anyone who has been in analysis knows this darkness—the anxiety stirred up by unveiling unconscious secrets, the frightening I–thou intimacies of the therapeutic process, the unbearable doubt and uncertainty, the reencounter with trauma, the registration of unrecoverable loss. The willing surrender to a process with the examined life as its only apparent goal and with no end in sight, to put it in the extreme, is daunting. Who wants to disturb one's life for so speculative an outcome? Only those with no other choice, only those who can afford the expensive last resort of psychoanalysis.

Last resorts would seem to put you in the victim position. But the New Left wanted victims to be victors, identifying with the oppressed Third World and at the same time seeing itself as vanquishing the forces of oppression. A rationalism ruled (amid all that LSD). The meaning of life was clear and universal: if you organized in your own interests, you would win the war at home, where new Third Worlds—people of color, women, marginal sexualities—were being identified. (That the New Left correctly criticized psychoanalysis for its falsely universalizing narratives— e.g., the oedipal story—did not cause it to reflect on its own tendency to endow its particular meanings on everyone else.) The public world owned by bourgeois (straight) white men could, it was thought, be explained and changed by praxis, that is, by theory-in-action. If that project succeeded, then, in a base– superstructure way, the contradictions remaining in the private domain where women reigned would resolve themselves. The personal was political.

Yet home, we were finding out, is precisely where one's own interests are least clear. The political is, in fact, personal. Marxism, to put it more evocatively, or social theory, to put it both more broadly and more precisely, needed psychoanalysis. Psychoanalysis takes up where social theory leaves off (Rubin, 1975). It comes bearing gifts: the interpretation of desire and "personal meaning" (Chodorow, 2000) a theory and course of action in respect to the inner life, and a guide to the symbolic systems of both psyche and society. Although social theory anatomizes the conditions of daily working and civic life, it does not unravel the personal and interpersonal tangles of domestic intimacy (and with which, New Left women were realizing, it is women's traditional cultural business to traffic). Social theory leads right up to the bedroom door, to the hearth of family and psyche. Then it stops, defeated by the messy, tangled intangibles of domestic life, the same untidy interiority that constitutes the meeting of minds (Aron, 1996) that constitutes psychoanalysis.

So, by the time I began training at the Postdoctoral Program in Psychotherapy and Psychoanalysis at New York University (1979– 1983), it was clear (at least to those of us in GRHS) that social theory needed psychoanalysis. We also knew what psychoanalysis did not: it needed social theory. Psychoanalysis, for all its unprecedented insight into the psyche, would not and does not admit of the complementary demand. Try it out: Marxism is a demand placed on psychoanalysis. It doesn't quite work, does it? Effecting the policing that Foucault terms regulatory practice, psychoanalysis erects quite solid walls against social theory. In a power-driven, myopic refusal of interdisciplinary challenge, it validates only two kinds of speech, the dualism of the biological and the psychical. It discredits, in other words, the third term, the social (and by extension the political), which nevertheless slips in on the normative or, what is in effect the same thing, the universalizing.

But why shouldn't psychoanalysis answer to social theory? So this book in effect argues or, better, tells by showing. Marxism may have predated Freudianism by half a century, but it had quite a lively presence on the cultural and political scene in which Breuer and Freud (1893–1895) penned "Studies on Hysteria." Its vitality during psychoanalysis' later florescence in the 1920s and 1930s is documented in Jacoby's (1983) *The Repression of Psychoanalysis: Otto Fenichel and the Political Freudians*, which also tracks its disappearance during World War II and the Cold War.[9] Every subsequent theory of human beings, Daniel Bell is alleged to have said, has had to reckon with Marxism (just as, we might agree, every school of psychotherapy must do in regard to psychoanalysis). Even Freud was stimulated sufficiently by it or, at least, by the political movements and social criticism it animated, to write a number of cultural essays, including "Civilization and Its Discontents."

As I trained in psychoanalysis, it was quite evident to me that psychoanalysis and social theory could speak to each other. I just didn't know at the time in what language the conversation could

---

[9] Consider the psychoanalytic luminaries who, inhabiting this nexus, received their intellectual formation during an epoch heady with progressive politics and psychoanalytic creativity: Sándor Ferenczi, Otto Fenichel, Edith Jacobson, George Gero, and Annie Reich. Some, like Wilhelm Reich and Erich Fromm, kept pushing for synthesis. Sadly, others, like Fenichel, abandoned their politics (Jacoby, 1983). According to Jacoby's moving account, their yielding was impelled more by their Holocaust-driven escape to an anticommunist United States (with its medicalized and antiintellectual psychoanalysis) than by the inherent incompatibility of two cherished and imaginative comprehensions of human possibility.

take place. Interpersonalism, with its focus on the connection between analyst and patient, and its attentiveness to the lived history between child and parent and, later, to countertransference and the person of the analyst, seemed promising. But its muteness on intrapsychic complexity felt like an obstacle. Correctly, I perceived that object relations theory was the route (although a nondoctrinaire Lacanianism might have offered an equally useful path, as it is now doing [see Malone, 1995, and also *The Journal for the Psychoanalysis of Culture and Society*]). But when, in the late 1980s–early 1990s, there bloomed an array of dialects—grouped now under the signifier of relational theory—that might permit the complicated conversation I envisioned, I was ready for them: object relations theories of all stripes—classical, postclassical, and in between; self psychology; interpersonal theory; intersubjectivity theory.

And so the point is finally sinking in. Otto Kernberg (2000), spokesman for American classical psychoanalysis, now argues that psychoanalytic use of interdisciplinary study can breathe life into psychoanalytic education. He advises dipping into not only neuropsychological research but history and sociology. Kirsner (2001), relationist in inclination, similarly warns of the intellectual sclerosis that shuts down the flow of psychoanalytic theoretical and clinical practice by shutting out interdisciplinary challenges. Perhaps, some might say, Columbus discovered America. But perhaps each discipline must reinvent its own wheel. That neither of these essays refers to any earlier critique of psychoanalytic myopia (e.g., Kovel, 1981) manifests the regulatory problem they bring to our attention. That they do not specifically notice a chief contemporary conduit through which social theory's challenge to psychoanalysis has traveled issues from their participation in a chief regulatory agency: patriarchy (Aron, 1996; Stern, 1997; Pizer, 1998; Dimen and Harris, 2001; Dimen and Goldner, 2002).

Feminism

Reenter feminism, and, with it, the third term to psychoanalysis and social theory, and, as well, the trip from dualism to multiplicity. Feminism has had particular cause to complain of both psychoanalysis's refusal to acknowledge the power structures contextualizing it and social theory's refusal to acknowledge the inner life. If psychoanalysis is a demand placed on Marxism, then feminist theory obliges both to stretch for the universal truth to which each lays claim—and, in stretching, to recognize their limits. Historically, social theory focused on ordinary life, on the lived, material foundations of society, and the class structure built on them. Hence the third term of this book's title, *Power*. Following in close historical succession, psychoanalysis studied what social theory did not—the elements of inner life and their foundation in unconscious and intersubjective processes. Hence, the title's middle term, *Intimacy*. Neither discipline, however, comprehended the other's subject. The role of the intrapsychic in social life, the place of society in internal process—this dialectic emerged in both fields as a determinism, whether that of matter over mind or that of mind over matter.

Feminism picked up where social theory and psychoanalysis left off by addressing what they left out—the "Woman Question" and, with it, myriad others. Hence the first term of this book's title, *Sexuality*. If your perusal of human life includes the Woman obliterated by Mankind, you encounter what the remaining half of the world does, thinks, feels, and dreams, and you have to find a way to conceptualize it. Reciprocally, Woman leads on and back to vital, nearly untouched issues. Reclaiming the materiality of women's lives puts a new spin on old, often dualistically phrased debates about sexuality, the relation between subjectivity and social life, and human nature. Insofar as this inquiry is accompanied by a social movement—feminism—there arrive with it many social theorists and psychoanalysts who are also women and who are asking, from within their fields, questions that might have been asked before but never had to be or could be answered until the Second Wave of feminism.

The Second Wave's prime intervention is the critique of gender. Man, as explained in Section I, is historically the universal human being in both social theory and psychoanalysis. But as long as "Man" stands for "men" and "women," gender remains an invisible category and Woman a special one. Only when the Woman Question is raised does gender, and hence femininity and hence masculinity, become a problematic of general interest to both social and psychoanalytic theory.

Asking about Woman therefore cuts a number of ways. For one thing, it renders gender a critical tool to mediate between psychoanalytic and social theories. For another, it facilitates using those theories to reexamine and change both the psychology of gender and the social institutionalization of sexual difference. Women, gender theory recognizes, are represented by others, by themselves, and by culture as responsible for the life of the interior in a way that men are not. According to their traditional matrimonial and parental roles, women are meant to mind matters thought too trivial for the big heads of government and business. Femininity is to concern itself with the rearing of children, the running of households, the negotiation of interpersonal complexity.

Posed as gender theory, furthermore, the Woman Question brings up other, equally weighty differences of social hierarchy. In postmodern perspective, we have seen, the binary always hides a hierarchy. Masculinity and femininity sound like separate but equal parts of a balanced dualism, yet they are not. In public and private life, in job searches and appointments, in representational systems, masculinity still wins hands down. The dualistic "anatomical distinction between the sexes" has complex cultural correlates and elaborations, many of which are entangled in male domination.

The anatomical distinction, argue many feminist critics of classical psychoanalysis (Chapter 2 discusses the contributions of Karen Horney and Clara Thompson to this argument), has as much interpersonal and social as intrapsychic significance (see, e.g., Bernheimer and Kahane, 1985, on the Dora case). Psychically, it emerges in the matrix of the oedipal crisis, which is not only a matter of mind. It is equally and always a system of power in which the father dominates by laying claim to both his wife and his son (his relation to his daughter being not well theorized at all). This early patriarchal crucible of mental development is implicated in other power structures. Not only does patriarchy inflect the development of self, sexuality, and intimate relations. In a culture that uses difference as the nucleus of inequality, it laces class, race, sexual orientation, and ethnicity, creating gendered Selves and Others to whom similarities of political interest are strange; the strangeness of inequity, invisible; and inequity, inevitable.

Gender theory, we might put it, became the cup that runneth over. About 10 years into Second-Wave feminism, it began to be evident that gender, a contested category inscribed simultaneously in mental and cultural registers, demands to be seen from many perspectives. Gender is at once personal and social. Gender hierarchy is at once psychological, political, and historical. Patriarchy consists of a system of representations organized through symbols, beliefs, and mores. It is a structure that empowers and privileges men and women differently by assigning them, respectively, to dichotomized and differently evaluated public and private spheres. It instantiates heterosexuality as sexuality per se and imbricates it with power. Consequently, feminist theory not only insists that social and psychoanalytic theory take Woman and her implications seriously. It requires, perhaps in a way that no other discipline presently can, that these disciplines take account of each other, so that the relation between inner life and social process can be understood as the personal, idiosyncratic, and dialectically shaped event that it is.

Feminism is the third to Marxism and psychoanalysis. Arguably the legatee of the "Marx–Freud synthesis," it brings the political to psychoanalysis, the psychological to social theory.[10] But compatibility, if it is to obtain, must be dialectically refigured. If once we sought to fuse Freud and Marx, we now see, as this book proposes, that we need instead to make them talk to each other. To this end, they crucially need a third party, a third voice from a third place, to get them out of their dualistic deadlock, which is where feminism and multiplicity come in. Feminism contains a tension out of which multiplicity naturally grows. One pole of this tension insists on the "authority of personal experience." This ethic, forged in consciousness-raising groups, held that, no matter what you were told in speech and print about your place as a woman, your own perceptions of your own subordination and

---

[10] Early feminist interest in psychoanalysis dates back to the 1920s and 1930s, when many intellectuals and classically trained psychoanalysts sought to unite two of the three great and diverging arteries of 19th-century European thought, Marxism and psychoanalysis (Jacoby, 1983)—to put them in their chronological order; the third and temporally intermediate one is evolutionary theory, a critque of whose utility to psychoanalysis appears in Chapter 3.

capacities possessed as much authority as your parents' views, your clergy's doctrine, your professors' truth, your country's laws, your analyst's interpretations. By the same token, only by recognizing women's subjectivity could inner and outer experience be grasped in their intimate entanglements.

Curiously, feminist privileging of the authority of personal experience resonates with contemporary democratic developments in psychoanalysis. In the past, analysts saw themselves as authorizing patients to speak, helping them to find their authentic voices. A subtle shift has happened. Now many recognize the patient's authority as equal to their own (see Renik, 1998). This shift in power and paradigm has influenced my own clinical work, particularly my emphasis on countertransference (for example, in Chapter 5, in which, disclosed or not, it is narratively central, or in Chapter 4, in which its deeply personal side emerges in the universal problem of fecal odors in the waiting room).

The other pole of the tension in feminism insists on the radical, contingent difference of each woman's experience. Even as feminists sought to carve out a new category called Woman, Woman's coherence was disintegrating: there were simply too many of her. As women's historical and cultural and semiotic and intrapsychic variability came to the fore of feminist theory, Woman came to be a variably interpretable subject. Woman is not Woman, but women of different colors, classes, sexualities, politics, and so on. Woman has multiple, only partly commensurable histories and subjectivities. And, as she goes, so goes Man. Feminist investigations, sailing "the postmodern tide of uncertainty" (Benjamin, 1991, p. 278), question the possibility of any generally valid theory of subjectivity altogether.

From dualism to multiplicity. There's too much to say, wouldn't you agree? Notice the general public irritation with the cultural and legal requirements that not only gender, but also race and class be taken into account in, say, employment, journalism, or polite speech. Tenacious old prejudices, like racism, certainly figure into this rejection of "political correctness." But we might also be suffering what postmodernist literary critic Margery Garber (1992, pp. 16–17) calls a "category crisis." Consider the phrase "politically correct." Invented by the New Left to criticize its own rigid tendencies (e.g., Stalinism), it has, in one of those ironic twists of cultural fate, morphed into a weapon wielded by the right to condemn progressive politics.

But the popularity of the phrase also speaks to the troubles of dualism. There are now just too many new ways to think about society and too many new categories of person to think about. Familiar binaries can't cope. Garber (1992) argues that dualism falls apart as an organizing structure at just this sort of historical moment, when it can no longer represent the teeming mess of reality. Literature and painting register this disintegration through the unexpected figure of the transvestite, whose gender-bending thirdness is not the point but the means to represent the overflow of meaning (p. 17). As part of the general state of confusion, indeterminacy and contingency replace certainty and authority.

Time to shift gears again. To return to the personal part of this intellectual and cultural history, 1979 was such a moment of category crisis and excess, at least for me. It was when my writing cracked, the way Glenn Branca's Symphony No. 3 ("Gloria")[11] cracks about four-fifths of the way through, shifting from one plane of musical meaning, whose possibilities have been exhausted, to another. I was to participate in a forum, "Sex in History," cosponsored by the Mid-Atlantic Radical Historians Organization and the Coalition for Abortion Rights and Sterilization Abuse (CARASA), in which I was an activist. I was scared. I had too much to say and too little theory to do it with. I knew that sex was at once personal, political, and theoretical. I knew that it was a feminist matter. I knew it was a matter of the unconscious and of history and of practicality. How could I put it all—academics and activism; social theory, psychoanalysis, and feminism; mind, body, and culture—together?

I couldn't. So when a friend suggested that I write a set of notes, I gratefully obeyed. Unconsciously inspired by Susan Sontag's (1964) classic "Notes on Camp," the result of this proto-postmodern[12] experiment was "seventeen sexual propositions, or variety is the spice of life." Not only its provocative style but its novel form mirrored its thesis: sexual desire's variability, incommensurability, and mystery in, among, and between individuals, across time and place and disciplines as well. As such,

---

[11] *Music for the First 127 Intervals of the Harmonic Series.* Neutral Records, 1983.

[12] As Gayle Rubin (cited in Butler, 1994) characterizes her landmark "The Traffic in Women" (Rubin, 1975).

the notes appeared in the radical feminist journal *Heresies: The Sex Issue* (Dimen, 1981). The effort to publish them in a conventional scholarly venue is a story in itself; in response to academic critiques, I wrote several revisions in conventional essay format, only in the end to return to start and redo the piece as "Seven Notes for the Reconstruction of Sexuality" (Dimen, 1982). There had to be notes because there was no unified theoretical matrix for thinking about sex. Instead of a scholarly narrative that pretended to seamlessness, notes could register disciplinary fragmentation, question disciplinary boundaries, and indicate the "space between" in which something new might emerge.

Postmodernism

Postmodernism marks the voyage from dualism to multiplicity. It is distinguished not so much by a set of ideas as by a change "in the structure of feeling" (Huyssen, cited in Harvey, 1989, p. 39). Like any aesthetic, according to Harvey's (1989) dialectical argument, modernism harbored the seeds of its successor. "Real revolutions in sensibility can occur when latent and dominated ideas in one period become explicit and dominant in another" (p. 44). Modernism as an aesthetic movement oscillated in a tension, between, as Baudelaire thought, two poles: on one hand, "'the transient, the fleeting, the contingent,'" on the other, "'the eternal and the immutable'" (p. 10). How was this contradiction between flux and stability resolved? Through the Enlightenment's practical and philosophical answer: the idea of progress (p. 12). But this 18th-century optimism was shattered by the 20th century's moral, political, and technological catastrophes: "its death camps and death squads, its militarism and two world wars, its threat of nuclear annihilation and its experience of Hiroshima and Nagasaki" (p. 12). Emerging out of the chaos was, says Huyssen, "'a noticeable shift in sensibility, practices and discourse formations'" that came to be called postmodernism (cited in Harvey, 1989, p. 39).

Postmodernism is noted for its serious politics, multiple guises, absurdist style, and guerilla tactics. Reacting to modernism's technocentrism, rationalism, and commitment to absolute truth, it privileges difference, fragmentation, and indeterminacy. It maintains a great distrust of the social control impulse inherent in all universal, totalizing discourses (Harvey, 1989, p. 9). Its "central values—heterogeneity, multiplicity, and difference" (Flax, 1990, p. 188) mock attempts to define it. "Like the category 'feminist theory,' . . . 'postmodern philosophy' does not correspond to any actual or unified discourse" (Flax, 1990, p. 188). Rather it comes in many flavors: Derrida's ontology, Rorty's epistemology and the history of philosophy and Lyotard and Foucault's "relations between truth, power, legitimation, and the 'subject'" (p. 188). Thumbing its nose at authority, it regards all truth as the product of power struggles aimed at social control. Its specific critique of power is often indirect, its impudence twits academic self-importance, and its self-irony reveals the uncertainty and provisionality in all attempts at final truth. It nudges you to write in bits and pieces.[13]

Postmodernism having taken academic root during the 1970s, it's not surprising that, when, in 1982, I spoke to GRHS about women's subordination and its relevance for psychoanalysis, I found myself speaking in tongues. Feminism, I have noted, has always valorized the personal. But this "primal stew" (Rose, 1984) of ordinary life can't really be told linearly or abstractedly. You have to get right down in there, inside the activities of buying a carton of milk or changing your tampon or taking your estrogen or speaking to your boss or playing with your kids or fighting with your lover. And you have to show how gender hierarchy inflects each of these prosaic moments.

Trying to convey what it feels like to be a woman walking the streets of patriarchy, I wanted to register the cacophony of internal voices accompanying you in response to the sexism you routinely encounter as you go about your daily business.[14] For example, I

---

[13] It draws on multiple and intersecting disciplinary sources: the "rediscovery of pragmatism in philosophy, the shift of ideas about the philosophy of science wrought by Kuhn and Feyerabend, Foucault's emphasis on discontinuity and difference in history and his privileging of 'polymorphous correlations in place of simple or complex causality,' new developments in mathematics emphasizing indeterminacy (catastrophe and chaos theory, fractal geometry), the reemergence of concern in ethics, politics, and anthropology for the validity and dignity of 'the other'" (Harvey, 1989, p. 9).

[14] I was articulating, in my own way, what Tax (1968) had (we each, as I have said, may need to reinvent the wheel).

borrowed and fictionalized a friend's experience of sexual harassment in all its lewdness, intrusiveness, repulsiveness, and excitement. To render that complexity, I wrote not in notes but in different voices. In that second proto-postmodernist work, which evolved into what is now Chapter 7, I played with, mocked, and inverted both old conventions and new. I sent up not only psychoanalytic but feminist orthodoxies (for example, that women only hate and never love being sexually objectified). I played tricks on academically accepted, linear ways of putting all this serious tomfoolery.

That essay, "Power, Sexuality, and Intimacy," attempted to use disjuncture and juxtaposition to evoke, defamiliarize, and transcend the problem of dualism. Its splice of theoretical sections with personal anecdotes was intended to drop the reader into an unexpected space where the old might be seen anew. Concomitantly, it also argued that understanding sexuality and gender required a postmodern move: thinking on two tracks, social and psychological, at once. The high-theoretical synopsis of ideas that were to be spun out for a more general audience, that essay ironically received publication (Dimen, 1989) three years after my hybrid work of fiction and theory, *Surviving Sexual Contradictions* (Dimen, 1986), for which it was the working paper. But by the 1990s, academics' resistance to such novel(istic) forms had dissolved; formal and conceptual experiments were welcomed. One such experiment appears here as Chapter 8 ("In the Zone of Ambivalence: A Feminist Journal of Competition)." Originally written for a special issue of the *Union Theological Seminary Quarterly Review* on the then-unorthodox topic of aggression between women, it consists of a set of journal entries in response to which commentaries spin out.

What gained expression in those years in literary form emerged as content when I launched my psychoanalytic writing proper. If the way I said things in the 1980s was unconsciously informed by postmodern aesthetics, what I actually said in the 1990s sprang from postmodernist thought. In this, I was aided immeasurably by Judith Butler's (1990) prodigious *Gender Trouble*, which showed feminists how they might arouse the term gender from its complacent homogeneity. In Chapters 2 and 6, I trace "gender's" modernist origins and its postmodernist deconstruction. Combing through gender's tangles, I want to make its internal quality of differentiation known to a psycho-analytic audience, which, curiously, received that category at the moment of its dissolution (Harris, 1996c). Elsewhere, imagining the body as a Rorschach, I anatomize its several realities—psychic, cultural, gendered, political, and, as seen by Merleau-Ponty (1962), intersubjective (Chapter 4). Struck by psychosexuality's ambiguities in the popular and intellectual imaginations, I retheorize it through *Lust*'s doubleness in tension with libido's single-minded forward rush (Chapter 5). And, exploiting contradictions of psychoanalytic theory as well as sexual anxieties pervasive in clinic and culture, I probe the perversities of "perversion" (Chapter 9). —

Throughout, I am alert to the affinity between psychoanalytic and postmodernist technique. Deconstruction draws on psycho-analysis' method of reading between the lines. Turnabout being fair play, one may then direct deconstructive techniques to clinical and theoretical practices alike. Clinicians, I argue (see Chapters 3, 4, 6, and 8) can use postmodernist ideas and angles because, in fact, this is what they do every day. I want here to challenge Harris's (in press) deft statement that although we think postmodern, we practice in the Enlightenment (see also Fairfield, 2001). On the contrary, I would say that clinicians' ideas—for example, the self as self-identical and identity as coherent—may derive from the Enlightenment. But their listening process is postmodern. They listen as much for what patients do not say as for what they do, for what their dreams omit as for what they hold, for the gaps in their speech as for the continuities, for absent as well as present selves.

The Heterodox Frontier

To work in the intersection of social, psychoanalytic, and feminist theory is to operate in a series of *décalages*. You might think of *décalage* aesthetically. Imagine a parquet floor, with a pattern that repeats asymmetrically, its second instance beginning at the midpoint of the first. Or hum a round, a song pattern, such as, "Row, row, row your boat" or, if you're in a French mood, "*Frère Jacques.*" You sing the little song, then repeat. While you are singing the ditty's second line for the second time, someone else sings the first line. And when the second singer gets to the second repetition of the second line (and you are at your third repetition of the third line), the third singer starts off for the first time. And so on, round and round. The *décalage* from singer to singer and line to line is what makes the whole enterprise fun. Without this design for dissonance, which eschews Mickey Mouse symmetry, the song would rapidly bore.[15] The systematically staggered pattern, a constant renewal of an old design, makes things interesting.

Psychoanalysis absorbs changes in social and intellectual thought with "glacial speed," as Adrienne Harris (personal communication, 1995) has tartly commented. But the academy and feminism are equally stubborn, each in their own way. Psychoanalysts do not understand, I think, how indebted feminist thought is to social theory in general and Marxism in particular. They therefore have not reckoned how much, in hungrily incorporating gender theory and critique, they also will have to contend with social criticism (of, for example, power differences between men and women, between heterosexuality and other sexualities, and so on). Nor do they yet grasp postmodernism's debt to psychoanalysis.

By the same token, psychoanalysis' late recognition of feminism and postmodernism is matched by the academy's continuing refusal to acknowledge the contributions of clinical psychoanalysis. Eager to absorb the text-friendly reading methods provided by Jacques Lacan's linguistics-inspired theories, academics are comfortable with postmodernist detachment but uneasy with the consulting room's empathy-tuned intersubjectivity. As one professor joining a psychoanalytic feminist seminar said, with self-irony but real revulsion, "I don't want to have to help anyone." And, although feminism, for its part, may find itself more at home in the personal realm of caring and sharing, there is a danger, as I argue in Section I, that it will forget—or has forgotten—the political dimensions of its project, the problem of power in gender and sexual relations.

---

[15] It's a little like cross-modal attunement, which Beebe and Lachmann (2002) and Stern (1985) find so crucial to mother-infant self-in-relatedness, difference in sameness. Balance may be found but it is sequential or temporal (time constituting the third to the dualism of balance).

I want to conclude by noticing a tension inhabiting psycho-analysis, social theory, and feminism. Marxism and psychoanalysis share a focus on the truth beneath appearances, widespread in 19th-century thought and reaching into that of the 21st. Classical Darwinism argues that not the visible phenotype but the hidden genotype determines survival potential. So in Marxism it is not the observable contractual relations but the obscured class relations between individuals that shape their fates. According to psychoanalysis, our unconscious wishes and fears, not our conscious intentions, drive us forward, backward, and forward again. And postmodernism is nearly obsessed with absence to the exclusion of presence, with looking beneath, behind, between rather than at.

A special case, the feminist variant of this tension, may illuminate the others. As I discuss in Section I, feminism, like psychoanalysis, has two main but contradictory goals. One of these is ameliorative, the other revolutionary. This contradiction generates a tension, a paradox between the impulse to improve women's lives and the impulse to change them altogether. This tension appears in my thinking about women's lives, about the inequities of classism and racism, homophobia and sexism, about how to help my patients feel better. This contradiction does not trouble me, for it constitutes the problem of digging up the ground beneath your feet, a problem encountered in any situation of change, whether social or psychological.

I am, however, a little embarrassed by the contrast between my earnest, do-gooder wish to solve problems and my ironic sensibility. The contrast between earnestness or sincerity and irony is a poorly recognized tension in feminist thought. Earnestness—the wish to make things better—comes across as a mite naïve, in comparison to the world-weary sophistication of irony—the recognition that no good deed goes unpunished. In the tension, sincerity–irony, do we encounter the disjuncture between modernism and postmodernism? According to Marxist literary critic Terry Eagleton, postmodernism's irreverent rhetoric mingles with a schizoid style and "contrived depthlessness" (Harvey, 1989, p. 6). This habit of irony, while contrasting with self-deluding disciplinary claims to Deep Truth, also comes up short on depth. When compared with the passion of engaged politics and, we should add, of engaged psychoanalysis (see Benjamin, 1998;

Dimen, 2000), irony without compassion can ring a little hollow. The nihilism loitering around postmodernism ill suits clinically and socially progressive stances. Yet it is hard to relinquish the postmodernist point: one's Marxist utopianism and therapeutic zeal like as not blind one—me—to the inevitable backfire of the best laid plans. Enlightenment rationalism, some say, led straight to the 20th century's technofascism (Marcuse, 1955).

I seem unable to resolve this tension (this dualism of my own). Indeed, my difficulty in eliminating it may explain the literary forms—the third—I have chosen. Notes, fragments, dual and multiple voices (Merleau-Ponty, 1962), these heteroglossic forms permit a certain provisionality. A unified thesis is difficult to change, but you can always add another note. This flexibility is a good thing, because different languages, unveiling different features of reality, are differently useful (Rorty, 1989). Certainly, Chapter 9 ("Perversion Is Us? Eight Notes") reveals the contradiction between earnestness and irony in its strongest and perhaps most provisionally resolved form. There I approach the clinical and theoretical problem of perversion by thinking through a series of quotations from the psychoanalytic and culture theory literature and from my process notes. The chapter's note format demonstrates, I find myself hoping, that the only way to help my patient is by cleaving to postmodernist ironies. Here, perhaps Rorty's (1989) cooler understanding of irony helps: the "opposite . . . of common sense," irony means an awareness that one's language (he calls it vocabulary) is contingent and fragile, that the terms in which one describes oneself "are subject to change" (p. 74). I hope, in other words, that, in telling by showing, I negotiate the Scylla of cynicism and the Charybdis of Babbitry.

You never know. It may be that what I have been doing to resolve the tension is choosing not to resolve it. And perhaps that paradoxical choice is yet another provisional resolution of dualism. Both–and. In contemporary psychoanalysis, the relation between dialectics and paradox is not so clear. Maybe it is no longer so clear in social life either; perhaps there never was going to be, as so many believe and believed, a single, universal solution to economic injustice. For psychoanalysis, anyway, paradox may be how we presently understand contradiction (Benjamin, 1994, p. 93), and out of that understanding emerges contingency—

possibilities for multiple answers to old questions, varied solutions for varied problems on psychic and social fronts alike.

Why, anyway, should we have to choose? Earnestly recognizing that problems exist and invite solution, we might also keep in mind that solutions come and go. We could ironically reflect that, as poet Norman Fischer said at his installation as coabbot of San Francisco Zen Center, "There's no end to trouble." Or, like the late Stephen A. Mitchell (1986), we might borrow Nietzsche's metaphor of the sandcastle you build at the shore, knowing that the wave will knock it down but building and rebuilding it anyway. The triple crossroads of psychoanalysis, feminism, and social theory at which this book stops is only the most recent way of asking time-honored questions about sexuality, intimacy, and power that are nigh universal in the West.

According to the late Pierre Bourdieu (1977), each culture generates two kinds of question. On one hand, there are the questions that may be asked, those within the "doxa" or orthodox systems of knowledge. On the other, there are the questions that are commonly thought to be unaskable (and therefore not usually asked), those pertaining to "paradoxic" regions of knowledge. In any discipline, work can proceed within the received paradigm, to switch to Thomas Kuhn's (1972) instantly classic, but also unfortunately instantly clichéd characterization of Western science. Or, struggling to make the paradoxic intelligible, it can break through to the "heterodox" frontier, asking unconventional questions about the paradigm's odds and ends, which themselves furnish the raw material for new knowledge and new paradigms. Owen Lattimore (1951) held that cultural change tends to occur at cultural borders, the regions of Otherness where diverse ways of being, doing, and thinking meet, clash, mix, and change. In my work, I have been journeying toward and along that border. Here is a record of how I got there and what I found. Welcome to the border, to the heterodox frontier, where you think the unthinkable, speak the unspeakable, and ask whatever you want.

I

The Story So Far
Psychoanalysis, Feminism, and Politics

When I went to high school, my mother, or maybe it was my father's mother, told me that it didn't matter whether I got good grades. What mattered was that I asked good questions. I still think that's what it's all about: impertinent, fact-challenging, even preposterous questions. Facts change, as we see in Chapter 1's account of women's sexuality. But imagining the unimaginable in the face of familiarity's foreclosure, which Chapter 2 suggests is key to psychotherapy, takes thinking outside the box. Section I locates psychoanalysis, feminism, and social theory in their shared intellectual history. Positioning them as the mutual friends, enemies, and interlocutors they are, it sets forth the questions about sex and gender, mind and body, culture and politics that this book takes up.

1

The Engagement Between
Psychoanalysis and Feminism
A Report from the Front

> Now, in a line of associations ambiguous words (or, as we may call them, "switch-words") act like points at a junction. If the points are switched across from the position in which they appear to lie in the dream, then we find ourselves on another set of rails; and along this second track run the thoughts which we are in search of but which still lie concealed behind the dream.
> —Sigmund Freud, "Fragment of an Analysis of a Case of Hysteria"

Psychoanalysis Makes a Map

Toward the end of his hilarious *Small World*, which spoofs the international academic conference circuit, David Lodge (1984) constructs an antic scene that could not have been written had not both psychoanalysis and feminism pervaded academia in particular, and intellectual life in general. Angelica, a rising literary critic, is presenting to the Modern Language Association a paper on the genre of romance (the novel in which she appears is, after all, subtitled *An Academic Romance*). Rife with sexual reference, her essay reveals the woman who, at once central and marginal to psychoanalytic thought, has uneasily entered the psychoanalytic stage, glad to have joined the nervously welcoming company of players, but not wholly sure that it's a good idea.

Angelica's theory unfolds in terms whose debt to Sigmund Freud states itself:

> If epic is a phallic genre, which can hardly be denied, and tragedy the genre of castration (we are none of us, I suppose, deceived by the self-blinding of Oedipus as to the true nature of the wound he is impelled to inflict upon himself, or likely to overlook the symbolic equivalence between eyeballs and testicles) then surely there is no doubt that romance is a supremely invaginated mode of narrative [Lodge, 1984, p. 366].

Phallic. Castration. Oedipus. Need I say more?

No, but also yes. That I don't have to detail these terms appertains to the first point I am making. The parodic extreme of Angelica's theory dramatizes how necessary Freud's theory of sex is for contemporary literary criticism, to name but one of many fields of thought. Who can think about sex without thinking of psychoanalysis? Whence the language to discuss in public the erstwhile private parts of the body? Where did we get what literary theorist Harold Bloom (1986) has called the nearest thing to a cultural mythology that Western intellectuals share, the story of how you grow up, become a sexed creature? In teaching us how to speak about it, psychoanalysis may be said to have invented sex as we in the 21st century imagine we know it. Freud's theory of desire, his scheme of psychosexual stages (elaborated by Karl Abraham, 1924, into a well-known but terminally boring theory of normal sexual development), and his narrative of sexual conflict that, drawn from the origin myths of Western culture, claims to account fully for what we might call the normal neuroses of modern civilization—these constitutive ideas make up a culturally central story of erotic passion, which, by the same token, they also engender.

The intellectual salience of the Freudian psychosexual story—its capacity to bridge the culture–psyche dualism—does not mean, however, that it is always correct. Cultural myths regularly accent some truths at the expense of others. One truth Freud omitted or, better, mistook, was that of women. Since his time, many have risen up to correct his reading of human nature as though two genders were one, and male at that. Take the erogenous zones in psychoanalytic theory. "Oral," "anal," "phallic," and so on, designate bodily sites of arousal and chart stages of growth. At the same time, they map ideas and allegiances. Body parts operate in psychoanalytic theory much as they do in the unconscious, as "switch-words," to use the versatile metaphor for dream process that Freud comes up with in recounting his treatment of Dora. Freud's anatomical map of a brave new sexual world plots a passage that begins as though generic to *Homo sapiens* but ends in masculinity: in a failure of nerve, it inscribes things female on a "dark continent" (Gay, 1988, p. 501), a metaphor burying in femininity the underproblematized (white) racism of psychoanalysis (but see Abel, 1990; Doane, 1991; Gilman, 1995; Walton, 1995; Tate, 1996) and indicating yet another taken-for-granted dualism, white–colored.

The psychoanalytic map of sex is currently being redrawn. Angelica, following such thinkers as philosopher Derrida, uses, for example, the metaphor of "invagination," once a medical and now a literary term that describes

> the complex relationship between inside and outside in discursive practices. What we think of as the meaning or "inside" of a text is in fact nothing more than its externality folded in to create a pocket which is both secret and therefore desired and at the same time empty and therefore impossible to possess [Lodge, 1984, pp. 365–366].

Does invagination, as a concept, bear a slightly sexist charge? If so, Angelica deploys sexism against itself to redress the gender balance tipped, in theory as in life, toward men: "I want to appropriate this term and apply it, in a very specific sense of my own, to romance." She begins with a feminist critique: "Epic and tragedy move inexorably to what we call, and by no accident, a 'climax' and it is, in terms of sexual metaphor, an essentially male climax—a single, explosive discharge of accumulated tension" (p. 366).

In literary view, Angelica is saying that reading is like sex. But, she wants us to ask, whose sex? She knows that for all the feminist revolution, for all the social critiques of sexual prejudice, still, when we think sex, we think Freud: we use his ideas to think *with*, if only to correct them.

Angelica corrects. This classical psychoanalytic thinking about sex that so informs literary criticism usually has, she says, only one sort of sex in mind: male (and heterosexual male at that, although Angelica, or rather Lodge, isn't concerned with what is, for far too many, still too fine a point). Literary theorist and poet Roland Barthes (yes, there are a lot of French scholars in the story of psychoanalysis and feminism) also succumbs. He

> has taught us the close connection between narrative and sexuality, between the pleasure of the body and the "pleasure of the text," but in spite of his own sexual ambivalence, he developed this analogy in an overly masculine fashion. The pleasure of the classic text, in Barthes' system, is all foreplay. It consists in the constant titillation and deferred satisfaction of the reader's curiosity and desire—desire for the solution of enigma, the completion of an action, the reward of virtue and the punishment of vice [Lodge, 1984, p. 366].

Foreplay

Foreplay is that which Freud told you that you shouldn't spend too much time doing, lest you sicken. To reach adult health, you should relinquish the infant's omnivorous pleasure in nongenital zones, focus on penis and vagina, and achieve the correct and healthy aim of sex—discharge from penis into vagina. You split sex into two: healthy, single-minded intercourse between dichotomized sexes versus infantile, sickening polymorphous perversity that proceeds on its multiflavored way without regard to gender propriety. Oh, yes, health and normality have their tragic consequences. Instead of practicing perversities, we become normal, that is, neurotic (a psychoanalytic paradox perhaps better known in Europe than in the United States; see Chapter 3). In sexual terms, you must complete the action, climax the sexual story, survive *le petit mort*. Orgasm quenches the flames of foreplay but also, sadly, douses desire. Ordinary unhappiness is the price of civilization, and accepting it is the way one accedes to authority.

Angelica suggests, however, that at least one literary genre escapes the polarity between forepleasure and endpleasure. Not surprisingly, this genre's sexual style is, in her view, female.

> Romance, in contrast, . . . has not one climax but many, the pleasure of this text comes and comes and comes again. No sooner is one

crisis in the fortunes of the hero averted than a new one presents itself; no sooner has one mystery been solved than another is raised; no sooner has one adventure been concluded than another begins. The narrative questions open and close, open and close, like the contractions of the vaginal muscles in intercourse, and this process is in principle endless. The greatest and most characteristic romances are often unfinished—-they end only with the author's exhaustion, as woman's capacity for orgasm is limited only by her physical stamina. Romance is a multiple orgasm [p. 366].

"Romance is a multiple orgasm." It *is* funny, isn't it? What a clever parody. Too clever, however, by half. Angelica's critique, you see, slips up a bit. She, or rather her creator, David Lodge, who I think must begin to take his share of blame as well as credit here, forgets one tiny (although not always literally so) detail, a detail Freud didn't forget, although many other psychoanalytic theorists of sexuality do. Read on.

One of the young men [in the audience] said, if the organ of epic was the phallus, of tragedy the testicles, and of romance the vagina, what was the organ of comedy? Oh, the anus, Angelica replied instantly, with a bright smile. Think of Rabelais [p. 367].

We should all be so quick on our feet! But not quick enough. Angelica does not remember the one organ whose sole function is erotic, the one that we might call, in these computer-wise days, the dedicated sex organ. You know which one I'm talking about, don't you? (This is the teasing portion of the essay—the foreplay, if you will; it gets more serious, to the point, very soon. Just wait.) Yes. That's right. The clitoris. In literary theory as parodied in *Small World*, the clitoris, the organ of pleasure, has no genre of its own. Strange, isn't it?

Or perhaps not. The psychoanalysis on which Lodge, like other literary critics, relies is, you see, a psychoanalysis of the book. In the Book of Freud, which is what literary critics know best (even, perhaps, better than the clinicians who practice psychoanalysis and for whom, as is well known and to which I later allude, whole new sets of books have emerged), the clitoris occupies a secondary and immature place. In the Book of Freud the female sexual organ most, if not first, importance is the vagina. And thereby hangs a well-known tale (or, rather, no tail at all, which is, after all, the tale's point). In Freud's version, vaginal orgasm tops the scale of maturity and mental health; the clitoris is but an instrument to be manipulated (literally) so as to get the vagina to work.

Theories are often like dreams. Their meanings are as multiple, their language as ambiguous. Let us riff, then, on Freud's observations about dream interpretation in the epigraph to this chapter. In dream association, ambiguous words, or "switch-words," act like "points" at a railway junction: they shift the tracks on which the associative—or, in this case, theoretical and, as must already be obvious, political—train of thought travels. The clitoris is one such switch-word or, if you will, switch-point. Its task, "male" in its biological homology with the penis, is to transmit "excitation to the adjacent female sexual parts, just as—to use a simile—pine shavings can be kindled in order to set a log of harder wood on fire" (Freud, 1905b, p. 221). Log? Penis, he means. The real reason the clitoris must yield its excitement is not to pleasure the vagina but to ensure a warm welcome for the penis. Behind the dualism of clitoris and vagina lies, or stands, the one of the penis.

Feminists Make Waves

In 1968, 63 years and three generations later, those were fighting words. The magnitude of the recent feminist revolt against Freudian tyranny over the female body can be measured by the fact that, in 1990, this "strangely inappropriate identification of the cavity of the vagina with a burning log" could be called, in the cool, urbane sarcasm of the high road, "less than illuminating" (Laqueur, 1990, p. 235). Around 1970, however, when some women were very, very angry (of course, we're still angry, but now some of us often get to say so in print), the vaginal orgasm was officially declared a myth (Koedt, 1968).

The feminism of that time saw in the psychoanalytic construction of the female body the pernicious machinery of patriarchal power. Freud's definition of the clitoris as male organized women's sexuality for men's pleasure: the penis wants the female vagina, after all. The myth of the vaginal orgasm also served men's power:

as medical and political switch-point, it "emerged out of the long historical repression of female sexuality in the interests of men's control over women's reproductive capacities" (Segal, 1994, p. 36). Freudian psychoanalysis made women adapt to the repressive, oppressive, bourgeois role of accepting, compliantly smiling housewife and mother. Not only that. In a dialectical move of the sort that Foucault (1976) would later theorize, psychoanalysis secured a power base for itself: by debasing the clitoral orgasm, it aggravated the problem of frigidity that it then called on itself to cure (not bad for business, as Kate Millett, 1970, pointed out six years earlier). Buoyed by Masters and Johnson's (1966) empirical research that claimed to demonstrate a unitary orgasm, the second wave of feminism deposed Freud and (re)captured the clitoris.

How different from the first feminist response to Freud. Horney, who began her campaign in the 1920s, was angry, too. Her sarcasm was equally urbane and no less biting (e.g., Horney, 1926). Her arguments, however, were professional, not political. While she followed the sociologist George Simmel in noticing that psychoanalysis was part of a masculinist culture, she worked then from within the clinical psychoanalytic fold. Not chiefly interested in the clitoris, Horney wanted, instead, to rescue the vagina from its developmentally secondary place; unlike the second wave of feminists, she did not question its orgasmic primacy. She wanted to show that penis envy is not bedrock, that femininity is as primary as masculinity.

Horney, and, in other voices, Ernest Jones (1927) and Melanie Klein (1928), took on Freud's theory of phallic monism: all children believe there is only one sex—male—until that catastrophic recognition of lack, differently traumatic for each sex, that only men have penises; women do not. Surviving the cataclysm of castration fears and anxiety is, in Freud's (1925a, 1931, 1933) view, prerequisite to healthy, mature femininity and masculinity; on it, furthermore, rests his theory of desire, neurosis, and human nature. Horney (1933) contradicted: if boys are born boys, girls are born girls. The vagina's sensuality, at least equal to that of the clitoris, is demonstrably present from infancy onward. She concluded by arguing that "behind the 'failure to discover' the vagina is a [culturally motivated] denial of its existence"

(p. 160). Freud's (1933) response to this strong argument is tendentious, categorically stipulating the nonexistence of infantile vaginal sensations (Freud, 1933, p. 118). This preemptive strike not only foreclosed argument but hinged psychoanalytic legitimacy on belief in the dogma of phallic monism (Fliegel, 1986).

Although Horney's intervention was evidently not the final answer—nor, as we shall see, is there one yet—it was the first sign that the center of Freud's theory of sex, a red-hot manifesto for sexual liberation bound up by a blue-blooded scientific pedigree, doesn't quite hold. Psychoanalytic subversion contends, *tout court*, that humans desire. Psychoanalytic conformity insists that they procreate. The classic psychoanalytic theory of sexuality is torn between two masters, sex and reproduction, a conflict of loyalties whose contradictory effects are visited on women. In the classic psychoanalytic story, libido is always masculine; women, insofar as they lust—and indeed they do in Freud's account—are male. Female desire is defined, hence nullified, by procreation or, more precisely, by Freud's desire. Sex as reproduction was Freud's royal road to legitimacy: if the psychoanalytic theory of desire could be linked to the great chain of cause and effect running all the way back from biology and Darwin to physics and Newton, it would be shown to be true and could take its place in the noble roster of modern sciences.

Anatomy, or, rather, biology, was destiny—for Freud. There were two prizes in the battle between Freud and the feminists: one, overt, was female sexual subjectivity, the other, covert, was Freud's scientific legitimacy. He sacrificed the first to win the second, a sacrifice symbolized by the instrumentalization of the clitoris on the psychoanalytic map (that this strategy failed is the story, as I have indicated, of contemporary psychoanalysis and feminism). Hence his perhaps guilty exasperation in asking Princess Marie Bonaparte, "What does a woman want?" (quoted in Jones, 1953, p. 421). What his question disavowed, his affect acknowledged: Women do desire. They want sex. They need it. He knew it, and he dissociated what he knew.

Surely this dissociation of women's sexual desire registers the shock of feminism. Freud's theories of women, as well as his asides on feminists, are littered with splitting and contempt, the defensive strategies characterizing the divided mind variously termed hysterical, borderline, or dissociated. Think, for example, of

Freud's (1931) famously weird reference to "the fact" of female castration that, if faithful to fantasy, nonetheless splits off the factuality of female anatomy (p. 229). Recall his manipulative and condescending exemption of women analysts from femininity: the negative features of femininity did not, he said, apply to them, they were exceptions, "more masculine than feminine" (Freud, 1933, pp. 116–117). Remember his rage at the nameless lesbian, for whose unnecessary "treatment" he tried to account (she was "in no way neurotic"; Freud, 1920b, p. 158, n. 2) and whose ire he explains by jibing, "In fact, she was a feminist." It is she whose gender he changes, in a midparagraph pronominal slip of the pen, from female to male (pp. 150–151; see Harris, 1991, who was the first to note this slip).

Three's Company

One might say that Freud's dissociation of women's desire renders feminism a ghost come back to haunt psychoanalysis (and it is to tell you about this that I have sketched the fight between Freud and Horney, who serve here less as actual historic intellectuals than as switch-points to intellectual history). Get rid of women as active desiring subjects, solve the "enigma of womanhood" (Freud, 1933) by equating femininity with passivity, and you get rid of feminism. It's that simple—and that complicated. Women's desire, and feminism, are not forgotten, they are disavowed; they are dissociated, not repressed. When we dissociate, or more precisely, when we projectively identify, we attempt to eliminate something that belongs to us by projecting it into some other being or thing, we next feel it was never part of us in the first place, and then we have it return to us as the other whom we hate with a debilitating passion. The dualistic strategy of hiding the two behind the one always backfires.

All of this suggests that there was something for psychoanalysis to get rid of. And there was. The early psychoanalytic world was, equally, a feminist one; the late 19th and early 20th centuries were the temporal home of first-wave feminism. Horney may have been Freud's specific target (Freud, 1925a, 1933), but she was only one of many advocates of women's desire in the psychoanalytic orbit. The pseudonymous Anna O, Josef Breuer's patient who is said to have invented "the talking cure," was Bertha Pappenheim, a founder of German Jewish feminism (Jackowitz, 1984). Other feminist contemporaries adopted and revised varied portions of the psychoanalytic understanding of women's desire (Anderson, 1992). Later luminaries in the arts, like H.D., sought out Freud and others for surcease of psychic suffering.   ❧

I am proposing a dialectical view: psychoanalysis and feminism come in a package. Psychoanalysis and feminism are causes (as both labeled themselves; see Alexander, 1992) with much in common, such as their "questioning of the moral status quo," and much to fight about, like their conceptions of femininity (Anderson, 1992, p. 73). Between the two lies a complicated tension. Their paradoxical engagement consists in their inter-implicated evolutions. Each, of course, has its Enlightenment pioneers, for example, the Marquis de Puységur for psychoanalysis (Ellenberger, 1970, pp. 70ff.) and Mary Wollstonecraft for feminists. As full-blown movements, however, psychoanalysis and feminism are creatures of the 19th century. Embroiled, they not only constitute one another, they have never lived apart; to wit, the timing and context of Freud's antifeminist remarks "make it unclear whether it was he himself or feminists who first chose to make psychoanalysis a center of ideological struggle" (Chodorow, 1989, p. 175). Just as psychoanalysis synthesizes and articulates in one convenient place the ruling ideas of patriarchy, thereby constituting both an attack on women and a means for feminism to deconstruct sexist ideology, so feminism exists as a pressure on psychoanalytic thought (Rubin, 1975). Conversely, the predominance of female patients suggests a diagnosis of psychoanalysis as "itself a symptom of women" (Forrester, 1992). Not only, then, should we restore to psychoanalysis its opposite number, but, as I am about to suggest, we need to recognize how, together, psychoanalysis and feminism triangulate with social theory.

If psychoanalysis plots desire, it also records a changed and changing sexual landscape, whose alterity alters it. The "dark continent" had already begun to explore herself by the time Freud declared her Man's terra incognita. Exploration continued after him, now enhanced by a scientific imprimatur of desire that, nevertheless, required women's masquerade as a good wife, dutiful daughter, or token woman (Rivière, 1929). What went around came around: Two generations later, feminists addressed a different sexuality than Freud and Horney. Indeed, the Second Wave's focus on women's sexuality, departing from earlier bourgeois feminisms, is likely a psychoanalytic legacy (see also Delmar, 1986, p. 27). As Freud's first feminist critics pushed him to articulate his misrepresentation of women's sexuality, his assumption that women want and need sex reciprocally reconfigured erotic experience together, if only by speaking the hitherto taboo truth. Sex having become speakable, women then had a public language in which to say that they knew something about their own pleasure that Freud had denied (Laqueur, 1990, pp. 233–243). If Horney gave them back the vagina, they could then reappropriate the clitoris. As I suggest later, maybe it's not too late to have both.

In principle, however, psychoanalysis and feminism were at a standoff until, in the late 1960s, a third term broke the polarized tension between them. Social theory, to put it more broadly, or Marxism, to put it more evocatively, gave feminism what it needed to counter psychoanalytic misogyny: the idea that the Woman Question had a history and a future. Woman's place, her desire, even her erotic anatomy were contingent. So were Man's. Historically constructed and socially contextualized, the battle between the sexes was cultural, not a natural phenomenon. And there's more: it was a matter of power. Sex was political. Desire, and all the theories analyzing and regulating it, could be understood in political terms. As women and men were not equal, so women were of different classes and races, differences that correlated variously with family structure, gender role, and sexual possibility. All that psychoanalysis took for granted about the human sexual question became, suddenly, destabilized. The governing narrative of psychosexual development, the familial frame for subjectivity, the culturally central arrangements for the heterosexualization of desire, these could now be called into question.

Fortified with social theory, feminists could turn to psychoanalysis for what they needed. And need it they did. Although social theory illumines the political dimension of their sex, it only flirts with the personal. Yet, as feminists soon saw, "the personal is political" holds especially for them, insofar as women's lives are defined by the personal in a way that men's are not. Social theory unveils women's social role. But it does not unpack those interpersonal, personal, and intimate matters historically deemed women's business. Enter psychoanalysis, bearing interpretations of women and desire, a theory and course of action in respect of the inner life, a construal of early object relations, and a way into the representational processes composing the symbolic systems of both psyche and society.

In a now triangular space, feminist theory mediates social theory and psychoanalysis, challenging both to exceed their premises. This triangulation completes a historical process. As Jacqueline Rose (1986) also argues, it continues a project, the "Marx–Freud synthesis," begun in the 1920s and 1930s and then largely suspended during World War II and the Cold War. The project uses psychoanalytic insights into interior life to understand, in order to alter, "the internalization, effectivity and persistence of some of the most oppressive social norms" (pp. 6, 8). The debate over psychoanalysis and politics (for which Freud's quarrel with the Marxist psychoanalyst Wilhelm Reich may perhaps here stand as a symbol) coincided with that over women, but the two controversies were not to engage until a half century later:

> It is rather as if the theoretical/clinical debate about female sexuality and the more explicitly Marxist debate about ideology and its forms were historically severed from each other—at least until [second-wave] feminism itself forged, or rather, demonstrated, the links [p. 8].[1]

With the exception of de Beauvoir's (1949) *The Second Sex*, all important contemporary feminist accounts of psychoanalysis emerge from this one historical and political moment—the Women's Liberation Movement, when, taking de Beauvoir's prescience to the next level, the personal is political came also to mean that the personal is theoretical and that the theoretical requires validation by the personal (Chodorow, 1989, p. 213).[2] Works by hostile critics such as Shulamith Firestone (1970) and Millett (1970), as well as by admiring critics and revisionists, such as Gayle Rubin (1975) and Juliet Mitchell (1974), respectively,

---

[1] This coincidence is not surprising. See Prologue, note 9.

[2] If a single paper can be said to represent this moment, it is Rubin's (1975) "The Traffic in Women," in which Marx, Freud, Lévi-Strauss, and Lacan are all

primed, in the early 1970s, the psychoanalytic feminist effort to explain how "ideological processes are transformed, via individual subjects, into human actions and beliefs" (Rose, 1986, p. 7). Between Rubin's (1975) work, which launched contemporary gender studies, and Mitchell's (1974), which facilitated the anglophone-feminist appropriation of Jacques Lacan's theory of sexed subjectivity, lies a field of tension that holds the contemporary encounter between feminism and psychoanalysis.

Enter Foucault, Laughing

Which feminism, however? one might ask. Which psychoanalysis, for that matter? Psychoanalysis and feminism each may have begun as one thing: psychoanalysis saw to the psyche, feminism to women. As they traversed the 20th century, however, the tides of change swept through them. The fault lines behind their internal uniformity[3] opened into a montage of interests, theories, practices, and constituencies. The meeting of practices, say, of feminism, psychoanalysis, and social theory, produces new ideas, new allegiances and alliances, new enemies. Now there are many feminisms: white, black, Third-World, Jewish, socialist, Marxist, [grassroots], liberal, cultural, structural, [academic, lesbian, heterosexual], psychoanalytic and so forth" (de Lauretis, 1990, p. 116). Likewise, as the psychoanalytic century has worn on, many psychoanalyses have materialized: (neo)Freudian, object-relational, interpersonal, self-psychological, ego-psychological, Lacanian, Kleinian—one could go on—as each splinter group schisms yet again. From dualism to multiplicity.

---

hoisted on their own petards in the service of both illuminating and calling for a new theory of what she then called the "sex/gender" system. Mitchell (1974) argued contemporaneously that this theory was at hand; Lacan would provide the means to route Marx through Freud, so that women's sub-ordination might be explained. Later, Rubin (1984) redivided sex from gender, arguing for distinct, if mutually implicated, theories of each.

[3] On North American shores, for example, feminism already possessed fault lines dividing abolitionists and their adversaries.

So many voices, so little time. The noisy frontiers of psychosexual theory are a deconstructionist's delight but a rapporteur's nightmare. The report from the front must, then, be brief, a headline or two. For one thing, body parts no longer have quite the same place on the psychoanatomical map. In fact, they're hardly corporeal or sensate at all. Take, for example, penis envy (not, of course, that anyone would want to). In psychoanalytic thought, the penis was once a biological organ that little boys had and little girls wanted. Many objects, especially cigars, symbolized it. Not anymore. Now Freud's penis has become Lacan's (1955–1956, 1958) phallus, which stands for (a pun that is always intended) what all want and none can have: to be the object of mother's desire, an impossible state of grace and power accorded not even to father—it's *your* mother, not his own, who desires him, after all. That Lacan claims this law of desire as the true account of human culture is, as I suggest presently, a misleading bit of politics.

For now, the next headline: Never fear, mother is here. A near-absence in the Freudian corpus and still a wordless void in Lacan's cosmology—from which Julia Kristeva (1982, 1983) and, in other registers, Janine Chasseguet-Smirgel (1986) and Joyce McDougall (1995) try to rescue her—mother elsewhere receives the mark of psychoanalytic distinction, a symbol of her own. Thanks to Klein, who answered Freud's (1931) wish by excavating the "Minoan-Mycenean" stratum beneath the oedipal floor and finding there even more primal origins for civilization's discontents than Freud had thought (Klein, 1981), the breast now rivals the phallus. Klein and, perhaps more dramatically and certainly more accessibly, D. W. Winnicott (1975), both synonymous with object-relations theory, have created a new primal scene: one's first trauma is not the sight of father screwing mother but the feeling that the good breast has turned sour—a mother absent or too present, actively bad or just so plain wonderful that all you can do is hate her for the unbearably intense love she inspires.

Phallus and breast, however, are incommensurate. Even if mother has joined father at the head of the psychoanalytic table—or, rather, at separate tables, because Lacanian and object-relational theories do not really translate—different is not the same as equal This inequality is not quite a matter of paternal power. Men's unconscious awe of maternal power may indeed underlie, as

Dorothy Dinnerstein (1976) contends, the near-universal degradation of the feminine, perhaps undergirding their grip on public power. Femininity, moreover, is not passive (as Freud recognized in a famous footnote, 1930, p. 105, n. 3) but active, even, as Adrienne Harris (1989, 1997) writes, aggressive, sometimes similarly to men but also, as Carol Gilligan (1982) and Jean Baker Miller (1976) propound, differently.

Still, femininity remains, here as everywhere, the marked category. That psychoanalytic gender, explicated by Irene Fast (1984) and Ethel Person (1980), corresponds to gender injustice remains a knotty theoretical and, among clinicians, professional problem. Male and female belong to a gender hierarchy that privileges masculinity, which, in turn, has unconscious correlates that, Virginia Goldner (1991) explains, require not only decoding (a task furthered by academic psychoanalytic feminism) but also healing. By promising to lead to sexual health, developmental accounts of how girls grow up to become what boys are not, and vice versa, serve also as moral recommendations. Analysts, educators, and parents need Jessica Benjamin's (1988b) object-relational reworking of penis envy: the sense of inadequacy girls feel in the absence of paternal recognition has its partner in the repudiation of femininity that, as Nancy Chodorow (1978) shows us, engenders both masculinity as conventionally constructed and the "oedipal asymmetries and heterosexual knots" of marital intimacy.

Description, however, is often also prescription. Psychoanalytic and feminist theory slip between registers, between what is and what ought to be. In each, you can find yourself talking about one when you meant to be talking about the other. Many have noted theory's swivel-hipped action, not least Foucault (1976) in his answer to Marx. Domination, he explains, hinges only in part on capital and other material advantages. People also imprison themselves with a little help from their friends, Freud's (1925b, p. 273) three "impossible professions"—education, government, and psychoanalysis. If oppression consists in the force of law backed up by the force of arms, domination depends on what people tell themselves, both consciously and unconsciously. What we tell ourselves, however, draws on a matrix of assorted claims to truth These claims are established and reproduced by disciplinary institutions with participants who produce the knowledge systems underlying modern power regimes, work in which they take enormous pleasure (think of the intellectual enjoyment in the practices, both clinical and theoretical, of psychoanalysis).

Domination derives from constructed cultural practices—what Foucault terms "regulatory" practices—that, willy-nilly, people believe reveal the truth about themselves, their lives, their value, and therefore about the systems that produce those truths. Domination practices achieve this effect, suggest Italian anarchist, Antonio Gramsci (1929–1937), and French socialist theorist, Pierre Bourdieu (1977), by impressing the psyche at the level of the body, by what Bourdieu terms "symbolic domination." Hence, the centrality of sex, identified by Foucault as the modern pre-occupation. Indeed, the more nonverbal the symbolic, the greater its power. In contrast to, say, military discipline, in which constraints are overt, symbolic domination "is something you absorb like air, something you don't feel pressured by; it is everywhere and nowhere" and therefore nearly impossible to get away from (Bourdieu and Eagleton, 1992, p. 115). Entering silently through such significant psychosocial arteries as posture and gait, or through the prelinguistic semiosis of tone, rhythm, and prosody, linked by Kristeva (1983) with the Lacanian Imaginary and the maternal, domination is what one may fairly call a sadomasochistic fusion of power, knowledge, and pleasure that forges the very hearts and minds it engages, thereby securing body and soul so as to make the modern state run. As psychoanalytic feminism has begun arguing with regard to social conventions of female desire (Dimen, 1986; Benjamin, 1988b; and see Chapter 9), escaping one's own need of, loyalty to, and pleasure in domination practices, like any revolution, requires a special effort analogous to the problem, familiar to any clinician, of relinquishing a bad object.

The challenge is to remember the political while retaining the psychical. With one not-so-small quibble, one could agree with Rose's (1986) elegant phrasing of the problem:

> The difficulty is to pull psychoanalysis in the direction of both these insights—toward a recognition of the fully social constitution of identity and norms, and then back again to that point of tension between ego and unconscious where they are endlessly remodeled and endlessly break [p. 7].

The quibble is power: the social construction of desire is also political, a nuance that psychoanalysis resolutely denies in aid of its own institutional strength. In psychoanalytic colloquy, "politics" is a signifier sure to evoke the response, "But that's not psychoanalysis." It's like the old song: I say "tomay-to," you say "tomah-to." I say "political," you say "not psychoanalytical." Psychoanalysis entertains only two legitimate bases for speech, the biological and the psychical. It excludes, in other words, the social, which nevertheless sneaks back into discourse in the service of the normative or, what is effectually the same thing, the universal.

By suggesting a relation between power structures and the unconscious, Lacanian thought seems to meet this challenge. For Lacan (1977), building on structural linguistics as developed by Ferdinand de Saussure (1916) and Roman Jakobson (1962), whose work together led to Claude Lévi-Strauss's (1949) midcentury structuralism, sex is a place in and a matter of language, but language is itself a matter of law and culture. To be (psychically) sexed is to speak, to become a person, and to enter culture, all in the same terms. Butler (1992) puts it this way: "Whereas [in object-relations theory] gender appears to be a cultural determination that a pre-existing subject acquires, sexual difference [in Lacanian theory] appears to constitute the matrix that gives rise to the subject itself" (p. 140; see also Mitchell, 1991, who, like other Lacanian feminists, refuses the term gender, which Freud never used at all). Subjectivity is primally and multiply split, its coherence founded in a linguistic fiction, a single sex: one is either male or female. Alternative sexualities lost through this dualizing fiction endure, unremembered but unforgotten, perceptible only in "the gaps, silences, absences in speech" (Alexander, 1992, p. 109) to which therapists attend so closely for clues to pain, or in the abject spaces of a heterosexist culture, where culture critics such as Butler (1995) locate a marginalized and dissociated homosexuality that haunts mainstream heterosexuality with the melancholy of its loss.

Yet Lacanian theory defaults on its promise. It indicates the necessary discontinuities, prohibitions, and losses of sex. Its pointer, however, remains the phallus, an obdurately male symbol that eclipses female desire. True, the theory of the phallus as the (appropriately named) master signifier of desire, sanity, meaning, and culture, describes awfully well how patriarchy works[4] or, at least, how it represents itself as working (Bowie, 1991, p. 130). No one has yet adequately explained, however, why the phallus has to be the human key symbol.[5,6] We must agree with Elizabeth Grosz (1994): "the relation between the penis and the phallus is not arbitrary but is clearly socially and politically motivated" (p. 322). Grosz precedes this remark by insisting that "feminists cannot afford to ignore the a priori privileging of the masculine within [Lacan's] account, nor can they too readily accept Lacan's claim that the phallus is a signifier like any other." Jane Flax (1990) makes a similar argument using a slightly bizarre metaphor that is, however, appropriate to her subject:

> Lacan's claims that the phallus exists purely upon a symbolic plane, that it does not signify penis, and that any relationship between signifier and signified is arbitrary[,] are disingenuous. Would we be persuaded by Lacan if he claims that the mother lacks, say, "mouse" or that her desire for the child is to be the "waxpaper?" [p. 104].

The phallus is not a universal, but rather the ideology, the theory and practice, of patriarchy.

The final headline from the front, then, is this: If mother is here, can women's desire be far behind? The breast is a switch-point to mother's desire, not yet women's. And the phallus, I suppose, switches us to infinity. Lacanian theory, so subtle about desire's fluidity, uncertainty, and intractability, is remarkably certain about women's subjectivity. Female desire's unspeakability may describe its own social erasure: "Only the concept of a subjectivity at odds with itself gives back to women the right to an impasse at the point of sexual identity, with no nostalgia whatsoever for its

---

[4] Rose (1982) claims this putative veridicality as the principal reason that feminists should adhere to Lacan.

[5] A "key" symbol is an element of meaning (which would include what Lacanians call signifiers) that, in ethnographic perspective, simultaneously expresses and creates a culture's central ideas, describes and prescribes its values and behavior (see Ortner, 1973).

[6] Not only does Lacan shore up Freud's patriarchy, he strengthens it by eliminating the biological determinism clouding Freud's account. The phallus is not the penis, or so he insists: "The importance of the phallus is that its status in the development of human sexuality is something which nature cannot account for" (Rose, 1982, p. 40; but see Flax, 1990).

possible or future integration into a norm" (Rose, 1986, p. 15; see also Dyess and Dean, 2000). To represent that effacement by a falsely universal symbol is, however, to prescribe the practices of misogyny as timeless, fixed. But women's desire is, I am saying, not a single thing. It is many and as such gives the lie to the phallus. Even if object-relational gender theory (re)presents the normative structures it means to deconstruct, to theorize gender as social construction is still to index its historical multiplicity. It is to reveal the ambiguity, difficulty, and elusiveness of women's desire as the alternate truth of anyone's desire—present and absent, flaring, doused, flaming up again.

Encountering Paradox: Strange Hearts

And so I return, in closing, to sex. Or, more precisely, to sexual parts, to the erogenous zones with which our heroine, Angelica, was so delightedly, if virtually, playing when we last saw her. Nor, now that we're talking about structures of domination, is this a surprising place to end up. Considering that one of the best ways to control people is to reduce them by taking the part for the whole, this resurrection of body parts is mandated. If erogenous body parts are Angelica's switch-words for her theory of genre, they are society's switch-points for its theories and, therefore, its control of mind and heart. We might say that this strategy is tantamount to turning people into part-objects. And yet so often the erogenous body parts are switch-points to desire, excitement, sexual pleasure, and orgasm. You know this, I know this, even Kernberg (1995), who husbands classical psychoanalysis (see Chapters 4 and 9, this volume), tells us about the routine centrality of eroticized body parts to sexual excitement and satisfaction. It's old news to say that sex is a site of contradictions. What would be new would be to describe a strategy for dealing with them.

I suggest the trope and habit of paradox. Consider philosopher Teresa Brennan's (1989) paradoxical resolution of the false choice between object-relational and Lacanian feminisms: "sexual difference is not only the result of socialization but its condition" (p. 9). To put this another way, both psychoanalysis and feminism take on Scheman's enigma, working the problem of dualism over and over again (see Prologue). Resolving dualism means neither splitting nor collapsing. Instead, it means maintaining possibility: the mobile, dynamic space between binaries yields resolution that in turn give on to new complexity, to the third.

It's like having to choose between vagina and clitoris. Why bother when we can have both? The psychoanatomical map redrawn, our train of thought shifts tracks. Like bodies of thought and intellectual-political movements, sexual bodies are neither singular nor dual, neither whole nor part. They are multiple and require paradoxical thinking. We can agree with literary critic Valerie Traub's (1995) appraisal without giving up the body: "the elevation of the clitoris (or labia) as the sine qua non of 'lesbian' sexuality overvalues not only the genitals as a source of pleasure but the power of bodily metonymy to represent that pleasure" (p. 100). The problem, and solution, is that no single organ represents Woman's desire (much less anyone's). There really is no Queen to partner King Phallus, whose sovereignty produces the resistance inevitably triggered by domination. The refusal of feminists, of women, to be either same or other, which is the spirit inspiring Luce Irigaray (1985), transforms sexual splitting into paradox. Dissension in the feminist ranks matches the multiplicity of women's desire, a cacophony exceeding the body's symbolic capacity.

Women's don't want just the genitals. They, we, want whatever is erotic, you name it. Perhaps Lacan's mysterious and mystifying *jouissance* is nothing more than this mundane multiformity of sex, its "excess over . . . the bare choreographies of procreation" (Sedgwick, 1990, p. 29) symbolized not only by the distinction of clitoris from vagina, but by their concrete possibilities: women can, want, and do have both clitoral and vaginal orgasms, maybe not the same woman, maybe not at the same time, maybe not each time, and maybe alternately or simultaneously with other climaxes, like those of the "G-spot" (Whipple and Komisaruk, 1991) or anus or . . . who knows?

Like orgasm, psychoanalysis and feminism are open questions, uncertainties waiting to cohere, only to fall apart and then begin again, contingent on their time and place. Their relationship neither does nor should resemble a harmonious marriage or any kind of primal scene whatsoever. No, family therapy is not indicated. Rather, nonmonogamy is the treatment of choice; think of their *ménage à trois* with Marxian, Saussurean, and Foucauldian social theory. Their relations should always be tense, the radicalism of each, a product of their promiscuity (feminist intercourse with social reality, psychoanalytic congress with psychic reality), answering the other's conformist and dominating tendencies.

The uncertainty at feminism's heart is the necessary, vital, thirdlike tension between its two main goals, one ameliorative, the other revolutionary. On one hand, feminism aims to better the lives that women lead, hence, the Women's Liberation Movement. On the other hand, feminism aims to radically reconfigure what we mean by Woman, hence, feminist post-modernism. On the face of it, these goals would surprise no one. If you look into them, however, you find that they contradict one another. Feminism tries to empower women so that they can create the lives they want, but it also—and simultaneously—puts their desires into question, for it asks whether there are wants women have not yet begun, or dared, to imagine. Like any progressive social movement, feminism tries to improve what already exists, while at the same time it undermines the status quo. In doing so, it generates a tension, a paradox between the desire and need to better women's lives and the wish and necessity to redefine them.

The heart of psychoanalysis is equally strange. Indeed, it is this strangeness, the initial, revolutionary shock of psychoanalytic theory that Lacan's impossible language is meant to memorialize. Lacan wants to combat the ameliorating pull of clinical practice toward rationalizing the weirdness, "undecidability," and difficulty of the psychic interior (Rose, 1986, p. 15; Bowie, 1991, p. 196). The theory of the unconscious, so at odds with daily life and ordinary speech, remains the most radical of Freud's contributions (even though the idea of it had long preceded him; Ellenberger, 1970, *passim*). For it's here, in the once known and then repressed, or as some analysts are thinking these days, in the never known and dissociated (Davies and Frawley, 1992; Bromberg, 1994), that lives what cannot be thought. In the tension of conscious and unconscious lies the potential for psychic integration, which is to say, paradoxically, for personal change and meaning. The psychoanalytic session is a chance to say the unspeakable and think the unthinkable, to imagine what does not yet exist. It's not much fun: psychoanalysis offers individuals what feminism and other varieties of political action offer collectivities, the subversive opportunity of digging up the ground beneath your feet. But, like feminism; and, as we see in Chapter 2, gender, it's got possibilities.

2

The Third Step
Freud, the Feminists,
and Postmodernism

If psychoanalysis is at once a body of knowledge, a theory of human nature, and a method of cure, as Freud once said, then the way we think about people and the way we help them are mutually implicated. As the feminist critique shows, however, we do not always think about people, women and men, in the most helpful way. Despite the best intentions, our thinking often re-creates the problems we meant to solve in the first place. In fact, I argue that the reinstallation of gender stereotype is a major problem in one branch of psychoanalytic feminism, the re-creation of gender dualism, which impels what I call the Third Step.

The First Two Steps

The need to consider how we think about women and men is not, on the surface, self-evident. After all, it seems pretty clear that, in the ordinary course of events, women, for example, are women, mostly we know one when we see one, and we have a general idea of the difficulties they confront. We would just like to be able to help them figure out what they need to do to make their lives easier, if not better. Who women and men are, however, is not as clear as our conventional binary between female and male would intimate.[1] The multiple and conflicting views of women in

---

[1] Lacan (cited in Mitchell and Rose, 1982) argues something different: that you cannot ask "who women are," because woman's existence, located outside the symbolic order of language, cannot be spoken.

psychoanalysis epitomize this point: Freud (1924b, 1925a, 1931, 1933), for example, developed and embraced one particular characterization of women, but some people, like Horney (1923), disagreed with it immediately, even as others embrace it still.

Freud's view of women, which is what I call the First Step, articulated what anthropologists call "folk science," the often tacit prejudices that, in each culture, constitute common sense. Although Freud's work tends to be scholarly and revolutionary, still the main thrust of his findings in this area is to codify unexamined popular assumptions about women and, implicitly, men. It is well known that the stereotype of women endowed by his thought with scientific prestige is mitigated, particularly in footnotes, by his own doubts about its validity (e.g., Freud, 1905b, pp. 145–146, n. 1); there he allows himself to think of gender and sexuality as multiplicities, not dualisms. However, the last of his essays on femininity consolidates the following dualistic view: women are castrated, penisless men who suffer from penis envy and morally inferior, weak superegos. They can achieve femininity only by abandoning their clitoral—deemed "masculine"—sexuality in favor of the vaginal orgasm. Their only hope for feminine fulfillment is through mothering and the acquisition of the baby that would serve them as a symbolic penis. Even their mothering receives short shrift: the centrality of the Oedipus complex maximizes the importance of the father and minimizes the importance of the mother, whose gravity is more obvious in the preoedipal period.

Some might ask, perhaps understandably, why one would even bother to call Freud's theory of femininity the First Step. Indeed, it seemed backward as soon as it appeared, as evidenced in the intense dispute ongoing in psychoanalytic circles in the 1920s (see Fliegel, 1986) when Horney initiated the Second Step. Still, as will be no surprise to the readers of this book, Freud's ideas in his domain were an advance (Chodorow, 1994). For one thing, they put femininity and masculinity into question. Before that, gender (a notion that did not in fact emerge until the 1950s) was generally taken for granted; it was a given that people were male or female, men or women, and that was that (see Katz, 1990, for a discussion on the "invention" of, for example, heterosexuality). Second, if femininity and masculinity sometimes appear as given, they also turn out in Freud's thought to be achieved; even as an epigenetic unfolding of sexuality took theoretical precedence, there persists a dissonant concern to understand how women became women, how men became men (Mitchell and Rose, 1982, *passim*). The bold theorizing of women's sexuality also deserves emphasis; Freud's ideas on desire and sexual development are as self-contradictory and prejudiced as his ideas on women. For example, libido is always masculine, yet women in classical theory are sexual beings in need of sexual gratification.

Still, the main image to emerge from Freud's theory of women is that of an inferior being, and it was this that Horney (1923) and, later, the interpersonalist psychoanalyst Clara Thompson (Green, 1964) set out to attack. Horney was the first to criticize seriously the notion of penis envy. She argues, for example, that Freud's view of women is that of a five-year-old boy. In the boy's mind, girls once possessed a penis but have been punished by castration, a punishment also threatening him. Regarding the girl as inferior, he imagines that, unable to recover from this loss, she must also envy him; her envy, furthermore, endangers him. According to Horney, what is, in the little boy, ignorance of femininity's value, became in Freud a bias obscuring femininity's independent development, including the origins of penis envy in the evolving relationship between daughter and mother. Therefore, in a move more Freudian than Freud and about which I have reservations, Horney moots an independent, innate line of development of femininity, parallel to that of masculinity. Anticipating Fast (1984), she contends that each child envies the other's sex but that this envy is not the entire foundation of character. She also proposes—and, again, most contemporary theorists would differ here—that each sex is innately drawn to the opposite one, in other words, that heterosexuality is inborn.

Horney, like Thompson, also attributes some difficulties in women's lives, as well as in theories about women, to social conditions. She criticizes Freud's measurement of women's development by culturally defined masculine standards. She claims that his depreciation of a specially feminine sexuality and his ignorance of the powers and joys of motherhood derive from prevailing cultural misogyny (an idea that Chasseguet-Smirgel, 1986, repeats without attribution to Horney). Indeed, Horney suggests that psychoanalysis as a whole expresses culturally unconscious, envious fears of women's fecundity and of maternal power, and a retaliative wish to depreciate them. Thompson, in turn, locates *women's* envy in society (Green, 1964). She reasons that women's feelings of inferiority and injury, or what Freud would have called penis envy, emerge from their lesser social and economic standing. The envy women feel, she contends, has to do with their lack of economic and political power in a competitive culture, not their lack of biological organ (an envy we might now theorize in terms of the phallus; see Chapter 1).

To sum up so far: Classical theory, the First Step, interpreted feminine experience largely in relation to masculinity, which was itself the (unconscious) norm in psychology, culture, and psychological theory. The work of Horney and Thompson, along with occasional contributions by other critics of Freud's views about women, initiated what I am calling the Second Step, that is, the feminist, critical response to Freud (for an insightful overview, see Shapiro, 2002). The recent stream of psychoanalytic feminist theory and research, which I am about to survey, continues what Horney and Thompson began. Coalescing in the mid-1970s in the context of women's liberation as a political movement, it uses psychoanalytic and feminist critiques of classical theory to review feminine experience and personality, revalue nurturing and relatedness, and generate new interpretations of women, mothering, and gender-identity development. Accepting gender dualism as a given, this current of thought soon branched off in two main directions. One, which belongs to what journalist Katha Pollitt (1994) dubs "difference feminism," focuses mainly on the psychology of women, retaining masculinity and femininity as separate categories. The other branch, "gender feminism" (or as Shapiro, 2002, calls it, "egalitarian/gender critique feminism") looks at the psychology of gender. It theorizes the dialectics of masculinity and femininity as they manifest in psyche and culture. To my mind, the tension between these two schools of thought calls for a new way of thinking, a third, postmodernist step, which began to evolve in the late 1980s and is codified in Butler (1990) and which is addressed throughout this book but particularly in Chapters 3 and 6. Indeed, this tension evokes the central and necessary contradiction in feminism itself, which I described at the end of Chapter 1, as well as the sometimes troublesome, but in fact creative, tug-of-war between psychoanalytic theory and clinical practice, as I anatomize in Chapter 6.

Difference feminism is best known through the work of Miller and Gilligan. Miller (1976) and her colleagues at the Stone Center, Wellesley College (Jordan et al., 1991), elaborate a critique of standard notions of self. Departing from the by now classical theories of separation-individuation (Mahler, Pine, and Bergman, 1975), they amalgamate a variety of psychoanalytic theories to forge a new theory of women's development and character. In their view, the theoretical and clinical centrality of separation-individuation and its goal of autonomy reflects, in part, traditionally masculine experience and its model, the culturally primal vision of a man making his lone way in the public world (choose any lonesome cowpoke you want). This cultural and psychological ideal is true mostly in the breach, however; Miller is fond of pointing out that behind every "autonomous" man stands a support staff of women—wives, mothers, secretaries, nurses, and so on (as well as, we should add, lower-status men, whose subordinate status feminizes them). "Relatedness," in other words, is as psychologically and socially salient as autonomy. Indeed, an inquiry into women's experience reveals the lifelong importance of "the relational self," which arises from women's socialization and experience as they inhabit a world of caring for other and mutuality.

Miller's insights were fundamental to Gilligan's (1982) reformulation of moral development theory. Academic developmental and cognitive psychology, Gilligan shows, uses male subjects to create a standard of normality that upholds both Freud's view of women's moral inferiority and the later theoretical premium on separation. Although Lawrence Kohlberg's schema, her main theoretical frame and target, charts progress toward a morality of universal principles of justice, her model, rooted in a study of women's development, describes a developing morality of care and attachment that we may call "relationality." Challenging the paradox in which traditionally "feminine" traits also mark women's moral deficiency, Gilligan formulates an alternate, equally essential, but until now unrecognized, sequence of moral development leading toward "the understanding of responsibility and relationships" (p. 19). Morality, in this view, is not an abstract and given matter of the rights of individuals, but a negotiated path through the particularities of connection toward the care of the other as well as of the self.

Gilligan also drew on Chodorow's (1978), work, which may be regarded as taking a middle position between difference and gender feminisms (note, once again, how dualism, even the one in psychoanalytic feminism that I have proposed, falls apart). Using an object-relational perspective, Chodorow theorizes the overdetermined process by which women, in becoming gendered, come to want to mother. Moving the psychoanalytic lens back from the oedipal to the preoedipal period, she accepts separation-individuation (in contrast to Miller) and examines how gender development inflects it. With her focus on women's difficulty in separating from their mothers, she argues that feminine gender identity takes its deepest imprint from the preoedipal merger of child with mother; in the mother's fantasies, the girl represents the dependent child who she, the mother, once was herself. In contrast, masculine gender identity is informed early on by difference; the boy, embodying the mother's fantasies of autonomy, separates from a mother whose gender marks her difference from him and his otherness in relation to her. The girl, her gender identity defined by similarity rather than difference and thus steeped in relatedness, comes to experience herself as incomplete without some connection to another. Because attachment, in other words, becomes central to the girl's sense of self, she is in some sense always waiting for connection with child (not, as classical theory would have it, for a penis).

Benjamin (1988b) tells a new developmental story, too. In consigning women to otherness, or inferior masculinity, she argues, the psychoanalytic literature tends to leave the mother's existing subjectivity or agency untheorized. However, the child's emergent subjectivity requires not only separation and differentiation, but also mutuality (Benjamin, 1988a, b). It needs, first, recognition by a mother who is herself an autonomous subject, an independence that the child both enjoys and needs to notice. The psychological and cultural denial of the mother's own agency and authority, and the consequent doubting of them, render the child's self-assertion, autonomy, and independence uncertain. This dilemma exacerbates a normative conundrum, which gender-related splitting in relation to the preoedipal father solves unequally for boys and girls: how do children become independent from the one on whom they are dependent?

Equally critical for subjectivity is paternal mutual recognition (Benjamin, 1988a, b). Fathers, in identifying with sons, mirror their desire for autonomy and their need for healthy grandiosity. In contrast, fathers' disidentification from their daughters denies the girls these wishes and needs. Given the psychocultural denigration of women and mothers, boys consequently acquire a semblance of masculinized autonomy by repudiating the feminized relatedness which, emptied of desire, becomes the fate of little girls. The search to name and live their own desire problematizes women's lives; given normative heterosexuality, they tend to seek it in the idealized male Other: If they can't have it, at least they can have a man who has it or appears to have it.

To summarize this second part of the Second Step, the difference feminists have continued what Horney initiated, elaborating an independent line of female development that recuperates and valorizes certain aspects of femininity as traditionally defined— for example, nurturing, empathy, receptivity. The gender equality feminists, in contrast, study the dialectics of gender: to understand how little girls develop, for example, they analyze also how boys do not. In their view, one becomes gendered not by learning "a one-dimensional message that [one is] either male or female"; rather, one "absorb[s] the *contrast* between male and female" (Dimen, 1986, p. 8). For difference feminists, masculinity and femininity are distinct, mutually alien categories, the second of which is unfairly denigrated, a fact that their critique aims to reverse. For gender feminism, masculinity and femininity are part of the dual-gender system that divides up human possibility such that what girls are supposed to become, little boys are not, and vice versa. It is this hierarchical "system of difference" (Benjamin, 1992, p. 90), the structure that underlies the denigration of femininity and the idealization of masculinity, at which gender critique aims.

Toward a Third Step

That little girls and boys do not always turn out as theory and ideology say they ought to is one reason we need a Third Step.

You might say that the Second Step has told us both who women are and what they want. If women's traditional behavior, attitudes, and character have been revalued by difference feminism, if their strivings for autonomy and desire have been ratified by gender feminism, what else is there to think about? Surely we have our work cut out for us; all we need to do is follow the dotted lines: support what women are and support their strivings for what they are not yet.

Yet, if you think about it, the answers difference feminism and gender feminism provide for Freud's questions contradict each other. What women are, which is what difference feminism offers us, is not all that women want, which is what gender feminism tells us. This contradiction in psychoanalytic feminist *theory* manifests a split in women *themselves*.

Indeed, the theoretical contradiction is a symptom of a cultural split, the polarity of female versus male that, in rendering each pole totally different from the other, obscures the differences and divides the poles. Women are often of two or more minds about who they are and what they want, a nodule of conflict with clinical manifestations, as becomes clear from the extended case example in Chapter 6 (and see also pp. 75–76). To comprehend this, we need to recalibrate our concepts so that they incorporate diversity, variability, possibility.

From Dualism to Multiplicity

Instead of finding this internal contradiction or variability a problem, why not make it the beginnings of a solution? Instead of assuming that all women want the same thing all the time, we have to think that women differ between and within themselves: diverse categories of women want diverse things, and most women's desires vary from time to time. Difference feminism tells us about women's difference from men. *But we also have to understand how difference circulates through gender altogether*, so that we can explain how it is that any given woman might, on any given day or in a lifetime, be and feel more the way men do or are said to, than the way women do or are said to. *Mutatis mutandis*, the same holds for men.

What is required is to turn this contradiction into a paradox (Dimen, 1994), a point I illustrate by locating my discussion in a larger context, that of feminism itself. Paradox, according to Ghent (1992), is a contradiction that admits of no resolution. Or, better, the only resolution to paradox is another paradox. Instead of creating a false choice between difference feminism and gender feminism, then, let us view them as two poles of a paradox whose tension cannot be immediately, if ever, resolved. And then let us "milk" that tension "for all it's worth" (Benjamin, 1994, p. 93). Let us use this dialectical thinking, this struggle with complexity and irresolution, as a route to creative understandings. Arguably, the two branches of psychoanalytic feminism spring from feminism's contradictory motives. Gender feminism emerges from the impetus to destabilize, difference feminism, from the ameliorative thrust. Yet the very idea that we are going to make someone's life better says that we think it can be different from the way it is now. Inside the ameliorative motive lies the deconstructive impulse. And the very choice to destabilize the category of women recognizes the second motive force, the urgent necessity of attending to women's lives. The two poles of the paradox inhabit one another, much as do consciousness and unconsciousness (for this argument, see Prologue). Psychoanalytic feminism, like feminism in general, needs both motives, and the tensions between them to keep moving forward. We have to change women's lives, but not get so lost in the action of changing that we forget the imaginative basis for change, the visions of how things could be different.

The problem with difference feminism is that its conceptualization of women has gone too far toward the ameliorative pole. It has taken an oppositional path, reacting against the patriarchal system that feminism challenges by opting for the previously excluded side, femininity (Benjamin, 1994, p. 89). In doing so, difference feminism has re-created one of the main problems we set out to solve (much to the satisfaction of those who objected to change in the first place). By focusing entirely on what women's psychology is, it forgets to ask what women's psychology might become. Thus, it implicitly endorses the status quo. It also tends to omit past and present differences among women by interpreting women's psychology apart from its historical, temporal nature; although difference feminists acknowledge that culture inflects psychology (e.g., Miller, 1991, p. 181), their theory of women cannot track such variability. Difference feminism, in effect constituting Woman as a seamless, timeless, universal category, attributes to women exactly the sort of skills found in Victorian idealizations of femininity: interpersonal skills, mothering, nurturing, empathy.

This new stereotype is at least as homogeneous and undifferentiated as the classical model, if not more so (see Chodorow's account [1994] of the many different women who populate the pages of Freud's oeuvre). Let me offer a personal example: At a conference given by the Stone Center (1993), Miller was describing women's character formation, arguing that women derive their self-esteem from creating relationships. Suddenly, I felt an unexpected relief and happiness, as if a burden had left my shoulders or a familiar fog had cleared. I saw the problem, a disjunction at my core. I'm a woman, but I do not base my self-esteem or self-cohesion on creating relationships. I've been vainly trying to make it my core all my life and berating myself for my failure. Not only have I had to escape to social forces pushing me toward this culturally classic mold of woman, I've been trying to force myself into it—and crippling myself in the process. It's not that I don't create relationships. I do, and I'm good at it; I have a lot of friends. But doing so is not my core.

So, during the discussion period, I voiced these thoughts. I then added that I saw no way for Miller's theory to comprehend my experience without pathologizing it. This is not a problem of exceptionality. It's a problem of theory. Certainly, I don't like feeling left out of or stigmatized by their theory. But the rub is that it has no room for this and other sorts of difference among women or within women, such as those characterizing women of different classes, ethnicities, sexualities, ages, regions, and so on. Nor does it encompass differences within the experience of individual women, in particular, desires that conflict. In the view of women emerging from difference feminism, there is no space for multiplicity.

The solution I propose, a Third Step, is to incorporate a postmodernist perspective. Let us think of gender as multiply instantiated, ambiguous, overdetermined, and conflicted. Along with core gender identity, or the sense that "I am female" or "I am male" (Fast, 1984), goes "a treasure trove of characterological differences" (May, 1986, pp. 188). These characteristic differences are symbolized by different relations to gender, by varying images or representations of it. And I believe that as clinicians, if we look at either masculinity or femininity without looking at the contrast between them, we will be inclined to imagine fixed essences, hard-and-fast polarities. If we do not have in mind an image of this multiplicity, we are going to wind up either missing the aspects of our patients' experiences that promote growth or recreating the molds that got our patients into trouble in the first place.

What is required is a view of women that contains from the start a notion of multiplicity and variety. To return to the two motive forces of feminism, we need, in order to ameliorate women's lives, to destabilize the way we think of women. To do that, we have to push off from gender feminism by solving a discursive problem that it faces in turn, that it shares with difference feminism, as, indeed, with all psychological theory. In a sense, each of us unavoidably re-creates stereotype every time we use the words man or woman. That's how language works: We speak it, and we understand the customary meanings the terms evoke; if we did not, we could not communicate, at least not in words.

This process is a product of discourse, a term that refers to the idea that we enter and form ourselves through language and culture, which preexist us. Flax (1990) explicates this term, which Foucault made central to recent intellectual thought:

> A discourse is a system of possibilities for knowledge. Discursive formations are made up in part of sets of usually tacit rules that enable us to identify some statements as true or false, to construct a map, model, or classificatory system in which these statements can be organized. . . . The place, function, and character of the knowers, authors, and audiences of a discourse are also functions of discursive rules (pp. 205–206).

That there is therefore, no external standpoint, from which it is possible to claim to judge the truth or adequacy of an entire discourse, puts scientific notions of proof and truth into question. Furthermore, a discourse's foundations reside in power; in somewhat positivist fasion, Foucault claims "All knowledge rests upon injustice" (cited in Rabinow, 1994, p. 95). But this fact of power is excluded, masked in the discourse of humanism that we have inherited from the Enlightenment (Flax, 1990, pp. 205–206; for further explication of postmodern thought, see Prologue and Chapters 1, 3, and 9, this volume).

Therefore, each time we speak or write "woman," we evoke the dual-gender system as a psycho-social-political structure that divides human possibility between two categories. As Goldner (1991) says, the very language for gender reprodues the categories we want to change, the stereotypes we struggle to escape. Even gender feminism is not immune to this dilemma. Chodorow's answer to the question of how women come to want to mother seems to posit an absolute difference between boys and girls, male and female, men and women, even though it is a dialectical account of what she recognizes to be a cultural and evolving phenomenon. Benjamin has rewritten the psychosexual story in a way that makes us understand how women can have penis envy, not as psychological bedrock, but as an aspect of a historically contingent and changeable relationship to their fathers.

Nevertheless, the basic narrative remains: as in all psychoanalytic theories of development, females become women, males become men, and the dance of their development is a heterosexual pairing. These theories are clinically useful because they rework and expand our understanding of how we *represent* our own experience to ourselves, for example, in terms of paternal and maternal transferences. But they do not account for the way experience and self-reflection conflict with that representation. In the course of this, gender as we know it winds up being reproduced, not broken up.

But gender is not of a piece. The problem with stereotypes is not their falsity but their lack of ambiguity. According to stereotype, women do this and men do that, women are like this and men are like that. Sugar and spice, snips and snails. Such false clarity lurks in the models of women, and men, preferred by both difference feminism and gender feminism. There is no place in such models either for internal conflict or for change. And, therefore, there is no place *for* such models in psychotherapy. Clinically, we need models that envision change, in which gender is multiple, shifting, ambiguous, labile, sometimes present in our experience, sometimes not. As I show in Chapter 6, gender should be an aspect of our patients' experience that we question, not assume.

One postmodernist view of gender, penned by historian Joan Scott (1988), reads:

[O]ften in patriarchal discourse, sexual difference (the contrast masculine/feminine) serves to encode or establish meanings that are literally unrelated to gender or the body per se. In that way, the meanings of gender become tied to many kinds of cultural representations, and these in turn establish terms by which relations between women and men are organized and understood [p. 37].

Take, for example, the dichotomies of public versus private and work versus family, and notice how they pair up with masculinity versus femininity. Grounding the division of labor between men and women, this opposition between men outside and women inside the home shapes also how we understand them, even though it may have little or nothing to do with how women and men experience themselves or how they might otherwise be understood. A woman may, for example, feel herself defined by both her work and her family, even though the stereotype says she is defined only by the latter. She may experience herself in her work as committed to initiative and self-advancement, not mutuality, even though in the privacy of her home, her values reverse. Or she may feel her work does not permit her inclination toward mutuality to flower, and may, because of this conflict, try either to stay at work and change the way things are done there or to leave altogether for home or a different kind of job.

Gender, I am saying, is more complex, multiple, and discontinuous than stereotype allows. Organized on the basis of one dualism, or the opposition between masculine and feminine, gender incorporates many others. A dual-gender system lines up a set of oppositions in woman: father–mother, active–passive, aggressive–tender, dominant– submissive, right–left, good–bad, and so on. But if you look closely, these crosscutting binaries do not stay polar. In Chapter 6, I relate the clinical case of Dr. EL (here and elsewhere throughout this book, patients' initials have been disguised and displaced), a mature woman who did not want to cry because she would cry only on a man's, not a woman's, shoulder. When I later thought about this moment— and unfortunately I did so not during the treatment, when I did not know what to think about it—I came to muse on all the oppositions implicit in her statement and how they mixed.

What Dr. EL meant by "woman" here was, overtly, that she was heterosexual. But unconsciously she meant more than that. Being a heterosexual woman meant, in effect, both not being a lesbian and not being a child. For who cries on a woman's shoulder but, in fact, a child seeking comfort from mother? And what, in EL's unconscious, did it mean to be a child if not to be someone with the humiliating attributes, for her and others, of dependence, need, and passivity? So when EL said "woman," she meant many contradictory things, not only male and female, but also other oppositions encapsulated in them: child–adult, need–desire, active–passive, dependent–independent. And when she said, "I'll only cry on a man's shoulder, I'm not interested in women," she fused several separable oppositions in a culturally acceptable as well as ego-syntonic way, a fusion that we had to undo so that we could examine each experience independently as well as in relation to each other.

So with patients I now want to ask, overtly or in my mind, "What *is* it for you to be a woman? What is woman made of for you?" I think of their gender identity as always emerging, always in process, and, entertaining this possibility, I see many different but intersecting paths to take. With someone like Dr. EL, you could ponder her feelings about homosexuality, or her problems around dependence, or her issues about passivity. If you start thinking about her fear of homosexuality, you'll get to her feelings about being a female dependent on another female, which would take you to questions of passivity, then to questions of being an adult. If you see gender as multiply constituted, sewn of many parts, then no matter where you start, you'll be able to go to the other issues as well, all of which are interconnected in an ambiguous, not a determinative, sense.

Postmodernism is disturbing. Because gender identity is so elemental, so fused with one's sense of self, reconfiguring it is disorienting. Gender identity seems to be signed, sealed, and delivered in a seamless package. That it is not emerges in one patient's multiple and cross-gendered transferences. This clinical vignette, a case of Robert May's (1986), illustrates the post-modernist tenet that what seem to be entities are disjunctive agglomerations, seamed, not seamless, wholes:

> Among the ways, he has experienced his therapist are the following: as a cruel, dominating, and humiliating father; as a strong and admirable father; as a responsive mother, attentive to his feelings; as a noble mother ready to die to protect him; as a pathetic, failed father; as a depressed mother or lonely child who will die if left

unattended. Each of these visions of his therapist has its complementary view of himself, its own cluster of variously painful and pleasing emotions, its own more or less hidden and conflicted wishes. To the therapist's cruel father he is the humiliated little boy who feels ridiculed and taunted about his penis; to the therapist's strong and admirable father he is the idolizing son, or the lovely young woman who will capture the therapist's interest and excite him; to the therapist's suffocating mother he is the silent and resistant captive; to the therapist's pathetic failure he is scornfully triumphant; and so forth. These dramatic fragments of experience shift and alternate not only over the course of the therapy but also over the course of a session. The particular fantasy of the therapist holding him and having intercourse with him embodies at least: (1) his wish for warmth and physical contact from the therapist as a mixture of mother and father relating to him as an infant; (2) his need to submit sexually to a father as a reassurance against his own aggression and envy; (3) his attempt to be a cute and pleasing girl who will be spared the therapist's wrath; (4) his wish to incorporate (steal) some of what he perceives as the therapist's phallic power; (5) his attempt to be a woman for the therapist so as to rouse him from what he fears will be a terminal depression [p. 187].

All these fragments belong to this patient; sometimes they are gender congruent, sometimes not. May's point is that to assume one knows what masculinity is to this patient is to foreclose this multiplicity, indeed, to pathologize it. As Harold Boris (1986), a more mainstream psychoanalyst, writing not about gender but about Bion's dictum that we enter each session without memory or desire, cautions the following: "If the 10:00 patient is one we know to be a married man in his thirties, we know too much, for how are we to attend the four-year-old girl who has just walked in?" (p. 177).

Identity and Its Contradictions: Clinical Postmodernism

Having tried to make a case, first, for the need to talk about gender rather than about women per se and, second, for the value of seeing gender as multiple and conflictual, I want to conclude with a direct application of postmodernist theory, in concert with gender feminism, to the problem of multiple personality in women.

In Margo Rivera's (1989) extremely interesting and useful argument, the postmodernist questioning of the existence of unitary identities is clinically crucial. Postmodernism, she says, "deconstructs the very object we take as our given, as pre-given, the human subject" (p. 26). What we, as psychologists and therapists, take for granted is precisely what we ought, according to postmodernism, to be wondering about. We ought to be questioning whether "a coherent, essentially rational individual who is the author of her own meanings and the agent of her own production" (p. 26) can really be said to exist. Postmodernism abandons the belief in an essential unique individual identity. Rather, it sees internal life as a historical production, a creation emerging in the field of power relations as these are presented in language and, therefore, suffused with the conflicts of power and powerlessness. Human subjectivity is, in this view, like all reality. It is contingent, constituted culturally and politically through language.

Although language is a place where identities and social structures, psychologies, and social practices are constructed, it is also, as Rivera makes clear, a place where they are contested. Even as discourse constructs self-representations, it contains contradictions through which we struggle against its limitations, falsities, and oppressions, a dual movement not unlike the contradictory tension between the feminist motives to destabilize and to ameliorate. One of the ways in which social and political structures change is by people challenging the nature of their existence, their own identities. Indeed, we may regard this contestation as one of the reasons psychotherapy is both possible and necessary: the internal conflicts people experience and bring to therapy are a way of contesting the way they are constituted.

Seen thus, identity emerges as multiple, not uniform or unitary, as emergent not stable, differentiated not seamless, always contested. So, too, is gender identity.

> [T]he idea of natural, sexual differences masks the social opposition between women and men and the hierarchy between women and men. A postmodernist view of gender reveals how men and women struggle to fit themselves into the proper gender position [Rivera, 1989, p. 27].

This point illuminates my own experience of Miller's thinking; it helped me name an internal struggle I'd always had, solved a problem in my analysis, and, as feminist insights have often done, helped me to stop blaming myself.

Clinicians might benefit from Rivera's (1989) strong position: "A rich psychic life depends on failing to slip easily into cultural roles and relationships" (p. 29). The problem in multiple personality is, she says, dissociation, not multiplicity.[2] Accordingly, her goal with people with multiple personalities has become not to eliminate but to support each of the alter personalities as "I" and to encourage one central consciousness of all of them and of their conflicts. The construction of alter personalities exemplifies the way particular social positionings and practices are continually produced and reproduced. For example, each personality state will identify with a given position according to the role which that self-state learned to enact as part of the individual's overall means of surviving. "For every personality who identifies with one position (the compliant little girl, for example), there is often another personality who ferociously resists that position (the anti-social boy)" (Rivera, 1989, p. 25). Rivera departs from the Lacanian and deconstructionist preclusion of a central consciousness, however. Like Flax (1990, p. 101), she criticizes the postmodernist notion of the decentered self. Postmodernist theorists, they say, do not realize the luxury of having a central organizing consciousness that can recognize and authorize this internal, sometimes chaotic, multiplicity. As clinicians, we recognize the need for an experience of coherence on the basis of which we can perceive incoherence, conflicted feelings, and the possibility of change (1989, p. 28; see also Chodorow, 1995).

I am arguing, then, that we must see gender in this way, too. The Third Step is, in my view, to destabilize, decenter, shake up our idea of gender, just as we once revolutionized our ideas about women's place. Because popular as well as scholarly notions hold that gender psychology is unitary, that men are this and women are that, women—and men, too—are having a difficult time incorporating their own multiplicity. But denial of multiplicity, not multiplicity itself, is the problem. We are usually conflicted about our own relation to gender, even as there is an "I" who feels the conflicts and attempts to decide what to do about them;

---

[2] It is worth noting how classical a position this is: illness comes from getting rid of what seems to be discordant, whether by repression or by splitting.

for example, as relieved as I am of the psychocultural burden of having to be a woman as conventionally defined, I yet feel loss and strangeness because I don't fit the most familiar and valued model of my femininity even though I'm probably not going to be able to do so.

Similarly, many women were relieved by the Second Wave of feminism, which said that not all women have to be mothers, that there are other versions of femininity besides maternality. Impelled by need, or principle, or both they made their way into the white-, pink-, and blue-collar worlds. Some, however, soon began to find themselves in conflict with their new definition of their femininity. In consequence, they began trying to link it to its more traditional understandings or to abandon it altogether. Women's longing for the familiar conflicted with their embrace of the new. Indeed, the emergence of conflict in women's sense of gender accounts for the popular success of difference feminism: women are seeking a feminist way to revalue the maternally, domestically, and interpersonally oriented dimension of femininity.

Such conflict is ordinary. The normativity of internal conflict, the rock on which the house of psychoanalysis is built, is immaterial to difference feminism and insufficiently savored by gender feminism. Gender is routinely seamed, contested, even alienating. Rivera (1989) says, "Not only character but social control and resistance to it show up in multiple personality" (p. 27). The same holds for gender: not only gendered personality but also social definitions of gender and our resistances to it emerge in ordinary life. Beneath the layer of socialization, Rivera argues, is not a true self, but "a multiple, shifting and often self-contradictory identity made up of heterogeneous and heteronomous representations of personal experience of gender, race, class, religion and culture" (p. 29; see also Chapter 6, this volume). And beneath the layer of gender enculturation is not an essential gender, but an ambiguous, variably constructed, highly conflicted relation to one's sex (as Lacan argues—and argues that Freud argues; see also Mitchell and Rose, 1982).

Let's do something difficult and counterintuitive. Let's hold contradictory notions in our minds at once. Let us see gender as a container of multiplicity, both unitary and divided. Let us consider gender systems as simultaneously dual and multiple. I am asking us to believe that, at the same time, we can know and not know who we are, that we can say "I" even as our identity is multiple, unstable, and emerging, as, we shall see in the next chapter, is our sexuality. I am trying to find a way to be able to say, with safety and excitement, "I am female, but what that means I have yet to find out."

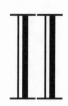

II

Mind, Body, Culture
Psychoanalytic Studies

Thinking, like psychotherapy, is as disorderly as it is linear, as divergent as it is convergent, as much mosaic as narrative. Ideas present themselves as they will. But they always need working up to. The concept of gender multiplicity explained in Chapter 6, and Chapter 5's deconstruction, demand a revised body, which is Chapter 5's task. Innovative notions of the body, in turn, depend on transcending that old dualism, Nature versus Nurture, which is what occupies Chapter 3. Long story short: Section II revisits Darwinism and psychoanalysis, plumbs the body's psychic and cultural versatility, deconstructs sex, and multiplies gender.

3

On "Our Nature"
or Sex and the Single Narrative

There's two kinds of people, those who give and those who take. The scorpion and the frog. Ever heard of 'em? A scorpion wants to cross the river. But he can't swim. Goes to a frog, who can, and asks for a ride. Frog says, "I'll give you a ride on my back? You'll go and sting me!" Scorpion replies, "It would not be in my interest to sting you, since as I'd be on your back, we'd both drown." Frog thinks about this logic for a while and accepts the deal. Takes the scorpion on his back, braves the waters. Halfway over feels a burning spear in his side, and realizes the scorpion has stung him after all. And as they both sink beneath the waves, the frog cries out, "Why did you sting me, Mr. Scorpion? For now we both will drown!" Scorpion replies, "I can't help it. It's in my nature."

From *The Crying Game*

In mid-July of 1993, a gay man interviewed on television said he welcomed Dr. Dean Hamer's finding that, according to the *New York Times*, "one or several genes located on the bottom half of the . . . X chromosome may play a role in predisposing some men toward homosexuality" (Angier, 1993). The finding showed, he opined, that there is nothing wrong with being gay. His actual words were, "I'm not gay because my parents did anything wrong."

This poignant, extraordinary statement just about said it all. So I use it here as my text, deconstructing it in order to indicate a relational way of thinking not only about homosexuality but about sexuality in general. This project, moving sexuality from dualism to multiplicity, engages a skein of ideas that loops through scientific and popular thought. I call this the Discourse of Nature, the main tool of which is a single narrative of normality, morality, and sex that, by masquerading as the mirror of nature, effects social control. If, I argue, you want a psychoanalytic theory of desire, then you have to give up the Discourse of Nature.

"My Mother Had the Face of an Angel"

Two sorts of nature show up in this Discourse. There's the kind that's the Law: Nature, the ultimate cause of all life forms, the one that's opposed to Culture, as in Nature versus Nurture. And then there's "nature," which, subjectively speaking, is what one feels about oneself, a sense of who one is, of who one cannot help but be.

Let us return to the text: I think we all understand what this man is talking about. I don't mean that we all know what it's like to be gay, that our problems are the same, that we're all the same under the skin, between the sheets. But we do know what it feels like to believe that the way we are, who we are, hurts our parents, that our "nature," as Neil Jordan's film *The Crying Game* put it, shames them. *The Crying Game* concerns itself, in part, with sexual nature: is it singular or multiple, fixed or fluid? The film tells a story of sex and politics through the encounter among three people. There is Jody, an endearing Afro-British soldier who, having been taken hostage by the Irish Republican Army (IRA), relates the tale of the scorpion and the frog to his guard, kind-at-heart Fergus. Fergus, on Jody's accidental death under a British army tank, goes to London to look up passionate, also Afro-Brit, male-to-female transsexual Dil, whom Jody had loved before his death. Even though Fergus has always thought of himself as straight, even though he threw up when, during their second sexual encounter (he had gotten a blow job in the first), he saw Dil's penis, even though he refuses a romantic engagement with her even until the end—still he comes to love Dil as helplessly as she loves him. *The Crying Game* closes with Lyle Lovett singing Tammy Wynette's "Stand by Your Man," as Dil visits Fergus in jail, where he is serving time for the murder (of his IRA lover, Jude), which Dil had committed. He tells her, in his own way, about the scorpion and the frog.

When Dil and Fergus have sex, is it heterosexual or homosexual? Who's manly here? Dil with her penis? The IRA? The British army? Who's womanly? Fergus with his kindness and self-sacrifice? Jude with her revolutionary's callousness? Perhaps, *The Crying Game* suggests, one's sexual nature isn't a given. Maybe it's a coming-to-be, necessarily unforeseeable.

These matters are momentous and troubling because of sexuality's cultural and personal meaning. Sex is about private desire, but desire is saturated with familial and social history. You may recall a moment from another film, *The Elephant Man,* when the protagonist, whose face bears the cauliflower lumps of Proteus syndrome, says to a beautiful woman visitor, "My mother had the face of an angel." Choked with tears, he pauses, then goes on to characterize his undesirability: "I was a great disappointment to her." If we didn't know what he felt like, we wouldn't choke up with him. We're familiar with the guilt, the shame and self-loathing, the helpless sorrow, the mourned or perhaps ungrievable loss, the yearning and the love. You don't have to be gay to have these feelings, and being gay does not mean you have to have them. But certainly some feel these ways because being gay in our culture means, somehow, to feel wrong, harmful, diseased.

It's no wonder, then, that our TV interviewee welcomed Hamer's news. His personal nature had been vindicated by Nature itself. He no longer had to blame his parents, and they no longer had to blame themselves—or him. There was nothing for anyone to blame anyone for. In the first reading of his words (I'll get back to the second at the end of this chapter), he was saying that he was gay not because his parents had raised him wrong but because that's what he was by nature—gay. There was no blame, no right, no wrong, just a natural fact. Just the facts, ma'am. No emotion.

But not just the facts. And lots of emotion. We all want biology on our side. It means something to find one's nature mirrored in what used to be called the facts of life, in nature. Biology, the discipline that gives official standing to the Discourse of Nature, vindicates and authorizes us. Studied, imagined, and in that way created by science (Fausto-Sterling, 1986; Haraway, 1989; Keller, 1992), biology becomes Biology. Serving to explicate, validate, and regulate Nature, the scientific discipline of Biology thereby also helps to create one's nature, the most private experiences of self.[1] Heterosexual people tend to be oblivious to this legitimation, just as white people usually don't note the color of their skin. It's what the New Left tagged "privilege"—skin privilege, gender privilege, class privilege. Here we are talking about sex privilege.

Neo-Darwinism, or If You're Not Straight, You Must Be Crazy

Heterosexuality's privilege has various charters. For the devout, it's Scripture. For the secular, including psychoanalysts, it's Darwinian evolutionary theory. Indeed, Darwinism has for intellectuals just about the same ethical and intellectual weight as religious doctrine has for believers. This parallel is no accident. In Western thought, the narrative of natural selection long ago supplanted the story of creation as the true account of the origins and fate of the human species (Lewontin, 1991). To the victor went also the spoils: in later 19th-century secular life, evolutionary theory came to carry the intellectual and moral charge that had until then been the exclusive property of religion.

Psychoanalysis in turn borrows from this nearly scriptural authority. The classic psychoanalytic theory of sexuality, which is in point of fact the only theory of sex psychoanalysis has (Dimen,

---

[1] Postmodernist psychologists, influenced by Foucault, have begun to describe the dialectical process whereby Biology creates Psychology. Cushman (1991), for example, critiques Stern's (1985) theory of infant development for its naturalization of one particular version of self. Stern's manifest contribution is the idea that relatedness is psychologically hardwired. It would appear, then, that his argument is more about culture than about nature. If, however, we ask who's doing the relating, Cushman observes, we find none other than the atomized Western self, situated by Stern's theory in a prelinguistic, presymbolic nature and thereby defined as originary.

1995), leans on evolutionary theory for scientific support, appealing to it as discoverer, purveyor, and arbiter of truth (e.g., Freud, 1913, p. 1 and *passim*; because examples are too numerous to cite, see Fliegel, 1986, pp. 13, 16, 26–28, for a summary critique; and Schafer 1977, p. 350). Even contemporary relational theorists, from Bowlby to the late Steve Mitchell, draw on one or another sector of Darwinian thought to validate their arguments (Slavin and Kriegman, 1992, pp. 33–54).

Darwinism comes in three main flavors. Evolutionary theory, as formulated by Charles Darwin, holds that life forms have evolved along certain paths through the process of natural selection. Species' adaptation to environmental vicissitudes is its principal mechanism: interaction between environment and phenotype selects for those genotypes that lead to the reproduction of the individual carrying them. If the individual can survive to reproductive age, that species has made it for another generation. This is a ruthless process: in their struggle for survival, individuals compete "for food, . . . space . . . [and] mates"(Ruse, 1992, p. 78). This innate competitiveness provided an apt metaphor for the second sort of Darwinism: arguing that cutthroat competition is natural and inevitable, social Darwinists (e.g., the late-19th-century sociologist Herbert Spencer) used "the survival of the fittest" to promote "laissez-faire capitalism as the force that would drive social progress"(Bowler, 1992, p. 193). In social Darwinist view, human progress justifies social cruelty in the name of species survival.[2]

The third sort of Darwinism, the one most relevant to questions of sexuality, intimacy, and power, is new. First as sociobiology (Wilson, 1977) and later as evolutionary psychology (Buss, 1994), it shares with the original version a singularity of narrative. But whereas traditional Darwinism concerns itself with species survival, the new variant focuses on genes and individual organisms. As Slavin and Kriegman (1992), psychoanalysts who have tried to adapt sociobiology and evolutionary psychology for therapeutic

---

[2] Mid-20th century accounts (e.g., Wynne-Edwards, 1962) argued to the contrary, suggesting that natural selection also favors the survival of groups and communities and, hence, cooperation. Some strict adaptationists (e.g., Thornhill and Palmer, 2000; pp. 107, 116) dismiss this perspective, although they point out that others agree with it.

use, put it, "all life forms—structures and, to some extent, behavior patterns—can be understood in terms of the built-in path toward reproductive success of the genetic material contained within the organism" (p. 56). Subject to the imperative to reproduce successfully, all organisms are driven to leave behind as many of their genes as possible in order to win the survival game. Indeed, genes themselves are thought to compete (Dawkins, 1976).[3]

If you follow this definition of sociobiology down the road to evolutionary psychology, you meet a fascinating reduction: "A person is only a gene's way of making another gene," quips Mel Konner (1985, p. 48), a sympathetic critic. This reductionism led the late Stephen J. Gould, a harsh critic, to call the new Darwinism "strict adaptationism," for it stipulates that every behavior has reproductive consequences and must be evaluated only along that one dimension. In effect, it "reduces all large-scale evolutionary phenomena to extrapolated results of natural selection working at the level of individual organisms within populations" (Gould, 1987, p. 218). Darwin called this the "struggle for existence." But modern evolutionists call it "reproductive success"(Gould, 1987, p. 218), in a terminological shift that makes all the difference in the world.

According to the new evolutionary theory, earlier Darwinians dropped a stitch: the theory of sexual selection (Trivers, 1972; Buss, 1994; Thornhill and Palmer, 2000). In Darwin's view, the difference between females and males in any species subjects the sexes to different selective pressures. Strict adaptationists have woven this proposition into a seemingly simple story. Females, bearing and then rearing the young, "invest" more than males in reproduction and sexual relations. Males' low reproductive "cost"—a moment of insemination—gives them very different survival needs. Because they bear and raise offspring, female animals seek mates as sires and protectors of them and their progeny. But they will not accept just any male. They wait for

---

[3] Gould (1987) distinguishes several categories of Darwinist thought: classical; strict adaptationism; "good sociobiology," mostly about nonhuman animal behavior; and "bad sociobiology," that is, "pop sociobiology" or "cardboard" Darwinism (pp. 25–51; see also Lewontin et al., 1984), which focuses on human beings. Others, such as the primatologist Haraway (1989), think there is no such thing as "good sociobiology."

those who look like they'll provide well and stick around. It's this female choosiness that converts the male instinct to reproduce into sexual drivenness. Because males are not guaranteed successful mating, they develop competitive strategies—for example, outwitting other males or tricking females—to achieve their goal of reproducing their genetic material (Buss, 1994; pp. 47, 73, 122, and *passim;* Thornhill and Palmer, 2000, pp. 53–54). Along the way, their cutthroat competitiveness heightens their sexual desire, even to the point where rape may be one of their procreative strategies (Buss, 1994; Thornhill and Palmer, 2000).

Now I must confess that I had a hard time writing the foregoing paragraph with a straight face. The idea that rape is Natural is, as you might expect, abhorrent to me. Strict adaptationists would argue that, in my revulsion, I am falling prey to the naturalist fallacy (Thornhill and Palmer, 2000; pp. 107–111 and *passim*). Science merely describes. It does not prescribe. My argument in this book is, however, that, when it comes to human life, the line between description and prescription is impossible to draw a priori. You need to have a debate before you can know—if you can ever know—which is which. You need to know a lot about both the metatheory governing strict adaptationist ideas and the historical context for their appearance on the intellectual scene. As Donna Haraway (1989) states, with characteristic excess and exuberance, "Like it or not, [strict adaptationists] write intertextually within the whole historically dynamic fabric of Western accounts of development, change, individualism, mind, body, liberalism, difference, race, nature, and sex" (p. 366). Sociobiology, for example, dates to the 1970s, which marks it as a reaction to the sexual, intellectual, and social upheavals of the 1960s. Evolutionary psychology, for its part, began growing in the neoconservative, robber-baron 1980s and came of age during the family-values 1990s. Each carries the values of its time.

For my part, the strict adaptationist narrative is more simplistic than simple. Perhaps one might have no quarrel with this account as a narrative of procreation. After all, you can't gainsay the universal process by which male and female genitalia meet, or at least spermatozoon and ovum join, and then begin to divide and differentiate into flesh and blood and bone. The trouble sets in when the selfsame narrative purports to tell the story of sex. All the great variety of human sexuality, including Freud's insights about bisexuality, reduces to a single version of "heterophilia," as psychoanalyst David Schwartz (1993) has brilliantly dubbed it. Heterophilia is the usually unarticulated, "overarching idealization" of heterosexuality that informs our culture and our theories of desire (p. 648). Following Foucault (1976), Schwartz distinguishes heterophilia from the negative—the prejudice termed heterosexism—by focusing on the power of knowledge to construct society: heterophilia is a set of attitudes, behaviors, ideas, and values that creates and re-creates hetero-sexuality as Sexuality. This construction explains why, when we say "sex," we tend to be thinking only of heterosexual intercourse. All other sexualities are afterthoughts, add-ons (Sampson, 1993). As codified in strict adaptationism, the effect, if not the conscious intent, of the heterophiliac Discourse of Nature is to reproduce the common cultural image of mating in which a guy chases a girl until she catches him.

Denying it all the way, strict adaptationism has a politics. Sociobiologists and evolutionary psychologists insist that their critics, especially feminism and Marxism (e.g., Wilson, 1977; Buss, 1994, pp. 211–214; Thornhill and Palmer 2000, pp. 23–124 and *passim*) are dismissable ideologues. But they refuse to recognize their own social commitments. The critics acknowledge their social program—indeed they claim that politics and science are always intertwined (e.g., Lewontin, Rose, and Kamin, 1984; Lewontin, 1991). But, as these critics (Lewontin et al., 1984; Fausto-Sterling, 1986; Gould, 1987; Haraway, 1989; Keller, 1992) contend, the new Darwinians claim to speak only—and the only—Truth.

Curiously, however, you do find strict adaptationists arguing for the morality of their position. They have only the good of society and people at heart, they say. Randy Thornhill and Craig T. Palmer (2000) conclude their book *A Natural History of Rape: Biological Bases of Sexual Coercion* with suggestions for family structures and child-rearing practices that will prevent rape. Surely this kindly advice has some bearing on politics. At the end of *The Evolution of Desire: Strategies of Human Mating*, David Buss (1994) says, "Ultimately, the disturbing side of human mating must be confronted if its harsh consequences are ever to be ameliorated" (p. 5).

This ideological commitment has other signs. How else to explain the odd departures from customary scientific logic found in sociobiological argumentation? They take three main forms: unnoticed contradictions, ambiguous language and rhetoric, and circular reasoning. Buss (1994), for one, waffles in his scientific zeal. Having led off with the thought that science can help us, he then contradicts himself. Acknowledging that the phrase, sexual strategies, as used in his subtitle, misleadingly attributes intent where none could exist, he says: "Just as a piano player's sudden awareness of her hands may impede performance, most human sexual strategies are best carried out without the awareness of the actor" (p. 6). If knowing what Buss teaches us will impede our sexual and reproductive performance, about which we are usually unconscious, then how, as he claims at the end of the book, can such conscious understanding help us exercise our unique "capacity to control our own destiny"? (p. 222).

Sociobiologists and evolutionary psychologists also play fast and loose with language. Where science favors precision, here fuzzy thinking comes in whenever it's handy. Consider the relationship between sex and reproduction. Strict adaptationism claims to tell a story of human sexuality (Buss, 1994), but its underlying principles craft a tale of parenting. Sexual selection, according to Robert Trivers, is governed by "the relative parental effort of the sexes in offspring reproduction" (Thornhill and Palmer, 2000, p. 33). I want to focus on the meaning and use of one phrase, parental effort. "Parental," it turns out, has only partly to do with parents, and "effort" only tangentially to do with trying. Females are said make a greater effort because theirs is the larger gamete: "the initial difference in parental investment—the difference in size between the sperm and the egg—has strongly favored other adaptations that reinforce it" (Thornhill and Palmer, 2000, p. 34). In other words, that the egg is larger than the sperm means that the female puts out greater parental effort and is therefore in greater demand. Their relative size has to do with their different contributions to ontogeny. As compared with ova, which contain nutrients as well as genetic material and whose numbers are great but fixed at birth, spermatozoa, produced in limitless bounty, hold no nutrients at all. In strict adaptationist view, they are "little more than genes with a delivery system" (Gould, 1987, p. 36), which means that males make a lesser parental investment. Consequently, they are the seekers, not the sought.

Now, I use poetic language myself. But I don't claim to be a scientist. Making gametes into parents endows Nature with culture. The unremarked doubleness of meaning in these conjoined terms, parental and effort, smuggles a psychology and sensibility—a subjectivity—into a putatively straightforward account under cover of objectivity and neutrality. Effort, as used by strict adaptationism, denotes the relative contribution made by males and females to procreation. But, as we ordinarily think of it, effort suggests a subjective sense of intentionally working hard. Now you might overlook this scientific appropriation of a vernacular term if the rhetoric of "parenting" also did not do double duty. Consider its range (Thornhill and Palmer, 2000, p. 334): from its common-sense meaning—the activities, psychology, and values of human parenting—to procreation among nonhuman animals, all the way down to the sperm and egg. But the familiar governs: when we imagine sperm and egg as parents, we are likely to see human parents working at being good at their child-rearing job. Because in the Euro-American West, we share a culturally particular idea of parenting—an adult man and woman with children in a nuclear family household—this loose usage projects an image with a limited cultural distribution onto a universal process.

Another linguistic sleight of hand places reproduction and sex in the marketplace. Writing of what happens when what Euro-Americans (or perhaps only North Americans) call "casual sex" ends in pregnancy, Buss (1994) says, "One act of sexual intercourse . . . requires minimal male investment [in contrast to the] nine-month investment by the woman" (p. 19). If she walks away, that is, she bears "the costs of that decision" forever (p. 20). The hazards and gains of casual sex cause women, like men, to seek "contexts in which costs are minimized and benefits increased" (p. 92). Such rhetoric—investment, costs, benefits—suggests, social Darwinian style, not only Nature as capitalism and individuals as entrepreneurs, but also sex and reproduction as utilitarian and instrumental. Indeed, quite serious sociobiological arguments have been made to just that point: altruism, for example, is now chalked up to self-interest in the form of helping those who are your closest genetic relatives before you help anyone else, so that your genes will survive (Dawkins, 1976).

When even plants turn out to be devious, surely it is time to wonder about hidden agendas. Buss (1994), a prolific and premier evolutionary psychologist, argues that orchids, by means of a structure that mimics female wasp genitalia, "deceive" male wasps of the species *Scolia ciliata*. Taking the gaudy flower for *la fleur* (as one of my Haitian college students called her genitals), the male brushes quickly over the flower's hairy surface and, while probing it "in an apparent search for complementary female genital structures," picks up pollen. The structure necessary for ejaculation having been absent, however, the male then goes on to the next "pseudofemale" (p. 153), which is then fertilized by the pollen carried on the male's genitalia. Orchids as cock teasers?

Finally, strict adaptationist reasoning is, at base, circular (Lewontin et al., 1984; Fausto-Sterling, 1986, pp. 160–161). Using the general research strategy of evolutionary biology, it draws on nonhuman life forms to illuminate their topic. But it does not do so in the inductive manner to which it lays claim (Wilson, 1977; Buss, 1994; Thornhill and Palmer, 2000), in which ideas emerge from data. Rather, sociobiologists overlay their data with cultural ideas. Here's how you do it: first, project patterns derived from human society onto nonhuman animals and then derive human behavior from the study of them. Then study apes and monkeys, fowl and insects. Next anthropomorphize them (Zuk, 2002). Give them cultural practices: implicitly endow, say, birds with marriage vows by saying that "doves experience a divorce rate of about 25% every season" (Buss, 1994, p. 11).

Go further. Regard insects as intentional creatures.[4] Discover the psychological and sexual richness of scorpionflies' procreative behavior. Males "prefer to provide mates with nuptial food gifts." However, if they don't have "dead insects or saliva masses" (Thornhill and Palmer, 2000, pp. 78–79) at their disposal and if they are endowed with a "notal organ" with clamps that seem designed just for rape, they will inseminate a female by force, especially if they are smaller or more asymmetrical than average (pp. 53–54).

---

[4] Describe, for example, a male of the *Johannseniella nitida* fly species, which, after copulation, leaves genital parts in a female's reproductive aperture, as doing so "in order to forestall reproductive takeovers from rivals" (Buss, 1994, p. 124).

Next discover in such phenomena the direct link between
biological reproduction and human sexuality. Say, with Buss
(1994), that what women want and what men want are universally
different. For human animals, describe the difference between
female and male investments as nine months plus 20 years versus,
at most, 20 minutes, respectively. Then argue that what women
want is men's care and protection (i.e., love and marriage) and
what men want is sex with many women (or girls), by force if
necessary. And then deem women's wishes for monogamy and
men's for promiscuity, and the consequent cultural battle between
the sexes, as natural, as written in the genes.

What you get is nurture painted as nature. A particular (cultural)
version of human procreativity and sexuality is said to be natural
and thereby re-created as universal. Yet beneath this circularity is
an even more subtle vicious cycle whereby the natural is equated
with the normal, the good, and the sane. There is but one way to
make sex and it just happens to be the way you make babies. Is
this anything but good? We might wonder about nonprocreative
pleasure sex and feel relief that its disturbances are regulated by
its reproductive functions. Indeed, you can see this family-values
unease in Thornhill and Palmer's (2000) neoconservative
suggestions for young girls. Rape being a consequence of males'
response to female choosiness—the chief selective pressure on
them—and young, pretty, fertile girls being the most common
victims of rape, we should be careful about coeducational activities.
Girls should be instructed in the dangers that men present
(pp. 180–181). Physical barriers should be instituted; for example,
e.g., summer camps should put a wide distance between boys'
and girls' bunks (p. 185). Sneakouts should presumably be
prevented by neochastity belts. What about locking girls in high
towers? Remember Rapunzel.

But parenting? Surely that is only healthy. Surely that is normal.
Surely that is sane. Surely that is good. A prescriptive moral to
the story hides in the strict adaptationist line of argument. Link
species survival to parenting and you endow a particular culture's
way of rearing children with the authority of Nature. Link
parenting with species survival and you burnish Nature with the
honor of modeling Western child rearing. The laissez-faire social
Darwinians used to think that Victorian society was civilization's

pinnacle and that evolution had been leading up to it all along. The strict-adaptationist acorn hasn't fallen far from the social Darwinist tree.

On this view, there's only one way to tell the story of sex: sex is reproduction. And reproduction takes place only one way: through the meeting and matching of those two beings whom we call parents, a male and a female who are so different that the twain shall meet only through their genitalia. Here is Gould's sarcastic summary: "males are aggressive, assertive, promiscuous, over-bearing; females are coy, discriminating, loyal, caring—and these differences are adaptive, Darwinian, genetic, proper, good, inevitable, unchangeable" (Gould, 1987, p. 36). Despite strict adaptationism's scientific shortcomings (Gould, 1981), despite, or because of, its service to moral ideals, cultural conventions of normality, and political forces (Haraway, 1989, pp. 320–322 and *passim*; Keller, 1992, pp. 33–43), it wears the badge of science and hence stands as a guarantor of (objective and neutral) Truth.

Heterosexuality is the singular behavioral hero in this story. Because the measure of any behavior is its contribution to species reproduction, heterosexuality, by matching penis to vagina, receives top marks.[5] Unsurprisingly, nonheterosexualities show up only exceptionally on the sociobiological map. When they do, it's to serve reproductive needs. Gould (1987, p. 47) cites sociobiologist Daniel Kevles, who saw in female pair bonding among ring-billed gulls on the Channel Islands a survival strategy providing greater opportunity for both females to be impregnated by promiscuous males. Thornhill and Palmer (2000, p. 55) cite feminist primatologists to argue that, among nonhuman primates, a female will pair-bond with another female to avoid rape, preserve female choice, and ensure their genes get reproduced through copulation with a superior mate.

Well, maybe. But homosexuality as erotic? Its usual absence is the clue to its value in this account: none. Despite its cultural ubiquity (Vance, 1991; Herdt, 1998), strict adaptationism offers no narrative account of it. "The origins of homosexuality remain

---

[5] A match that is, by the way, the founding trope of classical psychosexual theory—even, one might say, its ego ideal.

a mystery," states Buss (1994, p. 61). On these grounds, homosexuality might be argued to come and go like other traits lacking survival value, that is, randomly. In strict adaptationist eyes, however if it is females' nature to nurture and males' to prey, then women and men with other sexual natures are possessed of maladaptations and will disappear from the face of the earth. It is not far to go to think that the maladaptive is unnatural, that is, abnormal, hence ill or bad, immoral, insane.

The story of heterophilia constitutes the Discourse of Nature. Many disciplines participate in this Discourse, not only biology, but psychoanalysis, Marxist and other social theories, feminism, even anarchism (the anarchist Peter Kropotkin, 1902, used cooperativeness in nature as partial justification for the political program he set forth in *Mutual Aid*). If nature is thought to be the bedrock of human nature, and if biology has the final word on nature, then nature stands as a fount of truth, and everyone wants to locate their view of human society in biology.

As psychoanalytic participation makes quite clear, the terms of biological necessity, social normativity, and mental health are fungible in the Discourse of Nature. Many times, for example, Freud links his understanding of sexuality to Darwinian narrative, such linkage itself also being forged to moral precepts, assertions of social need, and models of mental health. This fungibility is evident in the literary structure of Freud's (1905b) "Three Essays on the Theory of Sexuality." Sexuality, beginning in poly-morphousness, has the potential for many story lines. As the narrative narrows, however, the requirements of procreation and species survival, the demands of culture, and the lineaments of sanity gradually come to imply and evoke one another (e.g., p. 229; see also Chapter 5, this volume). By the end, cultural stricture, psychic integrity, and reproductive survival speak in one voice. Sexual desire must conclude as a single narrative, the dual-gendered subordination of fore-pleasure to end-pleasure, in which (penile) discharge takes place in the correct (vaginal) receptacle.

Freud may argue that, "neuroses are, so to say, the negative of perversions" (p. 165). He may tell us that we fall ill because we inhibit nonprocreative desire. He may diagnose neurosis as the occupational hazard of civilization (p. 231; see also 1908, 1930). But the conventional Darwinian story of sexual nature is the story of cultural convention: if you don't do it the right way, not only will your genes not get reproduced, you'll wind up very, very sick. Heterosexual and potentially procreative intercourse is foregone at the cost of moral and emotional normality. Or, if you're not straight, you must be crazy.

SNAFU: An Excursion into Psychoanalytic Contradictions

Ahh, normality, that for which we all long but believe, deep in our despairing hearts, we will never attain. At last we're getting to the bottom of things. Normality is a torment equally of psyche, society, and, therefore, theory.[6] I have in mind here not only the Foucauldian (1976) critique (see also Chapters 1 and 9, this volume), according to which normality is constituted by knowledge, that is, by ideologies and regulating practices that activate and authorize patterns of domination. I also have in mind problems particular to psychoanalytic knowledge of sexuality, which routinely implies and entails developmental theory.

In my opinion, developmental theory customarily constitutes a theory of normality, of normal development. Put this another way. Many of you reading these words will have taken a course in "abnormal psychology." But have you ever taken a course in "normal psychology"? "No," you will say. But "Yes," you must answer, only it's gone under another name: sometimes it's called personality theory, most often it's called development. What these courses in the phenomenology of the normal teach is the process and steps of psychological, including sexual, growth and change.

To anticipate an objection: I am not suggesting we do away altogether with developmental theory. We require some way to think about change, if only because, with death and taxes, it's one of the few certainties. Still, current theories of psychological development won't quite do. The problem is not exactly one of final truth; the debatability of psychoanalytic truth (Mitchell, 1988, pp. 123–170) is intellectually desirable. The problem is

---

[6] Whether "normality" is an unavoidable and even necessary displeasure, which was Freud's (1908) contention, remains a matter too complicated to take up here.

more that of theory. Indeed, one of the juicy riddles psychologists and psychoanalysts have on their plates is how to theorize psychological change without imprisoning in normality the multiplicity of personal experience and the "multilinearity" (to borrow a term from anthropology; Steward, 1955) of psychological process (see O'Connor and Ryan, 1994, p. 16). Ken Corbett (2001b) and Harris (in press) are now fashioning multilinear theories of development based on chaos theory.

You see, whenever I think of the word normal (and let me apologize right away for referring to an experience that may be familiar only to provincial New Yorkers), all I can visualize is one of those electronic signs on the Long Island Expressway. You know, you're driving home after a lovely weekend in the Hamptons or Fire Island when suddenly you see it, the sign that strikes dread in your heart, the sign that says, "Normal Traffic Conditions Ahead." *Normal* traffic conditions? On what traffic reporters fondly dub "The World's Longest Parking Lot"? I don't know about you, but whenever I see that sign, I think, "Oh God, please, no, anything but that." They say there are no atheists in foxholes. I say, there are no atheists in the nightmare that constitutes normality on the Long Island Distressway.[7]

But wait a minute. Isn't that what normality is? A nightmare? Think of the classic World War II acronym, SNAFU. A military term, it evokes what psychoanalysts know truly defines the normal—the paradox, if you will, at normality's heart: "Situation Normal, All Fucked Up." Indeed, originally it is normality itself that makes the mess, at least according to the *Dictionary of American Slang* (Wentworth and Flexner, 1967, p. 493): "SNAFU. Original Army use c. 1940." The original Army connotation was that the situation was 'fucked up' owing to an excess of Army rules and routine."[8]

---

[7] David Bouchier (1994), a radio commentator, journalist, humorist, and sociologist, said all this perhaps a little more concisely. He described a suburban feeding ritual: "'Come on over. We're having a barbeque.'" What other message can strike such gloom and despondency into the suburban soul? Perhaps only "'Normal Traffic Conditions Ahead' has the same heart-chilling effect."

[8] By the way, most dictionaries define it as "Situation Normal, All Fouled Up," a normalizing and (what may be the same thing) deeroticizing gesture in itself (see, e.g., *The Random House Dictionary of the English Language*, 1966, p. 1346).

Freud, too, believed, as is well known and I've stressed, that order creates disorder. It's just the refusal to recognize this fact that's pathologically destructive.[9] Not only inhibition and neurosis but "civilization and its discontents" were, finally, Freud's ironic watchwords. If, then, neurosis is normative in civilization, what other meanings inhere in the notion of "normal"?

To put it another way, if we subtract the normative from the normal, what's left over? The excess, it seems to me, consists in the regulatory force of the idea of the "normal," a notion central to the power of psychoanalysis as a political and social institution. "Normality" is a powerful force because it seems to designate what's only good and right, that is, what's natural. This naturalness is, however, an artifact created by a discursive process that projects "assumptions about nature back and forth between biology and society in a vicious rhetorical circle" (Ross, 1994, p. 19). Spun 'round and 'round, the natural, the normal, and the moral become confused, one with the other, barely separable even on inspection.

Normalizing is central to psychoanalytic prescriptivity, that is, to its way of participating in regulatory practice. Mitchell (1993) notes this prescriptivity in an account of psychoanalytic homophobia. He identifies "an omnipotent ideal that placed the analyst in the position of arbiter of the good life" (p. 623). My qualm is that he localizes this admirably described power to name the normal within a mere two decades, the 1960s and 1970s. In contrast, many accounts situate psychoanalysis among the most powerful 20th-century institutions of social reproduction, whose job it is to re-create the status quo, that is, "the normal," each generation and every day (Kovel, 1981; Ehrenreich, 1989; Dimen, 1992).

Psychoanalytic thinking renders its own prescriptivity simultaneously normal, natural, and moral by creating a master narrative of human nature out of a particular sexual theory. Freud's compelling, universalizing story of human psyche, culture, and biology is a good example. In "Totem and Taboo" (Freud, 1913), his prime text on desire as the hub of human history, he argues that psychoanalysis will be key to a synthetic theory of human

---

[9] Levenson (1994) renders Freud's idea in a contemporary vernacular: "Maybe, as Mel Brooks put it, 'Life stinks' and recognizing that is a prerequisite for living successfully" (p. 706).

nature: "The beginnings of religion, morals, society, and art converge in the Oedipus complex" (p. 156). In a footnote, Freud first disclaims this centrality, saying he has just added one more factor. Then he goes on to insist that, even though people will resist this factor emotionally, it will have to be critical to the theory. Indeed, he himself is (perhaps genuinely) nonplussed: "It seems to me a most surprising discovery that the problems of social psychology, too, should prove soluble on the basis of one single concrete point—a man's relation to his father" (1913, p. 157, n. 1). Gender critique aside—although patriarchy is in many ways the point here—to establish a totalizing theory resting on a single, elemental cause is, in post-Enlightenment Western thought, a claim to Truth.

As both Marxists and postmodernists argue, however, claims to Truth are also claims on power. Take scientific notions of gender. Anne Fausto-Sterling (1986) argues that biological theories about differences between women and men serve power needs. Like Richard Lewontin (1991), she holds that systems of knowledge are created in the interest of ruling classes. A chapter begins as follows:

> Jobs and education—that's what it's really all about. At the crux of the question "Who's smarter, men or women?" lie decisions about how to teach reading and mathematics, about whether boys and girls should attend separate schools, about job and career choices, and, as always, about money—how much employers will have to pay to whom and what salaries employees, both male and female, can command [p. 13].

If Fausto-Sterling and Lewontin hold that knowledge is power, Foucault (1976, 1988) proposes the converse. Seeing knowledge as produced rather than controlled, he gives equal time to the formulation, "power is knowledge." In cultural ethos, institutions, and people, there is a will to knowledge constituted by a political economy of sex, immanent in which are strategies of power (1976, pp. 12, 73). The state wants to ensure orderly behavior, not only to punish crimes ex post facto; its interest is in the internalization of social control. "The more peaceful (i.e., controlled) the population, the more the state's power is legitimated and assured" (Flax, 1990, p. 208). Such social control, or domination, depends on manufactured truths, and therefore on the systems that produce them: "There can be no exercise of power except through the production of truth. These 'truths' reflect the 'facts of human nature' as revealed by biological and human science. These discourses tell us what it is to be human" (p. 207). As we have seen, strict adaptationist theories of sex-as-reproduction instruct us quite insistently in these matters.

Scholarly disciplines create a politically efficacious view of human life by claiming to find its source in Nature and thereby to demonstrate its truth, goodness, health, normality. Simultaneously forged are "[c]oncepts of deviancy, illness, maladjustment, and so forth," for they "are products of the same discourses that create the normal" (p. 207).[10] Sexuality is key to this socially controlling view of human nature. A plethora of disciplines—"demography, biology, medicine, psychiatry, psychology, ethics, pedagogy, and political criticism"—produces the truth of human nature by creating "sexuality" (Foucault, 1976, pp. 25–26, 33).

Sexuality, in turn, becomes divided into Natural and Unnatural. For example, demography emerged as a scientific discipline when, in the early 18th century, the category of population became for European states a social control problem distinct from questions about people as political actors. "At the heart of this economic and political problem of population was sex: it was necessary to analyze the birth rate, the age of marriage, the legitimate and illegitimate births, the precocity and frequency of sexual relations, the ways of making them fertile or sterile, the effects of unmarried life or of the prohibitions, the impact of contraceptive practices" (pp. 25–26). The resulting analyses, by dividing and classifying, rendered some sexualities natural, others not. The unnatural became a particular dimension in the sexual domain, covering everything outside of marital sex (p. 39).

This continuing production of new discourses on sex (of which the present contribution, let it be noted, is one), or what Foucault calls *scientia sexualis,* permits "something called 'sexuality' to embody the truth of sex and its pleasures." This socially naturalized creation called sexuality is the correlate of the discursive practice of the *scientia sexualis,* which defines sex as being by "nature," vulnerable to pathology and therefore requiring therapy, containing meanings requiring decoding, situating concealed

---

[10] "Failure of disciplinary practices becomes the basis of 'experts' to ask for more resources and power to pursue and exercise their knowledge in the name of the public good" (Flax, 1990, p. 208).

processes, a center for multiple and indeterminate causalities (p. 68).

From a postmodernist perspective, the truth of the Natural is social and political, and as such is subject to deconstruction. If, then, we look into the heterophiliac Discourse of nature, we find that the natural is not self-evident, undifferentiated, eternal bedrock. If natural defines the normal, the normal seeks its validation as a moral category by claiming its natural origins. To put the matter even more complexly and therefore more accurately; if natural–unnatural is a key binary for evolutionary theory, then normal–abnormal, sane–mad, and healthy–unhealthy are key binaries of psychoanalysis. In turn, these dualisms interchange with the good–bad, the right–wrong, and the moral–immoral that anchor the system of cultural conventions we call morality. This entire set of binaries forms the matrix that confines psychoanalytic thought about sexuality, leading it along the straight and narrow to an unintended destination.

Desire and Evolution: On the Winding Road to Ambiguity

If we elaborate on these complexities, contingencies, and ambiguities that I have been indicating, the seams in the Discourse of Nature begin to show and split. To recapitulate: if species survival is reproduction's goal, it's the biological organism that's usually taken as the main evolutionary product. If so, then the question that strict adaptationism insists we ask is also the question that, according to psychoanalysis, the incest prohibition excites: how is one of those products, those individual organisms, made? We want to see the primal scene up close. A theory, whether psychoanalytic or evolutionary, that starts from this (oedipal) question (and obsession) tells a single story that inevitably winds up naturalizing and normalizing heterosexuality.

Contemporary biological theory, in other words, does not adequately describe the species that psychoanalysts, at least, want to understand, a species that is more than its genes.[11] What

---

[11] This assertion would probably hold for most species; the difference is that human beings think and write about it.

psychoanalysts want to know is what is either flattened out by evolutionary psychology or of no interest to Biology. The mating game, which psychoanalysis, evolutionary psychology, and popular culture commonly think of as Natural, is, finally, irrelevant to contemporary evolutionary science. If relational thought has moved up toward the social, Biological thought has shifted down to the microscopic. Population biology, for example, cares little about the primal scene. Nor does it address sexuality in any way recognizable to psychoanalytic thought. In these molecular days, most biologists think about genes, not individuals; they study gene pools, not species (let alone social organizations like actual parenting, the nuclear family, and their psychodynamics).[12] In exasperation, Keller (1992), a mathematical biologist, damns mainstream biological thinking for representing the essence of life as nothing more than a string of amino acids (p. 96 and *passim*).

It is an ethnographic truism that the human species requires more than its amino acids to reproduce. The nature of human nature is, as anthropologists like to say, cultural as well as biological—and therefore inherently various (Lévi-Strauss, 1949, pp. 3–25). Gould (1977) quotes de Beauvoir, who said that we are *"l'être dont l'être est de n'être pas*—the being whose essence lies in having no essence" (p. 259). As three contemporary Marxist biologists put it, "The only sensible thing to say about human nature is that it is 'in' that nature to construct its own history" (Lewontin, Rose, and Kamin, 1984, p. 14). This construction is inevitably a social process. No human being survives as an isolate; put a baby down alone on a desert island and see what happens. The unit of survival is society or culture (Steward, 1955), not the individual organism.

Society, we have known since the turn of the last century, is a level of organization unto itself. With Émile Durkheim and Franz Boas,[13] we have thought of culture as a phenomenon exceeding and preceding the individuals who make it up. To its discredit, strict adaptationism seriously misunderstands this idea. Tendentiously, Thornhill and Palmer (2000) take a behavioral tack: "If the referent of 'a culture' is restricted to what can be identified by the senses, a culture is seen to consist of no more than a number

---

[12] Indeed, the reproduction of the species is in some sociobiological texts merely in service of the reproduction of the gene (Dawkins, 1976).

[13] Not to mention Marx and Engels.

of individuals interacting in certain ways" (p. 129). Not only do they here ignore the fact that their own referents are not "restricted to what can be identified by the senses" (recall the capitalism of insects), they also deny that social institutions have an existence apart from the individuals who compose them. Thus, they refer to "the specific environmental influence of other individuals (commonly referred to as 'culture')" (p. 142). By this definition, their own scientific tradition would consist of nothing more than individual bench scientists. On this view, in fact, there could be no such thing as a "tradition." nor, come to think of it, could there be progress either: without tradition, there would be only the daily reinvention of the scientific wheel.[14]

That human beings are cultural, that cultures differ and change—these facts will not surprise you. The question is what these commonplaces mean for psychoanalysis. René Spitz (1957) provided one answer: put a baby down in a crib and don't talk to it, he said, you'll see what happens—it dies of apathy. Winnicott (1960), of course, supplied another: there's no such thing as a baby, he proclaimed rhetorically, to dramatize his point that the infant exists only in an environment mediated by the maternal object, only in a relational context (p. 39, n. 1). The human species is not only biological, not only cultural, it's also relational. We are as much part of the context as the context is part of us. This relational context must be reproduced if the species is to survive. Now, what does this mean? Leaving aside the reproduction of social relations and institutions (which is culture's job and which, ultimately, must also be accounted for, but not within the confines of this essay; see Dimen, 1992), we might say what we're talking about is object relations and the desire drenching them.[15]

---

[14] What, I wonder, do strict adaptationists make of Kuhn's (1972) epochal *The Structure of Scientific Revolutions?*

[15] To speak of object relations and desire is, in a sense, to speak two languages whose compatibility requires some mechanism of mutual translation. I think about the problem thus: In relational perspective, the intrapsychic and the interpersonal are mutually constituted; from this already postmodernist angle, there's no chicken and egg, each is always already there. The intrapsychic comes into being and takes on its meaning and value in the charged, desiring field between persons, while, paradoxically, that field is realized through the inner worlds of the participants. And so our question about the evolution of the human species and what is natural in it entails a specifically psychoanalytic discussion of object relations, of the internal representations of self and others

Yet once we admit desire into the Discourse of the Natural, the whole story of the natural normality of heterosexuality explodes. The idea that sexuality roots most importantly in evolutionary, reproductive requirements loses credibility and meaning. Desire, a concept whose elusiveness fills "Americans, pragmatists to the core" with dread (Levenson, 1994, p. 692), can be most efficiently defined by what it is not: "Wants, needs, can be met. Desire is another kettle of fish entirely" (p. 692). Desire is about lack, absence, longing. Unlike need and demand, it is fundamentally unsatisfiable, a permanent, driving incompleteness. The yearning in which it manifests itself can be approximated in language but is, finally, unspeakable and ambiguous (Mitchell and Rose, 1982, pp. 1–58).[16]

However intensely felt, desire becomes sensible only through culture. Lévi-Strauss's (1949) characterization of the universality of the incest prohibition could apply as well to desire: "Culture has at all times and at all places filled this empty form, as a bubbling spring first fills the depressions surrounding its source" (p. 32). Lacan, in a certain sense, is correct in saying that desire is unspecifiable in the absence of the symbolic order (Mitchell and Rose, 1982). To put it more humorously, desire is like invisible ink: it won't show up unless it gets wet. But what w(h)ets it is culture: the coloring, flavoring, meanings of the without which it could not be represented and, unrepresented, could not exist.

More graphically, desire denotes what Freud (1905b) calls "sexual impulses—in the ordinary sense of the word" (p. 134), sexual desire as we vulgarly think of it, sex in all its concreteness, physicality, and excitement. Yet even before Freud, who understood sex as biological drive, anthropological researchers were teaching that no particular sexual desire is natural (Morgan,

---

as they are contextualized by emotion and value. In my view, emotion and value inhere in the desire in which object relations are suspended. From a feminist perspective, Jaggar (1989) argues for the intermixture of emotional and social value: just as social values always carry an emotional charge, so emotions are always permeated with social values.

[16]The debate on desire is intense, complex, and current. Of chief contemporary psychoanalytic interest is whether or not it is intersubjective, and if it is, how intersubjective. Levenson (1994), Stein (1998), Benjamin (2001), Dimen (2002), and Goldner (2003).

1870, in the United States and Tylor, 1889, in England).[17] Human organisms cannot and do not exist without cultural form, without social institutions, language, and so forth. Cultural forms, furthermore, vary, if not infinitely, then very, very widely. Because they do, human desire must be malleable, as Margaret Mead (1928), agreeing with Lévi-Strauss (1949, p. 32), put it—or, as I am putting it—multiple. It must be ready for anything, which means it must also be ready for nothing in particular. It must be nonspecific or, what is the same thing, omnivorous. In any event, it can't keep kosher.

Is this a long way to say what Freud (1905b) did in brief, that desire is polymorphously perverse? Not quite. The full force of his idea is unfelt unless the understanding of sexuality slips the dualistic leash. It's no longer enough just to point out Freud's obligation to Darwinism. And it is equally insufficient to argue, dualistically, that Nurture dominates Nature in the domain of sexuality (or, indeed, in any other domain; for example, intelligence). Sexual theory requires freedom from the determinism that psychoanalysis, like many other fields, has employed as an explanatory and rhetorical strategy. Determinism is part of what Flax (1990) calls the "Enlightenment metanarrative" (p. 30). In postmodernist view, it is a story of how human progress takes place through the application of reason to human life. This linear reckoning of cause and effect underlies all Western disciplines and knowledges, constructing their search for singular truths.

My argument for psychoanalysis, like Gould's (1987, 2002) for Darwinism, is to give up all determinism.[18] It may seem, for example, that desire's cultural variability demonstrates its independence from Nature. But oppositionalism always restores what it topples. The argument that cross-cultural variation disproves biological determination won't quite wash. As told, it

---

[17] Indeed, cultural relativism and an appreciation of cross-cultural diversity reach far back in Western thought, not only to Montaigne but even to Herodotus.

[18] In Gould's (1987) view, the natural world, constituted as a strict Darwinian's purview, contains many ambiguities (pp. 13–14) that could be better appreciated by a view of "biological potentiality" (Gould, 1977). He pleads for a nondeterminist, Darwinian theory of contingency and interactivity capable of attending, without reductionism, to diversity, complexity, and ambiguity.

substitutes one determinism for another, making Nurture not Nature, Culture, not Biology, the prime mover. Therefore, the culturalist strategy, used without critiquing determinism, leaves sexuality and desire as *tabulae rasae* to be inscribed according to cultures' needs (see, e.g., M. Harris, 1989). But because, in the determinist game, that which is closest to the physical wins; desire, once constituted, emerges, yet again, as Biology's unambiguous, undifferentiated, uniformed servant (see Thornhill and Palmer's, 2000, p. 110, critique of Harris's cultural materialism).

We need to find a third beyond Nature versus Nurture, and that's going to take us into ambiguity. Look at the quite different implications of polymorphous perversity from a postmodernist perspective. Desire's prime quality is its contingency, of which its vaunted cultural malleability is a consequence. In introducing their definition of "wish," LaPlanche and Pontalis (1973) say, "Any general theory of man [*sic*] is bound to contain ideas too fundamental to be circumscribed; this is no doubt true of desire in Freudian doctrine" (p. 482). To render this experientially; the confusion we experience in trying to decode desire is the decoding. Desire is ambiguous. Sometimes it is focused and precise, sometimes it's elusive and inconclusive. Desire is discontinuous, shifting. It is what waits to be given definition within and between selves. Among the diverse meanings it has received, all situationally plausible, are the classic linkage to reproductive goals; the equally classic Freudian delinking of drive, aim, and object; the Lacanian gap between the Imaginary and the Symbolic; and object-relational yearning for attachment.[19] When desire emerges as an indeterminate end in itself, as, with its passions, impossibilities, and pain, it often is; a quantum leap has been taken, and the rest is history—and psychoanalysis.

---

[19] Evolutionary psychologists and other sociobiologists might wish to look at the primate record for evidence of ambiguity in the nonhuman realm. See de Waal and Lanting (1997) as well as Haraway (1989), who suggest that we might be better off thinking in terms of contingencies, not determinisms. Except in the most general sense, which renders it meaningless, biological determinism, a theory not of ambiguities but of linearities, irreversibilities, and dualisms does not work for sex.

Between Instinct and Object, Clinic and Culture

We should sever the tie between psychoanalysis and the Discourse of Nature. Determinism suits the Freud (1905b) who wed desire to procreation, not the Freud (1930) who queried the abrogation of ambiguity in, say, the commonsense matching of masculinity to activity, femininity to passivity (p. 105, n. 3). As such, it skirts the 20th-century paradigm shift from either–or to both–and— from positivism to uncertainty, relativity, and contingency, from empiricism to social constructionism and deconstructionism. Its logic—the Discourse of Nature—figures nature in the image dear to the heart of a heterophiliac culture.

Psychoanalysis should not only forgo its classical grounding of sexuality in the requirements of evolutionary survival. It should also forget the postclassical presumption that what's Natural is not sex but attachment. On close inspection, this seemingly revolutionary theoretical advance is but another dualistic reversal. The classic sexual dualism—sex drives attachment—morphs into the postclassical relational dualism: attachment directs sex (see Chapter 5 for a more extended discussion of this reversal). Either–or.

If Freud missed something about relatedness, this naturalizing of attachment overlooks something about desire. "Excitement," Adam Philips (1988) observes,

> tends to turn up in object relations theory as a defense against something reputedly more valuable. . . . The implication . . . is that freedom is freedom from bodily excitement. As though in states of desire the self was, as it were, complying with the tyranny of the body [p. 71].

Object relations theory, by subordinating the erotic to relatedness, smacks of a certain Puritanism that may be discerned in, for example, Winnicott's "distrust of, or dismay about, the nature of instinctual life" (Phillips, 1988, p. 71). That psycho-analytic Puritanism (an oxymoron that André Green, 1996, delighted in exploiting) is, itself, regulatory practice hardly needs demonstrating and is argued in Chapters 5, 7, and 9.

What I am suggesting and initiating is a deconstruction of psychoanalysis's use of biology, its participation in the Discourse of Nature that is the foundation for its regulatory power. Psychoanalysis and the Discourse of Nature are historically mutually constitutive: the idea of Nature informs the theory of human nature which, in that vicious rhetorical cycle, recreates a sense of givenness. Yet Nature lacks a common meaning, even as it seems to be common sense (Ross, 1994, p. 250); everyone, from conservation biologists to sociobiologists, from economists and politicians to poets, means something different by it—females, race, social convention, personality (for examples, see Haraway, 1989, pp. 82, 140, 153, 251, 280).

For psychoanalytic purposes, the idea of the Natural is not so much wrong as too coherent: either Nature or Nurture, heterosexual or homosexual, masculine or feminine. It's certainly true that, given that the human species reproduces itself biologically through the union of spermatozoon and ovum, a penis and vagina that, you might say, want each other are critical for the propagation of species, as is, therefore, a psyche appropriately coded for a set of heterosexualizing institutions, like marriage, parenting, and the family. However, this reproduction doesn't just happen; to borrow de Beauvoir's pronouncement on women, heterosexuality is made, not born. Its presence depends on the cultural construction of two opposing genders (Butler, 1995; Chapter 6, this volume), the similarities between which are systematically minimized and the differences sharpened (Rubin, 1975).

Dialectics, not determinism, is what's required. I agree with Ogden's (1994, p. 15) argument that Freud's "struggle with the limitations of" linear, positivistic thought reveals his and his followers aspiration to science as a cover for psychoanalysis' dialectical spirit. In Euro-American culture as we know it now, that which potentiates reproductive heterosexuality also undoes it. Desire must flower for heterosexual—and procreative—activity to occur. If it does, however, then so do impulses and tendencies—polymorphous perversity—that may contradict procreative sex and the normative structures housing it. As Freud's (1905b) theses on the direct relation between neurosis and sexual inhibition suggest, many psychological and cultural events must take place if one is to be turned on by people of only one sex, whether of one's own or the opposite's. Being excited by the Other doesn't just happen. It requires a context potentiated by the one- and two-person work/practice/activity of relatedness.[20]

I recognize, at this point, a likely objection: at the very moment when homosexual desire seems to have received the same scientific imprimatur as heterosexuality, that is, when it's gotten a place at the genetic table of life, I am arguing, "Oh, let's just forget about reactionary old Nature." The problem, however, is not nature, but the rhetorical (as well as material) use we make of it. Nature has been and is used both popularly and scientifically to condemn homosexuality. Maybe the tide has turned. But tides turn again. Scientific theories ebb and flow with public opinion. The Discourse of Nature, in other words, is not on the side of the angels, or, better, of those who are customarily demonized. Appealing to it is like carrying a loaded gun to fend off assailants: you're more likely to get shot than if you weren't packing, and, finally, it doesn't remove the cause of the crime.

Of course, once we exit the familiar (should I say familial?) expressway to Nature, we travel an anxious byway, which brings me back to an alternative reading of this essay's initial text, a single, spoken sentence whose curious syntax sings a vital and necessary anxiety. One of the accomplishments of a normalizing theory of sexuality is that it provides landmarks in an otherwise open and sometimes seemingly endless sea of desire. Even its inherent pathologizing serves as a guide of sorts: if it pathologizes you, well, at least you know where you are, you've been wronged or you are wrong, but you do have an identity. Right–wrong. Dualism is reassuring: "I'm this, not that."

The television text with which I began, however, rejects all theory. It reads, if you remember, "I'm not gay because my parents did anything wrong." We have so far taken this to mean, "I'm not gay because my parents did anything wrong but because that's how I naturally and rightly am." On this understanding, we have interpreted the sentence's anxious overtone as related to the self-

---

[20] It was, after all, to explain this by no means self-evident phenomenon that Freud (1905b) wrote the "Three Essays" after all. That he there recapitulated cultural prejudices of homophobia and sexism, and that he created a one-person psychology compatible with the biological determinism to which he looked for confirmation and authorization, serves as fodder for a contemporary reinterpretation of sexuality.

righteous emotional and moral demand placed on theory to exonerate children and parents from a psychologically and socially harmful, unfair blame. And we have seen that, in validating this demand, the text has recourse to the facts of nature, taken to be morally unblameworthy, neutrally true, an explanation beyond explanation.

Still, if you consider the text's negation, the placement of the "not," then another meaning emerges. We've heard, "I'm gay not because my parents. . . ." But the actual sequence is, "I'm not gay because. . . ." The "not" refuses the predicate beginning "gay because." There is, says the text, not "gay because." There's only "gay." "Gay" neither wants nor needs explanation. Do we, the syntax asks, say "I'm heterosexual because. . . ."? Don't we explain only that which is somehow "different," which sticks out, calls attention to itself as unnatural? Explanations only harm, suggests the text; they pathologize, stigmatize, and delegitimize.

One reason, we can conclude, that there is to be no "gay because" is that homosexuality should be understood as natural, normal, just like heterosexuality which, as "the absent standard" (Sampson, 1993) of psychological and political normality—like masculinity, the "unmarked category"—neither wants nor needs nor receives explanation. Gay should receive the same privilege as straight, including what we might call "SNAFU privilege," the right to be fucked up without having your desire stigmatized because of it, or the right to have your sexual problems addressed without having your sexual preference pathologized. Like heterosexuality, gay identity should be the uncontested base of identity politics as well.

One can only agree. And yet. . . . It's not my job here to opine on identity politics, whose exigencies often require what Spivak and Rooney (1994) have termed, in regard to women, a "strategic essentialism," which in this case might mean using Darwinian theory as a claim to truth and power. It is more imperative that I address what I find troubling in this implicit refusal of explanation, which I think emerges from an anxiety born of ambiguity. For one thing, if we don't provide explanations, someone else will: you need a position to counter the hydra-headed forces of homophobia, misogyny, and so on. For another, refusing explanation refuses what we do know, that one's experience and history and one's own personal individual nature have something to do with each other. One's personal nature is a complicated output of multiple constructions, happenings, meanings: a contingency (Rorty, 1989), not a determinism.

To refuse explanation is to refuse the complexity of desire and the tangle of pain. Sex is not uncomplicated, to put it mildly. Its scariness is not always intrinsic to its excitement. In entailing as much unpleasure as pleasure, sex doesn't always provide as much joy as it might. If we don't usually want to look a gift horse in the mouth and ask why we're having a good (sexual) time (Stoller, 1979; Goldner, 2003), we do tend to want to know why we're not. Absent explanation, there's no way to figure out what's wrong. Who or what causes sexual (and other psychic) pain? Sometimes the villain is the Other, sometimes it's us. Sometimes we blame our parents because of the pain sex brings us, but are mistaken to do so: the pain may come from social prejudice, or it may emanate from the grievous losses we all meet on life's trail. Sometimes, however, we are right to hold someone else to account: people make mistakes, and sometimes we even collude in those our parents make.

How to understand these complications and ambiguities? There are a variety of routes. One is traditional, to posit binaries that eliminate ambiguity: the normal–evolutionary–heterosexual versus the pathological–unnatural–queer. But there are others: for example, Chodorow's (1992) argument from a classical position that all sex, including heterosexuality, should be interpreted as compromise formation. I am proposing a third route, one formed in the main tension or, perhaps we may call it, paradox, in Freud's sexual theory. I want to suggest that there are many possible narratives of sexuality. As Haraway (1989) insists, evolutionary theory can and should support deconstruction into multiple accounts. As Chodorow (1994) argues, sex and romance, even within the United States, are inspired by as many fantasies as there are subcultures.

Classical psychoanalysis provides much room for postclassical multiplicity. Recall this footnote to Freud's (1905b) "Three Essays":

> The most striking distinction between the erotic life of antiquity and our own no doubt lies in the fact that the ancients laid the stress upon the instinct itself, whereas we emphasize its object. The

ancients glorified the instinct and were prepared on its account to honour even an inferior object; while we despise the instinctual activity itself, and find excuses for it only in the merits of the object [p. 149, n.1].

Note, first, the two sexual stories Freud finds in Western history. The Greeks, and their practice of male homosexuality, value sexual passion (although the object they dishonored might well have been women). Freud's turn-of-the-century contemporaries, in contrast, excuse the drive's vagaries on account of the value of the object—love justifies passion.

Note, secondly, how this quote establishes two poles of a paradox: on one hand, instinct, in Freud's problematic term, or, as we might nondeterministically reformulate it, desire, and, on the other, object, or better, object relation. Freud's theory of sexuality developed, I think, in the tension of this paradox. As time went on, his thought followed the pattern of the "Three Essays." Pulled by the discourse of the Natural to pathologize nonheterosexual desire, it succumbed increasingly to the object pole, making sense of sexual activity in terms of object choice and forgetting desire.

But we do not have to go that way. We can tell sexuality with many narratives. Oddly, even sociobiology has this potential. If you read the strict adaptationist narrative carefully, you see, in fact, two narratives, one for females, the other for males. That heterosexuality consists of two realities is, of course, a feminist commonplace. But what we should note here is the variety inherent to the evolutionary psychological story. Haraway (1989, pp. 316–330, 349–367) argues that such narrative multiplicity shows up in the work of Darwinian feminists who study nonhuman primates and use their findings to reconstruct the path of human evolution. Focusing on females, who had been overlooked by earlier primatologists, these feminist scholars construct a world of "inherently differentiated and heterogeneous females" (p. 365). In *The Woman That Never Evolved*, for example, Sarah Hrdy (1981) argues for a femaleness that is aggressive as well as nurturing, but not passive; self-interested and altruistic, but not self-sacrificing; competitive and cooperative, but not compliant. Such a view of early human females and their primate ancestors, as expounded by Fedigan, Hrdy, Small, Smuts, and Haraway, regards them as "committed to reproduction, but not within a maternalist discourse" (Haraway, 1989, p. 365). Instead, their reproductive fitness is a function of many variables, including choice of mate, elicitation of male protection, both competitiveness and cooperativeness with other females, and females' ergonomics.

Although, then, in Haraway's view, there can be a productive interaction between biology and critics of biology, still feminist sociobiology omits what is most important and interesting about human beings. It "leaves intact an ethnocentric logic of sexual politics and a deep (re)productionist ethnophilosophy translated into a technostrategic language of universal investment games" (p. 366). It handles difference only "categorically," as "the motor of antagonism" (p. 367), not as the seed of creativity and connection. Erased are the complexities of desire and culture for males as well as females, the relational contingencies and meanings of mating and fertilization, and "all the ambiguities of the term reproduction as applied to organisms that neither make copies of themselves nor reproduce by themselves" (Keller, 1992, p. 132).

Let me wrap up with a mini case vignette that illustrates the clinical value of thinking about sexual desire in terms of narrative multiplicity, both—and rather than either—or. IM came into treatment with a fear about his sexuality. Was he homosexual? He had other, not unrelated sufferings, principally a malaise that, as our work progressed, he identified sequentially as an ogre and then as a loneliness that had become his friend. But his work on his object choice took a more circuitous route, and I followed its twists and turns.

I had no idea what he wanted in the way of sex. I knew that, like others of my patients, he didn't want to be homosexual. He dreaded the social consequences. He feared the ostracism, the loss of unquestioned acceptance, the shame accompanying those loses. He craved the convenience of being part of a straight couple. He anticipated that, should his parents become cognizant, they would die. He couldn't imagine telling his friends. He believed that at his Wall Street office, where machismo was king, he would be shunned and maybe even fired.

IM was dating women when he started treatment. But occasionally he would go out, late at night, to a gay bar. Once in a while, he would pick up a man and they would flirt or, rarely, go back to his apartment for a tryst. Was he basically heterosexual, with a taste for homosexual acts on the side? Because Ms. Right never seemed to come along, was he after all really gay and just denying it? Was his problem one of intimacy, not sexuality?

Perhaps the most important clinical intervention I made was my explanation of my point of view. Right now, I suggested, neither of us knew where he was going to wind up. Nor did I see how we could know. Gender and sexuality are not a matter of either–or. Nor are they fixed. Rather, as I would put it now, they are emergents, contingencies. Person (1980) writes that most people experience their sexuality as revealed, not chosen (p. 620). But this revelation, I would add, may be an ongoing process. It's not so much that people are, as Alfred Kinsey (1948, 1953) described, possessed once and for all of degrees of homo- and heteroerotic preference. There is more to anyone's sexual preference than meets the eye at any given moment, and psychoanalysts need to be open to the possibility of subtle or radical changes in it (see Chapter 6). So, I explained to IM, with each roll of the dating dice, we, or at least I, would keep an open mind. Maybe he was gay. Maybe he was straight. We would find out.

I will say, however, that I did emphasize his reluctance to pay nondrunken attention to his homosexuality. Once, when he was complaining that he couldn't decide, I exclaimed, "But you haven't dated a man!" One evening, he told me, he found himself in a gay bookstore. This venture encouraged me to suggest he look at Bruce Bawer's (1988) *A Place at the Table*. Bawer's is hardly a book about multiplicity. Rather, he argues that gay people simply want to be normal. They want to be just like straight people: to be in couples, marry, create families, be invited to, or give, Thanksgiving dinner. IM didn't want to march in the Gay Pride parade, wear leather and chains, dye his hair pink, or kiss his boyfriend in public. Maybe he was queer according to what he did in bed, but not in how he wanted to live. Queer wasn't his nature. He took up my suggestion, bought the book, and said, "This is me!" So, I thought, here we are: he is gay, after all.

But then he met a woman who seemed like a really great match for him. She was sophisticated, liked sex, was easy to talk to. A midwesterner too, she seemed to him like home. He felt safe telling her about his homosexual encounters and desires, and she confided accounts of her own sexual explorations with women and men. They had fun, they took trips together. There was even the possibility that they could be together while he would have homosexual affairs on the side. I thought I was hearing wedding bells. It was April. June, I conventionally thought to myself, was coming.

Of course, when he terminated his treatment right around that time, I did voice my doubts and hunches. But he would have none of my thinking that his relatively sudden wish to leave treatment could have anything to do with any ambivalence about his new intimacy.

His return to treatment was just as sudden. They had been on a trip out of the country, and had been unable to bring their marijuana with them. And so, when, on the second night in their four-star hotel, they started to have sex and he had a panic attack, he understood that the answer to his sexual question was still out of reach. Marijuana, as it turned out, had been their constant sexual companion. Without it, he couldn't do it. And so he returned to treatment, and wended his way slowly out of that relationship, into homosexuality, and, finally, once again out of treatment.

My point is that he had to sustain doubt, find ease in uncertainty, and be open to any possibility. I had to join him in that wandering, even as I, and he, understood that he wasn't going to be joining Act-Up. And he had to have the opportunity to reconstrue himself. Relieved of the idea that his object choice had to be either/or, he could lounge around in sexual options until his own desire revealed itself to him through his own struggles with himself, his engagements with others, and his therapy with me.

We can resist the lure of Truth's closure, as Mr. IM learned. We don't have to tell one story as we try to know our nature. IM's narrative was unfinished when he left. I'll never know its end. I've run into him a couple of times in the neighborhood we share. He goes to another therapist, a man who does a lot of body work. IM has a boyfriend. He goes to a gay church. I don't know whether he's come out to his parents. He seems to be happy.

What is best about psychoanalysis is its appreciation of particularity, argues Corbett (2001b). Instead of causal stage narratives, he proposes "dynamic analyses of subjective phenom-enologies . . . in which patterns are modified by the contingent and often paradoxical structure of subjectivity" (p. 323). Writing of culture, anthropologist Clifford Geertz (1973) calls this "thick description." Although norms and universal regularities catch that which most marks human development, says Corbett (p. 324), they don't get what is "most interesting" about it, "the way in which the repetition of patterns or averages is never exact, the way in which it can occur only with variance." Gould's (1977) argument about what's most compelling about the human species is cognate: "Flexibility may well be the most important determinant of human consciousness; the direct programming of behavior has probably become maladaptive" (p. 257).

This vantage point has its complexities, of course. Appreciating contingency, we must accept ambiguity. Yet by entering the ambiguous, charged space between the poles of paradox, we can recoup what was best about Freud's delinking of drive, aim, and object without subscribing to the normalizing Discourse of the Natural. Perhaps we can construe two parallel and paradoxical processes, one in which relationship governs the erotic and another in which erotism governs relationship. We can move the body outside the discourse of Nature into questions of embodiment (see Chapter 4). Our thought can encompass a necessary tension between the amorphous sea of desire and a developmental process that provides experiences of coherence, in which hetero-, homo-, and other- sexuality are mutually constitutive, not a sequential and hierarchical binary (Butler, 1995). By thinking this way, we could render sexual desire, like gender, a contingency, an outcome of "acts of interpretation" (Harris, 1991, p. 213). Perhaps then development itself, even stages, might emerge as efforts of meaning, not givens (Corbett, 2001b; Harris, in press).[21] Perhaps the shame and the blame, inhering so often in desire as to seem essential to it, could emerge as the constructions they are. Paradoxical thinking suits the ambiguity of sex, and even, as we shall see in the next chapter, that of the body.

---

[21] As Harris (1991) argues, to view sex, object choice, or gender as grounded in biology ("the real") disregards what's fundamental to "Freud's radical intervention in our understanding of personality. Biologically determined theories keep such experiences as gender and sexuality outside the system of meaning itself. To be meaningful, these experiences must be understood as symbolizable. Gender, then, and the relation of gender to love object can be understood only by acts of interpretation" (pp. 212–213).

4   The Body as Rorschach

> All neurotics, and many others besides, take exception to the fact that *inter urinas et faeces nascimur* [we are born between urine and faeces]. The genitals, too, give rise to strong sensations of smell which many people cannot tolerate and which spoil sexual intercourse for them. . . . there exist even in Europe peoples among whom the strong genital odours which are so repellant to us are highly prized as sexual stimulants and who refuse to give them up
> —Freud, "Civilization and Its Discontents"

Consider the body a Rorschach. In its doubleness of form, in its bilateral symmetry, it even resembles the inkblots routinely administered by psychologists to assess character and sanity. The body might not be a blank slate, but it is surely treated like one. Yet, if it is a surface, it is also a cavity. An armature of bones with a carapace of skin housing the organs of life, it is animated not only by the pulsing blood and guts nestled in the corporeal interior but by something less tangible. Psychoanalysis names this interiority "psychic reality": "whatever in the subject's psyche presents a consistency and resistance comparable to those displayed by material reality; fundamentally, what is involved here is unconscious desire and its associated phantasies" (Laplanche and Pontalis, 1967, p. 363). That psychic reality is as real as physical reality was Freud's earliest point. Conversion hysteria, in which objectionable thoughts and emotions turn into bodily suffering, is a cornerstone of classical psychoanalysis (Breuer and Freud,

121

1893–1895). The mind expresses itself by transforming the body; conversely, when the mind can do no more, the body takes over.

If the body is a fact, it is also an idea that situates theoretical debate, dispute, and change. Originally and starkly biological and sexual, the psychoanalytic body has all along carried other, often discordant meanings of mind and culture. Using several clinical case studies, I propose to deconstruct the classical body, which, as it turns out, is but one of many representations of material reality. I read the body through three lenses—bodymind in culture, embodiment in the consulting room, and bodies in patriarchy. Through this chapter parade embodied patients and analysts; disembodied theorists; bodies gendered, raced, and aged; smelly, respiring, hungering, and lusting bodies. Many dualisms prance about, too, and many thirds are called for.

Psychic Reality, or the History of the Bodymind

The body is what it is and what we make of it. Different practices make for different bodies. It may be, for example, that Jacques Lacan, living much in his head, found his corporeal body rather more ineffable than, say, a dancer might. For him, the body, as all biology, incarnates "the Real," that which, mutely resisting symbolization, cannot with any certainty be known (Žižek, 1996; but see Butler, 1993). Impervious to our ideas of it, this cipher body is a brick wall into which all systems of meanings run. Others feel the body as both transparent and substantial. Listen to Irene Dowd (personal communication, 1999), a dancer and neuro-muscular educator whose sensibility might in fact define embodiment: "You speak of 'the body,'" she laughs. "I *am* my body. I am aware of myself as a physical being all the time, of how I change according to what I am doing and how I am moving." The dancer knows her body as the theorist knows his words.

Still, even in the dance world, the body and its activity exceed representation. Consider the fate of Labanotation, one of many sorts of transcription that are to dance what the score is to music. Created in 1940 by Ann Hutchinson Guest, Helen Priest Rogers, Eve Gentry, and Janey Price, it has largely yielded to video (Zina Steinberg, personal communication, 1999) and video's ability to capture the body's signature mobility. Yet, finally, dancing must be taught hands on, in three-dimensional flesh, kinesthetically activating multiple sensory mnemonics (Schachtel, 1959)—not just sight and sound, but touch and, possibly, even smell and taste.

In clinical psychoanalysis, it is bodies' psychic meaning that counts. Marie Cardinal (1983) tells of intolerable vaginal hemorrhaging that eluded medical healing. Psychoanalysis was her last resort. Her analyst forbade all talk of her physical suffering; for that, he said, she might consult her physician. His interest was how her mind represented her body. Much pain and many years later, when Cardinal could fathom her mother's madness and thereby own a hatred that, disavowed, had maddened and sickened her in turn, she found serenity at last, while losing her psycho-somatic bleeding forever.

The body's psychic reality is contingent, an effect of history, of the fourth dimension, time, inhabited by the body in all its immediacy. Psychic reality forms a palimpsest through time, across time, in layers of time, each layer surviving into the present and stretching toward the future. Unlike linear, one-damn-thing-after-another historical time, psychic history is as layered as a Napoleon, as curvy as Einsteinian space.

Recall Freud's (1930) brilliant but flawed use of spatial absurdity to figure the temporal impossibility of mind. The mind, says he, is like Rome, only more so. In this "jumble of a great metropolis" the present neighbors immediately on the past. Hard on one building, dating from, say, the city's birth, is another from, perhaps, the Renaissance. Except that in the mind's montage, these two structures hold the very same spot at the very same time:

> In the place occupied by the Palazzo Caffarelli [1580] would once more stand—without the Palazzo having to be removed—the Temple of Jupiter Capitolinus [of the sixth century B.C.E.]; and this not only in its latest shape, as the Romans of the Empire saw it [between the first and sixth centuries C.E.], but also in its earliest one, when [in the sixth century B.C.E.] it still showed Etruscan forms and was ornamented with terra-cotta antefixes [p. 70].

Notice, however, that Freud does not speak to what one might call architectural embodiment, an omission, perhaps telling of the psychoanalytic tendency to reify, that I am addressing. Had he factored in the way these buildings were used, another palimpsest or two would have surfaced: the Palazzo served as the German

Embassy until 1918 and, for a moment after 1925, as the Museo Mussolini.[1]

Embodiment may be conceptualized as bodymind (Wrye, 1998), a both/and that we can employ in working through the Cartesian dualism between subjective mind and objective body. An interleaving of psyche and soma, private epochs, interpersonal history, and public convention, bodymind situates extreme individuality. Opening that "frontier between the mental and the physical," where Freud (1905b, p. 168) presciently but dualistically locates instinct, bodymind denotes not two polar functions but a third area: the body as "the subject of perception [in] a dialogue with the world," as Maurice Merleau-Ponty sees it (Reis, 1999, p. 384).

In its contingency, bodymind is a perfect fount of mystery for the endless probing of the "unique individuality" (Wolstein, 1975) that constitutes clinical psychoanalysis. Think of the skin-ego, conceived by Didier Anzieu (1989) as "the original parchment which preserves, like a palimpsest, the erased, scratched-out, written-over first outlines of an 'original' pre-verbal writing made up of traces upon the skin" (p. 105). Perhaps the self is written plurally on the body. For Harris (1996a), memory is a series of drafts, not a single snapshot. At any given moment, any given body may inscribe an orderly developmental sequence, but it may also speak in tongues, with memories registered and layered in flesh and sensation, just as paintings of the fauna needed and revered by Paleolithic hunters were superimposed through the ages one atop the other on cave walls.

Bodymind moments record a life. Take Mr. HC for instance. He puts together, during his treatment with me, a series of accidents that lead him to recall the central trauma of his childhood. At age five and then again at age seven, he had a broken collarbone. He fell off the roof, he knows. Here and there he details the bloody fights with his father that pockmarked his adolescence. Somewhat later on, he mentions that, at age two, he was wearing an arm and shoulder cast (dead white plaster strangely bright against young white skin, as I saw in a black and white snapshot that he sent to me after the therapy ended). He fell off a chair, he thinks.

---

[1] Natalie Kampen (personal communication, 1999), a historian of Roman art, kindly supplied the foregoing dates and the data.

We work these memories until, he tells me that, one night at 2 A.M., he awakened in panic. His cat, hunched at the foot of the bed, was hissing and growling, her ears flat in terror and hostility. HC has been visited by a memory of evil: he remembers going to the dentist, when he was seven, in a foreign country where his father was working for an international company. He remembers sitting, frightened, in the chair; he remembers crying out; he remembers his father entering the office, chiding HC for being a baby, climbing onto HC's lap, and then forcibly holding HC's jaws open so that the dentist could do his work. At the procedure's end, HC recalls in horror and humiliation, his father smiled and then spat in his mouth. Or, he muses a few sessions later, did his father only drool? Whatever.

Humiliation, having entered HC's mouth and soul, became systemic. The week after he entrusts me with this flashback, he force-marches himself through his shame over rotting teeth. After the fact, he confides that he has visited the dentist for the first time in 30 years. Only slowly and with extreme terror, getting the shakes every now and then, does he impart all the details. He reveals to me his lonely courage when, at 13, he siphoned off into a large juice glass a little bit of liquor from every bottle in the living room cabinet. Then he took a pair of pliers and went into the woods, where, drunk, he healed a month-old toothache by yanking the backmost molar out of the lower right side of his jaw.

As HC and I cautiously weave between the troubles of present and past, he fashions out of these superimposed layers three images, three little boys—aged two, five, and seven—who become imaginary companions. Shards of his fragmented psychic self, each imagined little boy begins to have his own memories, each slowly and in pieces tells the story of his own injury, none accidental and all having something to do with a very angry and alcoholic, abusive, and adored father—and a mother who did not intervene. After a while, the boys grow older and merge into one: by the time HC left treatment, he had as his imaginary companion his own 18-year-old self, a psychic construction that, he told me with remarkable insight, signaled his self-acceptance, a sign that he had taken himself to his bosom. Later came a final, color photograph of him standing in front of his new store with his new boyfriend.

The Mind–Body Problem in Psychoanalytic Theory: Anatomy Is Destiny?

If, for Freud, the body was first and foremost sexual, it now seems protean, versatile rather than sexual. Bodies are charged with emotion and value as well as history. Instead of a contradiction to be resolved, then, the mind–body problem may be a paradox to be explored. Primally and profoundly, classical psychoanalytic metaphor plumps for biology: as hunger rules the body (Freud, 1905, p. 135), so libido steers desire. At the same time, psychoanalysis renders the body the mind's creature: the hysteric's body (Breuer and Freud, 1893–1895) obeys the laws of psychology, not biology. This plethora of meaning and practice, which might be rephrased as the mind/body problem, constructs a polarization ripe for undoing.

Notably, though, indecision and contradiction, not paradox, govern psychoanalytic thinking about the bodymind across the century. Examine, for example, that classic soundbite, "Anatomy is destiny." Now, as you probably know, this immortal claim has nothing to do with the "psychical consequences of the anatomical distinction between the sexes" (Freud, 1925). Rather, it denotes the condition of human birth and its effect on sexual desire: *inter urinas et faeces nascimur*—we are born between urine and feces. Most people, Freud (1930) contends—not only "neurotics" but "many others besides" (p. 106, n. 3)—do not like to think that they enter the world, head first, through the region of the body dedicated to waste disposal. One's downy little head, with its still unclosed fontanelle, passing through a corridor situated between the twin sewer pipes of urethra and anus?

At this point an illogic emanates from an unarticulated contradiction. Freud has been plumbing a "primary repelling attitude . . . toward sexuality" (pp. 105–106, n. 3), which he links to the atrophied sense of smell in *Homo sapiens*. This linkage is understandable for an epoch in which the genitals were thought to be hardwired into the nose (Gay, 1988, pp. 56–57). Leaning on Darwin, Freud (1930) deems diminished olfaction biologically adaptive, an "organic defence . . . against animal existence" (pp. 105–106, n. 3). *Homo sapiens* having gained bipedal locomotion, the highly corporeal sense of smell, so intense for other mammals, became a shadow of its former self; the rather less visceral sense of sight took over as prime erotic stimulus. As the capacity for olfaction wasted away, so too did sexual desire and with equal evolutionary advantage.[2]

Freud seems to have been unaware of the puzzle: if you can't smell, why would the odor of sex bother you at all? In one place, we learn that disgust is as innate as the upright posture it accompanies, whereas elsewhere we learn that it sets in only after birth. Freud's footnoted argument has the poor, innocent baby, born between urine and feces, receiving from the world's Welcome Wagon the gift of a nigh-traumatizing stench, but lacking the physiological or emotional tolerance for it. And yet, as Freud (1930) explains in an earlier footnote, "The excreta arouse no disgust in children." Disgust is learned, not inborn, acquired not inherited. Indeed, it is taught: "Here upbringing insists with special energy on hastening the course of development which lies ahead, and which should make the excreta worthless, disgusting, abhorrent and abominable" (pp. 99–100, n. 1).

The contradiction between mind and body in psychoanalytic thought constitutes a productive tension. If we step into that tension and construe the relation between mind and body as paradoxical rather than oppositional, then we find a third term: both mind and body, it turns out, inhabit culture, a triangulation that Freud recognizes but for which his system cannot account. "Accident," as Freud repeatedly terms it throughout his studies on masculinity and femininity, not "constitution," causes the feeling of disgust that "seems to be one of the forces which have led to a restriction of the sexual aim" (Freud, 1905b, p. 152).

Freud's illogical but culturally sensible argument predicted what the 20th century was to bring: those smooth, deodorized, but nevertheless (or therefore) very sexy bodies, posing on the page and prancing on the screen, their minimalism signaling the erotics of corporeal excess, and of its control. His thought anticipated Norbert Elias's (1939) documentation of its cultural context: 19th-century Europe's "incitement to cleanliness" was potentiated, Sue Shapiro (1996, p. 306) suggests, by that new

---

[2] "The diminution of the olfactory stimuli seems itself to be a consequence of man's raising himself from the ground" (Freud, 1930, p. 99, n.1). Freud argued similarly, Gay (1988) tells us, in a letter of 1897 to Wilhelm Fliess.

technology, indoor plumbing, which, initially available only to the rich, eventually radiated a civility aspired to by all. As down there became "down there," toilet training in particular and socialization in general fell into line. Dirt in the new regime was for animals, not human beings. And all things anal—from the products and process of human excretion to olfactory pleasure— became *de tro*p, a fastidiousness about bodily functions that children were, through upbringing, to acquire. Meanwhile, of course, repression, both psychical and theoretical, left *urinas et faeces* sparkling with desire.

Freud and the Nitty-Gritty Body

The immediate is not unmediated. Take another look at the epigraph to this chapter and imagine it in its original form, as a footnote on a page of "Civilization and Its Discontents" (Freud, 1930). Like heat, the distinctive odors of the groin practically rise from the bottom of the page. Here as elsewhere, footnotes memorialize the contradiction of the good ship Freud: hot sex in the hold, cold science on deck. The result is Freud's legacy: paradox. In the red-light districts of "Civilization and Its Discontents," the pungent body lives on. Just as culture, Freud says, cannot disavow childhood's corporeal excess, so, we see, he cannot disavow the dirty pleasure of adult sex. But he does try to palm it off, first on animals, then on children, next on the Other. For animals and, implicitly, for the animal in us, Freud points out, sex and its carnal pleasures know no shame. Think, he scolds, of how we betray our "most faithful friend," the innocent dog, whose shameless bliss in putting head to crotch so as to smell, lick, and clean incites our shameful contempt and whose name is one of "our strongest and commonest terms of abuse."

When it comes to the animal in the human, however, Freud gets on his high horse and gallops away. A strange thing to say, I know, given that the sexual body may rightly be judged a psychoanalytic creation (Foucault, 1976). But the only way Freud could memorialize the erotic appeal of the nitty-gritty body was to project it outward and downward. Projection (Laplanche and Pontalis, 1967) "is always a matter of throwing out what one refuses either to *recognize* in oneself or to *be* oneself" (p. 354). Freud knows that not all human beings so disdain the scent of sex, that some have a different erotic sensibility. Typically, he tells us about it. Having taken some pains to argue that human sexual malaise is universal, he turns right around and says the opposite: "in spite of the undeniable depreciation of olfactory stimuli, there exist even in Europe peoples among whom the strong genital odours which are so repellant to us are highly prized as sexual stimulants and who refuse to give them up" (p. 107, n. 3).

Faced with a contradiction—the robust appetite of some unidentified European peoples versus the squeamishness known to him from his patients, his acquaintances, and, possibly, himself[3] —he articulated his confusion in a way that permits one to infer at least an ambivalence on his part about the relationship between anatomy and destiny. On one hand, the "result of [Darwinian] research coincides in a remarkable way with commonplace prejudices that have often made themselves heard" (Freud, 1930, pp. 105–106 n. 3). To be concrete, most people, according to popular belief as well as his own clinical data, recoil from fellatio or cunnilingus, consistent with evolutionary exigency. Their oral erotism thus restricted to mouth-to-mouth contact, their sexual pleasure likewise contracts. "Nevertheless," he says, the universally adaptive advantages of these prejudices "are at present no more than unconfirmed possibilities which have not been substantiated by science" (pp. 105–106, n. 3). Carnality is not lethal: nose to groin, some "peoples" relish the intoxicating mix of urine, feces, and sexual fluids and rather defy you to take their pleasure away.

In the miasma of Freud's unease, all the inferiorized, all the abjected Others—the body, sex, peasants, Jews, the racially and sexually stigmatized, women—begin to look pretty much alike. They are made to identify with what he dislikes, and therefore disidentifies from, in himself. If, in identification, one "assimilates an aspect, property or attribute of the other and is transformed, wholly or partially, after the model the other provides" (Laplanche and Pontalis, 1967, p. 205), in disidentification one disassociates oneself from it. Freud's disidentifications create a strange and potent stew of country, class, race, and gender. His sense of his

---

[3] Gay (1988) writes that Freud's "sexual activity seems to have tapered off "after age 37" (p. 162).

ethnicity, and hence his class pride were, in Sander Gilman's (1995) argument, equally a dilemma about racial and gender identity. In *fin de dix-neuvième siècle* Austria, Jews were docketed as a mentally and physically defective race, an anti-Semitism with which, Gilman contends, Freud colluded by scotomizing his roots and identifying with his nation.[4] In the same breath, according to Gilman, Freud's unconscious effort to expel from his own bodymind the dregs of his abject Jewishness fed his denigration of women like an underground river.

A Body That Stinks and a Body That Thinks

The Body Relieved of Embodiment

As soon as Freud brings the body out of the closet, he shoves it back in. The case of women is paradigmatic. Ponder the joke that Freud (1930) uses to illustrate his claim that a "quota of plain aggression" invariably accompanies Eros: "The love-object will not always view these complications with the degree of understanding and tolerance shown by the peasant woman who complained that her husband did not love her any more, since he had not beaten her for a week" (pp. 105–106 n. 3; on the sado-masochism in this joke, see Chapter 9, this volume). Ho ho. The efficiency with which this pleasantry fuses sexism, classism, and racism sure hits that funny bone. The conditions are ripe for projective identification: "a mechanism revealed in phantasies in which the subject inserts his self—in whole or in part—into the object in order to harm, possess or control it" (Laplanche and Pontalis, 1967, p. 356). Here a self-that-can-insert injects into an other-that-can-receive the fear, hatred, and contempt that so often mark the intimacy of enemies. Why can't Freud tell that joke about one of his bourgeois patients instead of a stereotypical woman from an Austro-Hungarian village? That she lacks ethnicity is probably part of the humor: she is an "other," not a "self."

---

[4] We might then wonder whether, if only figuratively, his reviled eastern European Jewish forebears were those very "peoples" who defiantly prized "strong genital odours . . . as sexual stimulants."

Subordinate and rural, one of "them" as opposed to "us," she is also a woman, the butt of both her man's aggression and Freud's.

We seem to be dealing with a misogyny as old as Aristotle, whose phrase, translated probably by St. Augustine,[5] Freud borrows (albeit without citation): *"Inter urinas et faeces nascimur."* Why does Freud not notice that those smells that he presumed vaporize sexual desire belong exclusively to those in whom the birth canal is found? To put it differently: the people who love that region of female anatomy *inter urinas et faeces* are, literally and figuratively, peasants. In Freud's thinking, maleness may serve not only as "a critique of femininity," in John Toews's (1998, p. 78) canny phrase, but also as an assessment of any abject category whatsoever—peasants, Jews, bodies, excreta, reprogenital aromas, and so on. Admire Jonathan Swift's (1732) satiric vision in "The Lady's Dressing Room":

> Thus finishing his grand survey,
> The swain disgusted slunk away,
> Repeating in his amorous fits,
> "Oh! Celia, Celia, Celia shits!" [p. 451].

Now Strephon, the poem's protagonist, meets what Freud considered to be Man's fate:

> But Vengeance, goddess never sleeping,
> Soon punished Strephon for his peeping.
> His foul imagination links
> Each dame he sees with all her stinks:
> And, if unsavoury odours fly,
> Conceives a lady standing by [p. 451].

Strephon sees a woman who reminds him of sex. He smells something noxious and imagines a woman. What a mess![6]

---

[5] I have attempted to discover who actually translated Aristotle. Norman O. Brown (1959) names St. Augustine, although Seth L. Schein (personal communication, 1999), a classicist, speculates that it was St. Bernard of Clairvaux.

[6] Brown (1959) chides scholars for ignoring what both Freud and Swift had to say about anality (p. 180) but does not notice the gendered aspect of either the omission or his correction.

The mistaken equation that causes Strephon's particular malady
—foulness = femininity = foulness—becomes, in Freud's thought,
a disease common to humanity. We can read the associative chain:
men = Man = human, while women = ? Once again, the
unconscious equation of humanity with men inflects Freud's view
of the sexual world. Doubtless there are women who have no
taste for the aromatics of their own repro–excreto–genital region
nor, for that matter, of men's. However, the nauseated people for
whom the association between the condition of their birth and
the smell of sex is so intolerably close that it snuffs out their sexual
desire are, without a doubt, men. Stench, thy name is Woman.
Bye-bye Sex.

Or, better, good-bye Body, hello Mind. Have you wondered
why Rodin's *The Thinker* took a male form? Feminism has chastised
Western culture for reducing Woman to her Body. Carolyn Bynum
(1991), writing of 13th century women mystics and eucharistic
devotion, says, "To put it simply, the weight of the Western
tradition had long told women that physicality was particularly
their problem" (p. 146). But, with feminist philosopher Iris
Marion Young (1990), we might note another drift: the classic
Western body, for psychoanalysts as for everyone, is male. It is,
however, a body that neither feels nor knows itself. An object-
body, it is free of the stresses and strains, the stinks and smells, the
weaknesses and wetnesses and mortality and, most important, the
senses of the ordinary body that are in European history made
the property of women (Grosz, 1994) and that link women to
Christ who himself had a human body (Bynum, 1991, pp. 204–
206). It is a body suited to Descartes's *cogito,* which subordinates
the boundary-losing, emoting body to the separating-individuating,
cognizing mind.[7]

A body that thinks, not a body that stinks. As Young (1990)
argues, the ordinary absence from philosophical considerations
of women's socially ordained and highly embodied concerns—
housework, child rearing, the negotiation of interpersonal life—
bares the secret Western premise that "the body" is male. The
female body may be the West's own private Rorschach, the artist's

---

[7] Flax (1983) has linked this body precisely to the two-year-old, and, Corbett
(personal communication, 2002) adds, a male at that, as can be seen in the
move from the emoting to the separating-individuating, cognizing mind in the
case of Little Hans.

often headless muse. But a body with a head, a body that thinks? Rodin's sculpture concretizes the body latently conjured by that third-person neutral, "he," which, officially but a literary convention, actively and repeatedly constructs a particular type of body for all to see—the "abstract individual" of capitalism with a white, Anglo-Saxon, Protestant, uppermiddle-class, heterosexual, male body whose main feature is its head borne on a hefty fist.

Recovering Embodiment

Embodiment has lived a sort of secret life, hidden away by gender hierarchy (Jaggar and Bordo, 1989). Abjected on the margins of adult corporeality, preserved in the private domain ruled by women, both venerated and abominated in Western culture, the female body also and equally memorializes embodiment, body as source of experience, knowledge, meaning. Woman is the prime, although not the only, vehicle, selected by Freud, as well as by Western culture at large, to transport the abject aspects of human experience away from the civilized center of daily life. Perhaps the conundrum in Sherry Ortner's (1974) classic question, "Is male to female as culture is to nature?" is a body that stinks as much as it thinks.[8]

As quickly as Freud tears off the fig leaf, he slaps it back on. On one hand, he is trying to liberate his readers: Look, you may think that all this carnality belongs only to lower types like peasants, but the truth is, you the civilized want it too. We know that far from our cosmopolitan capitals exist many strange orders of folk who relish the aromatic stew of ejaculate, vaginal fluids, urine, feces, sweat, and hair. But this dangerous, exciting preference, which we sophisticates regard with a fascinated and horrified disgust that "the sexual instinct in its strength enjoys overriding" (Freud, 1905b, p. 152), really resides close by, so near as to be almost one of us. Like the adjacent genital, excretory, and reproductive zones, these crotch lovers are intimate neighbors, living "even in Europe." If they won't relinquish their olfactory delight, well, then, maybe we don't want to either.

---

[8] Even Lévi-Strauss (1949) agreed that although women may be treated like objects—"signs"—they are also fully sentient human beings who use signs themselves.

On the other hand, Freud has been engaging in a little anality of his own, dichotomizing the body, keeping one part and expelling the other. The body he knows is the body as the object of scientific knowledge, "the body known as a third-person observer knows any object in the world" (Sampson, 1996, p. 604). Studied, interpreted, and governed by mind, to which it is inferior, this object-body reproduces gender hierarchy, a part of the unknowing, but knowable world called "she" by the probing scientist (Keller, 1985).

The body that has disappeared from psychoanalysis is the body of experience, the body known from the inside out, not outside in. Embodiment renders the body a source of knowledge differently available to the person living in that body than to the person watching that body. This ostracized subject-body is certainly the sexual body, but it is equally the sensed body, the body of pleasure and pain, the body made of emotion as well as of thought, unconscious as well as conscious signification, the body of psychic reality, the paraplegic's "body silent" that loudly compels our attention (Murphy, 1987).

Like as not, the embodied body involves other bodies. As Elsa Beatriz Cardalda (personal communication, 1993), a Newyorican poet and psychologist, puts it: "Our boundaries are made of people." Encrypted by culture, the subject-body inhabits a liminal world of other subject-bodies. Such multiplicity is marginal to Euro-Western representation, contend anthropologists Beth A. Conklin and Lynn M. Morgan (1996). In prevailing North American imagery, the body is a material entity, subject to natural, not social, processes and incarnating cultural ideals of individuated personhood: "It is disciplined, controlled, restrained, and autonomous—a kind of private property" (p. 664). In contrast, among the Wari' of the Brazilian rainforest, bodies are construed as thoroughly social, "constituted through interpersonal exchanges of body fluids and foods." Puberty, for instance, is thought to be brought on by social, interpersonal, and psychological events: heterosexual intercourse triggers menstruation, while killing an enemy begets puberty in men.[9] Fatherhood in this non-

---

[9] Conception, in turn, is said to occur when enough semen accumulates following many, closely sequential acts of sexual intercourse. Pregnancy, in other words, "is evidence of a sustained relationship between a man and a woman."

monogamous society is plural: "Any man who has sex with a pregnant woman contributes semen to form the fetus' body and has a claim to biological paternity" (p. 671). Even prenatally one's boundaries are made of many Wari', unlike the Euro-Western embryo, always already "interpellated" (Althusser, 1971, pp. 173–183) as an unambiguously boundaried and singular subject.

Working the Tension by Multiplying the Body

Instead of splitting the body in two, let's multiply it. Consider Merleau-Ponty's (1962) phenomenological solution to the mind–body dualism: the body is neither subject nor object but both. He speaks of "the metaphysical structure of my body," which is at once "an object for others and a subject for myself" (p. 167). Here is the mind–body dualism's third: *An object for others and a subject for myself.* In Merleau-Ponty's paradox, the body always involves other minds, existing simultaneously for self and for other. The body can be both subject and object, rather than one or the other, because (at least) two people are involved in it, each from a necessarily different relation to it. No one can know my own body from the inside as I do, nor can I perceive it as you can from the perspective of your own embodiment, which is external to mine. The body's psychic location, in this new response to the universal Rorschach, is invariably doubled.

How helpful Merleau-Ponty's stance can be in reflecting on psychotherapeutic embodiment, which, we are now understanding, is always intersubjective. An object for others but not yet a subject for herself, AB's body was her medium; on it she performed the psychical and social inscription of flesh, blood, and bone, which everywhere endows the mortal bag of guts with structure, identity, and reality (Scarry, 1985; Santner, 1996). At first, AB's life was "desolate." Unfocused, she could not cohere work life or career, nor did any of her love affairs, whether gay or straight, furnish that "sense of aliveness" which Winnicott (1971, p. 158) calls "the self." Her psychic life was lived externally, on her body. For 15 years, since her late teens, her body measures had worked overtime both to create a sense of meaning and thereby to keep her sense of realness intact.

Anzieu's (1989) idea of the skin-ego illuminates both AB's dilemma and her solution. Her body was a bad thing: it was, she thought, fat, as well as, or because, female (and she dreamed once about a flabby older woman somewhere behind her—me, of course, also repellently female, in the chair behind the couch). Trying to redraft her body, AB would starve, or gorge and vomit, and drink. She would mark her skin by the "delicate self-cutting" that relives and masters the threat to psychic existence posed by childhood traumas (Kaplan, 1991, p. 369). Pain is a way to feel and so to know one is alive (McDougall, 1989). If to cut oneself and not die is to mark one's aliveness by reminding oneself that the skin-envelope (Anzieu, 1989) works, AB's cutting gave her life.

AB had been trying to make a psychic skin all by herself, an effort curiously incarnating the century-long contradiction between theoretical and clinical psychoanalysis. If psychoanalytic theory has trafficked in a "one-body psychology" (Rickman, cited in Laplanche and Pontalis, 1967, p. 278), clinical psychoanalysis has in effect functioned as a two-person field (Mitchell, 1988), a disjuncture we may now be set to evaluate and remedy. Construing the body, paradoxically, as simultaneously subject and object may be one way to navigate this tension between the theory of an individual mind and a therapy of two (see Shapiro, 1996).

Much as several buildings can occupy the same site in the Rome of the mind, maybe one body is always also two or more. At the beginning of treatment, AB was dwelling in a one-body, one-person psychology. What helped was the recognition and experience that two of us in two bodies were working together in the same space and time. "There is no meaningful individual body ego without the interface—the holding, looking, touching encounter of the social other," writes Harris (1996a, p. 371). AB needed to let her one become two until her one could take its own place in the world.

Although Anzieu (1989) calls it the skin-ego, touch-ego might be a better appellation. The skin-ego surprisingly echoes Merleau-Ponty's (1962) subject–object body, even though it adumbrates a one-body psychology. In fact, it is intersubjective—"the mental image of which the Ego of the child makes use during the early phases of its development to represent itself as an Ego containing psychical contents, *on the basis of its experience of the surface of the body*"(Anzieu, 1989, p. 40, italics added). Arising in tactility, in the primal sensuality of being held by a caretaking (m)other, the skin-ego is in fact a third, existing somewhere in the space between embodied persons, a two-person psychology in a one-person bodymind.

AB needed me to touch her, to be both the family who did not hold and the therapist who did. I was to contain images of her health and illness both, to see the creative side of her self-destruction. Certainly there were times when I incarnated the parents who held neither physically nor psychically. Countless sessions began with my silent prayer that she stop yelling at me as though I were the cause of her persisting anguish. My holding failed her quite concretely, too: although I had noticed her anorexia very quickly, I was long blind to her alcoholism.

AB needed me both to hold her in mind and to let her go to the mindless edge of mad embodiment. This allowance communicated what she unconsciously wanted me to imagine and what, in fact, I did imagine: her as separate, intact, integrated, and alive. For much of the analysis, I was the skin-ego she needed to develop for herself through the analytic touch-ego. That she could survive my failure, and I her disappointment in me, testified to our mutual psychic sturdiness. Looking back, at the close of her analysis, AB said she had not only needed to fall apart, she needed me to let her do so. She had needed me, like the neighbors who heard her nightly screaming, to notice the pale scars cut into her olive skin. But she did not need me to try to stop her. Like the patients described by Khan (1979) and Eigen (1993) who seclude themselves for long periods, failing either to work or to carry out their social lives, she had to risk all to (re)gain her own wish to live.

Even Analysts Have Bodies: Projective Identification, Anality, and Relationality

The nearly simultaneous entrance of women, embodiment, and the person of the analyst on the psychoanalytic stage is no accident. Women as analysts incarnate the clinical commonplace that analysts use their bodies when treating psyches; countertransference, like transference, registers somatically (e.g., Davies, 1994; Harris, 1996a). Patients employ the bodied analyst as both dumping ground and sounding board, eliminating what they cannot abide by making their analysts both concretize and experience it. Analysts, probing their embodiment (Shapiro, 1996), deepen the surface they provide for patients to inscribe their interiority. Ogden (1994) describes how analysts use "reverie" to reflect not only on fantasies but also on corporeal sensations and imagery in order to intuit a patient's unconscious process (Reis, 1999, p. 389).

Projective identification, as a bodily state of mind that bleeds into intersubjectivity (Schore, 1996; but see Reis's, 1999, critique), is immensely valuable in limning countertransference embodiment. Initially a signature of Klein's (1950; Klein et al., 1952), one-person psychology, it now emblematizes relational, two-person thought and practice (Sands, 1997) because it signifies at once interpersonal process, individual psychodynamics, and unconscious communication. The language used to describe it can evoke the corporeality of intersubjectivity, that is, the touch-ego: recall AB, who both "touched" me and got "under my skin." Now I want to tell you about Mr. JG, where skin-ego and touch-ego tangle with projective identification and all the disturbing affects to which beings are subject where bodies and appetites mingle with gender and sex.

It is early morning. I am alone in the office. I had a very rich meal the night before. I use the toilet. A smell lingers. I use the bathroom spray. JG, my first patient, arrives. He has noticed the spray, he says. In fact, he adds, he's noticed the odor behind the camouflage. I freeze. Like an automaton, I follow the rules. I ask what this experience is like for him. "Smelling your shit is comforting," he replies with a private smile. "It makes me feel close to you." Somehow I am not comforted. In fact, I am humiliated.

Yes, it did occur to me that JG really did feel relief because now we could both recognize, together, that I, like him, had shit that stank, that we might have a common humanity in many other ways. But that we could not explore his feeling of safety, even pleasure, in our shared human predicament—that he would respond to no more questions, that I could find no observation that interested him—told me that other matters were at stake.

Excretory embarrassment perfumes the psychoanalytic air. Who is easy with shit in the analytic office? "I won't talk to my therapist about shit," Marcelle Clements (1985) wryly confides. "As far as she's concerned, I haven't gone to the bathroom in the three years she's known me, and I hope she has therefore deduced that I have in fact never gone to the bathroom and that excrement has nothing at all to do with my life on any level whatsoever" (p. 69). Only recently are analysts studying how they use their physicality in psychotherapy (see, e.g., Shapiro, 1996; Aron and Anderson, 1998). None, however, writes of personal odors. Fools rush in.

A female analyst and a male patient, middle aged, white, face to face: the patient needing relief not of body but of mind, the analyst embedded in her body and, for the moment, bereft of her mind (Rosenfeld, 1987; Josephs, 1989). A horrifying and fascinating moment. How difficult it is to have an analyst with a body. For JG, my body (like his mother's and wife's) contained both extraordinary hope and crushing disappointment, all the goodness in the world and all the badness, a "great burden," as he put it, for him, but for me too, one that I carried with uneasy delight. Now the private body that excites disgust and may not go out in public had been caught, naked, in the peculiar public privacy of the analytic office. Cut off from the good body and saddled with the bad, JG fell into anxiety, from which he could flee only by making me feel awful.

Shame aromatized the room that morning, mingling there with the love and hate that marked our relationship. The intensity of this moment of therapeutic impasse suited perfectly the primal quality of our intimacy, which had bloomed almost instantly when we began working together nine years before. In an atmosphere thick with projections and counterprojections, we felt deeply connected and shared periods of profound anger and difficulty. Reacting to JG's rageful and assaultive suffering, I would feel a combustible and paralyzing mix of seemingly endless fury and empathy. It is fair to speculate that, after all these years, I was fed up with his sense that nothing was ever good enough, as well as with my own helplessness; but I had resisted probing my ambivalence until my body took over, as bodies will do, and, overflowing, forced a countertransference enactment (Davies, 1994; Sue Shapiro, personal communication, 2001).

That, in this clinical drama, I felt not only my own but JG's shame was part and parcel of our relationship, my job, and our joint patriarchal heritage. The classical proposition that shame is developmentally connected with matters of toilet training, power struggles, and hence the anal stage, is sufficiently familiar (Erikson, 1950). A clinically more enlightening move locates shaming in a relational matrix. According to current argument, the erogenous zones are exciting not in themselves but in the unconscious context in which they matter (Fairbairn, 1954). To take the example most famous among clinicians, the mouth is erotic because it channels not libido but relatedness (Sullivan, 1953): it's great to get together with mother and get fed, an excitement symbolized by the breast (Klein, 1961; see Chapter 5, this volume, for further discussion of the theoretical reversal between libido and relatedness).

This humiliating anal encounter between JG and me enacted the best and the worst about our relationship. My experience of shame, and his shaming of me, complied with his need that I temporarily hold all he hated in himself until he felt sufficiently uncontaminated and undamaged and therefore resilient enough to take it back. As the analyst whose job it is to bear the patient's projective identifications, I was, in the transference, the parent whose job it is to contain and process the child's intolerable affects (Bion, 1977). Our enactment epitomized our power struggle over shame: an unconscious demand on his part and a conscious acquiescence coupled with an unconscious refusal on mine, that I dispel, by embodying, the atmosphere of humiliation that he has always inhabited, an anxiety-ridden, bodily state of mind to which a solution had unexpectedly presented itself—my body's serendipitous betrayal of me, as bodies betray everyone, lingering like footnotes at the bottom of the page to mark the cost of civilization.

That my failure was his triumph depended, finally, on patriarchy and its gendered splitting of emotional labor between mind and body, nurturance and aggression (Benjamin, 1988b; Dimen, 1991). With me, the woman, as the omnipotent (m)other, processing and therefore identified with the abject (Grosz, 1994), JG could be the man whose body could be counted on to stay in control. During those few minutes in which my messy (female) embodiment became the center of our attention, JG could expel into me the narcissistically wounded and castrated boy who had rectal surgery three times before puberty, whose mother's rages terrorized the family, whose father suffered bouts of depression, and whose twin sisters were born shortly after his first surgery. Gone was the disappointed, bewildered, and shamed six-year-old whose beautiful mother repulsed his amorous advances. Erased was the humiliated twelve-year-old who agreed with his father's dismissal of his pubertal anxiety as girlish. For the moment, JG could be strong and I could be weak, he the mocking adult and I the shamed child, he the male and I the female. But perhaps, I see now, there was an additional exchange. Perhaps, if JG ever returns from the hiatus he took two years later, we might analyze the possibility that on that dreadful morning we also enacted a conventional heterosexual split: he as a man shouldered the aggression that I as a woman could not sustain in my effort to nurture his narcissism and contain his abjection.

Clitoridectomies, Psychic and Otherwise

So far, I have been considering how to break out of several principal instances of the mind–body dualism—mental–material, masculine–feminine, cognizing–experiencing (or thinking–stinking). I have reframed mind–body as a paradox to be explored and proposed several thirds for doing so: embodiment, bodymind, the intersubjective body. I want now to add the idea of culture, which evokes two more polarities, body–culture and mind–culture. Curiously, this move shifts us to both the margins and the center of psychoanalysis. On the one hand, it directs us to look at power and how it inflects the bodies we know. On the other, it brings us back to sexuality—and its pains and pleasures.

If "the 'book' from which the children learn their vision of the world is read with the body" (Bourdieu, 1977, p. 90), children's knowledge of their bodies also always passes through the sieve of culture. Think of, say, facial scars, whether acquired in duels by 19th-century German noblemen or created in puberty rituals for Nuer boys and girls. Consider the butt lifts and hair implants, pierced ears and noses and earlobes and lips, the circumcisions and clitoridectomies found here and there in human history. Bodies are inscribed with ideas and values that announce to self and other what a person is and is to be.

Culture, however, is shot through with power. Silently, power enters psyche and intimacy through diverse arteries that convey social meaning, for example, posture and gait (Mauss, 1936). Power slinks in on semiosis, the tone, rhythm, and prosody animating the primal experience of mothering (Kristeva, 1983). Most obviously, power becomes internal through sex, through acts performed on the genitals to beautify, sanitize, and sex the body. Even physicality, seemingly self-evident—the body as only biological and never psychological, or only spiritual and never earthly, for example—is "an effect of power" (Butler, 1993, p. 2).

But the body's politics are amazingly tortuous. As both object for others and subject for oneself, the body holds great symbolic, representational, and communicative capability. Indeed, the more nonverbal the symbolic, the greater its effect: nonverbal representation inhibits discrimination between subject and object, self and other, which is why, in the play of power, the body is often a route to the mind. Domination, we have seen (Chapter 1), marks the psyche by marking the body (Santner, 1996). At the same time, resistances to symbolic domination also take advantage of this body–mind fungibility.

Look, for example, at the clitoris and its adventures, both psychoanalytical and political. When Princess Marie Bonaparte, psychoanalyst and student, patient, and benefactress of Freud, elected to cut her clitoris to fit theoretical fashion, it would have been difficult to say whether her act was a strike for or against freedom. Her sad and slightly bizarre story, so different from Cardinal's (1983), allows us to begin pulling together the many and varied threads of which this chapter is woven: psychic reality and embodiment, sexuality and gender in psychoanalytic thought, psychic process and cultural politics. An independent-minded sexual intellectual, Bonaparte was nevertheless, in her own view, "frigid" (Bertin, 1982; Appignanesi and Forrester, 1992). More exactly, she enjoyed clitoral sensation and orgasm but mourned simultaneous, penis-in-vagina orgasm.

Disposed, perhaps by trauma (Bertin, 1982), to dissociate incompatible truths (Davies and Frawley, 1994), Bonaparte risked a masochistic sexual odyssey that enacted psychoanalysis' century-long ambivalence about the body. In, possibly, a paternal transference to Freud (Appignanesi and Forrester, 1992, p. 340), she agreed on libido's masculinity but firmly disagreed that vaginal life depended on clitoral death. Instead, she held that women are innately bisexual; that the clitoris situates both masculinity and female eroticism; and that vaginal orgasm in heterosexual intercourse is the most desirable form of climax.

Bonaparte's theory of her sexual unhappiness foundered on psychoanalysis' unsolved mind–body problem. In the matter of orgasm, psychic reality held sway for everyone but her. If psychoneurosis caused sexual difficulty for some women, genital anatomy turned out to be erotic destiny for others. In tall women like herself, she believed, and her research seemed to confirm, "largish gaps" between clitoris and vaginal opening "were not . . . favourable to normal transference of" sensation from clitoris to vagina, representing "a real stigma of bisexuality" (Bonaparte, 1953, p. 150).

Oedipally rebelling (Freud had tried to dissuade her), Bonaparte turned to surgery. Genital operations were then, as they are now, no strangers to Western medicine (Freud, 1920b, p. 171). "Some turn-of-the-century European and American doctors used clitoridectomy as a cure for masturbation and so-called nymphomania" (Walley, 1997, p. 407). When one Professor J. Halban (whose gynecological writings are referenced by Freud, 1905b, p. 319) claimed a surgical cure for anorgasmia, Bonaparte hired him—twice—to move her clitoris nearer her vaginal aperture so that penile thrusting might stimulate them simultaneously. To her despair, the perfect orgasm never came (Bertin, 1982, pp. 170, 181; Appignanesi and Forrester, 1992, p. 337).

That the clitoris is so often an article of dogma would be funny if it were not tragic (Flax [2002] assesses the matter similarly). Certainly the "fetishized" clitoris (Traub, 1995, p. 90), not to mention the penis, is a form of symbolic domination. Far-fetched though it may seem, clitoral psychopolitics connects psychoanalysis and international politics. Dramatizing this odd coupling are Bonaparte's meetings with Jomo Kenyatta, then anthropologist Bronislav Malinowski's student and later Kenyan anticolonialist, prime minister, and president. In the 1930s, Bonaparte, circulating by virtue of station and intelligence among political and cultural elites, sought him out to discuss clitoral excision among his people, the Kikuyu (Bertin, 1982, pp. 191–192), a fortuitous but not accidental historical conjuncture.

The sadism in Freud's dichotomy between the immature clitoral orgasm versus the mature vaginal orgasm is, of course, old news (Koedt, 1968). More interesting is the way the various excisions of this little bit of flesh fuse feminist and colonial iconography. There is no need to rehearse the feminist critique, beyond emphasizing that this psychic and cultural clitoridectomy (Bonaparte, 1953, pp. 153–165; el Saadawi, 1980, p. xiv) inferiorizes the clitoris relative to both penis and vagina. But do recall that Freud's anatomical map locates female matters on that famous "dark continent,[10] a European colonialist epithet for Africa that hides in femininity another body matter—the unconscious and institutional racism to which psychoanalysis, like all disciplines, is heir, a legacy that, until practically yesterday, received hardly any attention at all. In classical psychoanalytic theory as well as the culture in which it grew, (heterosexual) male desire, as feminists have been pointing out since 1970, is the governor of sexuality, and female desire is his servant, a colonialist model if ever there was one.

Both mind and body are at stake here. The clitoris attracts patriarchal prurience (Freud, 1905b) because it is a route to psychic reality, to hearts and minds as well as sex. Literally and symbolically, Alice Walker (1992) insists, the clitoris embodies sovereignty; in psychoanalytic terms, clitoral embodiment underwrites the self's place in psychic and cultural representation. When, cries Nawal el Saadawi (1980), girls "in Egypt, the Sudan, Yemen, and some of the Gulf states" (p. 33) are ritually cut at age 7, as she herself was, the mortification of their sexual flesh not only violates their bodily integrity, but hobbles them as citizens of country and world by deforming their capacity for autonomous thought.

How do you draw the line between routine care of the body and domination? between consent and submission? between violation and self-expression? Female genital mutilation (FGM[11] a label already drenched in moral outrage) raises these questions in explosive terms. The controversy kindles anguished argument because it pits one central tenet of Western enlightenment

---

[10] Which, as he confessed in a 1928 letter to protégé and biographer Ernest Jones, is how he regarded the adult woman's sexual life (Gay 1988).

[11] See the website: www.fgmnetwork.org/intro/fgmintro.html.

feminism, control over one's body, against another, the need for multiplicity in understanding and setting feminism's agendas.

The politics are delicate. Western feminists have not only been advised to butt out (el Saadawi, 1980, p. ix) but also asked to complexify (Spivak, cited in Apter, 1992a, p. 51). So it might further the international conversation to note the dilemma and splits created by the paradoxical, ambiguous body, object for others and subject for oneself. Friends and foes of clitoral excision range from mothers and daughters to politicians. For many women in the Third World, this sacred ritual surgery makes their daughters both sexually pure and marriageable (Walley, 1997). Publicly embarrassed by el Saadawi's polemic, Anwar Sadat stripped her, a physician, of the post to which he had named her, Director of Public Health. By the same token, those girls and mothers who do speak out report the horror of the assault and the danger and punishment of protesting. And at the United Nations, Hillary Clinton charged: "It is no longer acceptable to say that the abuse and mistreatment of women is cultural. It should be called what it is: criminal" *(The New York Times*, March 5, 1999, p. 36; see also Toubia, 1993, and Schroeder, 1994).

Negotiating the Scylla of relativism and the Charybdis of colonialism, First World feminists are challenged to hold plural identifications while taking a stance on the practice itself (see Abu-Lughod, 2002, for similar reflections about veiling). At stake are crucial debates: competing ideas of bodily integrity; the rights of children and the question of who defines them; women's choice and voice. Currently there is no way out of the contradictions of the ambiguous, intersubjective bodymind caught in cultural and international hierarchies: alternatingly legal, cultural, and moral, what is for some the routine care of the female body is for others symbolic domination—and here let us not forget breast implants.

Freud's Body, Buddha's Body, or the Politics of Multiple Orgasm

Rebel with a Cause

As an idea, the clitoris rebels against the phallus, the symbol of the permanently erect penis, which for Lacanians represents desire, the social order, and language. What a perfect example of symbolic domination, of patriarchy using the body to sell itself as the only version of sanity. How else to understand why Lacan attended so little to what Bowie (1991) dubbed "the everyday uncertainties that beset the male member" (p. 125)? Lacan, Bowie notes, missed an excellent opportunity to see that the penis' unpredictability "make[s] it into a dialectician par excellence, a nexus of signifying opportunities, a fine example, in all of its modes, of the Freudian *fort/da*" (p. 125).

Although the penis, in its prosaic vicissitudes, might well symbolize multiplicity, uncertainty, and democracy, that representational job falls to the clitoris. In psychoanalytic iconography, the clitoris, the third to vagina and penis, occupies the discursive place of multiplicity. Talk about Rorschachs. Shoved to the margins of society, the female body, with its savage little clitoris, becomes rather like a wild animal on the outskirts of civilization. "On the one hand," says Thomas Laqueur (1990), "the clitoris is the organ of sexual pleasure in women. On the other, its easy responsiveness to touch makes it difficult to domesticate for reproductive, heterosexual intercourse" (p. 240). In the realm of the penis, the clitoris begins to seem like an unruly citizen and therefore has to be put in its place.

Perhaps it is the clitoris's excess that has had to be excised. In Kernberg's (1990) summation of his thoughts on sexuality, the clitoris appears only as a dubious absence from the list of erogenous zones attributed to girls (pp. 23, 30). Odd, isn't it? In the classically sexual body of psychoanalysis, the clitoris is dedicated to pleasure, unlike the vagina and penis, or the urethra and anus, which combine, variously, reproductive, excretory, and sexual capacities. So how come it disappears in the survey of psychosexual anatomy conducted by the American dean of contemporary classical psychoanalysis?[12]

The clitoris, in my view, is as protean as the body itself. Recall its links, whether in Freud's Vienna or Kenyatta's Kenya, el Saadawi's Egypt or 1970s feminism, to autonomy and rebellion. The body, I have been arguing, is versatile, multiple in its meanings, flexible in its capacities. In the *décalage* between object for others and subject for oneself, bodily materialization is ongoing, "never quite complete;" bodies "never quite comply with the norms by

---

[12] Feminist critics, of course, give the clitoris its erotic due (see Schor, 1981), although, oddly enough, they occasionally forget the vagina (e.g., Wright, 1992).

which their materialization is impelled" (Butler, 1993, p. 2). Sex is variously sited not only on the body (Foucault, 1976) but between bodies and minds.

In a manner approaching transcendence, genitally traumatized persons manifest this erotic versatility. Through the use of cocaine, a quadriplegic man, 20 years after his injury, recovered for a period of 10 years a sense of genital excitement and gratification. With deep irony and gratitude, he writes in his autobiographical novel of his "astral ejaculations": he knows that his penis, clasped by his "clawed left hand's index finger and thumb," does not spurt semen, but he feels as if it does (Caldwell, n.d., p. 2). In an e-mail to me in August 1999, he explained further: "Tactile illusion is indeed odd. It took me very much by surprise. . . . I would have liked to be hooked up to sensors to see if any of the changes I felt were objectively measurable. The hot sperm . . . was extraordinary to feel, was very real—as was the sometime lifting of my hand by my erection even when my penis wasn't tumescing. . . ." He was interested to know of the "phantom orgasms" experienced by quadraplegics and paraplegics, even those with penile amputation (Money, 1961, p. 293).

Nor is he alone in his will to psychic transcendence. Regard the sexual pleasure that a strong critic of FGM, Hanny Lightfoot-Klein (1989), found among Sudanese women who, even though they had received the most extreme, pharaonic form of clitoridectomy, in which not only the clitoris but the labia majora and minora are excised and the vaginal orifice all but closed by sutures, found their way to realize sexual pleasure. Without dismissing the trauma of genital mutilation, Lightfoot-Klein records several verbatim accounts of heterosexual intercourse (pp. 85–86; for similar reports, see Hoodfar, 1997, p. 261). "It feels like electric shock going around my body," said one. "I feel as if I have had a shot of morphine," revealed another. "My body vibrates all over. Then I feel shocked and cannot move. At the end, I relax all over." A third confided, "It gets very tight in my vagina. I have a tremendous feeling of pleasure and I cannot move at all . . . for about two minutes." A fourth: "I tremble all over. My vagina contracts strongly, and I have a feeling of great joy." And, finally, a fifth reported, "I feel shivery . . . very happy. . . . It is a very sweet feeling that spreads and it takes hold of my entire body." In a chapter praised by an otherwise critical Ruth Hubbard (1999),

Natalie Angier (1999, pp. 77–78) both imparts similar data and contrasts two clitoridectomized American women, one who has orgasms and the other who does not.

Clitoral orgasm, move over. Vaginal orgasm, move over. Even penile orgasm, step aside. There is more than one way for women— and, as a matter of fact, for men—to come. Alice Ladas, John Beverly Whipple, and D. Perry (1982) identify an orgasmic continuum for women, ranging from the classic clitoral or "vulval" orgasm to the uterine or "G-spot" orgasm, with many a "blended orgasm" in between. They propose, as well, a parallel continuum for men: "orgasm without semen expulsion," "typical ejaculatory orgasm," and "nonejaculatory emission." Multiple orgasms, indeed. How wonderful, as Harris (in press) points out, to recoup what psychoanalyst Josine Müller (1932) believed: the site of female or any sexuality is never singular. For her, clitoris and vagina were equally female or, as she put it, "feminine." Oddly, even Freud, by arguing that there were two orgasms for women, the psychoanalytically incorrect clitoral and the proper vaginal, paved the way for the notion that there might be different strokes for different folks.

Is splitting the orgasm, and thereby dominating women, a way that psychoanalysis (and even a culture or two) handles the inability to tolerate multiplicity? One could argue that the clitoris is not one but many.[13] Remember its history: the seat of orgasm and

---

[13] Let us note half a dozen clitorides in Euro-American sexual history. There is, for example, the oral clitoris: the uvula, said second-century C.E. physician Galen, "gives the same sort of protection to the throat that the clitoris gives to the uterus" (quoted in Laqueur, 1990, p. 37). Then you have, of course, the penile clitoris. Whereas Galen and others following him thought of the uterus as a penis turned inside out—male and female being greater and lesser variants, respectively, of the same body—Kaspar Bartholin, a 16th-century Danish professor of medicine, pointed out their error: not the womb, but the clitoris is *the* female penis, . . .'the female yard or prick'" (p. 92). At about the same time, "Columbus—not Christopher but Renaldus" (p. 64) announced he had discovered what Traub (1995, p. 84) dubs the "Renaissance clitoris," the reproductive clitoris from which, if rubbed "'vigorously with a penis, or . . . even with a little finger, semen flies swifter than air. . .'" (Laqueur, 1990, p. 66). Then, in the 19th century, the demon clitoris rode into town, tinged with masculinity, always suggestive of homoeroticism, and therefore set up— by Freud—in gladiatorial combat for erotic dominion with the definitively female vagina. Finally, we should register a couple of 20th-century clitorides: on one

fertility until 1905 (Laqueur, 1990), the creature of the penis after that, and the insignia of the liberated woman in the 1970s, it narrates competing social forces. And even though vaginal orgasm, for example, was officially declared a myth in 1970—a fabulously emancipatory bit of feminist doctrine that may nevertheless require revision in the light of history and experience —some vaginas keep right on going and going and . . .

One More Rorschach Response

If the clitoris rebels against the phallus, what is the discursive place of orgasm? Perhaps a glance eastward, at one more response to the Rorschach body, may yield a clue. That, once upon a time, orgasm measured health and maturity makes sense for a body in which sexual need and gratification are modeled on hunger and its satisfaction. Suppose, however, the Buddhist body, one based not on appetite but on breath. Mark Epstein (1995) lays out the clinical and theoretical consequences. When the body is a hungry body, it "is experienced as an alien entity that has to be kept satisfied" (p. 145). Winnicott's account of the not-good-enough mother, Epstein reasons, yields either too little or too much food or mother, so that the child becomes, respectively, either deprived and entitled or engulfed and obliterated. He contrasts the Buddhist view: "When awareness is shifted from appetite to breath, the anxieties about not being enough are automatically attenuated" (p. 145). In mindful breathing, the body is a site not of demand or need but, simply, of being in the timelessness of the present, which is, indeed, the site of psychoanalytic space. A self located in its moment, connected to its past and sensible of its flow into the

---

hand, the liberated clitoris, which, distinguishing recreation from procreation, is queen of female pleasure, "a Pandora's box packed not with sorrow but with laughter" (Angier, 1999, p. 58); and, on the other hand, the lesbian clitoris, which, in Traub's (1995) view, has served the politics of identity by metonymically associating "female bodily orgasms . . . with an erotic identity" (p. 101), that is, female homosexuality. The feminist clitoris, suggests Haraway (1989) with light irony, is to create "multiply orgasmic, unmarked, universal females . . . possessed of reason, desire, citizenship, and individuality" (p. 356), "quite a performance" for the *mentula muliebris,* the little mind of women as it was called in 16th-century scholarship (p. 359).

future, produces echoes not only of "going with the flow" but also of free association.

It will not do, of course, to think of this solitary suggestion taken from the West's Other as a final, oppositional answer to the psychoanalytic body. Many questions remain: Would such a body be, any longer, the site, structure, origin, or symbol of relationship? of sex? How would we want to redraft attachment, desire, intimacy, maturity? If we start with the body as just breathing, not as endlessly longing, is the body still the site of excess? Or is the body's unspeakability produced by a particular discourse? Is it this sort of discursive construction, asks Butler (1993), that characterizes the Real? If so, can the Real never be known or spoken?

West–East? What about a third? Paradoxically, breathing can be mindful at some moments, sexy at others. For Lacan, the breath can be a cause of desire, which he sometimes defines as the demand for love minus the appetite for satisfaction; he speaks of "respiratory erogeneity," and deplores the paucity of its study (cited by Dean, 1994). Remarkably and persuasively, Fairbairn (1954) articulates breathing, sex, and psychic suffering. Starting from the premise that hysteria is "the substitution of a bodily state for a personal problem" (p. 117), he states: "The data upon which the theory of erotogenic zones is based themselves represent something in the nature of conversion-phenomena" (p. 121). After all, the theory holds that erotogenicity derives from the joining of mucus membranes to external skin. Why, then, does it not include the nostrils, which serve surely as fundamental a need as, say, the anus? (It is hard here not to think about the erotics of nose jewelry worn by women in India, men in New Guinea, and kids of all ages in Manhattan.) Indeed, he recounts two cases in which sinusitis qualifies as a conversion symptom. In one of these, the disorder was historically connected to childhood anal retentiveness that dramatized the impingement that a patient experienced from a dominating, possessive, and frustrating mother.

The point (as we probe sex itself in the next chapter) is to destabilize. As Shapiro (1996) observes, psychoanalytic conventions of the body iron out contradictory wrinkles in the name of scientific legitimacy. Resituating the body in relational tension reveals the wrinkles once more. Good. As we age into psychoanalysis (itself a discipline of maturity), they help us to appreciate the complexity that, face-lifted by science and linguistics from the experienced body, is entailed in working through the problem of dualism. Entering embodiment, we come upon affects, which may emblematize the bridge between body and mind, self and other (Schore, 1996).[14] Pain and pleasure are two such bridges, affects also spanning the two bodies posed here, the one that hungers, the other that breathes.

Two concluding anecdotes on affects as carriers of paradox: I recall a neighbor girl when I was a child, she was about five and I was ten. When she was unhappy, she didn't cry or scream, she would instead squat down and hold her breath until, blue in the face, she would faint. (Laughingly, her father would call her "Sarah Heartburn," much as my father did me, if for different reasons; as we now all know, the female body is not hysterical for no reason.) I don't know what was wrong, but I am sure that something was intolerable as long as she continued to breathe. Not breathing, she no longer had to feel.

By the same token, if you breathe, you feel, and not only pain. A meditation-minded psychiatric resident, wanting to integrate her two practices, began during our work together to bring her meditative awareness into the consulting room. As we worked on splicing psychoanalysis and Zen Buddhism, she found herself increasingly tolerant of disturbing affects (which would flood her while she was treating very ill inpatients) and therefore increasingly able to think in session. Neither of us, however, anticipated the personal spin-off from this professional progress. In our penultimate supervisory session, she rather generously and unexpectedly revealed to me that, during the previous evening's sex-making with her boyfriend, she found herself focusing not on her hungry body's need for what Lacanians see as illusory satisfaction, but instead on her breath, on each inhalation and exhalation, until she found herself, in the end, overtaken by the most extraordinary orgasm of her life.

---

[14] Sue Shapiro (personal communication, 1999) reminds me that William James was the first to speak of affects as bridges between mind and body.

5

Between *Lust* and Libido
Sex, Psychoanalysis, and the
Moment Before

> The only appropriate word in the
> German language, *Lust*, is unfortunately
> ambiguous and is used to denote the
> experience of a need and of its gratification.
> —Freud, "Three Essays on
> the Theory of Sexuality"

Sexuality is alive and well and living in psychoanalysis. You just have to know where to look for it—conduct a treasure hunt in which the prize is hiding in plain sight. At the same time, the reports of sexuality's death are not exactly wrong either. This apparent contradiction, really a paradox, deserves some unpacking. This chapter entertains three main themes: the psychoanalytic paradigm shift from sex to object relation; the problem of discharge and the solution of *Lust*; and the anxiety of erotic countertransference. These themes wind through a series of arguments: the history of desexualization in psychosexual theory; libido and the changing idea of nature in psychoanalysis; and desire and interpretation in clinical practice.

Rethinking Sex

Desexualization, André Green (1996), argues is rife. Nor is he alone in thinking so. When his provocative "Has Sexuality Anything to Do with Psychoanalysis?" appeared in January 1996, I consumed it not with admiring hunger but, for all its polemic against the post-Kleinian paradigm shift, with voracious envy: he beat me to the punch, got it into print before I did. Actually, though, someone else had said it before him. Thomas Domenici, then a candidate at the Postdoctoral Program in Psychotherapy and Psychoanalysis at New York University, critiqued the psychoanalytic flip on sexuality in an address in April 1993.[1] Drive theory, Domenici (1995) contended, sees affective and inter-personal needs as "an overlay upon a more basic template of sexuality and aggression" (p. 34). In contrast, object relations theory (to name but the most influential and general of the new psychoanalytic schools) reverses the matter, making sexuality the secondary precipitate of a desire for connection and intimacy (see Chapter 3).

Curiously, there was a flurry of psychoanalytic writing on sex even as Green was firing his initial salvo. In 1995 (when Green delivered his paper as the Freud birthday lecture at the Anna Freud Centre), four new books were published. Bach (1995) freshly sets a Winnicottian platform under the traditional binary of sex and aggression. McDougall (1995) finds dilemmas of psychic life and death embedded in sexual desire and practice. Kernberg (1995) couples classic psychosexuality with postclassic object relations. Last, the contributors to *Disorienting Sexuality*, an anthology edited by Domenici and Lesser (1995), deploy social con-structionist, feminist, and queer theory to interrogate the way sexual identity is construed in clinical and theoretical psychoanalysis. Then, in the space of 12 months, two major conferences took up the topic, the 1997 conference of the International Psycho-Analytic Association in Barcelona and the 1998 meeting of the Division of Psychoanalysis of the American Psychological Association in Boston.

There seems to be something in the air.

Of course, when an authority, a veritable tribal elder like Green (1996), anathematizes our unconscious omission, we notice it and hop to. But our psychosexual closets need even more of an airing than Green gives them; there exists, to use a more classical metaphor, a psychoanalytic bedrock that Green has overlooked.

---

[1] His remarks took place at the panel "Homosexuality and Psychoanalysis" at the meeting of the Division of Psychoanalysis of the American Psychological Association in New York.

Yes, Freud invented psychosexuality, and Green, like Lacan, is right to want to go back to him. I suggest, however, that we return to a different Freud, the prescient Freud of the footnotes, whose answer to questions that only now may be asked (Khan, 1979, p. 18) can put an entirely unexpected spin on this rethinking of sex. Yet before we can return to our point of embarkation, some reconnaissance is necessary, some assessment of the journey so far as well as some inventory of what we need to recover.

Where Libido Was, There Shall Objects Be?

Psychoanalysis has blown hot and cold about sex from its beginning. Even Freud (1905b) desexualizes when he carves heterosexual order out of the polymorphously perverse jungle, and he continues domesticating as he proceeds (e.g., Freud, 1911, p. 222; 1920a). Ferenczi (1933), for his part, names an often-transgressed divide between the language of adult passion and the language of childhood tenderness but nearly writes sexuality out of infancy in his attempt to write sexual exploitation out of parenting and therapy.[2] Dualistic flip-flops continue apace in the next generation, as object relations, ego psychology, and self psychology all contribute to the unsexing Green deplores. Fairbairn's (1952) pithy pronouncement that libido is object seeking, not pleasure seeking, brings objects into the circuit of desire but sends sex to Coventry. Sexual pleasure may seem to acquire a scientifically indisputable place in human necessity when Heinz Lichtenstein (1961) gives "nonprocreative sexuality" an evolutionary function; thus rationalized, however, it promptly and predictably becomes distinctly unsexy, sinking under the weight

---

[2] Lewis Aron (personal communication, 1998) argues that Ferenczi "did not abandon the idea of childhood sexuality but rather downplayed it as the origin of pathology unless it was made traumatic by parental abuse, misunderstanding, and deceit." Nevertheless, it seems to me that calling infantile sexuality "tenderness" and adult sexuality "passion" constitutes a desexualizing move. The danger is that, once the damage done by incest and sexual abuse is given its due, there is a tendency to deny infantile sexuality. The challenge is to hold both children's sexuality and adults' abuse in mind simultaneously (Harris, 1996a, b).

of its Darwinian burden as "the mainstay of identity" (Person, 1980) for the malleable psyche of *Homo sapiens*. Heinz Kohut's (1977, p. 226) substitution of Odysseus and Telemachus for Laius and Oedipus fashions a new father but startlingly omits sex altogether—unless you include homoerotics, which his image of a successful oedipal outcome specifically rules out. Even Lacan's (1977) return to Freud is oddly disembodied, the phallus signing an excitement that seems more cerebral than psychical.

Still, Green (1996) (and, for that matter, Lacan) is wrong to argue that, when it comes to sexuality, the contemporary critical shift in ideas is valueless. Our postclassical lens helps us to see our classical subject more, not less, clearly. The new thinking takes off from Melanie Klein's relocation of genitality in the preoedipal period, which "places sexuality squarely in the middle of the emergence and structuralization of the self in its relation to others" (Mitchell, 1988, p. 95). The developmental story changes: as individuals, we are no longer thought to go straight from birth to Oedipus. On the way, we pass through, even tarry a while in, and definitely take our sexual shapes from a maternal landscape (Laplanche, 1976) in which Narcissus can be seen looking into pools of desire. It is even noticed from time to time that not everyone traveling this road is male or heterosexual.

Key to this new thinking has been the contemporaneous insight of Fairbairn (1952) and Sullivan (1953) that introduces object relation as a third to the dualism of mind and body. Corporeal erotogeneity, Fairbairn (1952) argues, flames as much from relatedness as from body chemistry (or epigenesis). Likewise, psychosexual stages—oral, anal, phallic, genital, and so on—are not just corporeal but also interpersonal moments. Sullivan's example is the most familiar and famous: the mouth is an erogenous zone not because it just is but because nursing makes it a primal site of relatedness (and, as we saw in Chapter 4, the anus is exciting because it situates toilet-training power struggles). In this mode, Mitchell (1988) mines the sexual for such relational themes as search, surrender, and escape. Clinically, then, sexuality is reinterpreted. Technical questions now focus on how sexuality serves the need for, say, attachment or recognition or selfobjects. Furthermore, clinicians newly engage and theorize the preoedipal erotization of transference and countertransference (Wrye and Welles, 1996).

Sexuality has become a relation, not a force. If, with Freud, we thought that your sex is what makes you who you are, now we think that who you are shapes what sex you are and what sex you like. Clinical attention is less often on how the anatomical distinction between the sexes influences the psyche. More commonly, we think about meaning, not biology. We wonder how the intrapsychic, interpersonal, and cultural significance of the anatomical distinction inscribes desire. The self, we now think, is born in relationship, not in the continuously flowing impersonal excitement—libido—located by Freud beneath psychic process and structure.

Yet as is so often the dialectical case, the solution is a problem—or, in other words, *plus ça change*. Although it may look like our views of sexuality have been turned completely upside down, Freud's theory of sex reigns, if only unconsciously. The "sexuality" produced by the intersubjective world, to put it differently, is exactly the one that Freud had in mind. Look at George Klein's (1961) appealing argument about Freud's two theories of sexuality. In ego-psychological voice, he pits what he calls Freud's explicit structural-libido theory, which he claims lacks clinical relevance, against his (implicit) clinical theory. But what, in the end, does Klein really mean by the clinical theory of sex? Sensuality, not sexuality—"a capacity for a *primary, distinctively poignant, enveloping experience of pleasure* that manifests itself from early infancy on" and endures throughout life (p. 19). Like the other efforts to generate viable theses of sexual dualisms—sex and selfhood, sex and object relation, sex and clinical process, sex and corporeality—Klein's is good and sensible and useful. However, his clinical theory is manifestly not about sex, or, rather, it redefines sex as sensuality. In other words, we find here as everywhere else the desexualization that Green complains about. There remains only one theory of sex, and, yes, Klein is right about it. Libido theory *is* cold. But what does he offer instead? Something nice and warm. What happened to the heat?

On the Anxiety of Erotic Countertransference

Before I turn up the flame, let me say why I think our reconsideration matters. After all, you might be thinking that clinically we address sex the way we do anything else. Too true. Yet technique, try as it might, does not prevent countertransference anxiety, which is what, clinically, the eclipsing of sexuality shows up as. I have in mind the student who worried, two thirds of the way through my course on sexuality, whether it was unethical to ask patients about their sexuality. We have come full circle in 100 years, no?

Consider Freud's uneasy countertransference with Dora, Jane Gallop's sophisticated account of which illustrates an anxious approach–avoidance to sex that is time honored in consulting room, classroom, and text. Freud (1905a) fretted, Gallop (1982) reminds us, "that the reader might be scandalized that a psychoanalyst should discuss sexual practices . . . with an inexperienced girl" (p. 140). He instructs clinicians to be direct, frank, and fearless, medically dry; don't gynecologists unhesitatingly make their patients "submit" to the uncovering of their most intimate anatomy? Yet at the very moment Freud claims to speak most straightforwardly, his patriarchal attitude—and, I would add, his own anxiety—compel him to take what Gallop slyly terms a "French detour": "I call bodily organs and processes by their technical names, and I tell these to the patient if they— the names, I mean—happen to be unknown to her. *J'appelle un chat un chat*'" (Freud, 1905a, quoted in Gallop, 1982, p. 140). The proper doctor becomes, Gallop cleverly suggests, flirtatious, even titillating, simultaneously prurient and puritan: Freud, unconsciously using the French vulgarity for female genitalia *(chat* or *chatte*), "calls a pussy a pussy" (Gallop, 1982, p. 140). A slip of this order, even if it occurred only with his readers and not with his patient, suggests an underlying anxiety that we ourselves can recognize to this day.

Our slips are not dark corners to rush past. Contemporary clinical theory argues instead that we can and should put them to work. I am right, therefore, to make the anxiety of erotic countertransference my principal pedagogical concern. Anxiety prevents analysts from addressing sex where it is and makes them see it where it isn't. The solution, I have found, is to talk about sex not dryly, as Freud counseled with a prudence necessary to his daring venture, but seriously, with humor and pleasure. Read "Three Essays" with your genitals, I tell my students (some of whom have suggested we read with our other erogenous zones as well). Let the laughter bubble, let the puns come, let the eroticism permeate the room. Sex talk is, as I have argued elsewhere (Dimen, 1998; see also Gallop, 1988, p. 86), sexy talk because it is a performative:

> To talk sex is to do sex too. . . . Performatives constitute a paradoxical experience in which a word is not a word, an act not an act. They permit ambiguity to be experienced and, eventually but not immediately, named. Speaking desire is a performative, a speech act that constitutes the situation it declares, but at the same time is not an action. Its very ambiguity is what makes it erotically, affectively, cognitively, therapeutically powerful [Dimen, 1998, p. 83].

When we engage sex in clinic or classroom, we need to enjoy it, if only because sex talk is also anxious talk. When I teach, I want the class to think together about this anxiety as well as about the (possibly) anxiety-related sexual prejudices they share with patients and other analysts. If students can be at ease talking about sex with one another, they are more likely to be comfortable with patients and thereby let this particular taboo lift.

Why does anxiety commonly accompany erotic countertransference? The problem is general. No topic, with the possible exception of money, so renders analysts and others unable to think; no topic but sex is so filled with doubt, fear, shame, excitement. Witness the common popular agreement relative to Monicagate: if people will lie about nothing else (although Bill Clinton did lie about a lot), they'll lie about sex. Many rivulets feed the anxious flow. The return of the repressed, to be sure; we are haunted by what we forget. The culture matters, too. I agree with Green that psychoanalysis sports a fearsome puritanical streak (see Chapter 3). Does that Puritanism sustain another polarity, the professional versus the personal? If you talk about sex in public, then will you get excited in public (rather than in bed) and thereby appear vulnerable, needful, even, dare I ask, weak? And now in these relational days, we are uneasy with the ruthlessness Freud (1908) perceived—sex as amoral, focused on self not on other—that, disciplined by what he ironically called "civilized" sexual morality, accounts for "modern nervous illness." Today, too, we fear the law or, specifically, accusations of sexual harassment or the public sequelae of recovered memories; the threat of legal action and media exposure makes us edgy and cautious (Harris, 1996a, b).

We are, finally, intellectually anxious: we require a theory of sexuality that fits the sea change in psychoanalytic thought and practice.

Parsing Libido: The Idea of Nature in Psychoanalysis

Sex, if it is a fact, is also an idea. Like most ideas, it has weight, a body, you might say, of its own. Ideas are commonly thought to be accurate recastings of the facts they represent, molds giving the true outlines of the reality they encase. We tend to assume a one-to-one relation between an idea and the thing that the idea is about. Through ideas we can see, as through transparent glass, the "real" truth. Or so goes the model of thought with which we have been operating for 200 years or so (Harvey, 1989; Flax, 1990). In the 21st century, though, it makes sense to take account of an alternative way of thinking that has cohered of late—the postmodernist paradigm that, if the attacks now leveled at it by the academia that once adored it are any indication, has now joined the philosophical canon. What we, along with Freud and his critics, are unused to entertaining is that ideas have substance; they have color and shape.

When we write, talk, or think about "sex," we are engaging a reality even before we begin to study it. It is not so much that ideas distort a previously existing, true, and knowable reality. It is more that ideas possess a reality of their own. They constitute a sort of parallel universe that must be parsed so as to set in sharp relief the world it is meant to illuminate. Here I want to parse the idea of libido, core to which is the idea of Nature. Libido, we learn right at the beginning of "Three Essays on the Theory of Sexuality" (Freud, 1905b), is to sex as hunger is to food. "The fact of the existence of sexual needs in human beings and animals is expressed in biology by the assumption of a 'sexual instinct' [termed libido], on the analogy of the instinct of nutrition, that is of hunger" (p. 135). Sexual desire, this analogy suggests, is as natural as hunger.

The idea that sex is natural, not cultural, belongs to a wide, pervasive, and largely successful intellectual gambit on Freud's part. Freud was trying to construct the psychoanalytic equivalent of evolutionary theory: He wanted to make his account a master narrative (Flax, 1990) that, by explaining everything about how the mind works, would sway medical minds in particular and intellectuals in general. To do that, he needed the legitimation that Darwinian theory could provide (Schafer, 1977; Fliegel, 1986), the Discourse of Nature (adumbrated in Chapter 3). If the psychoanalytic theory of desire could be linked to the great chain of cause and effect running all the way back from biology and Darwin to physics and Newton, it would be shown to be true and could take its place in the noble roster of modern sciences.

Today, after a century in which all certainties have been smashed (Harvey, 1989), the rallying cry is that sex is cultural, not natural. Human nature, we now think, is a possibility, not a determinate. But psychoanalysis is only just catching on. As I contended in Chapter 3, the psychoanalytic reliance on Darwinian thought amounts to little more than an appeal to authority. Yet, as far as the psychoanalytic idea of nature goes, it is a case of new wine in old bottles. If, in 1900, sex was natural, now, post-2000, objects are natural. "Attachment is the new Nature," observes Ken Corbett (personal communication, 1998), "but its social construction is regularly overlooked." Over the course of the psychoanalytic century, psychoanalysis has remained faithful to Freud: It uses the selfsame strategy to achieve the elusive goal of scientific legitimacy but deploys it on different territory. "Where libido was, there shall objects be" may be said, as we have seen, to be the common metapsychological thread running through the diverse midcentury rereadings of psychosexual theory as described in the brief literature review offered earlier in this chapter.

Nature retains an honored place in psychoanalytic thought, but its contents have, astonishingly, changed altogether. What a mistake. Just as the appealing simplicity and parsimony of libido elide the rich complications of object relations, so the naturalizing of attachment denies the protean ambiguity of sexuality. Indeed, the binary opposition between nature and culture begins to make less and less sense in psychoanalytic perspective. Even in Freud's thought, sexuality is always both natural and cultural: libido is a fundamental energy, but it must be shaped, and the consequences of this construction are inevitably tragic.

Remember Freud's (1908) mordant conviction that the culturally desirable restriction of desire causes "modern nervousness." The repression of sexual desire, necessary for civilization, works like a hydroelectric dam. Rules forbidding sexual activities, say, masturbation or premarital intercourse, halt sexual energy's natural, continuous flow, making its force available for the building of culture. Built into this ingenious design, however, is a critical backfire. Sexual desire, constrained, may yield civilization. But it also produces neurotic anxiety, which in turn reduces the appetite, the lust, for life. One falls ill of repressed desire, and the rest, as they say, is history.

Seeing the double bind of sex is hardly to reduce it to the either-or of nature versus culture. Freud's real message was the irony of sublimation, as announced by the scare quotes in his title, "'Civilized' Sexual Morality and Modern Nervous Illness." What civilization gives with one hand, it takes away with the other. It gives us culture but takes away peace of mind. Hatred prevails over love of life. Fear of death dominates and neurosis—psychological distress—rules. This classic ambiguity is, I believe, more important in rethinking sexuality than the either-or that Freud buys into when he turns to Darwin (Young-Bruehl, cited in de Lauretis, 1994).

Sex and Technique: Libido, Discharge, and Catharsis

I propose, then, that, in probing the psychoanalytic idea of sexuality, we skip the 19th-century debate between nature and culture and engage the more contemporary tension between modernism and postmodernism. My strategy is, however, quite old-fashioned: I read the footnotes, using one dualism, text–note, as a third to negotiate another, modern–postmodern. As many analysts (e.g., May, 1995), literary critics (especially Marcus, 1984; Bersani, 1986), and other readers have found, to read Freud's footnotes is to discover a suboceanic world that puts in question the self-evidence and stability of the textual terra firma. Containing Freud's doubts, second thoughts, and contradictions, they are the seams in an otherwise seamless story (to switch to a domestic metaphor, whose appropriateness will soon be apparent). One customary function of footnotes (Grafton, 1997), of which Freud takes great advantage, is to manage theory's overflow, its inevitable inconsistencies. Freud's notes serve as a reservoir for competing ideas that, although they did not fit what he intended to say, may turn out to be relevant to what we want to say.

The first substantive footnote in "Three Essays" (Freud, 1905b) betrays Freud's inkling that libido was not an altogether satisfactory idea. "Science," his second sentence reads, "makes use of the word 'libido'" to designate sexual needs because the only available word in ordinary language is inadequate. Which word is that? In the note tacked onto this sentence, we learn: "The only appropriate word in the German language, _Lust_, is unfortunately ambiguous and is used to denote the experience of a need and of its gratification" (p. 135, n. 2, added 1910). Science wants precision, not ambiguity. _Lust_ does not meet this standard. It is contradictory, denoting, Strachey adds, either desire or pleasure. The meaning of _Lust_ is, in other words, doubled—both the longing for pleasure and pleasure itself—a meaning unavailable in the English homonym, lust. Both–and, not either–or.

What Freud gains in clarity by selecting only one pole of the _Lust_/libido dualism, he loses in complexity. Let us explore, here, the both/and that his text couldn't handle very well. That his explanation emphasizes semantics should not obscure the footnote's semiotic and discursive significance. Freud's discourse on sexuality contains, I want to argue, a slippage we must explore in order to rescue sexuality from the obscurity into which it has lately been cast. Following Laplanche's (1976) use of Foucault's theory of the "derivation of psychoanalytic entities," I suggest that the slippage between text and footnote corresponds to a doubled movement in sex that Freud senses but, committed to science and simplicity, cannot quite articulate.[3] In making biology the ground for libido by likening libido to hunger, Freud trims his terms, obeying science's demand for parsimony and consistency. In rejecting the doubleness of _Lust_, though, he strips sexuality of something vital. Perhaps there is a straight shoot from biological need to biological satisfaction; he has indicated, remember, that hunger is simple (although the convolutions of anorexia and

---

[3] For Bersani (1986), too, this doubling is simultaneously theoretical and experiential. Freud's (1905b) "teleological view of sexuality in the 'Three Essays' [represses] the counterargument of sexuality as a kind of historically non-viable phenomenon of a pleasurable–nonpleasurable tension" (p. 89).

bulimia qualify this suggestion considerably, as I am not the first to point out). The sexual way is, however—and it is Freud who teaches this—anything but straight.

I propose to rehabilitate this rejected (German) word *Lust,* and remodel it as a new idea that can revivify sexuality for postclassical psychoanalysis. Between libido and *Lust* lies a century of controversy, contest, and clinical change. If libido marks the ultimately straight and narrow of biology, *Lust* marks the contradictions, the twinned joy and suffering of the psyche. Libido and *Lust* render two competing psychoanalytic accounts of sex, one articulated, the other buried. Libido is the account we know, but *Lust,* a piece of sexuality hiding in plain sight beneath the text, is the account we intuit.

Libido's cardinal feature, its drive toward discharge, is rich with presupposition and implication, with models of body and mind, illness and cure, desire and action, social values and moral dicta. As a concept, it does much theoretical work. Let me review, condensing here Person's (1986) admirable summary. Not only an appetite demanding satisfaction, libido has psychological power: it is a force that registers sexual instincts in the mind and thereby partners the emotion of sexual longing. Alternatively conceived, libido is an energy that accumulates to produce "unpleasure." It mounts, surges, seeks release. Existing outside awareness, libido nevertheless serves to excite consciousness, there to be transformed into something the psyche wishes to get rid of.

Discharge is the bridge between sex and sanity. Classically, sex requires release, without which illness ensues. There is a psychic economy, and sex is central to it. It is not far from sex as safety valve to catharsis as psychic cure. I am referring, of course, to the "talking cure." Today, Anna O (Breuer and Freud, 1893–1895) might have said she "just needed to talk."[4] Then she called it "chimney sweeping"—a domestic metaphor appropriate to much of her life at the time and also true to the root meaning of catharsis, "to clean." Although this account of psychoanalytic cure is controversial (whether in fact Bertha Pappenheim got symptomatic relief but not cure), and although the therapeutic mechanisms are under debate (whether it was the mere act of talking or, rather,

---

[4] I am familiar with Borch-Jakobson's (1997) indictment of Breuer's account as a fabrication; this is not, however, the place to address his argument.

talking *to* someone that helped her), still Anna O's strong image of chimney sweeping accorded well with classical psychic economy.

Nowadays, we do not measure our work by catharsis; indeed, much of psychoanalysis may be regarded as a dialectical development in response to this early formulation. So, too, should we overhaul the discharge model of and for sex.[5] Discharge and sex do make a suspiciously perfect couple: sexual discharge and psychic discharge, the economics of body and mind, cure and sex. Freud, it is said, derived the sexual discharge model from economic theory (which he drew from Newton and Darwin). But what if the economic theory drew on the sexual model? Why did discharge become the psychoanalytically defining moment of sex? Did its physicality have something to do with the psychic centrality accorded it by theory? To put it a little differently: Were its origins more literal, at least as personal as they were professional? If, in the beginning of "Three Essays," of sex, and of psychological development, all sexual pleasures are equal, in the end only one is said to count: "end pleasure," or orgasm. The desired and psychically necessary completion of the sex act, end pleasure is defined as discharge. Discharge of what? Two things, we are told— force and, in Freud's (1905b, p. 207) phrase, "sexual substances." We have already seen what the force is: energy, libido. But what are the substances that are discharged?

My question is rhetorical (and a bit arch) and the answer obvious. Even if, as Steven Marcus (1965, p. 191) showed, Victorian pornography represents female ejaculation as discharge, in Freud's thought, discharge as substance appears to refer only to seminal emission. Contemporary research on female ejaculate notwithstanding (Ladas et al., 1983), only the orgasms of men routinely entail physical discharge—at least in the Euro-American view of these matters, for Tantric Buddhism, by way of contrast, teaches a sexual practice in which orgasm occurs without ejaculation (Odier, 1997).[6] In argument with, especially, Krafft-

---

[5] Although the approach I am suggesting agrees with the focus of Klein's (1961) critique, it provides a different sort of answer than the one he had in mind. He, too, observed that, in drive–discharge, sexuality is something to be gotten rid of, whereas in clinical theory, "sexuality is a pleasure experience to be elicited or pursued, with variations of aim" (p. 49).

[6] I am indebted to Sue Shapiro for alerting me to the significance of Indian sexual practice for my argument.

Ebing, Freud (1905b) recognizes the bias of this formulation: "Having been designed to account for the sexual activity of adult males, it takes too little account of three sets of conditions which it should also be able to explain. These are the conditions in children, in females and in castrated males" (p. 214). However, that he goes on to warn us against laying "more weight on the factor of the accumulation of the sexual products than it is able to bear" does not impel him to rethink further the implications of the discharge model. This is a task that confronts us now.

Maybe, as Robert Holt (1989, p. 184, n. 7) quite sensibly and perhaps humorously proposes, there was another substance at stake. He suggests that the original model for drive was not hunger but urination—a model that enables us to capture the drift but also the insufficiency of discharge theory. Although the implicitly invidious comparison between seminal discharge and micturition may ill serve the erotics of urination, it does bring out a certain grimness in the classic theory of psychosexuality. Revealed is the astonishing chain implicated by the figure of discharge: urine, semen, symptom, cure. At work here is the hydraulics of sex and psyche: the relief upon excreting urine, the release of ejaculating semen, the cathartic passing of the symptom, the calm after the storm of illness.

Can cleanliness and godliness be far behind? This often unquestioned imbrication of hygiene, sex, illness, and treatment is worth noting. If semen is a waste product, what does that make of sex? With Foucault (1975), we can observe here a sort of policing function, a moralizing tone that stands out when discharge becomes the exclusive metaphor for sexuality or, for that matter, for sanity. As hygiene, sexuality becomes a moral and medical matter subjected to the authority of doctors, clergy, therapists, and other guardians of the contemporary soul (Shapiro, 1996). The economic theory of sex, or at least the aim it attributes to sex, embeds sexuality in a model of health and illness, engineering and efficiency.

We can wonder as well about the moral force exercised by the discharge model on our clinical practice. Classically, what mattered was the interpretive climax: once the patient had vented, the doctor would know what was wrong and could then tell the patient what caused the illness—an authoritative (if also sometimes authoritarian) telling that was curative. Did things ever work out like that? Today we doubt not only the efficacy of this model of cure, but its veridicality. We work very differently now. We notice and value mutuality and enactments and the indeterminacy they sow (Ogden, 1994; Chused, 1996; Price, 1996); we employ a multiplicity of theoretical and clinical practices. We doubt. Is it the destination that matters, we have begun to ask, or the journey? What is the relative importance of interpretation, the process of arriving at it, and the relationship between analyst and patient?

The Mess in the Consulting Room: Lust, Chimney Sweeping, and the Moment Before

Additional interpretations of Anna O's humble but spectacularly layered metaphor of chimney sweeping are possible, and I begin here to show how *Lust* might serve to answer the postclassical questions raised in this chapter. I do not dismiss the power of catharsis in either the clinic or the bedroom. The parallel between ejaculation and catharsis is, for one thing, too compelling to set aside: Slighting female orgasm though it may, it salutes the gratifying conclusiveness of climax. And, in therapy, it does help to get things off your chest, even if analysis is interminable. But, although libido and catharsis befit a one-person model of mind, they don't do much for the two-person variety.

You *need* someone to sweep your chimney. Anna O did. She didn't say so in as many words, but she did. Think about it this way. Anna O didn't clean her own chimneys. In her socioeconomic class, you got someone in to do the work (usually young boys who were small enough to climb inside the tall, sooty towers). Breuer, too, was hired help, employed by Anna O's father to help her get well. Is it stretching the matter to suppose that, when Anna O spoke of chimney sweeping, she was addressing not only Breuer's need for her father's money (Borch-Jakobson, 1997) but her need for Breuer? What Anna O meant, I should like to interpret, is that she needed her analyst. In keeping with contemporary theoretical and clinical practice, the focus of which is equally on the inner world of psychic reality and on the external world of interpersonal and social reality, I want to argue that Anna O was trying to tell Breuer, in language that both admitted and denied her desire, that she depended on him.

Certainly we do not wish to avoid the metaphor's sexual implications, but we do not want to overlook its ambiguities either. Without a doubt, the image of the chimney, a passageway for heat and smoke, evokes the desirous vaginal interior, the phallic entry of the cleaner and his brush. *"Chimney-sweeping* is an action symbolic of coitus, something Breuer never dreamed of," writes Freud to Jung in 1909 (McGuire, 1988, p. 267).[7] Anna O wanted Breuer, so the account goes, to enter her chimney. She desired him sexually and is even said to have had a hysterical pregnancy as a sign of what she desired and could not have. Look again at the metaphor, however. Is the chimney, would you say, a phallic column or a vaginal cavity? Is it female? Male? Is entering the chimney to sweep it an act of female domesticity or an act of male labor? Is it a one-person or a two-person psychology? How can we choose?

Both/and. Like the ambiguous container in Henry Moore's sculpture *Internal and External Forms,* the chimney has both an outside and an inside, is both male and female, is an erect enclosure that is also an embrace. Proceeding from dualism to multiplicity, let us think of chimney sweeping not through the economics, but through the semiotics, of desire and therapy. Borrowing Foucault's (1966, p. xii) characterization of his own effort in *The Order of Things,* I propose a set of "corresponding trans-formations" in how we think about sex, how we think about the mind, and how we think about psychotherapy. Anna O's imagery is not only sexed and gendered. It also evokes the space of dependency and need that we associate with domestic life. Perhaps, upon noticing a chimney, a 19th-century Englishman, living in, say, Manchester, might think of mills and industry. But, if you are Anna O, you think chimneys, you think hearths, you think homes. Chimney sweeping smacks of a creatureliness, a bodily feel, a plenitude and messiness that are surely properties of both sex and therapy but drop out of Freud's elegant scientific reduction of desire to libido and his clinical understanding.[8] The domestic interior, surrounded

---

[7] I thank Steven Reisner for telling me about this letter; it is always reassuring to have Freud confirm one's independent assessments.

[8] 8 An absence that, we have wondered, can itself induce a little iatrogenic sickness. Was Anna O's hysterical pregnancy an answer to Breuer's unacknowledged sexual countertransference?

by the public world to which psychoanalytic theory and practice belong, situates intimacy, relatedness, and warmth as well as complexity, confusion, and the half-lights of bodies and minds growing into and out of each other—a viney, complicated mess, the same sort of mess that we find, according to Philip Bromberg's theory of psychoanalytic technique, in the consulting room (personal communication, 1991), the same sort of mess that we find in sex.

What about this mess? Certainly it has something to do with development, with the "relational excess of early human life" (Corbett, 1997, p. 501); with the ambiguities of intersubjectivity; with the complications of gender; with sex as, paradoxically, both ruth and ruthlessness. But before we can get to such both/and matters, we need to mess with the idea of libido just a little bit more. There is, hovering mutely on the margins of classical psychoanalytic thinking, an alternative theory of sex. I am referring to that word, *Lust,* tucked away down there in that profligate footnote.

If libido describes why you want to have sex, *Lust* says what it is like while you are having it. Let one of my students speak for me. One day, after class, he said to me privately, "I don't know why Freud emphasized discharge as the be-all and end-all of sex, why he thought the moment of orgasm is the greatest pleasure. As far as I'm concerned, it's the moment before, when you're just hanging on, and you want it to go on and on and you don't want to stop" (Mark Mellinger, personal communications, 1995). It would not then be exact to say that *Lust* is to libido as polymorphous perversity is to sexual intercourse or as need is to desire. I am trying here to suspend dualistic thinking. Hence, I do not suggest, either, that libido is to *Lust* as male is to female, even though, of course, the androcentrism of discharge theory is old feminist news, if perhaps newer psychoanalytic news. Neither feminism nor psychoanalysis, however, has noticed the other sexuality dormant at the bottom of the page and in the clinic. A different axis of tension is at work here.

Way down deep, *Lust* means not the conclusion of discharge but the penultimate moment of peak excitement when being excited is both enough and not enough, when each rise in excitement is, paradoxically, satisfying. Orgiastic. I would not want to do without orgasm—catharsis—myself. But isn't the pleasure of *Lust* equally central? A need calling for satisfaction, a satisfaction becoming a thrilling need? An excitement whose gratification is simultaneously exciting? Both "lost to the world" and in the world at once (Bach, 1998)? a doubling of feeling, a doubled and potently contradictory state whose end one craves and fears? If the closure of climax is devoutly to be wished, do we, or at least some of us, not savor it all the more because, in achieving it, we must let go of the extraordinary poignancy of sustained excitement in the moment before?

Two states ordinarily thought of as mutually exclusive—desire and satisfaction, or tension and release—in fact coexist in *Lust*. Both/and. Whereas libido puts a distance between need and gratification, *Lust* posits their simultaneity. The line between *Lust* and libido is therefore always on the verge of disappearing. Even though Freud (1905b) announces on the first page that he prefers the Latinate and scientific-sounding libido because it seems so straightforward, clear-cut (clean-cut?), and economical, libido never entirely satisfies him. Look at how, 65 pages later, it turns out that arousal and gratification are not always distinct in ordinary experience. "The concepts of 'sexual excitation' and satisfaction' can," Freud notes, "to a great extent be used without distinction" (p. 210). Two pages after that comes yet another footnote written not later on but in the first edition of the work: *"'Lust'* has two meanings, and is used to describe the sensation of sexual tension (*'Ich habe Lust'* = 'I should like to,' 'I feel an impulse to') as well as the feeling of satisfaction" (p. 212, n. 1).

Vicissitudes of *Lust* in the Clinic: Three Vignettes

Might we call this the pleasure of desiring? Ms. PS, a patient who, at the beginning of treatment, would leave her body when her lovers responded to her desire, was recently recounting her struggle with the shame, pleasure, and embarrassment of telling her husband just which squeeze or caress she likes him to give her. She associated to the lunch she would eat after the session: She always thinks she wants an empanada even though it always disappoints her. She recalled a short story about a woman who gives up smoking and discovers all the longings and cravings smoking had hidden. At the end of the story, the woman decides to go to a bad, overpriced restaurant so she can have the tomato soup that is always too salty, because that's what she wants. "Wanting the empanada," I said, "is almost an experiment, sort of holding something constant, sort of pure desire." "Yes," replied PS, who has been struggling with matters of desire and aggression, "it's not tied up with satisfaction, I don't know how to say this, it's the satisfaction of the desire, no . . ." She trailed off. The next session, she said, "It's enough just having the desire. No, that's not right. . . ." She ran out of words. There is no English word for *Lust*.

Clinical examples whet our analytic appetites. Certainly we want to know what an empanada means to Ms. PS, and we can easily begin to associate to its symbolic possibilities. Food in a pocket might have a particular meaning for a 32-year-old woman who wanted to get pregnant, as PS did. A Caribbean food might matter to a white antiglobalization activist identified with Latin American politics, as was PS. I chose not to pursue an interpretive line, however, because I felt that, at that particular moment, expanding her experience of *Lust* was more congruent with the psychoanalytic goal of the examined life.

Another patient, Mr. TK, suffered from his lust for me because it could not be satisfied. Not only was he, like Odysseus, bound to the mast, but he had done this voluntarily, and it frustrated and angered him. TK knew something about *Lust* already, however. As I was going off for summer vacation during our first year of work together, he gave me a letter in a sealed envelope. On the flap of the envelope, he had written, "Don't open this right now. Open it later. Later still. Later. Not now. Later. La—" As PS had run out of words, so the rest of TK's words ran over the edge, disappearing into the flap's foldover.

The unease of *Lust's* ambiguity shows up here. As relatedness, we now think, may nurture desire (e. g., Mitchell, 1988), so the suspended state of unconsummated desire might reciprocally hold relatedness. Perhaps, indeed, this state of suspended animation— feeling without acting—is a gift of the incest prohibition: the creation of intimacy in which, as Freud might have put it, undischarged libido generates the connective power of love. Think here of Jody Davies's (1998) recent argument: "We all have sexual desires on which we do not act—places in which such actions would be inappropriate and wrong. As adults, we can desire without the promise of satisfaction; we can want without having to possess. Perhaps this is the true legacy of Oedipus—the capacity to sustain desire for what we can never have" (p. 76). I feel obligated to acknowledge that one might find aggression hiding in Mr. TK's playful, teasing note. Such was not, however, my first response, and I did not offer such an interpretation. Indeed, I made no interpretation at all. I waited because, as I now understand my decision, I thought there was more than hostility offered to me. You might call his gift seductive. I would call it *Lust*.

Indeed, *Lust,* as an atmosphere, may yield more understanding than—one might put it—premature interpretation can. Having emerged for a time from a long, dark regression, Mr. TK had a new feeling. One day, after telling me about his yearning for another unattainable woman—a public figure, some 20 years older, like me, but black while I am white—he fell into a brief silence. Then, "Oh, this lust for you, it won't go away." Another silence. "But the lust does something good. It makes me feel close, hopeful about our relationship. It's not all good. It hurts. There is also a melancholy that is pleasurable, too." The poignancy of desire slips away when we focus only on discharge. Even so, it is not easy to hold. Here is Davies (1998) again: "Perhaps it is only the gentle survival of such a harsh reality that allows us to risk the potential humiliations and rejections of . . . adult mutuality and sexual intimacy" (p. 765). TK and I wavered in our ability to inhabit this ambiguous space with any degree of comfort, unsettled in the unsettling, inconclusive space of the examined life.

Lust thus reconceived has technical implications. Was TK's feeling for me sexual transference? Dependency sexualized? Just plain sexual? Just plain maternal? All of the above? Perhaps equally vital is the emotional climate of the consulting room. How do we sustain the state of desiring so critical to the analytic relationship— the shared states of feeling in which clinical discovery and creation take place? There is an excess of hypothesis, many potential routes that patient and analyst might take to achieve a state of intimacy through which one may "court surprise" (Stern, 1997).

The same fruitful indeterminacy holds for sexual counter-transference, which we are thereby enabled to enter in a mutative way. Another patient had been describing significant problems that one would have called marital had marriage been the relationship in question. Suspecting that my erotic counter-transference, unvoiced, had once before unconsciously communicated itself to Dr. FN and coalesced into a nearly home-wrecking affair, I decided to disclose my erotic feelings. Aware of the possible risks attendant on disclosure (Maroda, 1994, pp. 94–96, 135–138) but also aware of the potential rewards (Davies, 1994), I said that I would not act on my desires in any way other than verbal, and I did not reveal anything about my own sexual preference or domestic state. I suggested that this erotic countertransference might have a variety of sources that we could discuss; I had in mind projective identification, erotization of attachment, my own unresolved personal issues, and mundane sexual attraction.

This disclosure permitted us to enter and maintain a state of intimacy that, remarkably, yielded not only symptom relief but fundamental change. "No one has ever said anything like that to me before," said FN, who had been through a range of treatments over the preceding 25 years. What was new for this patient was not the revelation of another's sexual desire, a form of relatedness uncomfortably familiar from childhood on. What was novel and even shocking was my interest in noting and maintaining a state of mutual desiring that itself became an object of shared experience and knowledge rather than an occasion for discharge. If one wished to put what happened next in classical language, one could say that libido and *Lust* together made Eros, the life force in its binding aspect, which has, at least for now, triumphed over Thanatos (Freud, 1920a). FN's "hysterical misery," I hesitate to say (because it seems too good to be true), began turning into "ordinary unhappiness." The route taken by this transformation has been, however, postclassical—the one-way street of catharsis meeting the two-way street of connection. For the first time, FN felt me as a presence in the room, a person, and things began, slowly, to change. The symptoms of chronic fatigue syndrome have been gone for some time now, their place taken by the psychological distress kept at bay for so many years. Now we contend with anger, fear, anxiety, terror, sadness, and loss. "I am no longer the 'walking dead,' " FN puts it, "I have come alive."

That final vignette is meant to illustrate the intermediate space of *Lust,* the unconsummated, pleasurable, ambiguous, difficult, and clinically potent space my patients and I inhabit, and I have tried to recount it so that the medium is the message. Did you notice I haven't mentioned FN'S gender? Do you care? Why? My silence is, I know, a bit teasing and mischievous, but there is a point. There are many ambiguities. Let me mention two. One is the relation between technique and turnout. We are not, as I suggested in the Prologue, scientists, and we therefore cannot predict (for a recent discussion of psychoanalysis as science and the Grünbaum debate, see Curtis, 1996; Fourcher, 1996; Jacobson, 1996; Protter, 1996; Schwartz, 1996). FN's analysis is not over, and, to be sure, we do not know what will happen between now and termination. Like any clinical act, my self-disclosure grew in a matrix made equally of technical and metapsychological generalities and the particularities of the individual case; FN is a person able and more than willing to inhabit potential space, and we have shared similar thunderous moments in regard to dilemmas of attachment as well as desire. (Final disclosure: FN, a Jewish feminist of a certain age—like me—is a woman who lives with a woman self-described as "a lesbian separatist in the 1970s and a queer activist in the 1990s.")

The second ambiguity is gender. When we meet sex in the clinic nowadays, we are tempted to think gender, and so we should. The entrance of gender theory into psychoanalysis—or, as Benjamin (1984) has put it, "the convergence of psychoanalysis and feminism" in the object-relational model—is something of a phenomenon. A fringe element as recently as the early 1980s, the discourse on gender has become absolutely central to psycho-analytic colloquy. Gender theory has so convincingly responded to the classical conundrum of female desire that not only does André Green (1997) himself agree it needs attention, but much of psychosexual theory falls these days under its rubric, as Benjamin (1997) notes. Still, now that we remember gender, we have to be able to forget it, too. As I suggest in the next chapter, the psycho-analytic situation has both gendered and gender-free moments—creating a tension that we inhabit all the time. If, to put it differently, we subtract gender, then what's left of sex? A lot, I suspect, and it is that to which I have been attending in this essay. There is sex as well as gender, and it is time to retheorize sex.

Between *Lust* and Libido

When we read below as well as above the line, Freud's distinctions blur. Not only do excitement and satisfaction fade into each other. Not only do the two acts into which the play of sex is said to be clearly divided also lose their identities. A new account of sexual experience takes shape, one that disturbs the smooth surface of theory, one as messy as sex ordinarily is. What happens in the experiential and conceptual—one might say intermediate—space between what Freud taught us to think about as "fore-pleasure" and "end-pleasure"? Something sexy, I think. And something, of course, complicated and difficult. (Hence the urgent question occupying pundits and politicians alike: Is oral sex sex?) On reflection, "sex" in Freud's (1905b) "Three Essays" and, therefore, I would argue, in the back of our minds is always confused (see Chapter 3). Sometimes, sexuality means heterosexual intercourse; other times, polysexuality; still other times, reproduction. On one page, sexuality denotes specifically and originally genital excitement that tends to flood into other body parts; on the next page, the entire body is an erogenous zone. Sometimes it signifies arousal, and sometimes it signifies climax. It may connote a driving force or a psychic structure or a relationship. I do not reject this confusion. On the contrary, I find it appropriately recursive.

Psychoanalysis has lost its innocence, swept through by the sea change in 20th-century thought. Marshall Berman's (1982) remarkable appreciation of the modern (note, not postmodern) spirit sums up the spirit of the new psychoanalysis: "a desire to live openly with the split and unreconciled character of our lives, and to draw energy from our inner struggles, where ever they may lead us in the end" (p. 171). If libido fits the classical model of cure, then *Lust*— the unconsummated moment before—is a signifier more suited to the clinical stance taken today. Think about current metaphors for the space of psychoanalytic work—transitional, potential, intermediate (Winnicott, Ogden, Bromberg). Think about a personal relation mediated by the impersonalities of time and money in which belief is willingly suspended and analysts and patients proceed like Odysseus bound to the mast—an Odysseus more suited to the psychoanalytic task than the one invoked by Kohut—"exercising restraint while yielding to desire" (Wilner, 1998).

Let's situate sex in the space between libido and *Lust*. We might begin our thinking about this ambiguous location through both the dialectics and the grammar of space. I juxtapose two unlikely bedfellows. We can say, with Ogden (1994), that, like consciousness and unconsciousness, neither libido nor *Lust* "holds a privileged position in relation to the other; rather they stand in a relation of relative difference, each constituting the other through negation" (p. 60). And we can return to the erotics of breath (see Chapter 4). Listen to Daniel Odier (1997), a Tantric master who writes of the power of the comma, the space in the text standing for the space in life:

> Between two breaths, there is a comma. Between two feelings or two ideas, there is a comma. Between one gesture and another, there is a comma. . . . All life experiences are followed by a comma. . . . Our life is too often like a text without punctuation [but] all of a sudden, there is a rupture, a silence, a void, a comma, and true life—what Freud later called Eros—"begins" [p. 151].

Before moving on to the deconstruction of sexual difference itself in the next chapter, let's play one more riff on Bromberg (1998). Standing in the space between libido and *Lust,* a space giving on to the potent debates animating psychoanalytic thought today, we can look back at our origins. Recall Freud's (1905b) preface to "Three Essays": "For it is some time since Arthur Schopenhauer, the philosopher, showed mankind the extent to which their activities are determined by sexual impulses—in the ordinary sense of the word" (p. 134). *In the ordinary, quotidian sense of the word.* For all the peregrinations of his theory, all the impossibilities and confusions as well as illuminating truths, all the many questions to be put even to this one remark, this is what Freud was trying to explain: sexual experience as it was and is commonly supposed—concrete, graphic, exciting, hot. Contemporary psychoanalysis and feminism, each for different reasons, contest the idea that sexual impulses determine our activities; they follow the Freud of the footnotes who knew that there was no such thing as ordinary sex. But classic psychosexual theory won't let go of our imagination for a good reason: it remembers the sheer materiality of sex, the body, the mute excitement (Bowie, 1991, pp. 49, 141; Stein, 1998) to which our theories of desire attempt to give meaning.

6

Deconstructing Difference
Gender, Splitting, and
Transitional Space

In an early session, Dr. EL (whom I mentioned in Chapter 2), then 43 years old, held back her tears because, she said, "I don't want to cry on your shoulder." When I questioned her reluctance, she replied that the danger lay in the shoulder, not in the crying: she would cry only on a man's shoulder; she was not interested in women.

I want to understand EL's reply by thinking about gender. More precisely, I want to think through the *problem* of gender by thinking through the problem of dualism. More than race or class, gender has, for the last generation or so, at least in the United States, been the dualism of dualisms, a representational power in clinical practice, theoretical work, and daily life alike. Gender dualism is routinely conceived a matter of difference. But what is difference? In this chapter, I look into—deconstruct—difference so that its dynamics, silenced by being taken for granted, may emerge in their complexity.

That masculinity and femininity are different goes without saying. But in what ways? Under what conditions? Are males and females, actual men and women, as absolutely Other to each other as these two categories, masculinity and femininity? How gender categories manifest—in identity, character, style, and behavior—varies enormously. When it comes to gendered categories and gendered beings, paradoxes and contingencies abound. Variations in gender across history and culture; the similarity of personality, passion, and psyche across gender—these well-known facts require us to break into the rigid standoff between masculinity on one hand, and femininity on the other by creating a third—the space between. As we do so, we will see how gender dualism leads us into many other dualisms circulating through psyche and society.

— 7

The Space Between

In this chapter, I propose that at the heart of gender is not "masculinity" or "femininity" but the difference between them. When we look into that space of difference, we find that gender is not an essence but a set of relations (May, 1986). My thinking is located in two intersecting contexts, feminist and psychoanalytic. The first may be described as "the critique of gender," a phrase whose ambiguity is deliberate. I mean to suggest, simultaneously, gender as critiqued and gender as critique, gender as a concept that not only requires scrutiny but can itself illuminate other matters of mind and society. Reciprocally, understanding gender depends on the second, psychoanalytic context. Three Winnicottian concepts are at work: selfhood, splitting, and transitional space. These concepts can further the clinical relevance of the critique of gender.

I speak in this chapter of gender's possibility, of its present as well as its future. As a feminist, I am interested in gender revolution. As clinician, I am keen to patients' needs for help. Surely changing ideas about gender can feed (or flow with, or both) larger social changes. But they can also address immediate personal dilemmas. By defamiliarizing the emotion- and value-laden notions of "femininity" and "masculinity," the doubled critique of gender I offer can help to peel away what we think gender is (and believe it ought to be) from what it might be. Deconstructing gender stretches the clinical imagination about what patients' inner worlds are like and, given the chance, could be like.

Gender and Self

EL's wish to cry only on a man's shoulder spoke to two matters, one of gender, the other of self. Yet it is misleading to separate these two problems. As a brief overview will show, gender and self ordinarily entangle. Conventionally, "gender" denotes the psychological and social dimensions of the biological category of sex. This characterization sounds like a clear enough division of epistemological labor: "sex" refers to Nature, "gender" to Nurture. But it is not. Dualism's clarity is illusory or, at least, temporary. As we saw in Chapters 3 and 5, sex is itself so full of meaning as to elude stable definition; and the dualism, nature–nurture, which describes the sex–gender binary, falls apart when closely examined.

And, for a third, what gender seems to denote is one thing, but what it actually connotes is another. As described in Chapter 2, the connotations of gender are so complex as to generate an enormous indeterminacy. The epitome of dualism in contemporary Euro-American culture (perhaps since the Enlightenment, suggests Flax, 1990), gender works as a kind of cryptography. Masculinity and femininity are a sort of cultural code signifying not only (anatomical and representational) sexual difference but other qualities, entities, and relationships that have nothing to do with it. Given this encryption, gender meaning invisibly webs with a great range of cultural imagery, which, in turn, informs how gender and sexual relations are lived and understood.

"Gender," like "sex," is not transparent. Rather, it is a dense weave of cultural significance. By the same token, the contrast masculine–feminine, representing what Freud (1925a) called the anatomical difference, addresses a variety of matters, not all of which are germane to sex, gender, or the genitals. This slippage from sex to culture not only provides us with our understandings of gender as personally experienced but informs gender as a social institution.

Another elision, equivalent in power to that from sex to culture, informs what we might term the mutual definition of selfhood and gender identity, such that problems of self may come to be coded in terms of gender, and those of gender, in terms of the self. "Self" may plausibly and usefully be defined as the subjective version of the ego. But, as I indicated in Chapter 4, I use it to denote a sensibility, not a structure: a feeling of being alive. This sense of aliveness and the sense of one's gender inhabit one another quite intimately. Let me evoke that intimacy of self and gender identity with a set of familiar questions: If I feel "womanly," am I

at my most "feminine"? Or am I feeling most fully "myself"? When
I do feel "like myself," does that feeling have anything to do with
my female identity? If I feel, by contrast and perhaps more
pertinently, "unwomanly," am I feeling somehow "not myself"?
If I am "not myself," is gender identity somehow also, and more
secretly, involved? And so on.

Would these puzzles even arise if self and gender identity were
not already in problematic relation? The entanglement of gender
and psychic development is a psychoanalytic durable. At its core
are several linked stories drafted by Freud and codified in the
literary and oral traditions of psychoanalysis: Oedipus; the penis,
the vagina, and the clitoris (see Chapters 1 and 4); activity and
passivity; and the id, ego, and superego. The complicated narrative
thus produced did not, however, unpack the gender enigma.
Throughout the history of psychoanalysis after Freud and Horney
(see Chapter 2), many have continued to study and theorize female
and male development (e.g., Deutsch, 1944; Kestenberg, 1968,
Fogel, 1986). The feminist entry into the ever-evolving story of
gender and psyche took wing when (as I have sketched in Chapter
1) the theorization of preoedipal life was sufficiently advanced to
take the mother into account, thereby allowing consideration of
gender's influence on parenting and child rearing (e.g., Chodorow,
1978). Subsequent work (Fast, 1984; Benjamin, 1988b) has led
to a new codification of the development of gender identity in
early object relations, as well as in the later Oedipal and postoedipal
phases (Benjamin, 1995; Bassin, 1996). Now efforts are under
way to retheorize this revised paradigm so that gender multiplicity,
the topic of this chapter, may be woven into the fabric of
developmental theory (Corbett, 1993, 2001b; Harris, in press).

We understand now that selfhood and gender identity crystallize
very early and nearly simultaneously in development, certainly by
the middle of the second year of life (Fast, 1984; Benjamin,
1988b). This developmental simultaneity creates a personal
problem. Although self and gender are structurally different, their
contemporaneous psychic birth makes them seem, even *feel*, joined
at the heart. Mutual encryption leaves their relationship
simultaneously unquestioned and questionable. The intrapsychic
proximity of sense of self to sense of gender identity often obscures,
not to say deepens, the complexities of gender representation thus
generated. At the same time, the contrast of masculine–feminine,

by collapsing many representations of selfhood *that are unrelated to gender*, can disguise, and even create, dilemmas of self as well.

Gender enters as a split, a concept I am using loosely (drawing on Benjamin, 1988b). "Splitting," in its psychoanalytic sense, signifies the divide in the self that, critical to a sense of difference ("I," "you"), is also used defensively. For example, it is mobilized to manage anxiety in the situation of parental narcissism and infantile need that led Winnicott (1975) to theorize true self–false self. In its cultural sense, splitting indicates the many dichotomies and dualisms paradigmatic in Western thinking since Descartes and of critical relevance to feminist and psychoanalytic thought. These dualisms, we will see, encode one another. Self and Other, masculinity and femininity, activity and passivity, and many other splits and dualisms show up equally, simultaneously, and interimplicatedly on psychic and cultural levels.

Sometimes the mutual coding of gender and self is directly translatable. For example, the conventional split between masculine and feminine in psychology and culture speaks also to pleasure, activity, and passivity. Pleasure in activity is wont to carry the valence of masculinity, whereas pleasure in passivity is charged with femininity, a split aligned with the traditional dichotomy in sex roles and in classical psychoanalysis (see Chapters 1 and 2). As this splitting has been challenged socially, it is more often questioned in the clinical situation, where one may suspect, for example, that women's sense of activity may be gender dystonic and therefore anxiety inducing, just as men's fantasies of passivity may express a fear of being homosexual, itself often code for the fear of being feminine.[1]

This example might seem straightforward, but the plot thickens. For instance, gender identity, normatively characterized as watertight, may in fact be porous (Harris, 1991). We do not always feel in gender, and when we do not, we feel anxiety, which makes us less likely to remember that sometimes one's gender resembles an ill-fitting garment. Like sex (see Chapter 4), gender is saturated with affect. When I asked a friend who had lost a tennis match how he felt during the game, he replied, "Like a girl" (he had had

---

[1] Famously, Freud's (1924) idea of "feminine" masochism, for example, refers only to men.

trouble wielding the racket). Clearly, "feeling like a girl" was not a pleasant experience for him. Still, was he anxious because he felt out of gender? Or out of gender because anxious about self? Or both? Why was losing incompatible with his masculinity? Or his heterosexuality? Is losing the same as castration? Does not losing also make us feel small? Castration, as Lacanians (Mitchell, 1982; Rose, 1982) and others (McDougall, 1995) have been thinking for some time now, maps onto other earlier losses—of, for example, the breast and hence of a sense of integration—that engender feelings of helplessness and loneliness. In losing, perhaps this man felt like a child as well as like a girl.

Or, Sue Shapiro (personal communication, 1990) suggests, maybe "feeling like a girl" represents a narcissistic wound: losing gender evokes all the other irrevocable losses of childhood that make us feel reduced and shamed. By way of comparison and contrast, another friend, who has always regarded herself as nonathletic, depicts her successful attempt to play squash by drawing a yapping, rushing Pekingese, which she reluctantly identifies as male. We might say that in her activity, she first and consciously experiences herself as not herself, as Other and, only second, unconsciously, and more painfully, as out-of-gender, as a junior, ridiculous male. If my woman friend experienced the narcissistic wound ultimately as gender loss, could my man friend have represented it finally by loss of self, by an encounter with the second-sex Otherness (de Beauvoir, 1949) that femininity represents?

Gender as a Set of Relations

One dualism leads to another. In critiquing the dualistic alignment of femininity with passivity and of masculinity with activity, we come upon a third—a whirl of dualisms orbiting in relation to the contrast masculine–feminine and to each other as well—self–other, preoedipal–oedipal, infancy–adulthood, autonomy–dependency, superiority–inferiority, heterosexuality–homosexuality. Contemplating this third reveals "gender" to be less a determinate category than something resembling a force field. Much like the atom, once thought of as substance but now construed as a set of interacting forces, so gender looks to consist not of essences but of complex and shifting relations among multiple contrasts or differences. Sometimes these contrasts remain distinct, at other times they intersect, and at still other times they fuse and exchange identities.

As a way of turning to how problems of self and gender may encode one another, let us focus for a moment more on activity and passivity and their relation to sexual difference. Recognizing the force field that marries the inherently unrelated contrasts masculine–feminine, self–other, and active–passive to one another permits us to understand, for example, that women's anxiety in activity may be a problem equally of self as of gender. On the other hand, this recognition also lets us understand that gender-neutral qualities of self, such as activity and passivity, can reciprocally organize and thereby evoke sexual and gendered splits. I have alluded, for example, to the fact that, for men, passivity may represent homosexuality and femininity.

An analogous, although not identical, slippage among activity state, object choice, and gender identity shows up in the experience of EL, whose refusal to cry on a woman's shoulder now emerges as a negotiation among dangerous polarities. Her response to my inquiry implied that she was neither a dependent child nor a lesbian, but an autonomous, heterosexual woman, and as such, her need for comfort was not a danger. To have admitted being a woman who wanted a woman's shoulder to cry on would have revealed what crying on a man's shoulder concealed, that sometimes she still felt like a child. The idea of leaning on a man defended against dependency longings because, in culture and psyche alike, heterosexuality lines up with, and symbolizes, adulthood and autonomy.

Sex, Gender, and Splitting: Clinical Reflections

Heterosexuality, even though it is classically (although not always in Freud; see Chapters 1, 3, 5, and 9) the object choice of choice, can and does serve to conceal and express splits in the self. Nominally heterosexual, EL had not had sex with another person in 15 years, although she did masturbate (which she refused to discuss). Having had one homosexual encounter in junior college, she later married a man 20 years her senior. He being mainly impotent, they had intercourse perhaps half a dozen times before a heart attack killed him three months after the wedding. Later, she had three major but short-lived heterosexual affairs; the last breakup so bereaved her that she resolved never to let anyone get close again.

These facts of her life, and those to be recounted, emerged slowly and painfully over the course of our work together. Contemplating our shared history now, I feel as I did then— dismayed, conscious of both reluctance and helplessness to grasp the full damage. Not untouched, I still was sensible of her wish that I respect her cocoon. Shielding her was her obesity, which, she believed, distanced men in particular. In her fat, she was like a great big baby, neither male nor female.

The gender ambiguity in my association reflects EL's sexual unease and ambiguity. Her attachment to a suspended heterosexuality masking childhood longings was a powerful means to disremember the sexual abuse that, from ages three to five, she experienced with her adored brother, nine years older than she. Almost daily, Johnnie would masturbate before her in the parlor at quarter to five in the afternoon while they listened to a favorite radio program and, in the next room, their mother prepared dinner. Torn between feeling special and feeling betrayed, EL never spoke of these encounters; she always believed that if she told her mother she, not Johnnie, would be punished; when she was older and thought about taking the story to confession (the family was Catholic), she would somehow forget.

Not only her flesh but her words protected her. I was both moved and paralyzed by the verbal fence EL planted around her private self. When, one time, she said, by way of explanation, "Johnnie set me up too early," she sounded like a forlorn child prostitute turned out by her lover-turned-pimp, a child now homeless but denying the despair of her psychic bondage to him. Yet, even as EL's speech (she often used clichés, for example) deftly dispatched emotion to some unreachable part of the galaxy, it served to consolidate her personal universe. Shattered, she wrapped the wounds of her amputated feeling in tried-and-true language that normalized her tragedy. At the same time, Johnnie's betrayal of her trust disrupted not only the consolidation of her selfhood but the emergence of her sexuality and gender identity. Was she female or male? She wanted to be both, and neither. While watching Johnnie's performance, was she watching and desiring her idol or identifying with him? Was she safe or in danger? None of this was clear. Her only relief was not to choose—neither to desire nor to be either gender (a dilemma identified by Harris, 1991).

Here, in summary fashion, is the sequence as it appears, in retrospect, to me, for it was not a narrative she could have produced herself. The cessation of the incest coincided with the birth of her younger sister (the last of five children) and the start of school, a traumatic concatenation of events that resulted in the tantrums for which she was punished after she started school. At the age of 5, she wanted to drown her newborn younger sister "because she wasn't a boy." She remembered the soothing excitement of clitoral masturbation when she was 8. Between the ages of 9 and 10, she frequently wore one of her father's cast-off ties, which she hoped would transform her into a boy. During her 11th year (when, after Johnnie's return from the Army, the incest recurred briefly until she put a stop to it), she began her avid consumption of novels and was at the time drawn to tales of pirates and potentates (thieves and kings, like her adored, ruthless brother). Torn between gender shame and pride, she was disappointed that menstruation was not a one-time-only event yet was humiliated that her first brassiere was her oldest sister's yellowed cast-off (delivered, to her embarrassment, by Johnnie as a present at a holiday dinner). By adolescence, she had come to hold what she regarded as the prejudiced opinion that boys should not be allowed to baby-sit. Finally, she feared sexually assertive men and preferred those who were shy and a bit unsure.

While gender and sexuality held their secret pleasures for EL, their main affective register was pain. Frozen between femininity and masculinity, on guard against fear and betrayal, and just out of others' reach, she came, in her adult life, to be cleft between body and mind, a cleavage that was apparently odd but, down deep, a source and sign of shame. Trained in physical therapy (by which she was supporting herself), she was finishing a doctorate, was already becoming known in her field, and had friends who were liberal, intellectual, and sophisticated. Yet she resided alone in her family home next door to her oldest sister in a redneck suburb. Her work life was also polarized. Her specialty within her field relied very much on concrete data, while theoretical abstractions found in other sectors of her discipline unnerved her. She preferred gothic and horror genres for extracurricular reading but generally found the news media too distressing to witness.

Splitting, in all its manifestations, characterized her psychic and intersubjective processes. Psychic processes took somatic form, her consciousness was divided, and she split the Other too (Laplanche and Pontalis, 1967, pp. 427–430). She overate and could remember nothing while gorging. Obese, she had myriad physical ailments and a minor cocaine habit. Between sessions, she would go amnesic, forgetting what had happened in the last meeting. In session, she would dissociate, losing touch with what she had just been saying or with what she intended to tell me. Doggedly, sometimes mischievously, she would balk at any suggestion that her acts, thoughts, or feelings had an unconscious meaning or origin. For nearly all of the treatment, she saw herself as the one attending to practical reality, leaving to me airy interpretations of unconscious meaning.

Still, the work paid off and the splits began to heal. Although she always remembered the facts of the incest and the sense of privilege she derived from it, she was, until a year and a half before we terminated, unconscious of her anger about it and the horror underlying it. At that time, EL began to follow the increasing media coverage of the sexual abuse of children, because she had just learned that there had been more sexual abuse in her own family. Johnnie, who had died in a freak accident at age 26, had left behind a wife and two children. His widow later remarried a man who, it turned out, molested both his stepdaughter and his stepson's daughter, that is, Johnnie's own daughter and granddaughter. EL's subsequent outrage on behalf of her niece and grandniece allowed us to probe her rage and despair about what had befallen her.

Following these insights, some behaviors changed while others hung on. As EL recovered her anger and sense of betrayal about the incest, she somatized less and her drug dependencies disappeared; she even stopped smoking. Nevertheless, her unwelcome obesity and her resistance to unconscious interpretation held fast almost all the way to the end. For reasons I come to later, we failed to undo some of the splitting in the transference and countertransference, in which EL embraced the manifest, the literal, the body, and I embraced the latent, the symbolic, the mind. Nor is it surprising that this split intersected gender as well. During one session, when she was in deep distress about her family's inability or refusal to appreciate her work, she spoke of her "inquiring mind." Together, we then discovered that, of her parents, brother, and three sisters, the only other person in her family who could also be so described was her father. If, therefore, her mind inquired, then it followed that she could not be female. But we were unable to explore the paradox that women, too, could have inquiring minds.

Desire in the Space of Difference

So far, the axis of my discussion has been splitting and its interface with the gender polarity: gender dualism, intersecting with other dualisms, either pole of which, rigidly clung to, may also signal splits in the self. But additional crosscutting axes introduce other considerations. Take, for example, desire. It, too, is dualistically organized. It is informed by gender as a dichotomous representational system that, making difference into splitting, manifests both culturally and psychically. In contemporary Western culture, desire has a heterosexual—or heterosexist, or heterophiliac (see Chapter 3)—template. This generates two models of desire, one split from the other. The first "honors, masculinizes, and makes adult the felt experience of 'I want.' The [other] demeans, feminizes, and infantilizes the state of being wanted, the felt experience of 'I want to be wanted'" (Dimen, 1986, p. 7; see also Benjamin, 1988b, pp. 85–133). Thus it creates of desiring and desiring-to-be-desired a split system perfectly suited to Plato's myth of men and women as opposite halves of a single lost whole.

This gender symbolism organizes life for the category of heterosexuality (Butler, 1995) but snarls men's and women's lives. Although gender and self are mutually implicated, self crosses gender boundaries. Even if gender inflicts selfhood's development (Chodorow, 1978; Benjamin, 1988), still the sense of self is known to men and women alike. This paradox of sameness in difference makes life interestingly complicated. If gender does not exhaust selfhood, then a psychic place for out-of-gender experiences and qualities would seem to exist. Even if desire codes masculine, for example, women might nevertheless have it. If they do, however, they may be anxious because it is gender dystonic. Whereas wanting-to-be-wanted might suit women's gender identity because it fits their femininity, it might by the same token alarm men because it curdles their sense of their masculinity.

Yet this baroque picture is even more complicated. Not only do personal background and cultural history contour constructions of desire for the heterosexual (Chodorow, 1994), the mix and match of desired–desiring, activity–passivity, and masculinity–femininity is contingent on object choice. Among many homosexual men, for example, wanting-to-be-wanted may take the form of an exciting passivity that confirms and produces a nonheterosexual masculinity (Corbett, 1993). At the same time, not every gay man is at home in passivity. And certainly stone butches, like my patient Ms. KS, dislike sex unless they can be the active giver who does not desire, never needs, and never receives.

The partial overlap between gender and self shows up in a particular dilemma many women find themselves in—and, I will suggest shortly, many men do, too. The polarity, wanting and wanting-to-be-wanted, cross-cuts not only the binary masculine–feminine, but the dichotomy, subject–object. This three-way meeting produces a primary contradiction, the "subject-as-object" (Dimen, 1986, p. 3). Subjects, in our cultural and intrapsychic representations, are men. The subject says, "I want." The subject, "Man," desires and represents authorship, agency, and adulthood. But women are adults and as such are expected to be subjects, too. However, at the same time, through conjoined psychic and cultural splitting, women are also expected to be objects ("object" here meaning not the intrapsychic representation of persons, as psychoanalysis uses the term, but "thing," as the vernacular has it). As inanimate things, women are represented to be without desire, to be the targets of the subject's desire. If subjects want, objects are there to be wanted.

In Western representational systems, then, women are expected to be both, the subject and the object. The development of femininity or of identification as a female, is, therefore, a compromise, almost, you might say, a compromise formation: part of gender's normal pathology (Goldner, 1991), femininity defends against the painful recognition that to live as a whole being, you have to divide yourself in half. As a defense mechanism, femininity is the process of learning to be both, to take yourself as an object and to expect others to do so, too, and all the while you know that you are a subject.

EL's is an extreme version of this double bind, an embodiment of a primary sexual contradiction. She split her identification as a woman into good and bad. On one hand, as a woman, you would want to be of a piece—a woman, not a child or a man; unwilling to weep on my shoulder, EL pronounces herself a woman. On the other hand, if being a woman means being both the subject of your own desires and the object of others' and therefore torn or suspended between these two positions—like EL, who, as a little girl, feared she would have been held responsible for her bother's sexual incursions—then perhaps you would not want to be feminine after all. So EL stopped time when the incest ceased; often feeling like a five-year-old girl, she walks with the rolling gait of a sailor, identifies as a heterosexual woman, and avoids sexual intimacy.

Hierarchy and Aggression Among Women

Examining the gendering of desire and the contrast subject–object or, better, subjectivity–objectification, returns us to gender as critiqued, because it introduces the particularly critical notion of hierarchy. The contrast power–weakness intersects all the others considered so far. As one literary critic describes the gender hierarchy's ambiguities, "gender refers not only to a polarity within a field of cultural information but also to the asymmetry between the two poles of that opposition" (Armstrong, 1988, p. 2). Or, to put it less formally and more whimsically, all genders are created equal, but some are more equal than others. Behind the two there is always and only one.

The contrast masculine–feminine, then, interfaces not only with inherently gender-neutral and a-hierarchial polarities but also with those trafficking in power. By way of the gender hierarchy characterized variously as "male dominance," "patriarchy," and "sexism," masculinity–femininity intersects with domination–

subordination, too. Indeed, so do all polarities, because, according to postmodernism, "binary oppositions are inseparable from implicit or explicit hierarchies" (Flax, 1990, p. 101). I do not want to recapitulate what gender politics has had to say, since 1949, about the effects of gender hierarchy on women. Instead, I would like to consider how this new contrast, power–weakness, illuminates masculinity as well.

That, in contemporary hegemonic Western representations, femininity is not essentially, but only contingently, a compromise between subjectivity and objectification, is revealed when we understand that men, too, can be the subject-as-object. In fact, this contradiction is what they, like women in the workplace, enter every Monday morning. On the job, most men have to follow someone else's orders with the same alacrity as though they had thought of them themselves. There, they, too, must be subject-as-object. They escape this contradiction only when they leave; even then, if they are Third World or in some other way stigmatized, they are not free from this sort of domination until they return to their own communities or homes. The difference for women is that hierarchy follows them everywhere they go. Most men may be "feminized" at work. But most women are stigmatized everywhere—at home, in the community, on the street—because they wear the contradiction of subject-as-object on their bodies. It may be, indeed, that the only time they are safe is when they are with other women. Even then, as I discuss in Chapter 8, not only the social hierarchies women inhabit but the relational structures of domination and subordination govern them almost as surely.

Indeed, hierarchy among women may have limited EL's treatment. I had hoped that, before she terminated, we would be able to negotiate the paradox that she, a woman of an active intellectuality, was in a room with me, a woman of like mind, a woman on whose shoulder she could finally permit herself to cry without threatening her gender, sexual identity, and sense of maturity. No such luck. Our mutual recognition of our mutual dilemma—being the subject-as-object—was impeded by barriers that drew on several dualisms: psyche and society, gender and sex, analyst and patient, parent and child.

One barrier was hierarchy, the most familiar in clinical discourse being the parental transference. With EL, I alternated between

mother and father. The power dynamics of the maternal transference and countertransference were, however, far stickier.
Unconsciously, the mother is a figure of power, an object of envy,
an incandescence of fear and love. In Dinnerstein's (1976) Kleinian
view, the preoedipal mother seems to the infant all-powerful, able
to starve as well as to nurture. In reaction, the baby feels rapturous
love and hatred. Conflicting with women's inferiorized social
position, this early maternal power creates "trouble between
women" (Dimen and Shapiro, n.d.). The "juncture of caring and
authority in one member of the dyad, that is, the analyst, painfully
juxtaposes the most primitive dimensions of the mother–daughter
relationship to the complications of femininity's social construction" (Dimen and Shapiro, n.d., p. 15).

That the mother is a sentient being with a desire and a mind of
her own (Benjamin, 1988b) intensifies the problem. Idealized as
she is, her mortality disillusions and incites retaliation. "The
profound longing for maternal nurturance conflicts with an equally
deep repudiation of women's subjectivity and authority, itself
rooted in, simultaneously, infantile love and hate, gender-identity
formation, and conventional sexual stereotyping" (Dimen and
Shapiro, n.d., p. 15). In adolescence, these feelings of repudiation
show up in the "competition, contempt, envy, and devaluation"
(p. 15) that so often obtain between mother and daughter as the
oedipal crisis resurfaces.

Sometimes, to avoid this mess, "a collusive pretense to a sisterly,
mutually nurturing relationship" (p. 16) emerges. Women, whether
mother and daughter or analyst and patient, may try just to be
friends. The daughter may feel that she cannot compete. Or she
may fear that, if she wins the battle, her victory will destroy her mother.
In particular, the anxiety that comes with aggression between women
evokes the dangers of preoedipal maternal destructiveness, dangers
that, in turn, incline women to excise aggression from their
intimacy and replace it with pseudomutuality. This excision not
only prevents them from understanding the creative potential of
aggression in politics and in analysis (Harris, 1989, 1997) but
can also threaten them with merging, a common solution to which
is splitting (Lindenbaum, 1985; see also Chapter 8, this volume).

Because preoedipal and oedipal transferences (and phases) are
yet another dualism, they often emerge entwined in the clinical
situation. EL would sometimes seem quite like a child who is full

of shame because she is excluded from parental intimacy. She would speak, for example, of the man who referred her to me as my lover. She would imagine us going to bed together and laughing about her. For my part, I empathized with her mortifying fantasy but found no way to surmount my countertransference and ease or illuminate her torment. Her fantasies made me anxious, too, because they entailed feelings of aggression—I the laughing, sexual, contemptuous mother, she the humiliated, desexed, raging, daughter. But aggression, as I suggested in Chapter 4, resembles activity in its gender dystonia for femininity and therefore for some women, especially those who, like me and EL, have experienced some version of sexual abuse by men (see my fictionalized experiences in Chapter 7; see also Dimen, 1986). Countertransference anxiety was less of a problem when my superiority to EL depended on my not being a woman. When I was the actively probing, thinking, and sometimes bullying father to EL's passively resisting, vegetating, and sometimes helpless daughter, my inter-pretations permitted her to engage her rage and therefore her ambivalent identification with her father. When I was superior as a woman, however, I became dangerous. Neither I nor EL could give words to the fact that, so often, I seemed to be the better woman: not only could I think, but I was thin. As winner of both contests, of minds and of bodies, I became the omnipotent pre-oedipal mother. I therefore remained, in EL's belief, incapable of understanding the shame, despair, and neediness she felt inside her fat. Instead, I was the impinging (Winnicott, 1975), engulfing mother who heaped her children's plates and insisted they eat everything, even when, as an adolescent, EL begged to be allowed to diet.

To some extent, EL was right. Like so many women who think of themselves as fat even though they are not, I could, indeed, imagine her anguish, but I could not cathect my empathy with her despair and self-hate. Unable to own my ruthless triumph in being the thin, thinking winner, I could neither join her feeling of humiliation nor use my aggression in the service of recognizing her own desires to be the woman warrior. Unreleased, my competitiveness, instead, became contempt. Sometimes, in her guise as an overweight five-year-old, she reminded me of no one so much as Jackie Gleason's brilliant television creation, the lower middle-class bus driver, Ralph Kramden.

Gender, Aggression, and Class

We come, then, to yet another barrier, the dualism of psycho-analysis and politics. In my work with EL, our class identities, I suspect, informed the countertransference—and perhaps the transference—in a way that I have been blind to until now. The work being over, I can speak only for myself. In the countertransference, I engaged, I believe, another instance of splitting, one based on social and cultural position. EL's class origins were not entirely different from mine. I, too, came from the suburbs, if from a rather more liberal community. But having managed to climb out of my origins into the intelligentsia, to which I now belong and whose bohemian trappings I treasure, I find some difficulty when my past confronts me. I can laugh and joke about it. I can even feel moments of identification. But to some extent, I define myself against my origins and draw my self-esteem from my upward mobility. Unlike EL, I am not torn. I would not go back for anything.

The splitting in which I engaged can be located in the space between the two classes traditionally identified by Marxist thought. Between the dualism of ruling class versus working class is found "the middle stratum" (Aronowitz, 1979), a class to which both EL and I belonged. Inclusive of the "impossible professions," this "professional-managerial class" (Ehrenreich and Ehrenreich, 1979) spans law, medicine, and middle management; social work, psychotherapy, and education; academia, government, and the fourth estate. Its work, crudely called mental labor, is better described as labor that fuses intellect and drive with great, although not complete, autonomy and self-direction (Ehrenreich, 1989, pp. 38, 78).

Professional-managerial work is a way of being as well as a livelihood. A means for power and prestige and a shaper of personal identity, it entails conceptualizing other people's work and lives (Ehrenreich, 1989, p. 13), and thereby confers authority and influence. Having come into being between 1870 and 1920, it was arguably the chisel that the then-emerging middle class used "to carve out" its own socioeconomic place, its own "occupational niche that would be closed both to the poor and to those who were merely rich" (p. 78). Finally, professional-managerial work enters, indeed, expresses, reflects, and generates identity because it permits creativity and discovery not only in work but also in one of its chief instruments, self.

This privilege renders the professional-managerial class an elite. But it is a highly anxious elite (Ehrenreich, 1989). For one thing, members of this class know that their power, license, and authority incite envy, resentment, hatred, and, I must as psychoanalyst add, idealization. For another, they, like their clients, also sometimes suspect, even if secretly, that, because they don't produce anything visible or tangible, they don't actually do anything real. Apparently unproductive, their work seems worthless. Nor can it match their own or their clients' inflated hopes for it. Because their only "capital" (Bourdieu, 1977) is "knowledge and skill, or at least the credentials imputing skill and knowledge" (Ehrenreich, 1989, p. 38), professional-managerials' high status is insecurely grounded. Unlike real, material capital, skill and knowledge cannot serve to hedge inflation, nor can they be passed on. They must be renewed by and in each person through hard work, diligence, and self-discipline.

Consequently, members of the professional-managerial class, like anyone in any class but the highest, fear the reversals that have catapulted middle-income people into homelessness and indignity (Ehrenreich, 1989, p. 15), a fear that Melanie Klein and Joan Rivière (1964, p. 109, n. 1) liken to that of children who imagine being orphaned or beggared as punishment for their unconscious aggression. They fear falling through the economic and moral safety net, hence Ehrenreich's (1989) apt title *Fear of Falling*. They fear "falling from grace" (Newman, 1988)—losing their wealth, their authority, their beloved work, and their identity as good, moral persons. Rooted in day-to-day professional-managerial work, then, this anxiety about felt fraudulence and looming loss is actually systemic in the role of analyst in class-structured society.

When such fears exist in the analytic session, splitting, amped up by projective identification (see Chapter 4), serves as a powerful defense. "You are the one who will fall, not I." The analyst becomes secure, the patient fearful. "I am powerful, good smart, attractive, sexy. You are not." The analyst's self-esteem is intact, the patient suffers the lonely torments of shame and insufficiency. Given the psychology of the professional-managerial class, defensive identifications can go upward and downward. In my countertransference with EL, I did not want to be pulled down. I have no doubt that, my sense of self and value tied to having gone up, she was going to be the one down. This countertransference projection may have been all the more intense because I was treating her at the beginning of my private practice, when I was highly insecure about my financial and professional success altogether. Professional-managerial psychology also meshes with other situations of domination. So I suspect that my falling back on my class superiority and elitism sprang from and fed the wellspring of mother–daughter aggression that lurked in my relationship with EL. I wasn't the lonely infant, the abused child, the fat girl. I was the unreachable, untouchable Mother. Had we been able to access our mutual aggression, would we have found our way to class hatred? Or vice versa?

It is, in retrospect, no wonder that EL presented as a split her plan to terminate her eight-year, once-a-week treatment; now that she no longer had to commute to Manhattan for therapy, she would have time to work on her obesity with a self-help group in the suburbs. There are ironies. Year later, she phoned to tell me, among other things, that I saved her life; I want to tell you this because of the grave doubts I have about my work with her. Some years after that, she also told me that she had her stomach stapled, lost her weight, and has never felt better in her life.

Difference and Transitional Space

In this chapter, as in this book, I am trying to create a space in which multiplicity can play. This space contains a creative and pleasurable tension. The idea of tensions is increasingly familiar in both feminist and psychoanalytic theory. It is also familiar in clinical work, where, however, it is not always such a pleasure. There, we—analyst and patient alike—dislike unknowns. We want answers. Certainly EL did and certainly I, looking back, do. Too quickly come by, however, answers can foreclose on the fertile complexities of uncertainty. Analytic work requires, instead, sustaining the tension. Faced with a dichotomy, the job is never simply to recall of the forgotten pole of any split but to hold "the paradox of simultaneity" (Benjamin, 1988a). This paradox, essential to both development and treatment, represents the Winnicottian transitional space where play occurs. Such pleasurable play was rare for EL and me, play being laborious when splitting dominates (Winnicott, 1971).

Classical psychoanalysis, as described in Chapter 5, regards tension as something to be eliminated. Postclassicism reevaluates it. Consider the constancy principle derived from biology. In Freud's thought, the organism is hypothesized to have a need to remain at a stable level of stimulation, free from excitement. It is this principle that accounts for Freud's (1970a) earlier, dialectical formulation of the pleasure principle as the reduction of unpleasure: from a state of stimulation—sexual arousal—the organism wishes to return to a state of rest—via sexual discharge. In the 1940s and 1950s, however, Edith Jacobson turned this principle on its head: pleasure came from tension's presence, not its absence (cited in Greenberg and Mitchell, 1993). Jacobson, observing the organism's interest in stimulation as well as in tension reduction, saw that what remains constant is not one state of being, but the relation *between* states of being.

> Rather than operating in the service of keeping the level of tension as low as possible, it is the function of the constancy principle as redefined [by Jacobson] to establish and maintain a constant axis of tension and a certain margin for the biological vacillations around it [cited in Greenberg and Mitchell, 1983, p. 321].

The pleasure inheres in an oscillation, not a steady state. As Greenberg and Mitchell suggest, pleasure is gained from cyclicity, the alternating reduction and increase of tension, not from its disappearance alone. Cyclicity, in turn, implies the oscillation between two positions, not an unvarying habitation of one; it suggests the importance of third, the space between. The pleasure of play, for example, lies in the repeated cycle between reality and fantasy. Famously, Gregory Bateson (1972) wrote of how dogs play, nipping at each other in such a way that it is never quite clear whether the nip is a nip or a bite.

For EL, nips were always bites. Whether alone or with me, she could not play. The sexual abuse she experienced interfered with her ability to enjoy the oscillations of her desire. Sex for her was always already someone else's: Johnnie's. And so she was inhibited from getting to know, on her own, her very desires, and their waxing and waning, as her own. Deprived, she suffered the depletion that occurs when difficulty in playing with reality leads to employing reality to defend against fantasy (Bassin, 1996). She could not afford to know her fantasy because reality was always too much with her. One way to describe EL's sexuality is in terms of a frightened and pleasureless holding to one position, an asexual attachment to a (masculine) heterosexual identity that is never played out, with or against, because it serves to defend against an inner world in which nips are always bites and, as such, too terrifying to enter.

Within desire, this pleasurable oscillation takes place between want and need. Desire is conventionally defined as wish, emergent in the psyche, and is thereby absolutely distinguished from need, rooted in the drives (Laplanche and Pontalis, 1967, pp. 481–483). I regard this definition, however, as a false dichotomy that intensifies polarization instead of illuminating experience. In contrast, I see the longing that characterizes desire as engaged with both want and need (see Chapter 7). Desire, maturity, independence, masculinity—these line up on one side. Need, infancy, dependence, femininity—these line up on the other. You can tell which side you'd rather be on, can't you? As, like Dr. EL, one tries to want and not need, one inevitably diminishes what one is trying to preserve—any appetite for living. Maybe, like her, one even eats too much to preserve psychic life. Although, then, mental health is defined, for example, by Lacan, as the triumph of desire—defined as want—over need, I propose a necessary, creative tension in the space between them. How else, for example, might we account for the common experience that "we all need someone we can lean on?" How, other than to feel both want and need for the other, do we negotiate the paradox of that Fairbairn (1952, pp. 34–35 and *passim*) called "mature dependence"?

"Difference," as I have been speaking of it here, is a paradox of selfhood. Autonomy and dependence, activity and passivity, heterosexuality and homosexuality, body and mind, selfness and otherness, subjectivity and objectification, superiority and inferiority, want and need, and I could go on: these apparent polarities are but diverse moments of the self, the passage between which might be regarded as pleasurable, even though when we leave the preferred polarity—when, for example, we transit from want to need—we are, as things now stand, extraordinarily uncomfortable.

What, then, of masculinity and femininity, which do not appear on this increasingly long list of contrasts? I might have said that they, too, are but different moments of the self. But I am not sure that they are because, in fact, I am not sure *what* they are. I am not arguing, as I once did, that, because masculinity and femininity are less determinate than conventionally thought, gender need not exist (Dimen, 1982). On the other hand, even though the ethnographic evidence for the predominance of dual-gender systems is persuasive (Cucchiari, 1981), the content of gender or the number of genders in any given system remains cross-culturally variable (Gailey, 1988), even subculturally variable within a single society (Chodorow, 1994). I would still make the same case for the possibility and pleasure of gender multiplicity (Dimen, 1982; see also Goldner, 1991).

Perhaps, as I proposed at the end of Chapter 2, it would be better to restate this position as a question: If masculinity and femininity were regarded as different moments of the self, what would each moment mean to a particular self or self-state? What is masculinity? What is femininity? In other words, I question these terms because, although we can name everything we think they are, on examination their meanings become uncertain. Therefore, I have used this uncertainty epistemologically; if, this chapter is asking, we assume nothing about gender other than that it is a socially and psychologically meaningful term, what meanings can we find out?

At the same time, I do not take the deconstructionist train all the way to its nihilist last stop of saying that things are only what texts say they are, that there is no ontology. I believe in the reality of gender-identity experience and of gender as an organizer in the psyche; as such, gender is variably meaningful, a variability that generates instability, invites inquiry, and offers richness. This "diagnosis" of uncertainty should not, however, be regarded as a failure of method or theory. Instead, as I have suggested in Chapter 2, it is a *sign* of what gender is (Rivera, 1989).

Gender, as an internally varied experience, is sometimes central and definitive, sometimes marginal and contingent. Consequently,

it is fundamentally and inalterably paradoxical (Goldner, 1991).
Harris (1991) evokes this ambiguity and complexity:

> Gender is neither reified nor simply liminal and evanescent. Rather,
> in any one person's experience, gender may occupy both positions.
> Gender may in some contexts be thick and reified, as plausibly real
> as anything in our character. At other moments, gender may seem
> porous and insubstantial. Furthermore, there may be multiple
> genders or embodied selves. For some individuals these gendered
> experiences may feel integrated, ego-syntonic. For others, the gender
> contradictions and alternatives seem dangerous and frightening and
> so are maintained as splits in the self, dissociated part-objects
> [p. 212].

To put it more figuratively, if life is a sea, then gender is an island.
Sometimes people drown in the sea, sometimes they are stranded
on land. I am arguing that we need the sea as we need the land,
and, to push this Winnicottian metaphor further, we also need
the seashore, where land and water merge (Winnicott, 1971).

The notion of transitional space can help us comprehend what
our theory has heretofore been able to handle only by splitting.
Gender identity, born in the space of difference between
masculinity and femininity, always retains the marks of its birth.
Therefore, although gender identity has come to be seen in
developmental theory as finalizing differentiation (Mahler, Pine,
and Bergman, 1975), I would suggest, counterintuitively, that it
does more: at one and the same time gender identity seals the
package of self and preserves all the self must lose. It serves to
bridge the archaic depths, the Impossible that underlies human
creativity (McDougall, 1985, p. 8) and the self, the psychic agency
that authors creation. Not only, as Fast (1984) has it, does gender
identity incline us to look for what we are not in the opposite-
sexed other. Alternatingly definitive and liminal, gender identity
also permits us to find in ourselves the excess we have had to
renounce so that we can also recognize it in the other, of whatever
gender (Benjamin, 1995). This view of gender tracks the progress
of "gender differentiation" from "overinclusiveness" to "gender
identity" (Fast, 1984); conceptualizes how access to the overinclusive
depths of the self might be conserved even as renunciation entails
their loss; and addresses *the capacity to identify with the opposite*

sex as a fundamental element in the mobilization of sexual desire" (McDougall, 1980, pp. 149–150).

This chapter ends, then, where it began, on a moment of ambiguity, because the space of paradox is where psychoanalysis works (Boris, 1986). There are many instances of paradox in the clinical situation. Look at gender's habitation of transitional space in my work with EL. The analyst may be a good mother, a bad one, or both; a preoedipal and oedipal father; sometimes a sister, a transference EL and I explored, and sometimes a brother, a transference that, unfortunately, we did not examine and that did not occur to me at the time. Imprisoned not only within my own gender but within a sense of femininity that splits aggression from nurturing (see also Chapters 4 and 8), I could not imagine then what seems likely now, that my inquiry may have represented to EL the early violation she suffered at her brother's hands.

Finally, because self and gender are not the same, we are not always gendered. Sometimes, as the orthodox position traditionally has it, the analyst's gender does not matter. Analysts dwell not only in the paradox of being sometimes female, sometimes male. They also live in the strangeness of gender multiplicity—single gendered, variously gendered, and even, at moments, gender free.

III

The Personal Is Political Is Theoretical: A Sampler

This section, whose three chapters sample the beginning, middle, and end of this book's history, gave me trouble. Chapter 7, published in 1989 (but written in 1982) was condemned by one of my readers: outdated, it had to go. I tried and failed to edit it into conceptual line with the rest of the book. Still I had to keep it. Analysts (Grand, 1997) and academics (Kulick, 1995, p. 21) alike have found it diversely useful. And, if some of its ideas creak, its structure still works, which is the point. In Section III, form and content evolve in tandem. Chapter 7 shows the postmodern fragmentation and heteroglossia that it cannot yet tell. It prefigures the conceptual shift from dualism to multiplicity evinced in Chapter 8's diaristic questioning of women's intimacy, and in Chapter 9's deconstruction of perversion via the orderly cacophony of notes from many sources. Section III travels from a time of certainty, when (as in Chapter 7) "women" and "men" were self-evident categories; through a middle period when their indeterminacy was nascent (Chapter 8); to the present moment of uncertainty and possibility, when, like perversion (Chapter 9), they are categories that we cannot exactly use but cannot exactly give up either.

7

Power, Sexuality, and Intimacy

There is a familiar myth that is sometimes, and wrongly, used to explain the origins of human sexual arrangements. This is the myth of the primal horde, the primal crime, in which the patriarch keeps all the women to himself and forces his sons to work for him; finally, the sons rebel, kill and eat him, fuck the women, and then, guilt ridden, promise to be good boys.

Many people have said a lot about what is in this myth (e.g., Freud, 1930; Marcuse, 1955; Brown, 1959), but few have noticed what is absent from it. The original primal crime had three parts: first, the patriarch's domination of his wife; second, her resistance—physical, emotional, behavioral—to his power; and third, her collusion in being less than she might have been, her participation in all those unavoidable moments when, because they are physically intimidated, economically dependent, or emotionally needy, women give in to patriarchy. Missing in this myth are women, their subordination, and, indeed, all that they symbolize—personal life, reproductivity, alterity.

This myth is both description of and prescription for capitalism, patriarchy, and the state. Its silence about women focuses the problem: Where is there, in this tale of power and sex, room for intimacy, for the knowledge and expansion of self achieved through knowledge of the other? How does an economy that exploits people and nature, all the while encouraging personal enrichment, create expectations for sensual pleasure? Where the political system attempts to control the person and psyche, even while celebrating individual autonomy, whence the self-trust and hope that creativity and generativity require? Given the pervasive inequality in our society, how can intimacy, which presumes a certain democratic and reciprocal attunement between people, obtain?

The Past

Addressing disparate regions of experience, these questions about power, sexuality, and intimacy cannot be answered until a missing link in the theory of patriarchy is forged. Patriarchy is both a psychological–ideological—that is, representational—and a political–economic system. Although theories of mind and society abound, no contemporary theory puts psyche and society together so that the whole story of patriarchy, including women's experience and its contradictions, can be told. The Frankfurt School's Critical Theory, in particular, has not lived up to its promise (Benjamin, 1978).

Perhaps the problem is one not of *ideas* but of *bias*. Perhaps the theoretical deficiency is methodological. Scholarship is conventionally based on "objectivity," on putatively value-free, detached, impersonal observation and analysis. As the feminist critique of science points out, however, this objectivist stance is actually quite personal, for it is based not on the absence of emotions and values but on their careful restraint. In fact, orthodox scholarship lacks a certain *kind* of personal (Flax, 1983; Jaggar, 1983; Keller, 1985).

In turn, then, perhaps the missing conceptual link in feminist theory is an engaged personal voice, saturated with feeling, values, and political protest, a voice such as emerges in feminist biography in which subject engages with subject.[1] But this politics of autobiography and biography should *not replace* the received patriarchal voice; rather, it should *juxtapose* it. The point is to use the different powers of both voices to generate a sense of opposition, difference, creative tension. The resultant third voice, retaining the personal power of the first and the intersubjectivity of the second, might thereby open a window on as yet unimagined, ungendered possibilities of speaking, knowing, and living.

Two such voices interweave here, a personal one, telling fictionalized stories of sexuality, and a public one commenting on them.[2] Sexuality is one of the most personal, engaged, and value

---

[1] See, for example, Perry (1989) and Ascher et al. (1984) for discussions of subject–subject engagement in feminist biography.

[2] Dimen (1986) develops this form more fully.

laden of voices. It is also one of the most theoretically demanding, for sex stands at the crossroads of nature, psyche, and culture. Accounts of sexuality, emotionally powerful and striking at cultural bedrock, beg for a response, provided here by a commentary fusing social, psychological, and feminist theory. As the commentary follows the triple problematic of sexuality, it traces the filigree of sexuality, power, and intimacy. Essential to its design are domination, the gendering of self, the division of labor between women and men, the gendered divorce of want from need, and the use of social reproduction to control desire.

I am a 37-year-old, heterosexual, middle-class white woman, wearing junior-sized clothes a shade on the beatnik side of trendiness. I am divorced and childless, and live with my cat and my plants in New York City.

I am walking home, and this shabby, drunk man is following me, saying, "Mama, oh mama, baby, please, I wanna fuck you, I give good tongue, oh sweetheart, Please."

"Oh, leave me alone, don't you have anything better to do?" I exclaim in annoyance.

He sniggers, then turns away.

After I get inside the lobby of my building, I wonder, What was that man trying to do? Did he want to degrade me, attack me, arouse me, flatter me, or simply tease me? Should I be angry or feel sorry for him? Why me, anyway?

The voices in my head immediately provide answers:

What do you expect when you dress like that? my mother responds rhetorically.

But it happens to me even when I'm wearing my down parka and my overalls, I explain in bewilderment, adding with some outrage, *How dare he talk to me? He doesn't even know me.*

Let me at him, I'll kill the bastard, growls my father.

Oh daddy, stop it, I reply, embarrassed by his passion.

My conscience asks, *How come you hear the pussy noises from guys across the street? You don't know them. Yet you notice what they say.*

I don't know, I mumble.

You know you love it, insists my own analyst.

Maybe, I admit grudgingly like a patient cornered on the couch.

You must have a pretty poor opinion of yourself if you get turned on by someone like that, comments an advice columnist.

I guess so, I say, feeling a little humiliated.

Well, you know, it makes sense that you hear it. It's dangerous out there, says the indignant, rational feminist voice in no uncertain terms. *One of out two women experiences rape or an attempt at it sometime in her life. You have to be alert.*

Maybe, I think. Soothed and vindicated, I stand a little straighter.

I think your reaction is disgusting, says the politically correct line-ist in me. *This man is but a product of his environment, his class, race, ethnicity, in short, of capitalism and the state. He is attacking not you but your* petit bourgeois *privilege.*

I'm sorry, I'm sorry, I reply, filled with guilt.

Perhaps he's compensating for his own feelings of badness, the psychoanalyst side of me counsels empathetically. *He projects his self-hatred into you, who, at the same time, remain the all-powerful, all comforting mother whom he now feels good enough to make verbal love to.*

Yes, yes, okay, but, still . . . I argue in increasingly louder tones with these contradictory voices. *Still, I don't know him. He doesn't know me. Is the noise coming from a person like the noise of an ambulance siren? Do I have to hear it so I get out of the way and don't get run over?*

Don't let it upset you, dear, my kind uncle says (the one who used to engineer intense, flirtatious discussions in his den, with the door closed, with one or another of my teenage girlfriends). *Just ignore him; don't give him the benefit of your attention; don't dignify him by a response; it will just encourage him,* says my uncle, trying to calm me down and smooth things over.

I pause for breath. Then, frustrated almost to tears, I nearly shout, *My mind doesn't work as rationally as yours. How can it? My brain hears, my desire is stirred, I lose control of my body. On the street my body is theirs. I am a body on the street. Two tits and no head and a big ass. I am a walking Rorschach. My body becomes a cunt and I am sore from this semiotic rape.*

Domination

Feminine experience is often one in which mind and body, mind and matter, are joined and, jointly, are ripped off. And at times we collude in this evisceration of our subjectivity, even as we resist. The process by which personal life slips from one's grasp as domination tears it away is coiled in women's experience. And domination makes alienation possible.

Alienation usually describes the experience of work in capitalism, in which the pacing and productivity of labor are directed not by workers but by profit needs and the extraction of surplus-value from labor-power by capital. In consequence, work life comes to seem meaningless, and people look forward to "real life," to personal life, which seems easier to arrange to one's satisfaction (see Dimen, 1994, for an overview of alienation in psychoanalysis).

Yet, somehow, for women, alienation, or something like it, appears not only on the job but also in personal life. Every time a woman goes for a walk, her mind and her body are invaded by a social definition of her femininity that threatens to disconnect her from her own experience. This is the experience of domination, the loss of one's sense of and wish for autonomy, as a result of processes that play on one's doubts about the reality and validity of one's self, one's perceptions, and one's values.

Patriarchy is, first and last, a system of domination. But it differs from other systems of domination, whether racism, class structure, or colonialism, because it goes directly for the jugular of social relatedness and psychological integration: desire. Patriarchy attacks desire, the unconscious longing that animates all human action, by reducing it to sex and then defining sex in the politicized terms of gender. Paradoxically, however, sexuality, thus organized by gender, becomes reciprocally desire's sculptor, while gender simultaneously organizes part of desire into the self. Not only sexuality, but all manifestations of desire are thereby informed by gender; thus, the roots of desire, itself the source of personal experience, are steeped in hierarchy.

In patriarchy, gender denotes a structure of political power masquerading as a system of natural difference. The invisible fulcrum of the myth of the primal horde, gender builds on a highly variable and interpretable biological given, the anatomical difference between the sexes. Thus made the linchpin of patriarchy, gender is the way that consciousness of self, and so one's sense of empowerment, is most immediately experienced.

Or, at least, it is the way that many women become most immediately conscious of self. Insofar as this does not hold true for men, it is because human experience is linguistically, ideologically, and socially constructed as male, to wit, "mankind," not to mention the personal noun "he," so that men's experience of self is perhaps continuous with simply being human.

Women, in contrast, may be aware of having an unconscious sense through language that society counterposes them to men as Other. Culture makes women both human and nonhuman, and they know it, and they must both swallow and reject what they know in order to go from day to day. Where empowerment is thus unequal, intimacy cannot easily grow. But, to anticipate a bit, where experience of self is thus ambiguous, intimacy has a fighting chance.

She is eight. Her father, 41, and her brother, 5, are about to take a shower together. "Me, too," she cries, eager to see her father's genitals. "No, no, dear, little girls don't take showers with their fathers," says her mother, 40. Since when? she wonders. She knows what she wants. They know, too. Do they know that she knows that they know that she knows?

In seventh grade, if you wear green on Thursdays, they call you a dyke. If you wear a black sweater any day, they call you a whore. Somehow, she forgets and wears green on Thursday and black sweaters when she likes. At a party in a suburban basement rec-room, she finds herself suddenly alone on the couch, the only girl in the room, when the lights go out and all the boys jump her and feel her up everywhere you can imagine. The girls giggle in the laundry room.

A girl from another crowd tells her she looks nice in her black sweater. They become friends, sort of. She sleeps over at her friend's house one night. They bake chocolate chip cookies and listen to opera. Later her friend invites her into her bed to do what her friend's crowd has been doing for a while. She feels nothing, is frightened, and goes back to her own bed.

She starts kissing boys on the mouth at 11 and likes it a lot. She doesn't pet above the waist with boys until 15; she doesn't like it but does it anyway to be grown up. She won't pet below the waist until 17; then she doesn't want to admit that she has orgasms. She starts masturbating at 18. At 21, she has intercourse for the first time. She likes the fact that she's doing it; it takes her 15 years to like doing it. She uses her diaphragm every time for those 15 years.

The Division of Emotional Labor

Patriarchy constructs gender, and gender the psyche, through two divisions of labor. The first, the division of emotional behavior, interrupts the fluid motion of personal experience and freezes into two moments, "individualizing" and "relatedness." Individualizing is a mainstream cultural ideal. Connoting autonomy, agency, and singularity, it also suggests the kind of adult who is responsible for himself and no one else. Only the masculine pronoun will do here, for, in our culture, this is the masculinized part of selfhood, symbolized by the lonesome cowboy, the Marlboro man. It is associated with the universal and transcendent, with creation and achievement, with abstract rationality, with tangible and enduring products. The "self-as-individual" glows with the glamour of heroic, solitary, self-discovering travelers, from Odysseus onward.[3]

Relatedness suggests Penelope, not Odysseus. While Odysseus was out adventuring with goddesses as well as monsters, Penelope was at home, weaving his shroud by day and unraveling it by night; in other words, she was doing the dishes. She was on the treadmill of relatedness, caring for things because she was caring for people (Miller, 1976). Relatedness, then, connotes the personal and the interpersonal, the particular and the pragmatic, care and nurturance, and invisible, ephemeral processes and feelings—hence the symbol of relatedness, the Madonna, the woman with a child. Still, as revered as the Madonna may be and as adored the sweet child, they paradoxically represent a dependency and loss of self with which Marlboro men are notoriously uncomfortable. Relatedness pulses with ambivalence, with the love–hate for mother that starts in infancy and, in our culture, finally radiates out to all women (Dinnerstein, 1976).

Yet these two tendencies of selfhood are potentially genderless and, in fact, show up in men and women alike. Indeed, to try to achieve one without the other is psychologically and socially dangerous (Benjamin, 1988b), if possible at all. To attempt only individualizing is to become emotionally isolated; to attempt only relatedness is to lose the self by merging with someone else. Clinically speaking, the consequences of such attempts are two sides of the same pathological coin. Socially, the dangers of John Wayne in the White House remain too obvious to name. And the

---

[3] Benjamin (1980) shows how the sex–gender hierarchy masculinizes and idealizes the individualizing image of adulthood.

reverence for a "true woman," that is to say a wife–mother, can mutate into the scorn for someone who, because she is "only a housewife," can become a mad or bad one.

The Division of Economic Behavior

Although relatedness may be essential for sociality in general and intimacy in particular, it is often disparaged because of its role in the division of economic labor. The organization of commodity production, which "division of labor" usually denotes, actually runs on an unspoken, initial premise: whatever wage-earning work women do, they are assigned first to the domestic domain because, in ideology, they are biopsychologically suited to nurturing and, in practice, they are trained for it. There, they do the work which (a) is never done, (b) is absolutely essential to the society, (c) is not called work because it is not remunerated, and (d) is therefore denigrated, sentimentalized, and trivialized. This is the work of reproducing—physically, socially, emotionally—adult workers and the next generation.

That the first thing we want to know about a woman is whether she is married, and the second, whether she has children, testifies to the cultural conviction that all women should do this sort of work. Yet in this so-called natural place women are asked to perform the most unnatural of acts. The domestic domain is meant to alleviate the alienation that everyone experiences in the public domain. It is supposed to foster autonomy and authenticity and provide pleasure and satisfaction in an atmosphere of intimacy. At the same time, it must nourish both the young and the mature so that they can not only tolerate alienated labor but also, ironically, feed their self-respect with it.

To the degree that housewifery manages to achieve the one goal, it betrays the other. In other words, housewifery is a task made virtually impossible by its contradictions. Intended as an act of love, it also serves domination. It maintains one means of production, labor-power, at no cost to the employer through the same means by which it helps the state control the labor force. Some tensions generated by this no-win arrangement find expression in the savage ridicule and subtle contempt lavished on housewives even as they stand on pedestals.

— Social Reproduction

Other tensions emerge in the doctor's office. The guilt and anxiety generated by their double-binding work can drive housewives a little crazy, for which reason they sometimes consult therapists, social workers, and other members of the "helping professions." Yet when they do so, they become even more entangled with the contradictions driving them there. They participate with these very professionals in "social reproduction," in the daily and crossgenerational re-creation of these three connected things— individual subjectivity, social consciousness (or "ideology" [or representation]), and social relations. An intersecting personal and institutional process, social reproduction takes place, in the state, in both domestic and public domains, in kinship, educational, communicational, professional, and bureaucratic systems (Mitchell, 1963; Rapp, Ross, and Bridenthal, 1979; Weinbaum and Bridges, 1979; Dimen, 1992).[4]

Social reproduction expresses and informs desire by re-creating cultural contradictions within personal experience.[5] Steeped in relatedness, it is feminized by the assumption that, as the proverb in the East European *shtetl* went, "Life is with people" (Zborowski and Herzog, 1952). Child rearing is central to it, both practically and symbolically, for child rearing is the raising not of monads but of beings through whose sociality and participation in social consciousness society is recreated.

Yet at the same time that social reproduction cultivates and requires relatedness, it is, in the contemporary West, equally but dissociatedly steeped in individualizing. It represents to us the standard model of adulthood: it cranks out an Andy Warhol

---

[4] Social reproduction may be differently organized in other cultures (Dimen, 1992). Unlike Yanigasako and Collier (1987), I have confidence in the utility of this concept, which, in contrast to Harris and Young (1981), I define to include the unconscious, inner life.

[5] This phrasing begs the question of whether social reproduction must always re-create cultural contradictions in psychological life in any culture. Indeed, it raises and then begs the question of whether there is now or ever has been any culture lacking contradictions, thus implicitly addressing a central Marxist debate about "primitive communism" and the communist Utopia. A discussion of these questions is far beyond the scope of this chapter.

silkscreen of what we have in mind when we say, "But you're not supposed to need anyone else." Through images reduplicated in speech, print, pictures, and music, it makes us long to emulate the Marlboro man—someone who may sometimes want others but who will never need them. And it makes us hate to resemble women, whose very interest in relationships and intimacy seems mired in the mud of need.

The Gendered Divorce of Want from Need

By the same sexist token, social reproduction sunders want and need. Merged in infancy as different aspects of desire, need and want separate out as development proceeds. Although they continue to be kin to one another, they appear culturally as unequal strangers. Wanting, associated with adulthood, active will, and masculinity, is better than need, linked to infancy, passive dependency, and femininity. Adults (like EL in Chapter 6) therefore try to distance their dependency needs by regarding their longings for love, tenderness, and care as weak, childish, "womanish."[6]

These patriarchal judgments fuse with unconscious forces and political exigencies to make need alarming. The feeling of need is disquieting because, on the one hand, we come to know it first as a matter of life and death; it recalls unconscious memories of helplessness, of our once total, infantile dependence on others for care and love. On the other, neediness makes us anxious because in the state it signals the possibility of adult helplessness. Not only are we at the mercy of capital's vicissitudes, but when the keys to the halls of state are in the hands of those whose fingers

---

[6] In some cultures, for example, the !Kung San of Africa, where the individual is not a viable economic unit but can survive only by dependence on the extended family or community institutions, need and want may be neither so divided nor invidiously compared. In such kin-based cultures, where, if one person is homeless or hungry, it is only because everyone lacks shelter or food (Lee, 1979; Shostak, 1981), need may not be the source of shame that we find it to be in the state.

hover over the nuclear buttons, we are nearly as weak as infants are physically.

Still, *feeling need* is not the same as *being needy*. When gratification is foreseeable, longing, and therefore need, is as welcome as the hunger that rises with the smell of dinner cooking on the stove, as reassuringly exciting as sexual desire for a tried-and-true lover. When instead, frustration is anticipated, the *feeling of need* threatens to become a *state of neediness*, and, therefore, dangerous. And people are likely to be frustrated when unequal class, skin, and gender privileges distribute money, social know-how, and skills unevenly; when only a few may slake the thirst for success stimulated in all; and when the state disregards the quality of life, overvalues the military, and lacks either work that enhances material security and self-respect or political empowerment that cultivates need-satisfying autonomy.

As the need goes, so does desire. When social conditions render the gratification of adult needs uncertain, besmirch dependency, and thwart the realization of wants, wanting can come to feel like needing; depending on others for satisfaction becomes unwelcome; consequently, longing seems altogether unpleasant. As political and unconscious forces spiral downward together, we try to get a grip on things. We try to want without needing. But, having pulled in our psychological belts, we find instead that we have diminished what we were trying to preserve—desire, and, with it, sex, hope, and intimacy. When yearnings for the Other arise nonetheless, they seem too complicated to acknowledge. As soon as such ambiguity emerges, John Wayne gets on his horse and rides off into the sunset.

When I was 18, I had a boyfriend with whom I was very much in love and of whom I was very much in awe, two not unconnected facts. At that time, he and his friends were in love with a book, *The Ginger Man,* by J. P. Donleavy. So naturally I thought I should be in love with it, too. I tried. But, somehow, it was very hard for me to see myself as the free-wheeling, woman-served, and woman-leaving main character, a great individualist who loved planting his seed, but didn't like kids or wives. No doubt I took things too literally, too personally.

This was not the first time I had difficulty with literature that portrayed the wonderful life of adult freedom in male terms. In high school, I wanted to be a beatnik. I, too, wanted to go on the road, but I could never figure out what would happen if, traveling in Mexico in 1958, I got my period. Were you supposed to carry a supply of Kotex with you? How many could you carry? If you took all you needed, there wouldn't be any room for all those nice jugs of wine in Jack Kerouac's car. The only beatnik I know who even considered this question was Diana diPrima in *Memoirs of a Beatnik*. She describes her first big orgy, the one with the works, including Allen Ginsberg. As she takes a deep breath and decides to plunge in, so to speak, she pulls out her Tampax and flings it across the room where somehow it gets irretrievably lost.

A grand moment, that. Do I hear you thinking, How gross? Or, How irrelevant? Gross, yes; irrelevant, no. And that's the point. Having to worry about the gross mess becomes a part of life from puberty on. A nagging, stupid worry becomes a fact of life, not quite as unnoticeable as your skin. The same nagging worry included wondering whether they had any contraceptive jelly in Mexico, just when in the seduction I was going to put my diaphragm in, once it was in whether it would stay in, and, when it was time to take it out, where I would find the water to wash it.

The Strange Relationship Between Sex and Reproduction

For every woman—heterosexual, lesbian, young, old—sexuality is inextricably entangled with reproductivity, in other words, with procreation, relatedness, and sociality as felt and as socially instituted. This entangling is experienced in various ways. When it is conscious, then either you are thinking about birth control, or, if you are lesbian, postmenopausal, voluntarily sterilized, or fertile and wanting to get pregnant, you are relieved that you do not have to think about it. If you think about it a lot, you may have to stop your masturbatory sexual fantasy to figure out what kind of contraception will best fit the scene you have constructed. If you are less obsessional, and if you are heterosexual, you only have to interrupt your spontaneous passion to put in your diaphragm, if you have not already killed it off by having done so before hand. Or you may risk your health, and so your peace of mind, by taking a pill or having an IUD inserted. And if you decide to "take a chance," as the phrase goes, you can have the thrill of forgetting about having to remember not to get pregnant.

But even if the strange relationship between sexuality and reproduction is not consciously problematic, it still rests in the unconscious experience of women who grow up in patriarchy. In our culture, women are responsible for babies, not so much because they give birth to them but because theirs is the gender made socially responsible for relatedness. This responsibility places them in fundamental conflict. It roots women's gender identity in relatedness, even as their adult identity is defined by individualizing. For women, then, every act of sex is one of conflicted and contradictory decisions about contraries—self and a potential other, self and society, life and death.

These decisions, which all people face, become very ambivalent for women because of the state's abiding interest in them. The state uses women's experience to control social reproduction, which, in turn, comes the royal road to the domestic domain, intimacy, and, finally, subjectivity itself. The state tries to control the bodies, and so the sexuality, and so the desire, and so the minds of women, and thereby of the children they rear of the men and other women for whom they are nurturers and symbols of desire.

The state has two main sources of power of women. It regulates access to the material basis of procreation, that is, to contraception, abortion, and the technology of birth, deciding by legislation who will be allowed to get them, how, and when. And the state attempts to control minds by mystifying them. For example, women appear to make independent reproductive decisions for which they feel individually responsible; they are, after all, "individualized" adults. But, because they are "in-relation" to the state, their decisions have in fact already been made for them by laws restricting their sexuality, reproductive choices, and access to jobs.

This double-binding form of domination makes alienation possible by making women, and therefore everyone they care for, feel out of touch with, split from, ill-at-ease with their bodies and their selves. Reproductive matters—periods; pregnancies; children whose impulsivity and savagery require domestication; adults whose bodies and psyches, deformed by domestication and hard work, call out for care; the disorderly passions of intimacy and sex—these female matters seems quite chaotic, crude, even ugly. They are unappealing next to the apparently clean-cut, rational, and easily measured project of material production so central to capitalism.

In our culture, reproductive matters are to the politicoeconomic domain what, in symbol, the vagina is to the neat penis—messy. And the individual isolation asked of one and for which one hankers represents an attempt to make a neat product out of one's messy personal uniqueness. In contrast, personal development, like the rest of social reproduction—including questions of the beginning of life, the timing of death, intimacy—these are ambiguous matters.

Drink in hand, he leaned against the wall with an air of teasing, self-mocking arrogance, eyes soft from intoxication. His sensual anticipation was all-enveloping. "When we get home, I want to fuck you," he said lovingly. "I'm going to put it in you, and go in and out, in and out, real slow, for a long time." He jerked his hips slightly. "That's how I'll fuck you," he said softly. "And when I'm done, you'll look a lot better. It'll perk things up here"—he lightly touches her breasts—"and make things smaller here"—patted her waist—"and smooth things out here"—he caressed her hips.

An ancient ache cramped her thoughts, and all she could do was laugh. She wished he were taller and looser. Knowing he was sensitive about his slight stature, she consciously fed his vanity, telling him of the lean precision of his proportions, the beauty of his classic face, the grace of his genitals. Indeed, his body awed her, even as his insecurity stimulated in her a luxuriant contempt.

Their lovemaking was wonderful that night—as always. He did all the work—as always. He was hurt that she was not more grateful.

Heterosexual experience is sometimes stained by the social evaluation of reproductivity that mutates into socially validated hatred of imperfect female flesh.

Her tongue slid along the soft involuted folds of her labia, her tongue slid along the soft folds of her labia. She licked her clitoris, she licked her clitoris. They came together, not knowing who was who.

"Your name came up," she said later, "but I told them I didn't want you in the group." "Why not?" she asked. "Because I want to keep my personal life and my public life clearly differentiated."

Sexuality excludes neither the forces of the unconscious nor the forces of hierarchy.

He's going to take her hand, she knows it. His palm is slightly cool and damp and soft, and her chest tightens. She will pull her hand away as soon as she can, perhaps when they must part to let some people pass on the crowded sidewalk. Her flesh crawls from him so often that you would think she might say to him, This isn't working, I'm sorry, I want to leave.

She has won, he has buckled. Very clearly, he needs her. And so, no longer the one ravaged by need, she becomes the strong one.

Later, she lets her denial of the waves of revulsion force her into inactivity, and she lets him make a fool of himself. This is how she can cross the line into sexual desire, and let him make love to her, and pull away abruptly from his gentle touch.

As we try to sever want from need, we find that sexual needs, the need for intimacy, and even the need to make meaning of life, take on an unwholesome or frivolous cast. In unavoidable consequence, life begins to make less and less sense. Life is meaningless without wanting, but there is no wanting without needing and therefore no desire without need. As need drains from desire, so does meaning bleed from life. To eliminate need is to kill desire and therefore any appetite for living.

They roll around in bed, she younger, he older, he once fat and soft now thin and hard but with a fleshly sensual aura still, she smooth and roly-poly. Perhaps the champagne from the night before fizzes their spirits still. Moments of pure delight, and finally she climbs on top and rocks into the black-silver inner spaces of realized desire where she forgets what she's doing, and, for one dizzying, bubbly, sunny moment, does not know if he is male or female, her mother or her father, and she knows that she doesn't know, and that he is who he is, and she cherishes this instant of laughing madness.

He has a pretty good time too, not the same as hers, but pretty good.

It helps them both that he's had a vasectomy.

⸺

Ambiguity and Intimacy

Fortunately, sexual passion reunites need and want. Erotic experience is extraordinary, lying somewhere between dream and daily life. Sped by desire, it knows no shame and no bounds. In it, pleasure and power, hurt and love, mingle effortlessly. It is a between thing, bordering psyche and society, culture and nature, conscious and unconscious, self and other. Its intrinsic messy ambiguity confers on it an inherent novelty, creativity, discovery; these give it its excitements, its pleasure, its fearsomeness. Sexual experience entails loss of self-other boundaries, the endless opening of doors to more unknown inner spaces, confusions about what to do next or who the other person is or what part of the body is being touched or what part of the body is doing the touching or where one person begins and the other ends. This is sometimes pleasurable, sometimes painful, always unsettling.

If sexuality is ambiguous, intimacy is doubly so. The lonesome Marlboro man generates his opposite number, an image of a mutual, egalitarian, empathetic, nurturing, and self-renewing relation between adults. Yet intimacy proves elusive in the very society that thus spawns, indeed, necessitates it. Individualizing that excludes relatedness makes us desperate to be close to others. But, compelled to deny need, we fear to recognize our longing. In the absence of a culturally valid image of an adult who is permitted to need—mature dependence—we are thrown back on infantile experience. Infants, however, are unaware that bridges between separate adults must be built; they not only mistake symbiosis for intimacy but imagine that it is there for the taking, not the creating; hence the street hassler, whose desperate invasions obviate the delicate attention on which intimacy thrives; hence our lunges for intimacy and our equally passionate retreats.

Yet a model of maturity that might make intimacy more accessible stands in patriarchy's shadow, the worshipped and denigrated feminine omitted from the myth of the primal horde. Just as the personal voice juxtaposed to the scholarly can yield a creative tension, so relatedness in tension with individualizing might produce another, although rarely realized, cultural ideal of personhood: a person simultaneously distinct, autonomous, and related to others. Recognizing contradiction, this utopian model of maturity manages to accommodate the paradox of self and other, of connectedness and separateness. Built into it is the knowledge that you can experience your separateness only through knowing, sensing, and intuiting the other at the boundaries between the two, between self and other. You can care for or hate someone else only if there exists a "you" to care or to hate, a "someone else" to be cared for or hated, and the capacity to care for or hate or, more generally, be in relation to others.

In other words, this model of adulthood, emerging in the charged space between conventional masculinity and femininity, is tolerant of ambiguity, something which women must be at ease in order to survive under patriarchy. In our culture, women symbolize ambiguity—neither of nature nor of culture but mediating them (Ortner, 1974). They represent, as well, an alternate moral path, a winding one to be made, not one that, given, must be rigidly followed (Gilligan, 1983; but cf. Stack, 1993).[7] This morality of seeing "both" and "and," of grasping two points of view simultaneously, is at home with the discomfort of ambiguity. It is crucial to what is called "maternal thinking," preserved by the domestic domain as a utopian vision, if not an always realized practice (Ruddick, 1980).

The capacity to appreciate ambiguity is essential to intimacy as well. Unfortunately, in patriarchy, this capacity tends to be as absent from maturity as from the myth of the primal horde, not only because of ideals of adulthood but because of how the young mature. The primary assignment of early child care to women has guaranteed that the father, that is, the cowboy's unambiguous hardness, will institute differentiation of self from other, adulthood's beginnings, and therefore the foundations of adult intimacy (Mahler et al., 1975). Because this differentiation is stabilized by making unspeakable, and so preserving, the meltingness of Madonna and child, it makes every mother-reared person feel incomplete and unworthy. But feelings of unworthiness are a meager basis for the emergence of intimacy. Until differentiation by disavowal disappears and the ambiguity of self, other, and their connection is tolerable, intimacy will remain, at best, bittersweet, ambivalent, and partial, punctuated by horrid periods of distance and sweet moments of merging.

---

[7] Stack's research among African Americans in rural North Carolina and in Washington, DC, strongly suggests that Gilligan's thesis may be class- and race-bound. Using Gilligan's methodology, she found that adults in general tend more toward justice reasoning; among adults, men tend slightly more toward care reasoning, women to justice reasoning.

The Present Envisioning the Future

The myth is only one of tradition; its silence on women and intimacy bespeaks other possibilities for society and desire. Instead of the recurrent adolescent rebellion forecast by myth; instead of the stasis that regresses to quiescent death (Freud, 1930); instead of the childish return to the mother blown up into a guilt-free social order (Brown, 1959); instead of a naïve-passing-for-innocent belief in technologically created abundance (Marcuse, 1955); instead of a universalizing of what is merely a culturally normal heterosexuality[8]—the permanent revolution will have to be one of uncertainty, a continuous unfolding of desire. Unavoidably, therefore, it will be ambiguous. Such unfolding can emerge only in a social order that would provide the economic, political, and reproductive basis for reasonable trust and foreseeable self-esteem.

We will not see this in our time. The oedipal drama the preoedipal passion play must change, but all we have now are reruns. The intransigence of the patriarchal state is the reason that we must maintain a utopian vision of a society in which desire is empowering, not weakening, in which all parts of the self can come out of the closet—passion and need, will and empathy, the anger that, through a paradoxical love, can make our society realize its ideals of democracy and decency even while hell-bent on betraying them.

Sexuality is not the route to revolution. But it runs directly to desire, and constraint of desire leads directly to self-betrayal and social bad faith. We suffer not from too much desire but from too little. Our failures to rebel, our incomplete revolutions, are rooted in the repression of desire that, essential to sexual oppression, truncates hope. The utopian thinking of the 1960s counterculture that called for the liberation of desire is no longer fashionable, even on the left, even among feminists. We are supposed to have grown up, our eyes adjusted to the size of our stomachs. But such modish maturity mistakes the nature of desire. We must desire all

---

[8] As found in the entire Marxian corpus.

we can, no matter how much it hurts or how foolish or greedy it seems. We may not be able to get everything we can, but to adapt the Rolling Stones, only by wanting everything we can imagine can we get everything we need.

8 In the Zone of Ambivalence
A Feminist Journal of Competition

1. New York City. Sometime at the beginning of April 1990.
   Alice Bach asks me to contribute to a feminist issue of the *Union Seminary Quarterly Review,* which she edits. The issue's topic is to be "competition between women"; authors may write about it in any way they please as long as they also refer to a relevant scriptural text. Because the volume is to be interdisciplinary, Alice says that I, as a psychoanalyst and anthropologist, cover ground others don't. I'm intrigued—I know a lot about competition not only in theory but in practice (what feminist doesn't?); I've even written about it. I feel weird about the religious part.

As you will see, the "religious," or at least spiritual, part comes to seem less weird.

2. New York City. May 17, 1990.
   This morning, I unearth my old King James Bible, and then run out to buy the *Tanakh,* the Jewish Version of the Old Testament. I want to scan the tales of competition between women from which Alice had suggested we might choose. I'm drawn to the story of Rachel and Leah; their rivalry over fecundity reminds me of my late friendship with [*I'll call her*] Linda.
   This evening, at the restaurant where I'm eating dinner with [*amazingly enough*] a date, who should I see striding out from some recess in the dining room with a hurt and angry mien but [*also amazingly enough*] Linda? Her husband, following close behind with a determined step, looks equally distraught. I feel slightly embarrassed for them.

When I arrived home that night, I began officially to keep a journal, excerpted and periodically extracted here, in a notebook purchased for that special purpose.

3. New York City. May 18, 1990.
   This morning, I dream that Linda telephones me. Now that she's
   turning 50, she says, she wants to bury the hatchet. I'm moved to
   agree this is a good idea; an old friendship is worth resuscitating
   even if you haven't spoken to each other for five years (except
   when you can't avoid each other at a book party). Then she tells
   me she's having an affair. "Was that why you looked so, um,
   worried in the restaurant?" I wanted to know. "No," she replies.

My unconscious, having turned the merely embarrassing into
potential disaster, an ordinary public quarrel into marital betrayal,
was, it would appear, out for blood. Now, it seemed to be saying,
I can settle the score. Now I can get even with Linda for what she
got before me, as Leah got Jacob even when he was to have been
Rachel's. I can retaliate for Linda's literary grace and style and
her ruthless self-interest, which permitted her to borrow some of
my less attractive qualities and lend them to those odd characters
in her sardonic, avant-garde novels. For now, you see, I can write
as well as she, and she, no longer my friend, is fair game. I can tell
on her, make her look as bad as I want. Ah, revenge is sweet, not
only because of the mean things she said and did to me in act and
in print, but because she has a second husband and I don't.

When my first book was published, I brought it to a party at a
friend's house in the country. I wanted to show it to them, in the
same spirit, I suppose, as you would show off for your parents, parade
an accomplishment before them. I thought my friends would take
pleasure in my pleasure, identificatory pride in my achievement; I
had no consciousness of competing (which doesn't mean I wasn't).

I can't remember if Linda said it right there and then or if she
waited until we were back in Manhattan: "I feel like I have to eat
crow." I was stunned. After all, she explained, her manuscript had
just been rejected by her publisher, which meant that I'd finished
my book first. I hadn't been aware there'd been a race. I think I
thought we were sister feminists together, together letting our
different spirits fly, together making our separate ascents, she
climbing the literary latter, I, the academic one. How naïve. Still,
it was only 1977; Evelyn Fox Keller and Helene Moglen (1987)
did not publish their article on competition among feminists until
10 years later, and Phyllis Chesler (2002) wouldn't publish her
Woman's Inhumanity to Woman for another 25 years.

Not too long afterward, at a feminist conference we'd helped to organize, a prestigious American publisher approached Linda to write a new book based on the paper she had delivered. Although the same house (like half a dozen others) later rejected my next book proposal, one commercial firm did in the end give me a very large advance, much larger, indeed, than hers. Oddly enough, Linda was visiting me when my agent called with the news; while her presence was not all that kept me from tasting my triumph, my apprehension of her inevitable and painful envy certainly darkened my delight, even though, as my best friend, she was the one person with whom I'd have most wanted to share the moment. Much later she read, and disliked, the penultimate draft of my book. About a month after that, I challenged her for the first time in our 15-year relationship. And soon after that she imposed a silence that would last six years.

Both my books are now out of print. Whenever I poke around bookstores hoping for the small miracle that a copy of one or the other might still be on the shelves, I am compelled to look for hers (there are now two) and I always find them still in print, sometimes even prominently displayed.

Have I conveyed to you the right combination of hurt and pride, struck the right note of ambivalence between love and hate? There seems no way to write about this matter of competition between women without anxiety, just as there is no way to think about it outside the moral(istic) question: competition between women, is it good or is it bad? This concern, lurching between binary emotions, pervades Valerie Miner and Helen Longino's *Competition: A Feminist Taboo?* in which Keller and Moglen's "Competition: A Problem for Academic Women" is reprinted. Some contributors think competition is a positively good thing and ought to be embraced (e.g., Lindenbaum, 1985; Lichtenstein, 1987). Others, like Keller and Moglen (1987; pp. 48–56), argue that it sours only when denied; acknowledged, competition can be constructive and enriching for women. Still others hold that competition is altogether bad not only for women, but for feminism and socialism; either it serves the oppressor by dividing the oppressed against themselves (e.g., Muse, 1987) or, as a tainted means, it spoils the ends (e.g., Ackelsberg and Addelson, 1987).

At any rate, whatever their position, all the authors write in a moral discourse. For example, Keller and Moglen (1987) say that "as the doors to the ivory tower have swung open, as positions of influence and power have become available to women, we [feminists] have lost both innocence and purity" (p. 22). The irony of their tone ("Fallen creatures now, we look at one another's nakedness in dismay") only heightens the problem of morality and its slide into moralism. Being a good feminist, they remind us, has meant that we do not compete. Keller and Moglen (1987) then ask the question lurking in all our minds: "But what does it mean to be a good feminist in a real world where real power, real issue of professional survival, and real opportunities to exert influence are at stake?" (p. 35). Caught, I think, in the trap of political correctness, they offer, predictably and honorably enough, no satisfying answer. They argue that we must continue to be feminists even as we believe in "some standards of excellence— however drastically they must be revised . . . as a necessary source of motivation" (p. 35) and act on these standards in our attempt to improve our work and our positions. They ask how we can do this under conditions of political and economic inequality, and how we can keep that inequality from disrupting friendships and the feminist community. They suggest we look to other cultures for models (p. 37).

Whew! What burdens feminists hoist onto their backs! It's not only that we have to run twice as fast as men to get where we are and stay there. We also have to live up to idealizations of women that feminism has borrowed and installed on an altar. Unknowingly, feminists have worshipped a false idol: femininity. If men have always had more leeway to be "bad," women, according to stereotype, have always had to be good girls, which means, says journalist Ellen Willis (1984), that they always have to be better than they are. That this impossible ideal ignores the meanness of girls and women is striking. That girls' "relational aggression" (Talbot, 2002) is now being noticed signals perhaps a reaction against such unintended feminist stereotyping.

And here you can see how (although not why) morality becomes moralism: good girls are moral girls, girls who, when they become good women, privately guard the moral order contravened by public brutality; responsible for the ligatures of life, they are to make sure that what happens between people feel good so that people can also feel good about themselves, and life connects and continues. Good women are the people Gilligan's (1980) girls think they are supposed to become: they reject competition, they want to make sure everyone wins; not concerned with self at the expense of other, they are so often concerned with Other that they forget themselves.

No one has noticed the irony: *to be a good feminist, you must be feminine.* You must conform to gender stereotype—to femininity—because feminists are supposed to be good in the way that girls, and women, are supposed to be good. If you want to be a good feminist, then be a good, feminine girl and think about everyone but yourself. Free yourself from your chains by wrapping them ever more tightly around you, trapping yourself in anxiety and guilt.

No wonder it's so hard to think about this topic. Anxiety, in Sullivan's (1953) metaphor, is like getting hit over the head with a two by four: you know something happened but you can't remember what it was (Joseph Newirth, personal communication, 2002). Just so with morality-cum-moralism and the guilt with which it burdens you. When anxiety arrives, paradox disappears and political correctness beckons. I'd like to suggest one way to break these chains: Do what I did last summer. Forget about it. Drop out. Go to California.

4   Davis, California. August 14, 1990. The first day of summer vacation. I walk my friends' dog. Or, rather, she walks me, which puts me in a most uncompetitive frame of mind. Leashed as much to her will as to her collar, I let my own desire follow hers right out of my usual mind into forgotten expanses of rest and creativity and the "unthought-known" [Bollas, 1988]. And, as I bliss out, beginning to leave daily-life cares and woes behind for 3 weeks, who should pop up in my mind but Janis Joplin singing — "Mercedes-Benz"

Another friend, with whom I'm in general but not direct competition (nothing at stake but success, two psychoanalysts in a field way back when there was no institutional ladder for feminists, hence no specific place to be won or lost), openly and generously admired my having secured a second book contract. In self-deprecation (the emotional equivalent of spitting three times to ward off your friends' envy), I replied, "Oh, I have a Janis Joplin complex." After she heard the following story, she concluded, "I guess I don't have enough of one."

According to the *New York Times*, Janis once bought two identical pairs of gold sandals, about which she waxed ecstatic: "I love wearing gold shoes. It's like a breakthrough. It demands a whole kind of attitude for a chick to wear gold shoes. . . . Maybe only girls would understand, but it [feels] almost as good as singing"(Lydon, 1969, p. 44). She also told her interviewer what it felt like to bring that "whole kind of attitude" (and, I imagine, her gold shoes) back home to Port Arthur, Texas, where, although she had grown up an averagely privileged middle-class person, she nevertheless always felt deprived of respect, poor in esteem: "I read, I painted, I thought. I didn't hate niggers. There was nobody like me [there]. It was lonely, those feelings welling up and nobody to talk to. I was just 'silly crazy Janis.' Man, those people hurt me. It makes me happy to know I'm making it and they're back there, plumbers just like they were" (p. 40). Now, rich in money and power, she could *show* them: "People aren't supposed to be like me . . . but now they're paying me $50,000 a year to be like me" (p. 40).

Is that what it takes to make it—a Janis Joplin complex, a wish for victory emerging out of friendless hurt so deep it makes you want to kill? Or, at least, is that bottomless vengeance the minimum? And did Janis make it? Was the competition worth the candle she burned at both ends? Was it worth dying for, as she did the very next year? She left us a great legacy, didn't she? Don't you love her music? Don't you love her for being such a bad girl and "making it" anyway? (see Echols,1999, p. 306). (Or, at least, such a bad *white* girl, for there have been many black women, like Billie Holliday, who, while adulated, don't hold quite the same place in mainstream—read, "white"—cultural mythology as Janis, even if they were models for her art and life; there's another, sociopolitical sort of competition going on here, and I'll return to it later on.)

You may recall that, in "Mercedes-Benz" Janis sings about having to make amends, because all her friends own Porsches. "Amends," according to Webster's (1956), is "payment made or satisfaction given for injury, insult, loss, etc.; as he [*sic*] made amends for his rudeness." How puzzling. You might think that amends is what you have to make after you win, as, sort of, damage control. Yet this song suggests that you can make restitution by competing. For what offense, then would keeping up with the Joneses compensate? It's tempting to psychologize Janis and say she felt like a bad person for being a bad girl (or became a bad girl because she felt so bad about herself), and therefore she had to atone. But not only is she not my patient, she's dead and can't correct me as living patients can. I'd rather listen for the more universal connotations of her verse and suggest that the transgression requiring amends is one we spy not only in Janis's life but in our own—the offense of not having as much as others, of therefore not being as "much" as they, and thus, by comparison, being "rude" and uncivilized. The offense lies in the unpleasant feelings aroused in the "haves" by the "have-nots," in the emotional structure of socioeconomic hierarchy: those who have less envy those who have more, who, at the same time, feel guilt; hence the "offense" of homeless people.

"Mercedes-Benz" was, of course, satirizing the sort of competitive society in which having less than other people feels like, and is even regarded as, an offense against them. On the album in which it appeared (*Pearl*), Janis sets it up in that hoarse, squeaky voice of hers: "I'd like to do a song of great social and political import." But although she makes us laugh at the pain, she also renders this universal scramble for dignity a far more personal than political matter. Nor is it surprising that she does so, for her song predates our recognition that "the personal is political," a slogan invented the same year the article about her appeared (Hanisch, 1969).

It's too bad that, for most people who once believed otherwise, the political has now dwindled to the personal. Still, the inherently mutual implication of personal and political life, which is how I understand that now-famous motto, girds the form and informs the content of this chapter. How, I want to ask, can we understand competition between women or feminists (or between anybody, for that matter) as a tension, as simultaneously personal and political, multiply located in our hearts, our friendships, the structure of daily life, and the social foundation? How can we chart the political and economic forces giving rise to and shaping competition as we know it while also tracking the intrapsychic processes infusing it?

I intend to answer these questions by what I say and how I say it. One central disappointment of Keller and Moglen's otherwise germinal contribution was how little they told us about their relationship. When reading it, you really do want to know what their competition was all about and how, or if, they resolved it. Because you never find out, you're never entirely persuaded that the answer lies in scrutinizing other creatures. Why should we look so far afield when at least some answers might lie rather closer to home, in the personal lives of the authors, both of whom continue as successful professionals and feminists?

So I've chosen to take a risk here and let you in on some bits of the diary I impulsively began once I'd taken this project on. As you can tell, I'm going to interweave those bits with some thinking I've done about the matter of competition. I will be arguing, in the main, that competitiveness has an unconscious life as well as a social reality. It exists in both inner and outer dimensions, equally a graphic social drama of striving, winning, losing, and living to fight another day and a vividly felt but invisible psychic drama of desire, hate, and reparation. Like any behavior, competition is informed doubly by emotion and politics, which is the reason that the twin demons of anxiety and political correctness plague our thinking about it. This double plague makes competition a prime arena for the struggle between love and hate, which can only be resolved by ambivalence or by what Melanie Klein called the depressive position.

To ask how we can depict the paradoxical simultaneity of mind and culture is perhaps also to ask the following: how do we speak about an ordinary experience using the disciplinary languages that, divided, (mis)represent it? In these deconstructionist days, you might use discourse theory to cut you way out of disciplinary prisons. But still you find yourself in a moral(istic) hammerlock, because the anxious and guilty discourse in which competition between women is located keeps you from holding more than one thought in mind at once. Is it possible to step out of this discourse? Or is the only way out to get as deeply into it as you can?

5. Tassajara Zen Mountain Monastery, Jamesburg, California. August 16, 1990.
   On the afternoon of my first workday at Tassajara, my second day here, 27 hours after my arrival, plagued by hard anger and a

headache that began when I arose at five-thirty A.M. to do things
I either didn't know how to do (like sitting *zazen* [meditating]
and raking pebbles into Japanese garden–style order) or felt were
beneath me (like cleaning hurricane lamps and toilets), I steamed
in the sulfurous steam room, and then, lying naked on the deck,
fell unknowingly into a nap. When I woke under the blue sky
ringed with leaves, I found myself silently asking, "Is this, no this
isn't, France? Greece?" And then, to my horror, "Who am I? What's
my name?" I did not know where I was nor could I remember my
name. And that's, I guess, when I remembered why I came.

When I came to Tassajara, I had emerged from two years of
nonstop competing with close feminist friends and colleagues,
more aware of my defeats than my victories, burned out, beat,
mistrustful of those to whom I was closest. At Tassajara, as I
swabbed toilets or made beds still smelling of the night or cleaned
funky spinach in the kitchen, I felt myself losing and giving up
the insignia of those losses and triumphs. As I unwillingly
relinquished these signs of myself and settled queasily into my
bare corporeality, I quickly came to feel humiliatingly small. To
my surprise, I found myself reaching for my accomplishments,
my status markers—"I have a PhD, I used to be a full professor of
anthropology before I bravely gave it all up to become the
psychoanalyst I am now," and so on—as if to remember who
I was.

I'm not going to say, either, that I left Tassajara restored,
trusting, and hopeful, or cleansed of desires for prestige and power,
cured of competitiveness and its discontents, and certainly not of
the desire for its rewards. Zen, I came to understand, is (at least
in the American context) about being where you are. And if
competition is where you are, then that's where you are.

Thich Nhat Hanh (1990), a Vietnamese Zen monk, tells the
following story:

> There was a young man who liked to draw lotus flowers, but he did
> not know anything about drawing. . . . He went to a master, and
> the master took him to a lotus pond and asked him to sit there and
> look at the lotus flowers all day without doing anything, just
> breathing, and looking at the lotus flowers. . . . He did only that
> for ten days, and he went back to his master. His master asked him,
> "Are you ready?" He said, "I will try," and the brush and paint

were given to him. He was painting like a child, but the lotus was very beautiful. He was nothing but a lotus at that time, and the lotus came out. . . . At first he wanted to paint the flower but finally he became the flower, and his intention to paint was no longer there. That is why he succeeded in painting.

When I first read the story, my immediate reaction was, Well, if I'm writing about competition between women, do I have to *become* it? Do I have to live in that place of tension, anxiety, and, sometimes, horror? I don't *want* to live there.

Then the obvious became new: that is *where* I live.

Perhaps the inflamed presence of competition in my life has something to do with the interface of biography and history: second-wave feminist activists and scholars are maturing into the peak of their professions; if they at first engaged politics with a (now declining) vigor, they currently find themselves at that point in their individual career paths where they must secure their positions if they are to have or retain any influence or protection. Structure and desire, power and ambition, propel them into competition. Conversely, as Keller and Moglen (1987) suggest, as long as feminists were marginal, they not only believed competition was counterproductive but, out of a combination of naiveté and political ideology, imagined they were immune to it (p. 22).

The competition we encounter with shock, recognition, amusement, and dismay exists not only in academia and politics. Although it's not all there is, it's everywhere. Transcending the dualism between personal and political, it is the stuff of which the social pyramid, its hierarchies founded on scarcity, is made. Look, it appears even where we think it can't. For example, Longino and Miner (1987) describe themselves as "radical feminists and socialists [who] thus have two traditions behind us that seem antithetical to competition" (p. 1). Their own volume constituting a rejoinder in regard to feminism, I need only mention Lenin and Trotsky, or the Prague Spring and its consequences, or Tiananmen Square, to remind you of socialism's putatively noncompetitive spirit.

Going even further back (in cultural imagery if not actual time), competition is where Rachel and Leah live too. According to Genesis, Jacob was sent by his parents to get a wife from his mother's brother, Laban. Canny Laban, meanwhile, had plans of his own. He wanted to marry off his older and "weak-eyed" (*Tanakh*, Genesis 29:17) daughter Leah before his younger and supremely beautiful Rachel. Jacob, however, was already smitten, having run into Rachel before he met up with Laban. So Laban proposed a bargain: Jacob would stay and work for a month, after which he would receive some recompense. Jacob countered by offering seven years in return for Rachel. Laban agreed and, when the time came, duly made a wedding. Under cover of darkness, however, he had Leah, not Rachel, led to Jacob's tent. The morning after, Jacob was angry. Conciliatory, Laban told them that a week hence he could marry Rachel, too, but only on the condition that he serve yet another 7 years.

This power struggle between Jacob and Laban had its mirror image in the rivalry over desirability and fecundity between Leah and Rachel. Rachel may have had Jacob's love, but she was barren, while Leah was fertile. Their mutual envy set off many rounds of births. After Leah had borne four sons, Rachel had Jacob cohabit with her maid, Bilhal, who then produced two boys whom Rachel claimed as her own. Leah, not to be outdone, did the same with her servant, Zilphah, who likewise bore two sons to Jacob. Then, one day, Rachel, still enviously infertile, demanded that Leah give her some of her son's mandrakes (for fertility) and in return allowed Leah to sleep with Jacob that night. Lo and behold, Leah then had two more sons and, to top it off, a daughter. But, finally, "God remembered Rachel" (*Tanakh*, p. 46) and she had a son— Joseph (and the rest, we might say, is history).

It is worth noting that the battle between Leah and Rachel was fought on femininity's usual terrain: beauty and fertility. In contrast, my own struggles, as I have recounted them here, revolved around professional success. Yet the anguish that I, like other feminists, experienced about competing in this arena (and, in some cases, in the reproductive arena, too) with other (feminist) women, draws on this cultural history. In the Biblical story, you expect the men to wrestle each other to the ground, as Laban and Jacob did.[1] But the tale's shock is the fact that the women would

---

[1] The details of the later trickery that took place between Jacob and Laban over the next 6 years need not concern us here. We might note, however, the outcome of their competitiveness. Jacob, the smarter and more cunning of the

practically kill each other for the femininity over which they compete. Do the same passions, transposed from private to public life, infuse feminism?

I must have wanted to run away from the contradictions of feminism and their effects on me and my friends. But there was no escape. I am sure that, had I remained at Tassajara and let the total institution (Goffman, 1961) swallow me up (indeed, I was tempted), the matter of competition would have resurfaced in me, and between me and others, in the pores of my mind and in the spaces of social life (in the short run, for example, I might have wondered who, on a given day, had meditated most "perfectly"—an oxymoron—while in the long run, I might have wanted to rise in the monastic hierarchy). Competition would have come back up not only because Zen practice encourages the emergence of all experience but because I've grown up where I've grown up, as have most of the monks here. You can't be anything but racist in a racist society, misogynist in a patriarchal one, and competitive in a hierarchical one. You can dislike your attitudes, and do battle with them—that's what being antiracist, nonsexist, and noncompetitive involves, struggling against that which contravenes your values. But your struggle doesn't purge you of your faults, even though it may help you figure out ways to ameliorate their political manifestations, or to imagine their ultimate undoing.

Racism, sexism, competition. Hmm. I seem to have reentered the moral domain. I'd like to take the analogy back, but I can't.

---

two, managed to become richer and more powerful. For 20 years, Laban kept trying to cheat Jacob not only of wives but of livestock. In the end, he lost and had to let Jacob, his daughters, their maids, and all his grandchildren go. Maybe it's not so hard to understand why the older man might play tricks on the younger one. After all, God had already appointed Jacob as the founder of nations. How better to triumph over the man who is inevitably going to exceed you than by making him serve for twenty years to get what he ought to have received after only seven? The oedipal boy, it turns out, is right: Not only in his guilt-stricken fantasy, but in lived life, the old man, in this case his father-in-law, *does* want to get him. Sons often have the opportunity to do what their fathers couldn't; *mutatis mutandis*, the same holds true for daughters and mothers, as Keller and Moglen (1987) so poignantly remind us in their recounting of intergenerational competition among feminists.

Political correctness aside, I think it's right. So I'll try, at least, not to be moralistic (which, by the way, raises the question of whether it is any longer possible to speak about politics without being, feeling, or being accused of being moralistic, sanctimonious). If racism is the mark of imperialism and misogyny is the mark of patriarchy, then competition is the signature of hierarchy. Competition may beget pain that explodes into greatness, as it led to Janis's energy and music, or Billie Holiday's genius. But competitiveness between women, particularly between feminists, is, I will say without anxiety, often horribly painful and, in that sense, a bad thing, which doesn't mean we shouldn't engage in it. Here's why. (No, this isn't a detour; or rather, it is, but it's going to take us back to that most interesting dilemma, whether you can be a good feminist without being a good girl.)

6. Tassajara. August 19, 1990.
    How do I hate thee? Let me count the ways.
    I hate thee to the depth and breadth and height
    My soul can reach, when feeling out of sight
    For the ends of Beings and ideal Grace.
    I hate thee to the level of everyday's
    Most quiet needs, by sun and candlelight.
    I hate thee freely, as men strive for Right.
    I hate thee purely, as they turn from Praise.
    I hate thee with the passion put to use
    In my old griefs, and with my childhood's faith.
    I hate thee with a love I seemed to lose
    With my lost saints—I hate thee with the breath,
    Smiles, tears, of all the life!—and, if God choose,
    I shall but hate thee better after death [after Elizabeth Barrett Browning].

I cannot deny that a hatred equal in depth to love has accompanied the competitions in which I've engaged with my dearest friends. I'd like to deny it because, always inclined to be a good girl, I shrink from feeling such aggression in myself and from seeing it in other women. I'm probably not alone in this. The ideology of femininity contains no room for the intense hatred that Janis spouted in her interview, which most of us feel, at least on occasion, but would never publicize.

Still, if we're going to talk about competition, I think we have to talk about hate because, my own experience convinces me, competition does not occur in the absence of this passionate concoction of "resentment, contempt, frustration, envy, [and] rage" (Levine, 1991 p. 10). At its worst, this hatred between me and my women-feminist friends has threatened to unbalance me; short of that, as I have told you, it nearly destroyed a friendship. What I wonder, though, is this: Would the hatred have had such destructive power if Linda and I had been able to know it, singly and together, beforehand? But could we have known? Is there any way to discuss hatred without falling into moralism? Is there any way to let hatred be without immediately censuring the one who hates? Is it possible that politics tends to become moralistic when it encounters, without acceptance, the passionate and frightening emotion of hate?

Let's look at hate or, rather, the effects of ignoring it in one study of competition that justly became an instant classic. Joyce P. Lindenbaum's (1985) psychoanalytic examination of competitiveness and envy with lesbian couples avoids moralizing, but only, it seems to me, by helping hatred to an early death. Somewhat coolly, she defines competition as "a constructive process that can evolve when an experience of 'felt difference' occurs between two separate selves in relationship" (p. 204). Lindenbaum arrives at this definition from her psychotherapeutic treatment of lesbian couples who, she finds, often come to her because they have stopped having sex. This has happened, she argues, because their ease with the nonsexual merging of selves leaves them defenseless against the unconscious, primal, mother–child fusion that, in the extraordinariness of sexual union, permits ecstasy, but, in ordinary life, induces a terrifying loss of self. And their comfort with nonsexual merging has in part to do with their inability to distinguish, intrapsychically and interpersonally, difference from separateness.

Difference, in these relationships, has come to signify separateness, and separateness to signify the loss of the other and of the relationship. Envy emerges as a way to defend against this "felt difference," with its signification of loss and abandonment. However, because envy causes pain and threatens intimacy, the couples Lindenbaum treats attempt to erase it by doing what women, whether lovers, friends, colleagues, comrades, or kin, often do. They create a "pseudomutuality" or pseudolikeness in which, unfortunately, each partner then feels she has sacrificed too much of herself. They resolve the tension of difference by creating a singular, false likeness. To minimize this high price, the partners next create "pseudodifference": Each, in order to reclaim herself, protests too much her own distinctiveness and consequently feels neither real nor comfortable, but is more often uneasily aware of hatred's seeds, of anger with and envy of the other.

Lindenbaum's (1985) solution is not to eliminate but to institute competition in the relationship. There she thinks it can imbue separateness and difference with a sense of safety, and detoxify envy by giving it "benign expression" (p. 205). If one partner envies the other's success in a particular domain, she is to determine the domain in which she herself wishes to succeed; if it's the same as her partner's, then she should go for it, try to beat her partner. This displacement of aggression from envy onto the job of creating the desired quality in oneself deflects the wish to hurt the other. Thus purified, competition becomes curative and provides one

> with the opportunity to become competent. It is not an easy task, nor is it one that can always be accomplished. There is still the possibility of deep disappointment. . . . In undertaking the challenge . . . one has, at the very least, the experience of developing a particular aspect of the Self and observing that the Other is not destroyed by this success. When One gets better, the Other does not have to get worse [p. 206].

Maybe. If the competition is about, say, cooking, there are always more meals to be prepared and eaten; if it's about tennis, then there's always next year's Wimbledon. But sometimes, when one person wins and the other loses, that's it; the game's over and will never be played again. If the contest involves a job and there's only one to be had, then there's no second chance, as we learn from the anguished cases Keller and Moglen (1987, p. 35) recount, as well as from those with which we've had personal contact, either as winners or losers (I've been both). And without a second chance, hatred is likely to have its day.

Lindenbaum's (1985) model, while attentive to the psychosocial construction of women's personality, seems to ignore both the social underpinnings and unconscious matrix of competition.

Certainly, people who have experienced trauma during the first two years of life (Lindenbaum's thesis employs this preoedipal model) are likely to be threatened by the Other's difference and to regard that difference as a sign of their own inadequacy, triggering retaliatory, envious fantasies that envision the Other's destruction. And to be sure, because women's personalities tend to form by identifying with, not differing from, (m)others, hence are marked by permeable boundaries, and are thus suited to the tasks of relatedness, women are often threatened by difference in precisely this way (Miller, 1976; Chodorow, 1978).

But the drama of competition is not only internal, or even internal to couples. Competition is also an historical process, and competitiveness is a politically meaningful feeling. In our culture, the context for competition is a socially structured scarcity, a fact recognized by Keller and Moglen (1987, p. 35), whose faith in the value of competitiveness is less naïve than Lindenbaum's. Under these circumstances, where the means to wealth and power are unequally distributed, envy is as inevitable as competitiveness. Envy, a complex emotion that feeds hatred, consists, in part, of admiration. Founded in processes of identification, it shows up in the desire to emulate the other. Yet it is also destructive, containing a wish to destroy anyone who has something, be it quality, relationship, object, or situation, that one longs for, so that one no longer has to remember that one lacks it.

But loss also has a political dimension. Early childhood's losses meet, and find echoes in, the socially constituted deprivations, disappointments, and failures of adult life (see Chapter 7). When social losses cannot be reversed, the disappointment they entail borrows from the passions of early life, when any loss seemed irreversible (think of a frustrated toddler). Not infrequently, this helpless disillusionment finds expression in hatred of self, of others, and of the Other—other races and ethnicities; women; the powers that be; or those who, like Janis, are deemed "weird" because of their sexuality, style, or beliefs. As we have seen in Janis's own life, it can, under the right conditions, also turn into self-destructive hatred of one's own Otherness.

The power of hatred to scare us all and to threaten social order is one reason for the social significance of competition. Competition rationalizes hate by institutionalizing it. As my pseudonymous friend Nathan, whom I regularly consult on matters masculine, told me, "We used to joke that, before basketball games, we were going to sit in a room and have a hate session." That's why there's no such thing as "true" competition, as Lindenbaum's (1985, p. 206) positivism (or, perhaps, romanticism) would have it: neither emotionally nor psychically neutral, competition has cultural and psychological origins and functions specific to the society in which it is found.

"True" competition is only an *idea* in our own society. Liberals and conservatives alike cheer: "May the best man win!" Sometimes, though, the "best man" is not the one who wins the game as played, but the one who plays the game by pulling strings (Ackelsberg and Addelson, 1987, p. 223). Even though being socially and economically well positioned doesn't mean you *can't* be the best at what you do, it can be an awfully big help to the competent and incompetent alike. And this socioeconomic differential tends to brew hatred, both among the many, who envy and resent those who have, and among the few, who live in contempt, fear, and guilt toward those who do not.

Hate seems to negate love; perhaps that's one reason good girls eschew it. But, you know, I could not have hated my competitors as deeply had I not loved them well; as my adaptation of Browning's sonnet suggests, hate feeds on love as (and I will return to this thought toward the end of this chapter) love needs hate. Hate can flourish only where illusions once held sway, only where love has blinded us. And its very presence indexes our longing to love once more. Unpacking the dualism of love and hate requires a high tolerance for ambiguity and paradox.

If you taboo one sector of passion, you stunt the rest. I wish Lindenbaum had let her patients hate each other for a while instead of trying to finesse the bad-girl emotion of hatred by instituting competition. Counter to my own impulses, I want to argue that we must bring hatred, and all the other bad-girl feelings, forward. If we don't, we remain locked in the good-girl model of feminism. Here, then, the new rule: *to be a good feminist, you have to be a bad girl* (Echols, 1987). You need to know everything you weren't supposed to know when you were supposed to be a good girl. You have to know everything about what you can and want to be. Break the dualistic hammerlock: be bad as well as good.

In Lindenbaum's (1985) final case example, a woman envies her lover's fame as a public speaker, at first relishing a vicarious success, later wishing to be as skillful but fearing the damage such an accomplishment might do to her partner. Through therapy, however, she identifies and accomplishes her goal; she, too, becomes a public speaker, and now she and her partner playfully goad each other on, as part of what they regard as their benign competition. I agree with Lindenbaum's (1985) concluding comment on this couple, but I also think it undermines her entire argument:

> That one woman envies her partner's passion for public speaking does not mean that she must work to become a skilled public speaker herself. It is the passion that is envied. The capacity to be passionate about something is what must be examined and developed [p. 206].

But passion is subversive. Hate explodes love, making love burn all the more brightly. If passion, not competition, is the point, then the clinical task becomes understanding why this particular woman cannot own, and thereby define, her passion, including her hatred. To institute competitiveness in the relationship forecloses inquiry into the inhibition of her desire. Writing about black adolescent girls, Daphne Muse (1987) makes a related point, contending that competitiveness is particularly damaging to them because it puts their lives "in a box," packaging their quest for personal fulfillment into conventional goals (p. 157). Or, as another aphorism puts it, "You can't get rich playing another man's game."

Or can you?

7. New York City. November 11, 1990.
   Another dinner date, this time with *[let's call him]* Jim. I tell Jim about the article on competition, and its problematic, the moral(istic) discourse from which it's trying to escape. "What's the mystery?" he wants to know. "Competition is nothing more complicated than a good game of tennis." "Well," I suggest, "imagine that you've got an assistant professor in your department *[Jim is an eminent sociologist of liberal persuasion]* who's a wonderful teacher, but doesn't publish, so, when tenure review comes around, it's not up but out." Jim is silent, indeed, I suspect, uncomfortable. Later, when he tells me that I shouldn't be

worrying about competition, I can't figure out whether he's flirting or competing.

So what does Jim's tennis metaphor mean? It means that he was as unsettled as I by the hostilities embedded in competitiveness, but could not find words for his discomfort. Jim was on a date, a situation that (for him, at least) necessitated an intensification of his adherence to (heterosexual) masculine stereotype. So he turned to an appropriate convention to disavow his distress. He repudiated the feminine nurturing implicit in my example of the poor, tenure-seeking professor. Instead, he likened competition to the athletic arena, which is the context in which men many learn to compete. The sports model has several functions: As part of social ideology, it represents the meritocratic belief that, in any competition, the race goes to the quick; conversely, if the winners are, by definition, the best, then, also by definition, those who lose deserve to. If you believe this, then you don't have to worry about fairness of the conditions under which competition takes place and you can, thereby, invalidate any social criticism the defeated may make. Competition, whether in the stadium, boardroom, or lecture hall, thus becomes a completely self-justifying, moral(istic) system (Harris, 1985).

The metaphor of athletics also does some emotional housekeeping by clearing away the ambivalence of competition, in which you must recognize that, because your gain is usually someone else's loss, your pleasure comes at the expense of someone else's, and vice versa. One way Nathan learned to deny ambivalence, and thereby to remember the pleasure and forget the pain, is through competitive athletics. Finding out that "it's only a game," he said, minimized the hostility of triumph and voided the shame of defeat, so that winning contained only pure pleasure, losing only stoic hope. Furthermore, if it's nothing but a game, then any blows you give or take don't really hurt because you were only playing in the sense of pretending, and so, once it's over, you need feel neither remorse for beating someone else nor hatred of the one who beats you.

I hear, however, that there's another side to the story. Indeed, I have seen it in Picabo Street, or in Venus and Serena Williams, to name some contemporary heroines. There is, it seems, an intense experience you can get from competitive athletics that you can't get anywhere else. Too bad I didn't learn this when I was a kid. Competitiveness and its gendered meanings have a history. In my time, there were tomboys and girl jocks, but if you were striving for femininity *à la* Rachel and Leah, you wouldn't touch sports with the 10-foot pole that you were hoping to find on some boy's body. The association between athleticism and lesbianism was, for one, thing, far too dangerous for aspiring hetero femmes like me. So, even though, in the last generation, history was made before our eyes—think Brandi Chastain—you don't at my age begin to play field hockey or even tennis. Like many other women who are more comfortable working out alone than meeting an opponent or being responsible to a team, I go in more for individual endurance sports, like swimming or jogging. I grew up as one of those women who look down on team sports as "trivial . . . orgies of violence" (Ring, 1987, p. 60). And in the past, I would always find the interest women friends take in organized athletics slightly mystifying, amusing, and suspect: what a way to compete for men, no? (Lichtenstein 1987, p. 53).

Yet I have come to understand the four secrets that women like me were never let in on. One of these concerns the relationship between competition and self-esteem. I can't be alone among women in feeling that, if I lose the game, I am "a loser." Of course, if your narcissism is at stake every time you play a game, you can hardly take any pleasure in playing. Rather, under those circumstances, each game becomes "a life-and-death struggle" (p. 53). If, in contrast, you know that "each game is nothing more than a game," as "the most accomplished women athletes" do, then the aphorism, "It's only a game," takes on a new meaning: winning and losing are only about that one particular contest (p. 53). The competition is not, in other words, about you, it's about your performance, which is not, as Zen strives to teach, the same thing at all.

In this restricted sense, then, competitive sports are, in fact, morally neutral. Although I don't believe it's particularly easy to distinguish yourself from the game you played on any given day, nevertheless I can see that competition in this arena offers you the opportunity to evaluate what you do without judging who or what you are. Surely this is a great and valuable lesson, applicable to many different parts of life. It might, for example, be

exceptionally useful for women who want to resist the psychological and social compulsion to be better than they are. If you
can feel that your own performance is not a matter of your own
goodness, then you are freed from the anxiety that attends your
attempts to improve your performance: you can work to improve
what you do because you are already good enough.

Athletics can't be the only route to this capacity for dis-passionately
estimating one's strengths and weaknesses (a goal Lindenbaum would
have her patients strive for). However, it seems to be the major one
in our culture. Competitive sports nurture this ability by carving out
a sacred space from ordinary life, a space in which the normal rules
of politeness are temporarily suspended and ambivalence is irrelevant.
Defined as "play," athletics rationalizes aggression by splitting pain
from pleasure, as I have suggested. But within play itself, athletic
competition can make room for the irrational and thereby release
normally proscribed aspects of self, in particular, aggression and
hatred. Play, in Winnicott's (1971) classic definition, lies somewhere
between ordinary life and fantasy, and the pleasure we find in it
depends on nearing the poles without settling into one or the
other (see Chapter 6). I'm not ignoring the commercial side of
sport. But I am saying that, within the rules of the game, even
when its frame is money and fame, anything goes.

The opportunity to experience and reverse one's self-hate is
the second great secret known only by top women athletes. Thus
detoxified and brought under the sway of ambivalence, aggression
and hatred lose their power to paralyze, and what happens next is
Zen-like. Once you let these powerful emotions be, they let you
be; once experienced, they can be known and managed, and hence
no longer dangerous to you or anyone else. And then it becomes
possible to identify aggressiveness not only between you and your
opponent but within yourself. Many of the best women athletes
say that your most important opponent is not your competition
but "yourself, your negative internal voices" (Lichtenstein, 1987,
p. 53). Successful competition allows, indeed, demands that you
own, confront, and triumph over those inner voices. Regarding
these bad objects (Laplanche and Pontalis, 1967, pp. 188–189;
Rivière, 1936) not as a sign of your intrinsic badness but as
obstacles to your goodness, you can subordinate them as your
goal, whether it be a prize or a poem that pleases you more than

the one you wrote last. By knowing, accepting, even loving your own hatred of self and others, you can clear away the obstacles to your own competence, the goal that Lindenbaum (1985) set for her patients.

Which brings us to "the zone." The process of examining and standing up to your own internal voices confers and demands a certain toughness of spirit, which, the experts argue, is essential to success. The third secret to which many successful women competitors are privy is that "the race . . . goes not to the swiftest, but to the toughest" (Lichtenstein, 1987, p. 53), that is, to those who concentrate.

> [T]he ability to . . . focus so completely on this one event, moment by moment, stroke by stroke, . . . gives the athlete the tiny edge she needs to beat an equally talented rival whose attention might wander. [Chris] Evert Lloyd, a Zen Master when it comes to concentration, always cites this quality as the key to the game [p. 54].

Athletic competence requires what in fact Zen Buddhists call "mindfulness," absolute concentration on the present.[2] This ability, achieved only by sustained hard work, can put you into the altered state of consciousness that athletes refer to as "the zone." This ecstatic state is a seamless unity among mind, body, and the rules and tools of the time. Here's Evelyn Ashford, who as of 1987 held the world record in the 100-meter dash:

> Time stands still when you're racing. . . . When I'm free-flowing and everything's just working, it feels like nothing. It's effortless. You don't feel the track, you don't feel your arms moving, you don't feel the wind going by. It's just nothing. It's perfect (Ring, 1987, p. 65].

In the zone, there's not even competition anymore. And, as is well known, when Evert Lloyd could no longer be in the zone, she quit playing tennis.

---

[2] At Tassajara, the ritual schedule ensured mindfulness; for example, kitchen work was regularly punctuated not only by ceremonial chanting, but by a bell that commanded a 30-second respite from whatever you were doing so you could bring your mind back from wherever it had wandered to where you were.

Here, then, is the fourth and biggest secret of all: To reach this "state of grace" (Shainberg 1989, p. 38), you have to traverse the fullness of yourself, the entire spectrum of your personality, so that you know what your capacities and desires are. This means that you have to travel into those dangerous sectors of yourself, the places of badness and pain. You have to take the good with the bad without moralizing, which is in fact what you can and do do in transitional space. You must, in fact, encounter and accept ambivalence: You have to risk being a bad girl and hurting others even while trying to love them; perhaps you have to recover the meanness you relinquished to be a good girl. And, in the service of self-regard and self-love, you have to tolerate being hurt yourself, hurt by losing, hurt by what you don't like in yourself.

This argument holds not only in the athletic arena but in, for example, writing or making art; more generally, it holds when it comes to doing anything well. But according to femininity, if you're doing something active and it hurts, that means you're doing something wrong. Contrast masculinity's lesson—even if it hurts and even if you're scared, you do it anyway. There may be suffering and danger but there's also triumph and personal best. As psychoanalysis teaches us, all growth entails anxiety. As the sports masters say, "No pain, no gain."

Janis, to return to the heroine of this story, knew all about that. When she sang, she was "in the zone." Listen to her once again:

> I can't talk about my singing. I'm inside of it. How can you describe something you're inside of? I can't know what I'm doing; if I knew it, I'd have lost it. When I sing, I feel, oh, I feel, well, like when you're first in love. It's more than sex, I know that. It's that point two people can get to they call love, like when you really touch someone for the first time, but it's gigantic, multiplied by the whole audience. I feel chills, weird feelings slipping all over my body. It's a supreme emotional and physical experience [Lydon, 1969, p. 44].

And a spiritual one, too, so precious that those who experience it become superstitious. Like Janis, "[most] ballplayers—out of confusion, or perhaps superstition, maintain silence on the subject of the zone" (Shainberg, 1966, p. 38).

So, yes, you can get rich playing a(nother) man's game. Women have by now learned a lot from the traditionally masculine preserve of competitive sports. The girls who now have the chance to compete have a great advantage over those of us who came before them and did not. They have learned something about their own capacities, needs, and limits. They have reaffirmed in their bodies the sense of empowerment we all first felt as infants when we grabbed our first toy or took our first step. They feel powerful, not only in the sense of dominating or being dominated by others, but in the sense of being able. They know about "power to" as well as "power over." Yes. Competition is good for women (and feminism—even the ridiculous match between Billie Jean King and Bobby Riggs—helped them get there).

When the game is over, however, you still have to deal with ambivalence and the ease with which, in our society, "power to" morphs into "power over."

8. New York City. November 12, 1990.
   Linda reappears in another dream: I pass her in the subway. Her white and green sweater dress suits her curves, which I find as breathtakingly beautiful as ever. I walk quickly by, trying not to let her see me seeing her. But she does see me and, saying, "Hi, sugar," reaches to hug me. I'm just beyond her grasp. Still I turn, belatedly, thinking I should try to respond. "Oh," I say, "you seem upset." "Yes," she replies. "What—" I begin to ask. "No," she declines, hastening down the stairs with a smile that apologizes for her hurry.

Yes, it is indeed surprising that my unconscious has cooperated with this writing project by providing me with so much material. At the same time as I'm grateful, however, I'm nettled: how come Linda enters my sleep every time (all of twice) I have a date?

One thing I've learned in the course of reflecting on competitions with my dearest friends is that women have precious few ways to make up. The conventions of masculinity institutionalize ways of repairing the damage players inflict or receive: You play a game of basketball or tennis, one side or person wins, the other loses, and you all have a beer, slap each other on the back, and go home. But femininity doesn't cover this territory at all. You win the man or the bake-off or the girl, you birth the baby first, and then what? Feel smug and diss the loser? You might

wish to suture each other's wounds, or even your own. But
femininity provides no rituals of reparation that, in acknowledging
the need to repair, transform hate into love and thus restores
ambivalence.

Ambivalence is a good, both/and thing. If *ambi*, in Latin, means
"both" and "balance," and *valence* means "power" or "charge,"
ambivalence means both love and hate. Generally, ambivalence
suggests the state of being torn between poles. Hence its usual
connotation, the negative inability to choose between love and
hate. But I see another meaning, the amazing ability to hold love
and hate in mind at the same time, the capacity that Melanie Klein
says marks the depressive position. Instead of splitting love and
hate—so that the other person is always only either good or bad—
one balances between them. The depressive position is not the
same as transitional space, in which the two—parent and child,
prototypically—are not yet separate if even they are not exactly
one any more. In the depressive position, the child has gained the
capacity to recognize self and other as separate, which achievement
is accompanied by the layered recognition that one can hurt and
be hurt by the other, that therefore there are good and bad ways
to relate, and that goodness is morally better. We might reframe
the depressive position in terms of the ability to sustain paradox
(Benjamin, 1998), to negotiate "a non-dialectical opposition
which the subject, saying 'yes' and 'no at the same time, is incapable
of transcending" (LaPlanche and Pontalis, 1967, p. 28). Thus, in
the depressive position, you recognize that you can hurt the one
you love and wish, out of guilt, to repair the damage.

Ambivalence is no picnic. There are great risks. Recognizing,
for example, that you can hate the mother you love, or love the
mother you hate, hurts infinitely. And it requires hard work. If
love always, and unconsciously, turns into hate, hate does not so
effortlessly return to love. Sometimes you have to make sure the
return journey happens by consciously recalling the love from the
darkness. Hence my dreams about Linda calling me and seeing
her in the subway. But you need ambivalence in order to go back.
Without it, hate and love destroy each other. Hate obliterates the
other, love consumes the self. When you hate only, you see nothing
but badness and therefore wish to wipe the other off the face of
the earth. When you love and see goodness only, you can't make
meaning of the other's flaws, and so, wishing to wipe those flaws

off the face of the earth, you see only what you want to see, only
what you can love. In a way, when you love without hating, you
see only the self you wish you were, never the other.[3]

If seeing the other as the other is the trick, then seeing another
woman as the other is even trickier. Sometimes there is too much
identification between women. Femininity disposes women toward
a gendered identification with their mothers (Chodorow, 1978)
that makes them feel more comfortable in being alike. Difference
is therefore not neutral. Rather, it can be threatening. It may
intimate separation and abandonment. But it may also mean that
the other can be different in ways you don't like. As we have seen
in Lindenbaum's account of lesbian couples, one defense against
this difficulty is merging (see also Eichenbaum and Orbach, 1988).

Being alike can, in turn, make liking one another feel imperative.
There is an intrapsychic slippage from likeness to liking that has a
social counterpart. I have written elsewhere about an "ethic of
loyalty" between women, which, at least among women of the
same age, race, class, sexuality, and so on, "holds that women are,
in distinction to men, the same and, therefore, peers, equals whose
first obligation is to one another" (Dimen, 1986; see also Dimen
and Shapiro, n.d., p. 16). (Perhaps this ethic defines the good
girl dimension of femininity that mean girls are rebelling against.)
One component of this ethic is an emphasis on likeness and love
at the expense of dis-likeness and hate, enforced by the taboo on
women's anger and aggression, of which Keller and Moglen (1987)
make much. Indeed, this force toward likeness is one of the main
causes for conflict between the women in the examples they offer,
on the basis of which they argue that "the common association
made between identification and cooperation on the one hand,
and between separation and competition on the other, is too
simple. Under certain circumstances, cooperation may actually be
facilitated by differentiation and autonomy" (p. 27). To my way
of thinking, however, differentiation and autonomy are insecure

---

[3] The discussion of hate, love, reparation, and ambivalence originates, of
course, in Freud, but really begins with Klein and Rivière (1964) and continues
with Winnicott (1958), in which he argues that the analyst must tolerate hating
the patient, as the mother must tolerate her normal hatred of her baby, for only
in this way can the patient or infant grow to be a separate person.

accomplishments unless you can tolerate dislikable, as well as agreeable, difference, the differences that irritate as well as please you; this capacity in turn rests on the accessibility of all your emotions, from love to hate.

Nor does my dream tell how to achieve this ambivalence, though it tells some of its possibility. The dream's key lies in the color symbolism of Linda's costume. On one hand, the combination of white and green has never appealed to me; I find it uninteresting at best and slightly repellent at worst. In the dream, then, it's a sign not so much of difference or dissimilarity or unlikeness between me and Linda, as it is of dislike. I dislike this color combination as, in fact, I disliked certain of Linda's tastes. Not, of course, that I ever told her. No, our friendship was founded mostly on being alike, not on disliking, on loving, not hating. With our selves merged, I (perhaps we) feared the series of signifiers that skids from dissimilarity to dis-likeness to hatred.

At the same time, these colors have a personal meaning connected to sex, power, and competition: when I was in high school, I spent quite a bit of time knitting a white and green scarf for my boyfriend whose college colors they were. That I consulted my mother frequently about this fairly simple project—how long, for example, the scarf should be—suggests to me now, as I look back, that I was in considerable doubt about whether I had the right to my own man—or whether I wanted a man at all. Maybe I wanted to merge, emotionally and sexually, with my mother—or another woman? Linda?

To interpret the dream language, that Linda wears the same colors registers some dubiety as to my own autonomy, sexuality, aggression, and power—in short, about my claim to the phallus (and how long it should be) (laugh). For me, in this dream, Linda is the phallic mother, the omnipotent mother who can kill as well as treasure you (Dinnerstein, 1976), the sexual mother who, my first dream said, might fight with her husband and sleep with another man. I fear her seeing me seeing her because, if she does, that will mean I will be looking directly into the Medusa's face and thus will be at risk of being turned into stone by the aggression and competitiveness and hatred, both autochthonous and reflected, I see there. I am afraid to look straight at her and let her see any frank desire to acquire for myself the sort of sexual power she has had, for her possession of which I hate her.

For her possession of which I love her. Love pervades the dream too, emotionally, sensually, sexually. I love Linda's curvaceous body even though I hate what she clothes it in. And Linda loves me too: she calls me by an endearment my real mother might have used. She loves me even though I hate her. I love her even though she hates me. The Medusa, a terrifying image of maternal hatred and destructiveness, can also be read as a passionate and utopian symbol of women's personal power. Yes, the mother has the power, and "she's not deadly. She's beautiful and she's laughing" (Cixous, quoted in Suleiman, 1990, p. 167). Suleiman elaborates Cixous's argument, "the laughing Medusa becomes a trope for women's autonomous subjectivity" (p. 168) including, I would emphasize, her hatred, aggression, competitiveness, and love. For her, my, our ambivalence. I hate her for the same reason I love her, the beautiful power that ought also to be mine, could be mine if I could tolerate the ambivalence of loving and hating her, the ambivalence that made me embarrassed, both dismayed and happy to see her quarreling with her husband in public.

Life, however, is not a dream, and the longed-for phallus is, to say the least, elusive. According to Lacanian theory, no one, not even men, can possess the phallus. Not a penis, it stands, on one hand, for the desire to be the object of mother's desire; on the other, it represents the Law to which we are all subject (Grosz, 1992; Macey, 1992). Yet there is more. The phallus is, in fact, overdetermined. As "the [discursive] site where the social is reproduced as the biological" (Harris, 1989, p. 114), the phallus also refers to masculinity. As I argue in Chapter 1, Lacan may have codified the phallus' symbolism but he didn't make enough of its traffic with patriarchy. Symbolizing men's "privilege in a culture of hierarchy, the phallus comes also to signify that culture itself, the state" (Dimen, 1986, p. 131). And even if in Lacan's view, no one has the phallus, some sure look as though they do.

The phallus is, therefore, what we compete for. In a culture of hierarchy whose signature is competition, where possessing the phallus means that you can dominate other people, winning the game is not only about the ecstasy of being in the zone. Within the rules of the game, as I have argued, competitiveness can be a route to empowerment, competence, and self-possession. But as long as the game is played in an economy of scarcity, "power to" slides easily into "power over," and empowerment can slip under the steamroller of domination. That this elision takes place among everyone, including women and feminists, is the reason we worry about the capacity of power and its rewards to destroy feminism.

I want to argue, then, that competitiveness cannot safely proceed among women, especially feminists, unless we can do something to prevent "power over" from steamrolling "power to." As useful as competition has been for me and as much as I want and intend to go on competing, I also know, from personal experience, that the combat is deadly. I don't think the wounds of losing heal until you finally win—or redefine—what you want. And, although losing may help you figure out what you're good at and what you really want to do, the connections between you and others can be damaged during the time it takes to do that.

What I really want to argue seems naïve, jejune, good-girlish: Somehow, everybody has to win. But how could everyone win in a way that would not devalue the prizes? One way would be for everyone to agree to use competition only to get "power to," to enhance their own competence, sharpen their skills, know themselves, and get into "the zone." Yet, in an economy of scarcity, what would keep "power to" from becoming "power over?" How could a rule hold out against the hierarchical structure necessitating it? If one person, one woman, one feminist, sets her sights on and makes her way to the top of the pyramid, becoming, say, a media or academic star, then the game is over. "Power to" becomes forever devalued in comparison to "power over." Indeed, who of us can say she wouldn't reach for the gold ring?

Even this chapter participates in certain competitions between women. Each of its two main springboards, the article by Keller and Moglen (1987) and the biblical story of Rachel and Leah, differently overlooks the structures of political power that shape women's relations to each other. Keller and Moglen acknowledge that politically based scarcity influences competition between feminists, but they do not investigate how class and race inflect the conflicts between the women whose stories they recount. Their theory, located in psychoanalytic discourse and familial metaphor, weights the psychology of maternal and sororal intimacies. The story of Rachel and Leah similarly evokes experiences of loss, power, and envy in the familial domain; insofar as its protagonists are sisters, their socioeconomic positions are as identical as they can be, and thus their competitiveness is rendered far more in personal than political terms.

Although my formal and theoretical approach has been to redress the balance, so that the dialogue between the personal and the political never stops, nevertheless my focus has been women's experience of competition in its unconscious and social— particularly feminist—contexts, not the political structures dividing and joining women. It's a focus I choose not only because I like it, but because I think it leads to certain kinds of truth telling that more neutrally voiced approaches preclude; it allows, even, I would say, constrains us to look at both inner and outer reality.

But there are other kinds of truth telling too, some of which may be missing here. It's in this sense that I wonder how much my textual springboards have set my discourse: Having selected the story of competing sisters, for example, I chose not to talk about another suggested text, the tale of Sarah and Hagar, of the mistress and her darker-skinned slave who became a surrogate mother for her, whose political positions are as disparate and unequal as any can be. Certainly I haven't spent any time discussing what it means to have your servant fight your battles for you by bearing your child, as Rachel and Leah did. Indeed, I recall feeling overwhelmed just thinking about the challenge of analyzing competition between women of different classes, races, sexualities, and so on, and also meshing that project with the others this chapter already takes on, the simultaneous dialogues between the psychological and the social, the literary and the theoretical.

One thing I've learned in writing this chapter is that, in contrast to the political sanctimony to which we in feminism and on the New Left have come inured, the Bible speaks in tones that are cold and clear, but somehow unjudgmental.[4] The narrator (whose gender, at one time a hot topic [Bloom and Rosenberg, 1990], I'm not qualified to discuss) looks, sees, and tells us at length about Rachel and Leah, but does not comment on this tale of love, power, and arbitrariness. For example, Rachel, it informs us, is beautiful and young, barren and dishonest, and, finally, the one whom Jacob loves. Leah, ugly and older, gets to marry first and bear her own children first, but she will never be the object of

---

[4] At least in the translation I used, the new edition put out by the Jewish Publication Society, *Tanakh: The Holy Scriptures* (1988), and recommended to me by Alice Bach.

Jacob's desire. Good and bad, the story seems to say, cycle among us, alighting here, alighting there. No one deserves, no one is undeserving. Life is difficult, and life is worth it.

Not bad, and not far from Zen, wouldn't you say? And yet, also not far from Zen, the Bible accomplishes this unmoralizing stance by ignoring its own political context, thus creating the dilemma we often encounter when the political meets the spiritual. For, if the Bible does not comment on equal or unequal justice, neither does it remark the patriarchal and generally hierarchical structure that birthed it and that we have inherited. In effect, its lack of commentary endorses the authoritarian structure in which only some men found nations, and women rarely do. This silence constitutes an unacceptable acceptance, not in the Zen-like sense of recognition, but in a more complicit sense of authorization.

I think the only way to get beyond this impasse of two necessary but contradictory voices is not to fight it, but to stay right in it, to go in, as I said at the beginning, as deep as you can, to use both voices even at the cost of confusion. I believe that the non-moralizing voice has to be juxtaposed with informed political judgment, with, you might say, morality. We have to speak in Zen-like tones of acceptance, and we have to condemn and try to change what we believe to be wrong. If you want to change what you hate, you have to love it, which does not mean that you do not struggle against it.

Once more, women's work is never done. But instead of trying to solve all the problems I've suddenly stirred up here at the end of this chapter, I'd like to make a small utopian suggestion applicable to a limited sector of life, not as a solution, but as a stimulant. And I'm going to reach for a favorite Western vision of utopia, another culture. Although contemporary college students regard anthropologists as intellectual colonialists who exploit other, non-Western cultures to understand the West itself, to search for "the primitive" in order to recover or even invent a part of ourselves (Diamond, 1974), I nevertheless think it's worth the risk of political incorrectness to take up Keller and Moglen's (1987) suggestion that we let ourselves be influenced by what we see in the Other.

What I have in mind is a system of power in which, to get power, you have to give it away. One famous example is the potlatch practiced by the Kwakiutl and other peoples of the northwest coast of North America (Benedict, 1934).[5] The potlatch is a multipurpose ceremony that individuals hold to mark momentous events in their lives, such as marriages or deaths, as well as to stake a claim in social position. As practiced before European trading systems undermined and distorted the Kwakiutl foraging ceremony, the potlatch also had the social function of reducing disparities of wealth within and, sometimes, between communities. In anticipation of the ceremony, individual men or women would accumulate a variety of goods acquired or created in the course of hunting, fishing, and trading. At the ceremony, they would give these goods away to the assembled guests. As a result of this largess, donors would start, or continue, to climb through the Kwakiutl ranking system, while recipients might inaugurate or add to a stockpile that would permit them to do the same at another time. The more things that people gave away, the greater the prestige they would obtain; hoarding, in contrast, would reduce the public esteem they merited. In effect, then, the system by which prestige was acquired encouraged people to outdo one another by giving away more than they received.

The moral of this ethnographic story is that, in some cultures, one strength cannot be converted into another, but only exchanged for another. Power may be said to exist in multiple domains in each culture—economic, political, social, representational, personal. In our culture, if you get power in one, you can get it in another. In Kwakiutl culture, you had to give up one to get another. The "more difficult it is for power to be translated from one domain to another, the less power any one individual can have over another" (Dimen-Schein, 1977, p. 212). Among the Kwakiutl and other peoples, power is held in paradoxical suspension. Power in, for example, the material domain cannot be both retained and transformed into political or symbolic power. To climb in rank, the Kwakiutl had to convert the material basis for power into prestige, which in effect meant they were underwriting their own competitors.

---

[5] The classic account of the potlatch is found in Benedict (1934). A later, ecological interpretation, rectifying Benedict's misunderstanding of the post-contact potlatches in which goods were not only given away but destroyed, is found in Suttles (1964).

As I said, a utopian suggestion. I'm not proposing we follow such a model; it wouldn't work in a society whose hierarchy is based on scarcity and private property. I'm proposing we think about a way in which we might be able to recycle power so that one strength could not be converted into another. Suppose, for example, that, in one very small group of feminists, someone who won the competition for "power over" couldn't keep the prestige (or money) it conferred on her unless it were exchanged for something like "power with" (and thereby became collective)? Suppose we had a ceremony in which the exchange took place? Suppose, in the ceremony, unevennesses could be smoothed? Reparations for the wounds of inequity could be made? Love could reunite with hate? And women could make up?

I can't imagine it. Can you?

9.   Sag Harbor, New York. August 19, 1991.
     A few days ago, I found, in that last batch of forwarded mail, a letter from Linda asking whether we might try to reconnect. The penny dropped today: she's just about to turn fifty. I'm not sure I have the same desire, but I'll meet her to clear the air, and then see where we go from there.

I make no claim to prophetic dreams. But what I tell you truly happened.

10. Sag Harbor, New York. August 1, 2002.
     On the phone with Linda speaking from her cottage in Connecticut, I said I'd finished editing the book and sent it off to The Analytic Press today.

Linda and I are friends again. Not best friends, or, at least, not each other's *only* best friend. She still has a second husband. Maybe I do, maybe I don't. We've had our struggles, our envies, our difficulties with our mutual differences. But now we know these pitfalls and can talk about them. We have survived the near-death to which fear of ambivalence once led.

I don't browse the shelves any more to see whose book is displayed. Of course, I now surf the out-of-print web sites looking for my own last, lost book, but somehow it does not occur to me to look for hers. We made up. It's OK.

9 Perversion Is Us?
Eight Notes

Note 1. How to Talk About This: Anxiety and Disgust

Just signed the contract for *Flesh and the World*," writes Michael Bronski, a culture theorist. "We had talked about my writing about blood and cutting. . . . Am I ready for this? Usually I have no trouble writing about anything in my sexual history—s/m, public sex, intimate moments with a lover, piercing, sex as a salve for death, jerking off on death beds, piss, violence. . . . It's a great subject—and the essay is sure to be mentioned in the reviews as, well, cutting edge." Ten days later: "I have no idea what tone to strike—lurid, medical, religious, psychological, confessional? . . . Assume an honest, open tone and simply describe the experiences. Don't forget to mention that it was the most potent sexual stimulation I have ever encountered. Leave out the fact that we were on drugs (you wouldn't want to give cutting and blood sports a bad name)" [Bronski, 2001a, pp. 279–280].

What a tone to strike indeed? I was glad to find in Bronski (2001b)—a man who practices what (he agrees) would surely be named a perversion (p. 309)—the uneasiness that I, whose perversities do not run in this particular direction, feel, too. This chapter was not easy to write. It's not your usual essay. It is a set of notes, excerpts from clinical reports of my own, literary essays, psychoanalytic theory, notes accompanied by commentary, free association, developed thoughts, fragments of theory—a recursive form that mirrors and predicts my topic. Perversion in the context of multiplicity and discontinuity is a discursive construct that, when examined, begins to fall apart so that we must wonder, why do we still talk about it?

In a way, notes make an end run around anxiety. And anxiety shows up a lot around sex. You may not agree with Bronski's (2001a) assertion that "everyone likes . . . slasher films where sex and anxiety are bound together and released in the spattering of red fluid" (p. 280), but hundreds of millions of box-office dollars can't be all wrong. As Sallie Tisdale (1994) a Buddhist whose *Talk Dirty to Me* made *Newsweek* headlines, wrote, "The merging of two into one in orgasm, this blending of identity, combines bliss and anxiety in a strange stew" (p. 281). Sounds a little like writing, actually. But to write a coherent essay, you have to think in a straight line. When, in contrast, you write notes, you jig and jog, zig along until you meet anxiety and then zag away in another direction, hoping to come back to that anxious spot from another angle, sparking this thought here and that feeling there and that idea way over there, hoping that this little bit of fireworks will end in a pattern of power and significance. Anyway, it is more my mode to open questions up, not to answer them. "Psychoanalysis," Lawrence Jacobson (personal communication, 1997) says, "is not an answer, it's a question." Unanswered questions court anxiety. Anxiety, discovered a friend just embarked on the psychoanalytic journey, is a tool for change.

Perversion is a topic rife with anxiety. Tisdale (1996) is probably right when she says, "We all have an edge, a place where we are bothered." We can see this anxiety in Bronski's writing, which, notelike, combines excerpts from his journal with excerpts from his essay-in-progress. Puzzled by anxiety's presence, Bronski (2001a) reminds himself and us about his participation in other transgressions, "s/m, public sex, intimate moments with a lover, piercing, sex as a salve for death, jerking off on death beds, piss, violence." This anxiety shows up in psychoanalytic writing, too. I have in mind here some of the most significant recent thought about perversion—the work of Bach, Chasseguet-Smirgel, Kernberg, and Khan—which I want to use, historicize, and critique. Sometimes this anxiety is handled by demonizing the pervert on behalf of Western civilization, as in Chasseguet-Smirgel's (1985) *Creativity and Perversion*. Sometimes it is stilled by bringing perversion into the safe precincts of matrimony, as in Kernberg's (1995) *Love Relations,* or love, as in Bach's (1995) *The Language of Perversion and the Language of Love.* And always, even in Khan's (1979) extraordinary essay on foreskin fetishism, the anxiety is relieved by exclusion, so that however empathically the pervert patient is comprehended, the pervert is still the other guy doing alien and even disgusting albeit (or therefore) fascinating things. Perversion may be defined, after all, as the sex that you like and I don't.

Cutting and bloodletting. Are these perversions perversions—transgressions to end all transgressions, *la crème de la crème*? Do sexual blood sports carry the anxiety and shame, the stigma and danger, the horror and *frissons* formerly associated with your run-of-the-mill perversion? Maybe stigma leaps from practice to practice just as genes in certain species of corn jump from chromosome to chromosome (Keller, 1983). Homosexuality, for example, came off the diagnostic books quite some time ago, even if in the minds of some people, including analysts, it remains a perversion. Maybe, as the stigma lifts from one marginal sexual practice, it doesn't disappear but alights on another—from homosexuality to bondage and domination to bloodletting, from bloodletting to . . .

Do visions of slippery slopes enter your minds? Throughout these notes, I am noting anxious moments, and this is one: stigma lurks.

Our collective relationship to perversion is, we might put it, one of projective identification. Perhaps perversion brews anxiety because, as Stoller (1975) sympathetically suggests during the "sexual revolution," we depend on it to hold what we cannot bear to remember about ourselves. It fascinates endlessly because it serves multiple psychic and social functions. For the individual, Stoller opines, perverse practices redress the ancient humiliations of childhood. For the family, perversion siphons off aggression, serving as a scapegoat by containing the cruelty and hatred threatening family integrity and security. By thus preserving the family, it conserves a cultural cornerstone and, therefore, society itself. At the same time, Stoller contends, perversion, by soaking up the anxiety and aggression brought on by oedipal rigors, safeguards heterosexuality and, therefore, the species. Absent a sponge for the anger, resentment, and hostility generated by oedipal competitiveness, these agonistic affects fester, contaminating the desire for the opposite-sexed other required by reproductive sexuality. Does what Ferenczi (1933) darkly dubs "the hate-impregnated love of adult mating" (p. 206) require sanitizing?

What sex was to the 19th century, perversion is to us now. Once upon a time, sex situated taboo, transgression, stigma, shame, excitement, dangerous pleasure, anxiety. A century of revolutionary sexual thought and a generation of revolutionary sexual practice later, sex is at least officially disarmed. If Barney Frank is in Congress, where can the frontier lie? Now the kids pierce noses, tongues, and eyebrows (forget earlobes!) and tattoo everything—an intimate erotics of body and rebellion, the dark side of which shows up in the self-mutilations that some (Egan, 1997) deem adolescent self-hatred.

A moment of anxiety. Don't mention children and perversion in the same breath.

Note 2. Pathology and Suffering, Shame and Pain

When, three years ago, I asked Dr. MH whether I might use material from our work together for this chapter, he consented. Two days later, he said that, while he still felt comfortable with my writing about him, he found himself in a bit of shock. That I had included him as a pervert opened his eyes: "I had thought it was OK, depathologized. But now . . ." He trailed off, and I filled in: "It says something is wrong."

How do shame and suffering become one? When MH, with whom I have worked three times weekly for slightly more than five years (three years at the original time of writing), said "I had thought it was OK, depathologized. But now . . . ," his anxiety registered, in part, the ambiguous power of diagnosis. In the matter of mind—as opposed to body—to pathologize is simultaneously to identify the illness that needs cure and to stigmatize the badness that causes shame. From a Foucauldian perspective, this doubled power inheres in all disciplinary institutions. Schools and the education system, government and its manifold activities, prisons and the correctional system, hospitals and the medical system, the mental health care system and what the French call *les psy*—all these organized practices have a doubled power, the power to name and the power to blame.

How often one's patients express the anguished fear: "There is something wrong with me!" Not a few analysts had it, too, when they were patients—the fear that you are a fundamentally and irreparably flawed human being, damaged goods, not even human in fact, something unwholesome and decaying at your core. "There is something wrong with me" is a cry of shame, the narcissistic injury for which there are no words—the injury that, because it inhabits the Real and lacks representation (Žižek, 1996), often turns concrete, mutating into psychical or physical harm to self or others. MH complains of frightening fantasies of violence, of occasional outbursts of rage in the dangerous neighborhoods to which his clinical work takes him.

What is the "it" that MH (whose sexual interests I have altered) thought had been pathologized? This "it" is, at least on the face of it, not singular but plural. Included are erotic fantasies and practices of beating; fetishes, including shiny belts and photographs; the payment of money (itself possibly a fetish) for beatings as well as for massages and handjobs; secrets and deceptions (the enlistment of putatively unwilling partners into beating scenarios); exhibitionism and voyeurism while cruising; the photographing of consenting and unsuspecting subjects whose body type, rarely found, meets MH's needs; the secret touching of a shiny belt worn by someone with just such a special body. When, upon first consulting me, MH told me he was a pervert, he did not have in mind his overeating and overdrinking, although he was nearly as ashamed of these practices as he was of the others— and we might want to think of them as what Louise Kaplan (1991), writing in the feminist tradition, calls "female perversions."

How can MH remember that something is wrong without feeling bad about himself? He entered treatment having self-pathologized. A mental health professional, he knows a sexual perversion when he sees one. He also knows full well what people in general but also psychoanalysts in particular think about perversion—the uneasy mix of clinical and moral evaluation, the cloud of shame in which perversities are practiced and studied, the anxieties they provoke. He hasn't read Chasseguet-Smirgel's (1985) *Creativity and Perversion* and, he suggests, probably never will—he read this chapter but thought it too dense—but he would find right there a mirror for his self-hate: for Chasseguet-Smirgel, "perversion is the equivalent of Devil religion" (p. 9). MH came of age in the 1970s, during that decade's sexual free-for-all, an epoch against which *Creativity and Perversion* must be read. Saving civilization by reinforcing traditional signs of purity and danger (Douglas, 1970), this near jeremiad sounds a clarion call for a certain personal and moral sanity—and, I would hazard, purity, if we recall that the Latin *sanitas* means "cleanliness"—in the face of a presumed cultural degeneration.

In Chasseguet-Smirgel's (1985) view, perversion degrades psyche and culture alike. Out of de Sade's texts she distills a definition: the pervert wishes to obliterate the distinctions on which psychic structures and social orders depend. The pervert makes a double erosion—of the difference between the sexes and of that between the generations. Chasseguet-Smirgel points out that sex, in the Sadean texts, takes place not within the heterosexual adult couple but all over the place—between males and females, between males, between females, between adults and children. As dualism dissolves, disorder is created, and, as borders are violated, pollution prevails. Things out of place soil, Douglas (1970) maintains in her ethnographic treatise on pollution, and Chasseguet-Smirgel (1985), in turn, deems such soiling the goal of perversion, which, in its confusion of the sexes and generations and its proliferation of multiple sexual acts, goals, and pleasures, lives defiantly in the anal phase. It chews everything up, reduces everything to excrement, and thus embodies "a system of values [that] is only the first stage in an operation whose end is the destruction of all values" (p. 10).

Ouch. I don't doubt the hatred that wants to obliterate, the despair that annihilates. As a literary effort, *Creativity and Perversion* succeeds quite well: it riles you up and thereby captures perversion's intensity. At the same time, however, its formulations do not do much beyond demonizing perverts and amplifying self-disgust. There is a glitch, a contradiction, at the book's core. The theory of perversion advocated by it departs boldly from classical formulations, but the theory of the clinical subject by which it implicitly abides lags behind. In its view, not oedipal but narcissistic dilemmas generate the perverse solution. The inability to sustain loss, inadequacy, castration, and death; troubles of identity, of the fusion of ego and nonego, of the differentiation of self and other—these issues, unresolved, may find expression in perverse sexual practices. Although this argument sounds sympathetic to the narcissistic patient—we are all, Chasseguet-Smirgel (1985) announces early on (p. 26), open to the perverse solution because

it soothes wounded narcissism—*Creativity and Perversion* speaks
as superego to id. Distilling its definition of perversion from the
Sadean corpus produces an odd clinical picture: the crippled
narcissist, whether hero or villain, is a mature adult who can be
held to account for his ignorance of shared values. The patient is
deemed responsible in a way that, Mitchell (2000) argues,
contravenes the request that analysts, who agree to hold up the
side of reason, make of their patients—to surrender "to love and
hate with abandon" (p. 133). ⎯

In *Creativity and Perversion* (e.g., Chassequet-Smirgel, 1985,
p. 34), narcissistic perverts always fall short when compared with
neurotics. Those who relate examination dreams, for example,
might benefit from an interpretation of their wish for
unconditional acceptance. What they hear, however, is that they
wish to escape the law (pp. 30–34). Here patients are not said to
seek recognition or selfhood or connection. Rather, they are driven
by sex and aggression, especially the wish to ruin the parental
coupling. In *Creativity and Perversion,* intersubjectivity begets
no explicit clinical or theoretical attention (see Chapters 4–6, this
volume). On one occasion, Chasseguet-Smirgel tells us how she
felt, for example, speechless and ground up, experiencing, one
might propose, a sort of annihilation anxiety in the
countertransference (p. 112). With pervert patients, who are said
here to take the analyst's words as seduction or attack but never
interpretation, there lacks, she justifiably claimed, a space, a depth,
a third dimension—what Winnicott termed intermediate space.
"In such a situation," Chasseguet-Smirgel writes, "there are not
three persons—the analyst and the 'normal' part of the analysand,
investigating, and taking care together of the sick part of the
analysand" (p. 111). Instead, there is an excremental mess made
of parts of both analyst and patient—a mess that can paralyze the
analyst's mind.

But consider Chasseguet-Smirgel's take on her countertransference. It is as though the unsettlement is induced, solely
the patient's fault. Or at least Chasseguet-Smirgel neither
entertains the utility of a two-person psychology to illuminate
this impasse nor allows that she had brought any feeling or idea
or history of her own to it. Yet, if the message of her book holds—
that perversion shakes civilization to its core—then the analyst
herself must feel some unease even before she meets the pervert

patient. Perverse sexual practices challenge just those fundamental cultural values that orbit on the procreating couple and, in Chasseguet-Smirgel's view, anchor Western civilization. And it is clear that her clinical philosophy centers on these values: Hating life, perverts do not accept the primal scene as likely to produce a child and therefore cannot "form . . . a couple with the analyst so as to give birth to a child that would be themselves, re-created" (p. 116).

Yet what of the analyst's hatred? Or love? What of the analyst's reflection on these inevitable emotions? They do not show up in *Creativity and Perversion*. This absence creates a knot of affect, subjectivity, intersubjectivity, and the meaning of perversion. In Chasseguet-Smirgel's account, the bounded, cogitating, omniscient analyst stands front and center. Nowhere to be found, however, is the analyst who reflects on the personal and clinical (not to say cultural) meaning (Chodorow, 2000) of her feelings, who in the chaotic clinical mix of part-selves might be able to identify with the patient. Absent these dimensions of the analyst's subjectivity, the patient's subjectivity finds no purchase. Subjectivity is a shared state of mind. Residing not only in each being, but also in the space between, it is evoked in each person by the other. Benjamin's (1998) proposal that recognition of that other subject is the point of the psychoanalytic process seems spot-on. Stein's (2000) account of her own chaotic countertransference to a patient struggling with love, hate, and perversion illustrates how an analyst might go about this recognition without reifying or diminishing the patient.

That this recognition takes place through affect (Stein, 1991; Spezzano, 1993) complicates matters. Affects, to come at the problem from the other side, are by nature intersubjective. As Mitchell (2000) and Morrison (1989) see it, they are highly contagious. Lacking floors and ceilings, walls and doors and windows, they cannot but be interpersonal. Constituting the atmosphere of early object-relational life, affects challenge the dichotomizing separateness of "I" on which conventional "constructions of subjectivity, and the personal and cultural values associated with them, depend. In, for example, "anxiety, sexual excitement, rage, depression, and euphoria," Mitchell (2000, p. 61) writes, it is often impossible to say which person started what. So when the pervert patient is said to be hateful, might it be difficult to tell in whom the hatred first arose?

The analyst needs her theory of perversion (if this is a concept she requires in order to think about sexuality), but she also needs to know both what she feels about perversion—its affective meaning to her and the values embedded in that meaning—and what those perverse practices mean to her patients (see Stein, 2000). And then she needs to know how these two subjectivities together produce and reproduce the transference neurosis, the third space through which the analytic cure, such as it is, takes place.

Certainly Chasseguet-Smirgel's patient enjoyed grinding her up, but what, one might have asked, is this enjoyment all about? If chewing can be destructive, it can also be creative (Winnicott, 1969a, b): If you want to grind someone up, you may want to kill them, but you may also wish to take them in so as to metabolize their identity and thereby grow an identity of your own. Not to concern yourself with what perversion means to a particular patient is, in fact, to enact what Bach (1995) and Ogden (1989) would regard as a perversion of your own—to reduce your patient to a nonentity by annihilating his or her subjectivity, to confuse what the patient means to you with what the patient means to himself or herself, and thereby to violate the patient's (emergent) boundaries. This is an act of power and knowledge not without its own pleasures (Foucault, 1976).

To think in the way I am proposing requires a therapeutic balancing act. Maybe you don't like perverse sexual practices, but that's not your business. Assuming that no work gets done when an inclination, practice, or pleasure is cloaked in shame and disgust—when the superego shames the id, inciting further resistance—my initial clinical goal with MH was to question the self-loathing that clings to his practices like a stink. Trying to hold all my responses in mind, I negotiate between acceptance and rejection, attraction and repulsion, curiosity, disgust, and boredom—a sort of guarded neutrality, if what we mean these days by neutrality is some point of balance (see Greenberg, 1993, for a related idea). Neutral in the *I Ching* sense of "no blame": I try to stay the Zen course of accepting what exists because it exists. Guarded in the sense of analytic caution: ultimately this congeries of shame, disgust, and excitement, which no neutrality of mine can ever excise from a patient's or analyst's psyche or from their culture, must itself be explored.

But you can't do this condescendingly, as though one day your patient will scale the heterosexual heights. You really have to believe that his solution—the body type, the nongenital erotic practices, the genital contact acquired on the sly and through commerce—is, other things being equal, viable. MH needs to have his practices and preferences and affects protected and guarded, kept safe and whole, until he can decide whether he wants to keep them or change them or let them go. But he can't explore his shame until he feels safe enough to find out what's wrong, until he feels sufficiently acceptable to look at it without becoming it, to stand in the spaces (Bromberg, 1998) between his shamed and shaming states of mind.

Note 3. What Is a Perversion?

> Another difficulty arises from the circumstance that there is so often associated with the erotic relationship, over and above its own sadistic components, a quota of plain inclination to aggression. The love object will not always view these complications with the degree of understanding and tolerance shown by the peasant woman who complained that her husband did not love her any more, since he had not beaten her for a week [Freud, 1930, p. 105 n. 3].

Now, I don't suppose that anyone has previously taken this footnote, which you have already seen cited in Chapter 4, as relevant to perversion. You would more likely use it as Freud meant you to—as an example of the "quota of plain inclination to aggression" bedeviling us all. Aggression is not, however, a found object, a plain natural phenomenon; it is as constructed as we now understand sex to be. As Freud told the story, aggression has, to my mind, a rather perverse distribution. A woman waits for a man to exercise aggression, which to her signifies love. To turn this formulation around, the man agents aggression, and the woman receives it—he the subject and she the object. For him to love is to give aggression; for her to be loved is to get it. He is active, she is passive. He does, she is done to. Sound familiar? Why are we not surprised?

I will hold off on the obvious gender implications of this construction of aggression and power in Freud's thought. I want first to pull out another thread. When I began work with a supervisee whose problem was a difficult countertransference to a patient's sexual perversion, I asked what the perversion was. The supervisee missed a beat, then replied as though the answer were self-evident: "Sadomasochism." Specifically, the patient engaged in practices of bondage and domination and had as well elaborate fantasies of torture dramatized in photographs and videos. As we know that versions of perversion exist, however, we need to ask why perversion is often equated to sadomasochism as a matter of course.

A signifying chain links perversion, sadomasochism, gender, and power. Let me put this differently. In keeping with the *fin de dix-neuvième siècle* discovery that the abnormal reveals the normal, Freud (1905b) begins his "Three Essays on the Theory of Sexuality" with "The Sexual Aberrations." What he did not see, and what the second Wave of feminism, especially psychoanalytic feminism, did, is that the sexual order to which the aberrations and perversions were central is equally a gendered order. In psychoanalytic feminist view, gender is "no longer a consequence" (Goldner, 2003) of mind or body or culture but is, like domination in general, a principle informing all; it is "everywhere and nowhere" (Bourdieu and Eagleton, 1992, p. 115). Produced by patriarchy and heterosexuality, it is also always a matter of power—an argument too long and complicated for me to make here (Firestone, 1970; Millett, 1970)—a fact that certain psycho-analytic applications of gender theory tend to forget (e.g., Sweetnam, 1996, 1999).

Returning to Freud's "joke" about the peasant woman and her complaint, we may wonder whether sadomasochism and, next to it, aggression, as constructed in both psychoanalysis and culture, are always and everywhere gendered. I am not the first to indicate the paradox: all Freud's case examples of feminine masochism are men. As Kaplan (1991) put it: "The sexual perversions . . . are pathologies of gender stereotyping" (p. 196). Benjamin's (1988b) elaborate work on the interface of gender, subjectivity, domination, and masochism remains classic. Look at it this way: if gender as an elemental structure of dominance and subordination is so critical to psyche, soma, and culture, is it any wonder that we think of perversion as inevitably sadomasochistic?

Listen to the mix of sex, gender, and power in MH's fantasy: "I really am a ninny, a squirmy little faggot. . . . I am having a fantasy

of the heat pipe as a penis going into the ceiling. I am thinking of
men buttfucking each other. Then I think of Romans with helmets
on." I say, "They wouldn't be ninnies, would they?" "I hadn't
thought of that." "The wish to have those desires and not feel
like a ninny, to feel like a warrior." "Wanting to be taken care of is
to be a ninny. . . . That's part of men's attraction to women,
cuddling up, being taken care of, but real men take care of
women." So are real women ninnies? In a power structure,
someone has to be the ninny. In a power structure, weakness and
longings for closeness—call them ninniness and tenderness—tend
to fuse. In his transferential longings for care, does MH feel like a
ninny with me? Does he think I think his need for me makes him
a squirmy little faggot? I shall return to MH's longing for
tenderness, which is so crucial to current thinking about perversion
(Benjamin, 1988b).

Is wife battering a perversion? Like Freud's peasant woman,
Ms. NK, a painter, described the most satisfying sexual intercourse
as what she's had after her lover has beaten her up. Perhaps, she
wonders, the combustion of sex and violence originates in the
beating she got as a six-year-old at her mother's hands, a
punishment for drawing on the walls of her bedroom. Or possibly
it stems from her father's denied lust for her, manifested in his
humiliating attack on her teenage sexuality (one day he tried to
pull her shorts off in front of her brothers). The influence of
feminism on psychoanalysis, muses culture theorist Apter (1992b),

> may be shifting . . . what qualifies as perverse. Whereas traditionally
> attention has been devoted to determining the epistemological
> boundaries between, for example, sadism and masochism . . . , rape,
> abuse, incest and other forms of violence . . . may now increasingly
> come to be theorized psychoanalytically as forms of perversion
> [p. 313].

If, as Goldner (n.d.), cofounder of the Intimate Violence Project
at the Ackerman Institute, tells us, "one-third of all [heterosexual]
women will, at some point in their lives, be physically assaulted
by an intimate male partner—slapped, kicked, beaten, choked or
attacked with a weapon" (p. 6), that makes physical abuse almost
normative for the culture in general and for heterosexuality,
marriage, and (given that abuse is no stranger to homosexual
households either) even attachment in particular. If aggressive sex

and eroticized aggression are so at home in the nuclear family, can we say that the abnormal is at home in the normal?

Freud's joke about wife battering is a joke about power that also performs power, and the performance is patriarchal. Is it perverse of Freud to illuminate a shady sexual pleasure by attributing it to his social inferiors? Why else would he think it funny to tell a joke about a peasant woman waiting to be beaten? Yes, we all know that Freud was a man of his time, but, you know, he is also a man of our time. And I do know that television host Bill Maher would lampoon me—that is, if these notes were of any interest to the Nielsen ratings—for political correctness. Freud's humor at her expense (wit being, as he [1905c] said, a form of aggression) makes use of a binary—us (males) on high versus them (females) down below—that appears frequently in the psycho-analytic discourse on perversion; recall Chasseguet-Smirgel's (1985) distinction between the pervert and "ourselves" (p. 34).

Caution: regulatory practice at work. That's how Foucault (1976, *passim*) would put it. After the Catholic church, psycho-analysis is, in his thought, perhaps the exemplary disciplinary power—its pronouncements routinely enforcing social injustice through the apparent neutrality of objective science. Psychoanalysts are systematicallly caught in the clinical dilemma that I indicated earlier: the power to name is also the power to blame and to shame. It is not far-fetched to think that Freud, for example, was using this anonymous couple as a rhetorical device to needle the sexually uptight Europeans who constituted his audience. One job of psychoanalysis is, after all, to reveal to the suffering the thing that, denied, sickens them. Doing it at the expense of those who can't talk back is, however, the ultimate in bullying. How tenacious Freud's misogyny is, how on the beaten track is his class pride, and how truly ambivalent is his attachment to sexuality. When he implies to his readers that they like the same sexual practices as the lower orders do (see Chapter 4), he simultaneously liberates and imprisons, frees by naming and binds by shaming.

Note 4. Accepting/Disowning the Perverse in the Normal

No healthy person, it appears, can fail to make some addition that might be called perverse to the normal sexual aim [Freud, 1905b, p. 160].

It is difficult to comprehend the idea of perversion otherwise than by reference to a norm [Laplanche and Pontalis, 1967, p. 306].

In the shadow of the normal has lurked the specter of the pathological [Haraway 1989, p. 358].

Well, you can't say it much more loudly or clearly than that. Perversion is culturally constructed. By this, I do not mean the crude misapprehension that psyche is culture's clone. Rather, perversion links with a set of meanings and practices that render each other intelligible and habitable. To label something a perversion is simultaneously to identify something else not perverse. The normal, what does not need to be said because it goes without saying, serves in this discourse as a residual category. For example, Freud (1905b) defines his somewhat coy but ubiquitous and textually crucial locution, "the sex act," only once and nearly offhandedly, about 10 pages into his first chapter: We may think of the "normal sexual aim . . . as . . . the union of the genitals in the act known as copulation" (p. 149). On the next page, after pointing out that kissing is not a perversion even though it does not involve the sexual apparatus but rather mucus membranes that constitute the portal to the digestive tract, Freud defines perversions as

sexual activities which either (a) extend, in an anatomical sense, beyond the regions of the body that are designed for sexual union, or (b) linger over the intermediate relations to the sexual object which should normally be traversed rapidly on the path towards the final sexual aim [p. 150].

There's no way around it. Freud argues with but ends up joining Krafft-Ebing, who said, "Every expression of [the sexual instinct] that does not correspond with the purpose of nature—i.e., propagation—must be regarded as perverse" (cited in Davidson, 1987, p. 39). The normal is the heterosexual, the coital, the reproductive. Abelove (1991), a European historian covering the topic of sexuality, calls it "cross-sex genital intercourse" or "intercourse so-called": "penis in vagina, vagina around penis, with seminal emission uninterrupted" (p. 337). I call it PIV— penis in vagina.

Perversion and that inadequately specific term *normality* construct each other. Perversion is necessary in more ways than Stoller (1975) imagines. How do you know what's normal unless you know what's not, unless you have a boundary? How do you know what's not normal unless you know what is? In the discourse of psychosexuality, perversion and heteronormality constitute each other's limits. Perversion marks the boundary across which you become an outlaw. Normality marks off the territory that, if stayed inside, keeps you safe from shame, disgust, and anxiety.

The binary thus formed is, however, only illusorily clear. Even people who engage in normal sexuality, Freud says, tend to include a perverse moment or two in their ordinary sexual practice—a position that, we shall see, Kernberg shares, sort of. And they don't even find it a problem:

> Everyday experience has shown that most of these extensions, or at any rate, the less severe of them, are constituents which are rarely absent from the sexual life of healthy people, and are judged by them no differently from other intimate events [Freud, 1905b, p. 160].

Do you recognize yourself here? As a matter of course, Freud says, the sexual instinct enjoys overriding disgust. Perhaps, suggests de Lauretis (1994, p. 24), Freud deems the perversions positive; after all, the perverts, like the woman in "A Case of Paranoia" (1915) or "Leonardo da Vinci" (1910) or the unnamed homosexual woman (Freud, 1920), were not ill. Indeed, they lived functional if not happy lives, in contrast to the neurotics and hysterics who came to him because they could not live at all, for whom the solution was to transform "hysterical misery into ordinary unhappiness" (Breuer and Freud, 1893–1895, p. 305).

Note 5. Fixity and Flexibility

> If, in short, a perversion has the characteristics of exclusiveness and fixation—then we shall usually be justified in regarding it as a pathological symptom [Freud, 1905b, p. 161].

Not only civilization, psychology, too, has great difficulty, where borderline cases are concerned, in distinguishing with confidence what is still part of normal sexuality, what is perverse and what is neurotic or psychotic. . . . For instance, is it normal or not to demand that the love object must be tall or petite, fair or dark, very bright or rather simple, domineering or submissive, and so on? Perhaps we may accept the conditions just quoted as normal; when they exact that a woman limp or even have a false leg, or that the man wear spectacles, or that the woman wear black underwear during coitus, the difficulty of drawing the boundary becomes greater [Balint, 1956, p. 20].

Is it normal or abnormal to insist that the love object be only one gender or another? I remember during psychoanalytic training, around 1980, a discussion of a homosexual woman being treated by one of our male candidates. He was professing his liberalism: "I have no problem with her being a lesbian. [You can already hear the excess of protest, of course.] It's just that she's restricting her choices." I don't think anyone mentioned what Balint (1956) had noticed 25 years earlier—that those who are exclusively heterosexual restrict their choices, too.

Now that psychoanalysis has welcomed into the fold of mental health the homosexual as well as the heterosexual, how will we define illness in the sexual domain? Many have fixed on the criterion of flexibility. Khan (1979) observes "the limited nature of the fantasies of the fetishist" (p. 143). Kaplan (1991) and McDougall (1995) argue also for flexibility as a criterion of mental health. This criterion makes sense. Kaplan remarks on "the inherent flexibility" (p. 506) of our sexual nature—a flexibility that, according to Lacan (1977), defines desire. Lacan would contrast desire with need: need, like hunger, must have one thing and one thing only, food. Desire thrives on substitutes. It may be satisfied or deferred, turned into pleasure or babies or buildings or bombs. It may accept a blow job or PIV or a beating, a fantasy or a body, a belt or a breast or a picture, a male or a female or a transvestite.

Truth to tell, though, human beings aren't the only flexible sexuals, and they are not all that flexible either. For example, the sexuality of the Bonobo apes is far more versatile, serving not only as a source of pleasure, a means to procreation, or a tension-release mechanism, but as a tool of social cohesion and an expression of dominance and subordination (de Waal and Lanting,

1997). The Bonobo have intercourse, genital-to-genital contact, fellatio, and mutual masturbation, although anal intercourse has never been observed. Whether female with male, or male with male, or female with female, they do it variously, back to belly as well as belly to belly. They kiss and French kiss, they cuddle and groom and then go off to eat, or they do sex until they orgasm. Erotic excitement pops up at a great variety of moments, most notably, de Waal and Lanting think, when individuals are starting to compete for food or a sexual partner. Erections; "GG-rubbing" (clitoris moving against clitoris); mutual scrotal massage; pressing genitals against nongenital body parts—all these erotic events and acts "change the tone of the encounter" (pp. 109–110). They stop aggression before it spirals into fights that disrupt the group. Bonobo social life "is peppered," every 90 minutes or so, by brief moments of sexual activity (de Waal and Lanting, 1997, 105).

Human sexual limits stand out in contrast. In the 1960s, we said, "If it moves, fuck it." Most of us, of course, didn't do that at all, or, if we did, it was for about five minutes. Balint (1956), among others, notices that sexual preference is really not catholic, hardly ecumenical at all. Person (1980) maintains that most adult fantasies are fixed. Our "sex-prints" (p. 618; see also Stoller's, 1979, idea of sexual scripts) are not only individualized but quite unvarying and as such ground identity in a fluid society. Sexuality, at least in a utopian view of it, would seem indeed to be able to occupy a third place between fixity and freedom, one in which both the *jouissance* of the margin and the safety of the center obtain (see Corbett, 2001b, for a similar vision).

Are we all a little bit perverse? Well, so some argue, although not always in the most charitable way. Let's return to Chasseguet-Smirgel (1985) here and put off an evaluation of Kernberg's contribution just a little bit longer. Chasseguet-Smirgel says, "Perversions [are] a dimension of the human psyche in general, a temptation in the mind common to us all" (p. 1). As we have seen, however, her "we" is not so ecumenical as it sounds; it's really a dualism, not a pluralism. Unlike "us," for example, perverts hate the truth. "The perverse solution," she insists, "tempts us to replace the love for truth with 'a taste for sham'" (p. 26), a temptation to which "they" yield. I would have her consider Bronski's (2002a) struggle between his wish to represent the sexiness of cutting and . . . well, hear him out:

Journal entry of two days ago is complete shit. I know perfectly well what is missing from the essay: honesty and truth. . . . What am I leaving out? That as much as I loved Jim, I thought he was fucked up about sex and his own sexual desires? That his s/m practices, including cutting, were mostly vain attempts to break through the crushing repression of his southern boyhood and his horrible feelings about himself? That for the first year we were together (out of five) he would have to leave the room after coming, so he could be alone? That some of these times he cried?. . . The romanticism of our blood games—and my presentation of it—is countered by the fact that there was often blood dripped all over the floor and furniture from other men he brought home [p. 284].

A moment of anxiety. "Blood, mother, blood," cried Tony Perkins in *Psycho* in 1960. "Blood and AIDS!" we scream now.

Well, but who doesn't lie about their sexual pleasure? Bill Clinton's not alone here, you know. A patient once allowed that she liked being fucked from behind while in a forward bend. I asked her what she liked about it. She didn't answer. "Sex is funny that way," was all she wanted to say. Is there nothing you are ashamed of? As Tisdale (1994) puts it, "Tongues loosen during orgasm, things get said that would never be said otherwise" (p. 280). Remember Gordon Lightfoot's verse about the room where you do what you don't confess? Shame, excitement, pleasure, the overriding of disgust. And why *should* you confess?

Still, viewed from another angle, Chasseguet-Smirgel's (1985) diagnosis may contain a truth that her truth cannot encompass. Replying to a discussion of "Dr. Fell" (Dimen, 2002), Bronski (2002b) refers to my criticism of Chasseguet-Smirgel's assertion, shared culturally, that "perverts hate the truth." Surprisingly, however, Bronski retorts, "This phrase to me is delicious for, ironically, as a pervert, I believe it to be completely true" (p. 309). Perverts do hate the truth, he insists, but what truth is that? Chasseguet-Smirgel's idea works, Bronski suggests, because the pervert is always on the outside, always the other: "The 'truth,' as it is so carefully and lovingly called, is almost always what is held as a cherished belief by those in the dominant culture: those with power, those who have the power to name—and, as it follows, to name-call" (pp. 308–309). Truth, in Foucauldian view, is an effect of power, a form of domination that *les psy* embody in characterizing perversion.

There is, you could say, a bit of projection going on: The contempt and arrogance that Chasseguet-Smirgel (1985) or, in fact, Kaplan (1991), who remarks that the pervert's self-regard is as "the one with secrets of Great Sex" (p. 41), identifies in the sexuality of perverts shows up also in the psychoanalytic discourse about perversion. So often when "we" are all said to be perverse, what is really meant is, "There but for the grace of God go I." We may be merely tempted, but they, poor wretches, give in. MH may use his hatred of his sexual desires as a form of hate speech, as an expression of his self-loathing, but so does psychoanalysis. Psychoanalysis prescribes sexual convention even as it subscribes to sexual liberation, but, in the fashion of projective identification, it splits this contradiction in two and then denies having done so, a disavowal that on occasion shows up as a bit of hate speech itself.

Indeed, it may be the details of desire, the particularities of pleasure, that most incite disgust, challenge sexual conventionality, set off the alarm. I could elaborate on MH's beating fantasies and practices, his furtive touching of belts, his Peeping Tom photography, his veiled pleas for a beating. But, I submit, these somewhat expectable instances and aspects of perversion discomfit less than what actually turns him on. MH has a very particular preference. The object of his desire is a man possessed of a strong but severe face, twinkly eyes, and white hair; a belly that protrudes just a little bit under the belt line; and thighs that spread out when he sits down, forming a lap. In a culture of thinness and fitness, I wonder whether a taste for pooched-out bellies and full thighs on elderly men is more transgressive than all the bondage and domination in the world.

A moment of anxiety. Taboo, in Douglas's (1970) view, neighbors on pollution. Shame isn't far away, either.

Perversion and normality construct each other. It is only relative to a desire like Dr. MH's that heterosexuality and homosexuality look like models of normality. MH's desire tests flexibility as a criterion for mental health, or, rather, his very specific tastes remind psychoanalysis, and the culture that embeds it, of what is projectively identified away from the norm into the marginal, the restriction of desire that, Freud (1908) said, creates civilization and mental illness in one blow (see Chapter 5). MH is anxious when we discuss his taste and the photographs he takes of men who fit his fantasy. "But you can't get what you need otherwise" is his plaint. Advertisements and, for that matter, erotica and pornography do not feature softly paunched seniors with full thighs. You could, as MH does, make a case for the bellied woman in the body of the man he desires. But can you also entertain this? Maybe it's MH who is on the side of health. The rest of us, who hate the signs of age in ourselves and others—the softening flesh, spreading bellies, graying hair—defend against our certain death by fixating on the billboarded thin young people whom we would be so happy to resemble. To rewrite Laplanche and Pontalis (1967), "It is difficult to comprehend the idea of the norm otherwise than by reference to a perversion" (p. 306).

The discourse on perversion, I have been contending, seethes with moralism, my own included. I want to ask for a moment of cultural relativism, that moralistic discourse par excellence. Suppose MH had lived in 19th-century Euro-America, in which men's portliness, a form of conspicuous consumption, signaled prosperity. Or, as Lawrence Jacobson (personal communication, 1999) asked me, if MH had lived there and then, would he have been turned on by emaciation? Consider the following. While conducting graduate archival research, EL (described in Chapter 6) lived in an inexpensive, immigrant quarter of Paris. A white woman of some 250 pounds (an avoirdupois, you recall, that she unconsciously hoped would keep her from being an object of desire and that she later slimmed by stomach-stapling), she was troubled by the evident delight of North African men who gasped, in patriarchal pleasure, *"Une grosse femme."* Sexism is sexism, no? or No? In *Reconstructing Gender: A Multicultural Anthology* is Christy Haubegger's (1997) essay, "I'm Not Fat, I'm Latina." Or, as someone who heard me deliver this chapter orally complained, is this comparison racist?

Anxiety. You will think me a moral relativist, someone for whom all bets are off, no law applies, anything goes, from bloodletting to child abuse to . . .

Note 6. Fetishism and the Paradigm Shift

[The] meaning and purpose of the fetish . . . is [to] substitute for the woman's (the mother's) penis that the little boy once believed in and—for reasons familiar to us—"does not want to give up" [Freud, 1927, pp. 152–153].

Fetishism is a state of omnipotently but precariously controlled mania. Hence it is at once intensely pleasurable and frightfully vulnerable [Khan, 1979, p. 165].

Perhaps because we are all fetishists in one way or another, as Balint (1956) suggests, fetishism occupies an ambiguous place in the psychoanalytic theory of perversions. Sometimes it belongs, sometimes it is excluded. In the classical view, fetishism is not a perversion, because the fetish is what enables a man to be heterosexual, not homosexual. The fetish, symbolizing the mother's penis, demonstrates that castration does not happen: Mother still has her penis. With his fetish close at hand, then, he need not flee women for the imagined safety of another man and his penis. Rather, standing in for the destructive, uncannily penisless vagina so feared by the boy is, say, a leather boot the man insists his wife wear before they have sex, or a bit of fur he caresses, or the car about which he fantasizes, or the dress he wears at the kitchen sink.

This definition of fetishism held, in principle, as long as homosexuality remained a perversion. If sexual preference no longer separates the perverse from the normal, however, what happens to our understanding of fetishism? Even Balint (1956), writing 17 years before the removal of homosexuality as a diagnosis from the *Diagnostic and Statistical Manual of Mental Disorders*, argues that homosexuality is not a perversion. Why is that? His explanation is illuminating. For Balint, what determines normality is not sex but love—a stance that epitomizes the sea change that psychoanalytic thought underwent over the course of the 20th century. What drives human beings and binds them together is, to use slightly different language, attachment—not amoral, impersonal, imperious libido. Because homosexuals, Balint argues, experience "practically the whole scale of love and hatred that is exemplified in heterosexuality" (p. 17), because "all the beautiful, all the hideous, all the altruistically loving and all the egotistically exploiting features of heterosexual love can be found in homosexual love as well" (p. 17), we cannot argue for the perversity of their desire. (I could riff on the way that, even in

this prescience, heterosexuality still measures mental health:
Exactly what does "practically" mean? But never mind.)

As what we may call the *relational turn* has taken place, a new
psychoanalytic and probably cultural normality has been erected
and, along with it, a new clinical goal—not the derepression of
forbidden desire but the healing of the mutilated capacity to love.
As a one-person psychology has given way to, or at least moved
over to accommodate, a two-person psychology, fetishism, like
perversion, becomes interpretable in intersubjective space. Khan's
(1979) remarkable essay, "Fetish as Negation of the Self: Clinical
Notes on Foreskin Fetishism in a Male Homosexual," encapsulates
the paradigm shift in psychoanalytic thinking about fetishism in
particular and perversion in general. This exceptionally moving
and theoretically interesting piece of writing comprises two parts.
The first, a 30-page section, is severely difficult and is based on
the first, five-year phase of an analysis. The second, which reads
like a spare eight-page short story, arose from the second phase,
which took place a decade later.

The story behind the story told in this essay is that of the
relational turn. The first part is a Tower of Psychoanalytic Babel.
It attempts to have it all, to retain the classical model of fetishism
and sexuality while incorporating the language and findings, most
notably and rather surprisingly, of ego-psychology, as well as those
of object relations. The range of concepts includes: "ego
pathology," "the (breast) mother," "internal objects and early ego
development," "transitional object phenomena," "separation
anxiety," "pathological body-ego development," "disintegration,"
"bisexual primary identifications," "flight from incest," and
"defense against archaic anxiety affects."

In the second section, the struggle to integrate theories of
attachment and narcissism with drive theory has vanished. This
Herculean effort is no longer necessary because in the 15 years
between the two writings, from 1965 to 1979, the paradigm had
shifted. By 1979, it was possible to dispense with references to
the classical one-person model of genitality and drive and to focus
on matters of narcissistic integration and damage and of broken
and restored interpersonal relatedness, and so it was possible to
tell a simple, accessible story, a story of the negation and recovery
of self. As Khan (1979) writes, "The title of this paper reflects

largely the understanding of the fetishistic reveries and practices as we began to comprehend them in the second phase" (p. 139).

Fetishism, in Khan's (1979) view, is not about sex; it's about a state of mind. Things, or body parts, are used to regulate not sex but psychic equilibrium, which in turn is primally dependent on the quality of object relations. "What the patient had sought from his treatment was the assimilation of this manic sexual fetishistic excitement and affectivity into an ego-capacity that could be related to the self, the object, and the environment" (p. 165). The manic defense against psychic deadness, an idea Khan drew from Winnicott, defines fetishism. For this patient, it patched together the fragmentary psychic structure constituted by an idealized attachment to a highly narcissistic mother whose marital instability and depression pockmarked his early life with a series of losses. In arousing uncircumcised working-class boys against their will and ejaculating into their foreskins, Khan's patient was simultaneously repairing his mother, binding her to him, and reintegrating himself. Classically, Khan wrote, the fetish is an auxiliary means serving heterosexual gratification and defending against perversions, especially homosexuality. Postclassically, however, we could do worse than cite McDougall (1995, p. 174), even though she denies anything as disjunctive as a paradigm shift: Fetishism is a "technique . . . of psychic survival . . . required to preserve the feeling of subjective identity as well" (p. 237).

Note 7. Relatedness, Aggression, and Social Control

I feel like I'm not getting into the meet [!] of anything [MH].

I have deliberately widened the issue of perversion from one of sexual identity to one of identity in general in order to include . . . character perversions and also perverse relationships, where the other person is used as a functional or part-object. Perversion in this larger sense is a lack of capacity for whole-object love [Bach, 1995, p. 53].

What makes a good life? A good psyche? So often the answer to this question seems to depend on what a person thinks comes

first. Your idea of elemental human nature determines your idea
of mental health. With the early Freud, we postulated that sex
comes first, attachment second, and therefore the derepression of
sexuality became the clinical telos, achieved by the authoritative if
not authoritarian doctor pronouncing on the patient patient. Now,
with the relational turn, we have attachment driving drives (see
Chapters 1, 3, and 5). Now the relationship of analyst and patient,
opened up for intersubjective construction and deconstruction,
becomes a key clinical tool, object of knowledge, a goal.

"Perversion," writes Bach (1995) "is a lack of capacity for whole-
object love" (p. 53). A moment of anxiety, at least for me.
Perversion isn't about sex?

The new psychoanalytic vision of mental health, I have
suggested, matches a new cultural norm, which means really a
new morality. Specifically, it needs to be contextualized in the
"family values" ideology that came to the Euro-American fore in
the late 1980s–early 1990s as a sort of backlash against the 1960s
and 1970s. Against women's liberation, the sexual revolution, gay
liberation, and all manifestations of sexual multiplicity—the
contemporary intersex movement, for example—the nuclear family
once more stood firm, its dualisms of generation and gender intact.
That it became a political shibboleth is not psychoanalysis' concern,
but its cultural ubiquity should be. For it finds its echo and support
in every field of endeavor and investigation, including clinical and
theoretical psychoanalysis.

This sort of tangle, of values and theory and therapy, has always
been the background for everyday psychoanalysis. If sex, more
than any other matter, brings it out, perversion inflames it.
Perversion is so disturbing, so challenging of received and
ordinarily unquestioned norms. Its power to pollute the normal
reveals the sanctity with which the normal is endowed, provoking
a defense of normality, sometimes with a flare of outrage, as in
Chasseguet-Smirgel's (1985)*Creativity and Perversion,* and
sometimes with a canny redefinition of it, as in Kernberg's (1995)
Love Relations. Both these major works have been influenced by
the relational turn. Chasseguet-Smirgel, as we have seen, switches
the etiology of perversion from Oedipus to Narcissus, even though
clinically she keeps the classical faith.

Kernberg makes a somewhat different move. If Chasseguet-
Smirgel's account includes unnoticed inconsistencies between

theoretical and clinical stances issuing from the *décalage* of theory we have already seen in Khan's (1979) study of foreskin fetishism, Kernberg intentionally tries to meld the relational turn with the founding paradigm. *Love Relations* inscribes a developmental trajectory in which psychosexuality evolves as a complicated weave of corporeality, psychodynamics, and intersubjectivity. In a tour de force, Kernberg whips up a multiply-twinned solution, an integration of two capacities—for body pleasure and for "total object-relation." Kernberg (1976) writes that, at maturity, genital pleasure organizes body-surface erotism into the matrix of total object relation and complementary sexual identification (p. 185).

In this new, widely shared model, love and intimacy are the signs and criteria of health, if not health itself. If you don't have them, there's something wrong. Across the entire analytic spectrum, attachment and its vicissitudes are what we look at and look for as we sit with our patients. I am alert to it with MH. Perhaps in response to my being away one August, he said, "I feel like I'm not getting into the meat of anything." But what I wrote down in my notes was not *meat*, I wrote *meet*. As I was thinking both about this essay and about a feeling of impasse in our work, I decided (inspired by Gerson's, 1996, disclosure of his transcription error) to tell MH of my slip of the pen and to propose an interpretation: consciously he may have wanted his flesh, his meat, beat, so to speak, but unconsciously he wished to meet me, to encounter and engage me—and, further, this was an idea that did not yet seem safe to him, and so he needed me to hold it for him. To my surprise, MH agreed. He had been complaining the preceding six months that therapy had plateaued for him. He did not want to come to session. Nothing seemed to be happening. His sexual appetite had fallen off. Following my interpretation, we began speaking of his mistrust of me, of his doubt that I can hold him in mind. Now we approached the possibility of tenderness. We entertained the possibility that his fear of my pathologizing him is also a wish for me to be more critical of his sexual practices—somewhat, we thought, the way he wants to be spanked—to show him not that he is wrong but that something is wrong and needs fixing.

But I am trying to decipher what sense it makes to call MH's difficulty with love and intimacy a perversion—for that is how Bach and, I think, Kernberg, too, would label it. Interpreting sexuality in object-relational terms is now an indelible part of our view and technique. Consider Ogden's (1989) choice to "use the term 'perverse' to refer to forms of sexuality that are used in the service of denying the separateness of external objects and sexual difference, and thus interfere with the elaboration of the depressive position" (p. 166, n. 11). Perversion here still denotes sexuality, but only the sexuality that defends against object-relational dangers. What is really wrong in a perversion, then, is not sex but relatedness and, by implication, development if not character itself.

Caution: regulatory practice still at work. When perversion relocates from sex to relatedness, its moral baggage comes along. If psychoanalysis once refined polymorphously perversity into heterosexuality, now it fashions a model of mature total object relation as the criterion of mental health. Yet who among us can claim to have achieved that? Wholeness and totality in relatedness are as intimidating as a heterosexuality untroubled by the homosexuality it has renounced (Butler, 1995). Bronski (2002a), tricking with Jim, lived with Walta, "the love of my life," whom he might tell of sex on the side—as many gay men do—but not of the cutting. Do you, by the way, tell your lover everything? Vital questions of cultural value pop up here. Does whole-object love mean telling all? Some? Does the idea of whole-object love replace heterosexuality as the unachievable ideal to which we must, in aspiring, submit?

Yikes. I feel like I'm criticizing motherhood. I respect the intent of Bach's (1995) revisionism. The "capacity for whole-object love" is certainly a good thing. But it's also a case of new wine in old regulatory bottles. "There's something wrong" still turns into "There's something wrong with me," although the referent shifts from sex to love. Sure, for most of us, it's awful not to be able to love and be loved. But why call this absence, this suffering, this failure, a perversion? All that assigning this diagnosis accomplishes is to preserve a traditional discourse, perpetuate an oppression, and make people feel bad.

Must there always be stigma? "It's my body" is the claim made regarding parent-mortifying adolescent body practices such as piercing or, in the 1970s, the long hair guys sported or the bras women didn't. But adolescent rebellion may be equally cultural critique or, if you will, symptom. Perhaps kids mark themselves to remind their elders that, in our culture, stigma never disappears.

In the new family-values psychoanalysis, stigma hops from sex to relatedness, from abjected forms of sexual desire to the impaired capacity to love. Sex recedes, and relatedness steps forward, a relatedness that has its perverse and, implicitly, normal forms, a clinical as well as theoretical happenstance not without its puritan underpinnings (Green, 1996) and cultural contouring (see Chapter 5).

We return to Stoller's (1975) argument about perversion and aggression. Does psychoanalytic preoccupation, like stigma, jump from sex to love because of an uncontainable aggression? Where, that is, does aggression lie in this model of mature caring? Oh, yes, I know that you can get angry and repair and so on, but somehow the family-values version of intimate struggle doesn't quite capture the intensity and ruthlessness of fear and anger and rage marking long-standing intimacy. Let me remind you of a scene from *Taxi,* the old television sitcom. Latka, an immigrant from some unnamed Balkan state, has married Simka, his fiancée recently arrived from their homeland. To get a green card, Simka has to prove to the immigration officer that she and Latka are married. Naturally, the day they are to appear, she has PMS and (what else?) forgets the marriage license. Of course, when she arrives without it, Latka gets angry at her. The officer helps them out by posing a series of questions designed to let them show that they live together on a regular basis. Question after question, they fail. Finally, he asks them to name the last movie they saw together. Latka answers one thing, Simka another, they begin to disagree, they begin to fight, they lapse into Ruritanian, and the next thing you know they have spiraled into a vindictive, hate-filled screaming match that is, of course, hysterically funny—at which point the officer interrupts them and says, "Okay, okay, I believe it—you're married. Only married people fight like that."

Kimberlyn Leary (personal communication, 1996) has observed the short clinical shrift given aggression in the literature during these relational days. Particularly in the context of the two-person psychology that is so rapidly becoming the new psychoanalytic convention, aggression might seem a bit incongruous (perhaps in part having to do with the maternal dimensions of the two-person model and the psychocultural divorce of aggression and femininity; see Chapters 4, 6, and 8). Yet, as Freud's joke shows, aggression is ubiquitous, showing up not only between analyst and patient but between psychoanalysis and its customers. I am concerned, as I said earlier, with psychoanalytic participation in domination— in naming, blaming, truth framing, and shaming. You might think of this psychoanalytic re-creation of the cultural morality producing it as a sort of aggression.

This participation tends to be quite invisible and therefore all the more powerful, as revealed by an inspection of Kernberg's (1995) take on perversion. In his view, a healthy sexual relationship in fact encompasses occasional sexual engagements in which one uses the other "as a pure sexual object" (p. 58). This permission for part-object exploitation in sexuality corrects the drift toward purity that, I have been suggesting, infuses the new family-values psychoanalysis. In an act of liberation, it admits aggression into the sanctum of sanity. Proposing the Kleinian integration of love and hate as signaling mature object-love, it does us all a favor by reintroducing Freud's recognition of perversion's ubiquity and giving it an object-relational place.

At the same time, this redefinition of normality is an act of imperialism. Speaking from the center of psychoanalytic power, of disciplinary authority, it colonizes the sexual margins, allowing the conventional to own the unconventional without any of the risks of unconventionality. In a royal cooptation of the sexual revolution, Kernberg (1995) renders perverse erotics acceptable, but only under the condition that it be practiced by that guardian of nonconformity, the heterosexual, married couple: "If a couple can incorporate their polymorphous perverse fantasies and wishes into their sexual relationship, discover and uncover the sadomasochistic core of sexual excitement in their intimacy, their defiance of conventional cultural mores may become a conscious element of their pleasure" (p. 96). That heterosexual couples might readmit pregenitality to their bed, that they might acknowledge the erotics of pain, that, like adolescents who pierce and tattoo, they might get off on sexual rebellion—what a daring vision.

But then comes the stretch: "It is in the very nature of conventional culture to attempt to control the basically rebellious and implicitly asocial nature of the couple as it is perceived by the conventional social environment" (p. 96). Here I must protest: the couple's "basically rebellious and implicitly asocial nature"? Unnoticed here is the absolute legitimacy conferred by heterosexual matrimony and the corresponding marginalization and denigration of other forms of intimacy, as told by the absence of homosexual coupledom from the model of mental health in *Love Relations*. Kernberg (2000) has indicted psychoanalysis's neglect of ideas beyond its perimeters—not only those of science but of history and sociology as well. If, however, he had consulted the critique of psychoanalysis found in those disciplines over the last 30 years (e.g., Weisstein, 1970; Kovel, 1981), his own idealization of the marital unit would not have escaped his ordinarily critical eye. Maybe radical notions of all sorts flit like fireflies in the matrimonial darkness. But, in Kernberg's own *oeuvre*, the procreating couple still reigns as the navel of the psychoanalytic universe, a stable center of sanity and social responsibility. I don't understand, then, how it can also situate rebellion and asociality.[1]

Talk about a moment of anxiety. This time, though, it's not the anxiety of stigma or pollution or shame; it's the anxiety of domination.

These mystifying, double-binding pronouncements incarnate the Foucaultian nightmare. They exemplify the worst tendencies toward domination; toward naming, blaming, truth framing, and shaming; in effect toward stigmatizing and the participation of psychoanalysis in the cultural morality governing it. *Les psy*, argues Foucault (1976), belong to a new form of power, "a technology of health and pathology" (p. 45) that constantly attends to and scrutinizes its subject, becoming itself a domain of pleasure. The body is a principal route to the subject—hence, the centrality of stigma to this power structure and its operation. This theory may be paranoid but is not on that account wrong; at the same time that the maneuver proposed by Kernberg (1995) unlocks one ball-and-chain by authorizing aggression on the sexual side of intimacy, it snaps another one on. Reading *Love Relations,* you think you can't possibly get it right; Kernberg knows, and you don't. Either you love the wrong way, or you can't love at all.

---

[1] Natalie Kampen (personal communication, 2002) suggests that, if we take a historical view, it is possible to argue that all the work that society puts into instructing a married couple in their duties, responsibilities, and pleasures indicates an anxiety: what havoc might this new pairing of someone's son and someone's daughter wreak?

You enter the "perpetual spirals of power and pleasure" that Foucault (1976) argues inhere in the technology of desire in contemporary society (p. 44). This spiraling finds itself in the knowledge that psychoanalysis creates and exercises, knowledge in which power is sensualized and pleasure therefore enhanced. Power, knowledge, and pleasure are, to use Butler's (1990, *passim*) neologism, interimplicated. Always suggesting, engaging, triggering, or in fact constituting one another, they form a psychopolitical gyroscope, in which "an impetus [is] given to power through its very exercise; an emotion reward[s]the overseeing control and carrie[s] it further" (Foucault, 1976, p. 45). As I read Foucault, I begin to imagine his two paradigmatic models of social control, the confessional and the couch, and think about the one I know. I think about pleasures and powers and knowledges of the psychoanalytic encounter. "Pleasure spread[s] to the power that harrie[s] it; power anchor[s] the pleasure it uncover[s]" (pp. 44–45). And now listen to the darker side of the transference–countertransference embrace, a psychoanalytic sadomasochism that may glue the analytic couple, as well as the writer–reader couple: "the pleasure . . . of exercising a power that questions, monitors, watches, spies, searches out, palpates, brings to light" (the analyst's pleasure at probing, asking, knowing, helping) and, "on the other hand, the pleasure that kindles at having to evade this power, flee from it, fool it, or travesty it" (the patient's pleasure at resisting, the erotics of the repetition compulsion). Following Foucault, we must conclude that sadomasochism is the principal psychodynamic animating the desire and struggle for power fueling the infrastructures of contemporary society, and it shows up everywhere authority and hierarchy are found (Chancer, 1992), including, need I say, in psychoanalysis.

Anxiety.

Note 8. Shelter from the Storm?/Rabbit in a Bramble Patch

I like deep massage, I like being beaten, I like catharsis [MH].

He is just an alienated isolate in human society and lives from that stance [Khan, 1979, p. 170].

As if by will alone a single drop of crimson, scarlet, carmine blood forms and runs down my chest. It stops, and I stare at it in the mirror. I don't feel like a saint, I don't feel beautiful, I don't feel sexy. I just feel alive and begin to cry [Bronski, 2002a, p. 294].

The label of perversion is as clinically superfluous as we now understand the label of homosexuality to be. It is not a diagnostic category; it does not tell us what to do. Now we take our clinical cue not from disorders of desire but from struggles of self and relationship—splits in psyche, maladies of object love, infirmities of intimacy. My strategy of detoxification has had some success with MH. Focusing on his discomfort with his being, with his self and his obese body, we have checked, if not eliminated, the depredations and degradations of his shaming self, and cleared space for the possibility that he might after all be an acceptable person. We have opened a channel through which might flow his longing just to be, to feel, to be a held baby. Glimmers of self-acceptance come and go. Recently he was able to dance without embarrassment for the first time in many years. His self-loathing is occasionally less virulent, at times quiescent. We explore in a widening spiral the range of MH's sexual practices and fantasies, thereby rendering them not much more toxic than the other dilemmas of his life, than those of work and family, for example. As we explore, however, we must survive the periods of deadness that accompany the diminution of the manic defense.

Psychoanalysis offers shelter from the storm, but it is not without its dangers. We have to be careful, Emmanuel Ghent (personal communication, 1986) said to me once in supervision. He recapped the end of *The Iceman Cometh,* when, following Hickey's false promises of peace after sobriety, the punch leaches from the whiskey: "Bejees," says Hope, "what did you do to the booze, Hickey? There's no damned life left in it" (O'Neill, 1940, p. 154). Evaluating his patient's and his own accomplishments, Khan (1979) suggests that we be mindful of "the great hazard of the analytic cure of a pervert's self-cure" (p. 176). Khan's foreskin fetishist emerged from his biphasic analysis "a person real in himself, creative in his intellectual pursuits, unharrowed by that ungraspable anxiety in himself, and beginning to live a life which to him is meaningful, sentient and true, and has a purpose as well as a direction in terms of its future" (p. 176). At the same time, however, he "lives a life which, by ordinary standards, is extremely lacking in human contact. . . . He is just an alienated isolate in human society and lives from that stance" (p. 170). Of another patient, Khan wrote that the glow was gone: When the manic defense collapses, when the perversions cease, a certain liveliness, an "instinctual fervour and dynamism" vanish, too (p. 176).

I wonder, though. A great absence in Khan's clinical account is of his own concordant countertransference to perversion. Had he been able to empathize, might he have found a way to help his patients keep the glow or create it elsewhere? Victor Bonfilio (personal communication, 1999) says that unless he thinks about how he lost his glow and found a new one, he cannot be of much help to his patients who are risking all with the throw of those analytic dice. There are good reasons, based on the internal structure of Khan's arguments, to think that, theoretically speaking, the only acceptable glow is that produced by conventional forms of intimacy. Certainly Khan enjoyed his homophobia; Godley (2001), writing of his disastrous treatment with Khan, recounts a telephone call from Winnicott that Khan took in session, in which the two men shared "a giggly joke about homosexual fellatio" (p. 6). The "spiral of degradation" (p. 5) that constituted the treatment, as well as his posttreatment relationship with Godley, suggests, however, that Khan's own glow derived as much from cruelty as from married intimacy.

With Stoller (1979), I wonder about the link between the glow and aggression, even the imbrication of sex, death, and life. If Khan's countertransference problem was, you might put it, love, then mine is perhaps hate or, at least, aggression, which I know is one reason that anxiety has dogged this chapter. And it is not clear whether fear of aggression is my problem, MH's, or ours; we'll see. The effort of loving him, even as he wards me off with gestures and sentiments soaked in hatred, echoes my struggle to negotiate between the love speech of naming and the hate speech of blaming; the depressive position being always in precarious balance, love and hate are never far apart, and intimacy is always both challenged and made possible by aggression.

If you domesticate desire, take the hate away from love and the aggression from sex, whence the glow? In "More Life," an essay whose title is borrowed from a speech by Prior in Tony Kushner's play *Angels in America,* Corbett (2001b) proposes a new developmental theory of multiplicity: There are many routes to sanity, maturity, sexuality. Probably this is another of our jobs, to midwife more life. "I like deep massage, I like being beaten, I like catharsis," said MH. Certainly his manic defense fuses elements of both connection and sexuality. At the same time, his pleasure in the deathlike shattering of self born in the crucible of catharsis (Bersani, 1988) sounds familiar to many of us. Chodorow (1992) wisely connects perversion and liveliness: "If we retain passion and intensity for heterosexuality, we are in the arena of symptom, neurosis, and disorder; if we deperversionize hetero-sexuality, giving up its claim to intensity and passion, we make it less interesting to us and to its practitioners" (p. 301).

Of his final self-cutting, Bronski (2002a) declares "I just feel alive and begin to cry" (p. 294). He writes here in the midst of death, the plague of AIDS that stole his lovers from him. Pain and blood are signs of life. Perhaps he struggles with psychic death, too. In any case, is life after deadness not a decent goal? Certainly, Ogden (1997) would agree. Perversion, Ogden argues, shows up in analysis as a defense against deadness, even if his prescription is the family-values usual: "In a healthy development, a sense of oneself as alive is equated with a generative loving parental intercourse" (p. 143). Are there no other ways to represent life, exuberance, passion, and pleasure besides reproductive heterosexuality?

How can we prescribe health when we cannot know, going forward, what produces illness? There needs to be a way to back off from the authoritarian and dominating inclinations that psychoanalysis shares with other regulatory practices. Remembering doubt is one route; writing disruptively is another. As Kaplan (1991) writes, the anorexic was once a smart and compliant child who surrendered all "for the safety and self-esteem of becoming a narcissistic extension of Mother. Yet from a prospective view, . . . no sensible clinical observer would predict from observations of a girl's relationship to her mother during infancy and childhood an anorectic solution to the dilemmas of adolescence" (p. 458). This opinion echoes Freud (1920b): "The synthesis is thus not so satisfactory as the analysis; in other words, from a knowledge of the premises we could not have foretold the nature of the result" (p. 167). Notice the judicious contingency of his formulation, which Khan, for all his grandiosity, in fact shares. How different from the certitude marking Kernberg's

(1995) seamless narrative that appears to wrap everything up in the service of truth but also hides all the loose ends.

Notes pull on those threads, rupture the surface coherence, or at least I hope they do. In these notes both clinical and rhetorical, I have taken the liberty of leaving you with many open questions alive in both clinic and culture about our diagnostic categories, our standards of health and illness, of morality, and of truth—a strategy that I think is true to the passion of psychoanalysis past and present, theoretical and clinical. Something has gone wrong for MH, and he suffers because of it. To make it better, he and I need to find out what that is. It may be that, once we find the answer, we will discover that the books were telling the truth and the answer was there all along. Then, again, maybe we will create a new truth, one that works for him, or for us, or maybe even for others. We just don't know right now. I like to quote Pete Seeger (1995): "As my father used to say, 'The truth is a rabbit in a bramble patch. All you can do is circle around and say it's somewhere in there'."

Perversion, even in Freud's understanding, let alone in light of the cultural revolution that has taken place since the 1960s, challenges our intellect, our passion, our practice. My study group read this chapter and worried that MH might be recognizable in the psychoanalytic community. They wanted me to disguise him more. I was surprised. Although he is a mental health worker at a very high level, he is not a psychoanalyst, which does not prevent him from meeting psychoanalysts who might have read this. Still, he and I thought it important that he be identified by his title so as to say to the readers of this chapter that he is, if not of them, at least among them. This is, of course, a rhetorical strategy and, I hope, a performative one. If Chasseguet-Smirgel and Kernberg are right, then let us acknowledge their moral, perhaps even moralistic, but finally routine, familiar, and ancient point: Perversion is us.

What, after all, is pathology? If perversion can coexist with health, if its status as illness varies with cultural time and place, then, conversely, any sexuality may be symptomatic—or healthy. If all sexualities may claim wholesomeness, if all have a valid psychic place, then all are subject to the same psychic vicissitudes. Put yet another way, sexuality has nothing inherently to do with mental health or mental illness. You may be ill if you are heterosexual, or

transverstite, and healthy, if you are homosexual or bisexual, or
. . . whatever. By the same token, you, like Khan's fetishist or like
Barbara McClintock, Nobel laureate in medicine and discoverer
of jumping genes, may live alone, without the trappings of
conventional intimacy (Keller, 1983, p. 205). And who's to say
that there's something wrong—something wrong with that,
something wrong with you?

Epilogue
Some Personal Conclusions

There are many ways to write an Epilogue. One is to obey the old saw about making a speech: Tell 'em what you're gonna tell 'em. Tell 'em. And then tell 'em what ya told 'em. So here, I suppose, I should tell you what I told you, restate the book's message. Of course, this book carries far too many messages to repeat. So I'll just keep it simple and remind you of the main point: sexuality, intimacy, and power are, in my view of things as they now stand, so finely imbricated that you need every resource you can call on—intellectual, emotional, spiritual, corporeal, scientific, poetic—to understand them. And even then your understanding will be only provisional.

Yet another way to conclude a book is to reiterate themes foreshadowed in the prologue. Several underlying debates, then, have threaded through these pages: the problem of dualism; the counterpoint of form and content; heteroglossia and the tensions of multiplicity; the third, dialectics, and contingency; and the paradox of sincerity versus irony. These problematics inform, in what I hope have been subversive ways, a variety of contested matters: body, mind, and culture; sexuality and gender; intimacy and intersubjectivity; clinical and social theory; psychoanalysis, politics, and cultural change.

An epilogue can also comment on how the book has done what it set out to do. Recursion of form and content, and *décalage* have been my fascination. Structure and substance, now foreground, now background, have shadowed, mirrored, inverted, and counterpointed each other. Perhaps an emergent synergy has generated a third—a new idea in your mind, a new experience. I would like that.

If a prologue maps out the territory the reader is about to travel, an epilogue might also reveal, with some vulnerability, what the author hopes readers have found. Perhaps clinicians have come away from this journey wondering about the historical and moral implications of their work. Perhaps academics have begun to comprehend the personal consequences of theory, as well as the particularities of psychoanalytic theory as lived. I hope I have helped readers to remember the political while focusing on the psychical; note the connection between critical gender theory and clinical postmodernism; ponder the narrative multiplicity in biology, social theory, and psychoanalysis; imagine the body that stinks as well as the body that thinks; consider psychosexual theory by meditating on the ambiguities of *Lust*; and enter the force field of gender. I hope that the mix of voices in this book has reverberated personally, so that readers, holding the simultaneity of personal, political, and theoretical, will question their own normality and the way they generalize from it.

An epilogue could also lay out the book's intended disciplinary contributions. My indebtedness and devotion to the traditions of feminism, psychoanalysis, and social theory are evident. But I want more from each. I want feminism to cleave to women while questioning the category of Woman. I want psychoanalysis to cleave to the unconscious while attending to the political. I want social theory to register what it knows and imagine utopias, too. And, although I want each discipline to retain its identity, I want each also to be challenged by the others kibbitzing at its margins. Intemperately, I want everyone to hear and take seriously this three way conversation. I want everyone to speak in tongues and everyone to listen.

Okay. Enough about me.

An epilogue might also say what remains to be done in the fields of thought it inhabits. Three principal domains beg for deconstruction: aggression, intimacy, and developmental theory. Colloquially speaking, classical psychoanalysis posits two main drives, sex and aggression. Although I have chosen to study the first, the second deserves equal time. Indeed, in three clinical cases (Dr. EL in Chapters 2 and 6, Mr. JG in Chapter 4, and Dr. MH in Chapter 9), I have struggled with my own personal and clinical relation to aggression. Certainly it's time for women to fathom their own use and avoidance of it. Like Harris (1997), Chesler (2002), and others, I try to do this (Chapter 8), but the interdisciplinary theoretical work awaits. How do women make psychic as well as interpersonal room for the inevitabilities of aggression? What are those inevitabilities anyway? How do social institutions accommodate them? And surely men suffer as much from aggression's difficulties (see, e.g., Faludi, 1999).

Probably it's time for altogether more theorization of aggression's past, present, and future, inside and outside the consulting room. Relational psychoanalysts have often been accused by classical analysts as being "nice" to their patients. Although that's not all we do, this characterization does fit the stereotype of the nurturing model created by the "mother" of psychoanalysis, Sándor Ferenczi, on which relationists draw. But the clinical transgressions with which we are familiar on the part of not only our forebears but our peers (Gabbard, 1989, 2000; Davies, 2000; Pizer, 2000) indicate where psychoanalytic theorizing needs to go. If you can't have aggression experienced, enacted, and interpreted in the session, then, like as not, you're going to act it out sexually (as I suggest in Chapter 9).

Aggression is no stranger to intimacy, which also needs more inspection. In this book, intimacy is represented as it occurs between analyst and patient, between women, between lovers, between writer and reader. It is, however, undertheorized. What an interesting project its study would be. One might turn to philosophers (Socrates; St. Augustine; Buber 1923), social historians (e.g., Giddens 1992), and anthropologists (Crapanzano, 1980; Kulick and Willson, 1995). One could employ feminism's sociological side, which has relentlessly anatomized and criticized intimacy's dominant social forms—the nuclear family and heterosexuality (e.g., Gornick and Moran, 1971).

Doing one's homework, one would investigate the other side, the political right's family-values boosterism, too (Hewlett 2002). Wanting, finally, to limn intimacy's psychodynamics, one might consult psychoanalysts who work in the intersubjective mode (e.g., Ehrenberg, 1992; Ogden, 1994; Shapiro, 1996; Marshall, 2000), those who disclose their sexual and other countertransference (e.g., Davies, 1994; Maroda, 1994), and those who use their knowledge to address the general public in works such as the late Steve Mitchell's (2002) *Can Love Last?* You could (I would) even study the recipes for intimacy offered by *Psychology Today* and *O*. I would also track intimacy's vicissitudes in the changing sexual and domestic cultural landscape—homosexuality, bisexuality, transgenderism; single-parent families, gay families, blended families. Here help is at hand in Weston's (1991) ethnography of gay family life and Corbett's (2001a) clinical study of gay family narratives.

Third, as I have suggested in this book, developmental theory is a great, barely touched reservoir of undeconstructed stereotype, linearity, and homogeneity. Postmodernist "heterogeneity, multiplicity, and difference" (Flax, 1990, p. 188) are just about to reach its shores. I have already learned a great deal from Corbett (2001b); I look forward to his *Boy Hoods* (Corbett, n.d.) as well as to Harris's (in press) *Gender As a Soft Assembly,* both of which use chaos and complexity theory, in conjunction with psychoanalytic, feminist, and social theory, to illuminate and explain the multilinearities of psychological development. Recursively, these ideas will make possible greater freedom for growth and thought.

Just as an epilogue can ask for more research, so, noting how ideas change as a book gets written, can it suggest the need for new theory. In redrafting these chapters, I found myself beginning to think about sexuality differently and indeed have already begun to write about it from another position. Friends and colleagues (Karol Marshall, Stuart Pizer) have remarked to me that my accounts of sexuality are quite celebratory. What, they want to know, about the darker side? Taking their criticism seriously, I have started to pay more attention to psychosexual pain as lived and interpreted. Certainly Freud addressed the fundamental linkage between sexuality and suffering on one hand and aggression, intimacy, and development in its gendered and other aspects on the other. Postfeminism, postsexual revolution, postqueer liberation, and postclassical psychoanalysis, we are in a position to extend and improve on his offering. *Les chagrins d'amour* are accessible in countertransference, as well as transference, if we only have the courage to approach them.

My metatheoretical stance has begun to change, too. Over the course of this book, postmodernism has shifted ground. At first, it crept quietly into literary structure (Chapters 7 and 8). Then it stepped boldly into the theoretical center (Chapters 1–6). In the end, it took over both form and content (Chapter 9). But, as I noted in Chapter 6, postmodernism is not the end of the line for me. As the product of a dialectic, it must, I believe, contain the seeds of its own destruction. Surely modern–postmodern has become yet another binary that conceals yet another hierarchy, with postmodernism on top.

In feminism, social theory, and psychoanalysis, however, moves are already afoot subverting this new hegemony. Feminist scientists (e.g., Fausto-Sterling, 1986, 1993; Haraway, 1989; Lewontin, 1991; Keller, 1992; Gould, 2002) wish to preserve biological science while dismantling Biology. Marxist critics keep developing Marxism while decentering it (Jameson, 1991; Eagleton, 1996). Psychoanalysts (Leary, 1994; Elliott, 1996; Eliott and Spezzano, 1996; Corbett, 2001b) advance psychoanalytic theory while deconstructing it. Corbett (2001b), for example, writes, that feminist and queer theorists want to capture . . . human variance and—illuminate the non-normative margin." Postmodern theorists are aiming "to deconstruct naturalism, disarticulate identification, and relativize normativity" (p. 319). But what, Corbett asks, about the costs of privileging fragmentation at the expense of coherence? Perhaps, he suggests, the forces of "nonregulation" regulate. Perhaps the celebration of irony has ignored the value "of living in reliable relations with others" and "the possibilities of transformation through relation" (p. 321).   ▬

Is it time for the pendulum to swing the other way? I hope not. I wouldn't go back, either in time or theory, even if I could. I'm greedy, I want it all; I want both irony and sincerity. I hope for a third place beyond modern versus postmodern, beyond smash-the-family versus family values. The third, a concept that, as we have seen, is at use in many regions of psychoanalysis, seems clinically and theoretically valuable. I want it to be our guide. There is no end to theorizing, there is no final truth, there is only more truth. That's our third.

Yes. I know. More truth? How unsatisfying. Surely a sentence ends with a period.

Well, here's my closure. A conclusion might also concede its own limitations. The final chapter of Flax's (1990) admirable and useful *Thinking Fragments: Psychoanalysis, Feminism, and Postmodernism in the Contemporary West* is titled "No Conclusions." The indeterminacy of outcome has become, I suppose, something of a postmodernist cliché. But clichés contain truths: how could there be conclusions on sexuality, intimacy, and power anyway? For one thing, they inhabit the same magnetic field, their endless attractions and repulsions reinforcing and reshaping each other. For another, what they are inflects how we think of them, but what they are changes with historical events, the contact of cultures, and idiosyncractic innovation; they are ripe for chaos theory. Finally, because they are as much mental as material phenomena, what we think about them influences what they are, which gives us more to find out about. Ideas are contingencies that, albeit neither material reality nor cause, are part of subjectivity and social life. They, and their effects, therefore constitute "an objective component in the forms of life that [we] actually live" (Danto, 2001, p. 26). There they become part of history and influence how we live. This recursiveness means there's no end to wonder.

Often, as I wander the evening streets of Manhattan, I gaze into lighted restaurants. There I spy people—principally women, but men, too (as well as those whose gender is not necessarily revealed by their appearance)—who, seated across the table from one another, lean raptly into the conversation. So many people, so many words. Every single hour of every single day (New York City, despite 9/11, is still open 24/7). How come, I always wonder, there's so much to say? What on earth could they still be talking about? Sexuality, intimacy, power?

References

Abel, E. (1990), Race, class, and psychoanalysis? Opening questions. In: *Conflicts in Feminism,* ed. M. Hirsch & E. F. Keller. New York: Routledge, pp. 184–204.

Abelove, H. (1991), Some speculations on the history of "sexual intercourse" during the history of the "long eighteenth century" in England. In: *Nationalisms and Sexualities,* ed. A. Parker, M. Russo, D. Sommer & P. Yaeger. New York: Routledge, pp. 335–342.

Abraham, K. (1924), A short study of the development of the libido, viewed in the light of mental disorders. In: *Selected Papers on Psycho-Analysis,* ed. E. Jones. New York: Brunner/Mazel, pp. 418–502.

Abu-Lughod, L. (2002), Do Muslim women really need saving? Anthropological reflections on cultural relativism and its others. *Amer. Anthropol.,* 104:703–790.

Ackelsberg, M. A. & Addelson, K. P. (1987), Anarchist alternatives to competition. In *Competition: A Feminist Taboo?* ed. V. Miner & H. Longino. New York: Feminist Press, pp. 221–233.

Alexander, S. (1992), Feminist history. In: *Feminism and Psychoanalysis: A Critical Dictionary,* ed. E. Wright. Oxford, Engl.: Blackwell, pp. 108–113.

Althusser, L. (1971), *Lenin and Philosophy.* New York: Monthly Review Press.

Amariglio, J. L., Resnick, S. A. & Wolff, R. D. (1988), Class, power, and culture. In: *Marxism and the Interpretation of Culture,* ed. C. Nelson & L. Grossberg. Urbana: University of Illinois Press, pp. 487–501.

Anderson, H. (1992), Psychoanalysis and feminism: An ambivalent alliance. Viennese feminist response to Freud, 1900–1930. In: *Psychoanalysis and Its Cultural Context:* Austrian Studies III, ed. E. Timms & R. Robertson. Edinburgh: Edinburgh University Press, pp. 81–94.

Angier, N. (1993), Scientists find gay gene. *The New York Times,* July 16, p. A1.

———— (1999), *Woman.* New York: Houghton Mifflin.

Anzieu, D. (1989), *The Skin Ego,* trans. C. Turner. New Haven, CT: Yale University Press.

Appignanesi, L. & Forrester, J. (1992), *Freud's Women.* New York: Basic Books.

Apter, E. (1992a), Clitoral hermeneutics. In: *Feminism and Psychoanalysis: A Critical Dictionary,* ed. E. Wright. Oxford, Engl.: Blackwell, pp. 50–51.

———— (1992b), Perversion. In: *Feminism and Psychoanalysis: A Critical Dictionary,* ed. E. Wright. Oxford, Englb.: Blackwell, pp. 311–313.

Armstrong, N. (1988), The gender bind: Women and the disciplines. *Genders,* 3:1–23.

Aron, L. (1996), *A Meeting of Minds.* Hillsdale, NJ: The Analytic Press.

———— & Anderson, F. S., eds. (1998), *Relational Perspectives on the Body.* Hillsdale, NJ: The Analytic Press.

Aronowitz, S. (1979), The professional-managerial class. In: *Between Labor and Capital,* ed. P. Walker. Boston, MA: South End Press, pp. 213–242.

Ascher, C., DeSalvo, L. & Ruddick, S., eds. (1984), *Between Women*. New York: Routledge, 1993.

Bach, S. (1995), *The Language of Perversion and the Language of Love*. Northvale, NJ: Aronson.

——— (1998), Colloquium on sexuality in psychoanalysis, New York University. Postdoctoral Program in Psychotherapy and Psychoanalysis, March 6.

Bakhtin, M. M. (1934–1935), Discourse of the novel. In: *The Dialogic Imagination: Four Essays by M. M. Bakhtin*, ed. M. Holquist (trans. C. Emerson & M. Holquist). Austin: University of Texas Press, 1981, pp. 259–420.

Balint, M. (1956), *Perversions and genitality*. In: *Perversions Psychodynamics and Therapy*, ed. S. Lorand. New York: Random House, pp. 16–27.

Bassin, D. (1996), Beyond the he and the she: Toward the reconciliation of the masculine and feminine in the postoedipal female mind. *J. Amer. Psychoan. Assoc.*, 44 (Spec. Suppl.):157–190.

Bateson, G. (1972), *Steps Toward an Ecology of Mind*. New York: Ballantine.

Bawer, B. (1988), *A Place at the Table*. New York: Simon & Schuster.

Beebe, B. & Lachmann, F. (2002), *Infant Research and Analytic Treatment: Co-constructing Interactions*. Hillsdale, NJ: The Analytic Press.

Benedict, R. (1934), *Patterns of Culture*. New York: Houghton-Mifflin.

Benjamin, J. (1978), Authority and the family revisited: A world without fathers? *New German Crit.*, 4:35–57.

——— (1980), The bonds of love: Erotic domination and rational violence. *Feminist Studies*, 6:144–174.

——— (1984), The convergence of psychoanalysis and feminism: Gender identity and autonomy. In: *Women Therapists Working with Women*, ed. C. M. Brody. New York: Springer, pp. 37–45.

——— (1988a), Elements of intersubjectivity: Recognition and destruction. Presented at Relational Track Colloquium, December 9, New York University Postdoctoral Program.

——— (1988b), *The Bonds of Love: Psychoanalysis, Feminism, and the Problem of Domination*. New York: Pantheon.

——— (1991), Father and daughter: Identification with difference— A contribution to gender heterodoxy, *Psychoanal. Dial.*, 1:277–301.

——— (1994), Discussion of Judith Jordan's "The Relational Self: A New Perspective for Understanding Women's Development." *Contemp. Psychother. Rev.*, 7:82–96.

——— (1995), *Like Subjects, Love Objects*. New Haven, CT: Yale University Press.

——— (1997), In defense of gender ambiguity. *Gender & Psychoanal.*, 2:27–44.

——— (1998a), *The Shadow of the Other: Intersubjectivity and Gender in Psychoanalysis*. New York: Routledge.

——— (1998b), How intersubjective is sex? Keynote address at annual meeting of Division of Psychoanalysis (Division 39), American Psychological Association, Boston, April.

——— (2001), Two-way streets. Presented at annual meeting of Division of Psychoanalysis (Division 39), American Psychological Association, Santa Fe, NM, April.

Berman, M. (1982), *All That Is Solid Melts into the Air*. New York: Penguin.

Bernheimer, C. & Kahane, C., eds. (1985), *In Dora's Case*. New York: Columbia University Press.

Bersani, L. (1986), *The Freudian Body*. New York: Columbia University Press.

——— (1988), Is the rectum a grave? In: *AIDS: Cultural Analysis, Cultural Activism*, ed. D. Crimp. Cambridge, MA: MIT Press, pp. 197–222.

Bertin, C. (1982), *Marie Bonaparte: A Life*. New York: Harcourt Brace Jovanovich.

Bion, W. (1977), *Seven Servants*. Northvale, NJ: Aronson.

Bloom, H. (1986), Freud, the greatest modern writer. *New York Times Book Review*, March 23, p. 2.

———— & Rosenberg, D. (1990), *The Book of J*. New York: Vintage.

Bollas, C. (1988), *The Unthought-Known*. New York: Columbia University Press.

Bonaparte, M. (1953), *Female Sexuality*. New York: International Universities Press.

Borch-Jakobson, M. (1997), *Remembering Anna O*. New York: Routledge.

Boris, H. N. (1986), Bion revisited. *Contemp. Psychoanal.*, 22:159–184.

Bouchier, D. (1994), Cooking on the barbecue is man's work. *New York Times*, Long Island ed., July 3, Section 13, p. 1.

Bourdieu, P. (1977), *Outline of a Theory of Practice*, trans. R. Nice. New York: Cambridge University Press.

———— & Eagleton, T. (1992), Doxa and common life. *New Left Rev.*, 191:111–121.

Bowie, M. (1991), *Lacan*. Cambridge, MA: Harvard University Press.

Bowler, P. (1992), Lamarckism. In: *Keywords in Evolutionary Biology*, ed. E. F. Keller & E. A. Lloyd. Cambridge, MA: Harvard University Press, pp. 194–201.

Brennan, T. (1989), Introduction. In: *Between Feminism and Psychoanalysis*, ed. T. Brennan. New York: Routledge, pp. 1–24.

Breuer, J. & Freud, S. (1893–1895), Studies on hysteria. *Standard Edition*, 2:21–47. London: Hogarth Press, 1955.

Bromberg, P. (1994), "Speak! That I may see you": Some reflections on dissociation, reality, and psychoanalytic listening. *Psychoanal. Dial.*, 4:517–548.

———— (1996), *Standing in the Spaces: Essays on Clinical Process, Trauma, and Dissociation*. Hillsdale, NJ: The Analytic Press.

Bronski, M. (2002a), Dr. Fell. In: *Bringing the Plague: Toward a Postmodern Psychoanalysis*, ed. S. Fairfield, L. Layton & C. Stack. New York: Other Press, pp. 279–294.

———— (2002b), Sex, death, and the limits of irony. In: *Bringing the Plague: Toward a Postmodern Psychoanalysis*, ed. S. Fairfield, L. Layton & C. Stack. New York: Other Press, pp. 309–324.

Brown, N. O. (1959), *Life Against Death*. Middletown, CT: Wesleyan University Press.

Buber, M. (1923), *I and Thou*. New York: Charles Scribner's Sons, 1970.

Buhle, M. J. (1998), *Feminism and Its Discontents*. Cambridge, MA: Harvard University Press.

Buss, D. (1994), *The Evolution of Desire: Strategies of Human Mating*. New York: Basic Books.

Butler, J. (1990), *Gender Trouble: Feminism and the Subversion of Identity*. New York: Routledge.

———— (1992), Gender. In: *Feminism and Psychoanalysis: A Critical Dictionary*, ed. E. Wright. Oxford: Blackwell, pp. 140–145.

———— (1993), *Bodies That Matter*. New York: Routledge.

———— (1994), Sexual traffic: Interview with Gayle Rubin. *Differences*, 6:62–99.

———— (1995), Melancholy gender—refused identification. *Psychoanal. Dial.*, 5:165–180.

Bynum, C. W. (1991), *Fragmentation and Redemption: Essays on Gender and the Human Body in Medieval Religion*. New York: Zone Books.

Caldwell, S. (n.d.), Love note. Unpublished manuscript.

Cardinal, M. (1983), *The Words to Say It*, trans. P. Goodheart. Cambridge, MA: VanVactor & Goodheart.

Carr, E. H. (1961), *What Is History?* New York: Vintage.

Chancer, L. (1992), *Sado-Masochism and Everyday Life*. New Brunswick, NJ: Rutgers University Press.

Chasseguet-Smirgel, J. (1985), *Creativity and Perversion*. New York: Norton.

——— (1967), Freud and female sexuality: The consideration of some blind spots in the exploration of the "Dark Continent." In: *Sexuality and Mind: The Role of the Father and the Mother in the Psyche.* New York: New York University Press, 1986.

Chesler, P. (2002), *Woman's Inhumanity to Woman.* New York: Nation Books.

Chodorow, N. (1978), *The Reproduction of Mothering: Psychoanalysis and the Sociology of Gender.* Berkeley: University of California Press.

——— (1989), *Feminism and Psychoanalytic Theory.* New Haven, CT: Yale University Press.

——— (1992), Heterosexuality as compromise formation. *Psychoanal. Contemp. Thought,* 15:267–304.

——— (1994), *Femininities, Masculinities, Sexualities.* Lexington: University of Kentucky Press.

——— (1995), Gender as a personal and social construction. *Signs,* 20:516–544.

——— (2000), *Psychoanalysis and the Search for Personal Meaning.* New Haven, CT: Yale University Press.

Chused, J. (1996), Abstinence and informative experience. *J. Amer. Psychoanal. Assn.,* 44:1047–1073.

Clements, M. (1985), *The Dog Is Us.* New York: Viking/Penguin.

Conklin, B. A. & Morgan, L. M. (1996), Babies, bodies, and the production of personhood in North America and a native Amazonian society. *Ethos,* 24:657–694.

Corbett, K. (1993), The mystery of homosexuality. *Psychoanal. Psychol.,* 10:345–358.

——— (1997), Speaking queer. *Gender & Psychoanal.,* 2:495–514.

——— (2001a), Pomo stork: Nontraditional family romance. *Psychoanal. Quart.,* 70:599–624.

——— (2001b), More life: Centrality and marginality in human development. *Psychoanal. Dial.,* 11:313–335.

——— (n.d.), Boy Hoods. Unpublished manuscript.

Crapanzano, V. (1980), *Tuhami: Portrait of a Moroccan.* Chicago: University of Chicago Press.

Cucchiari, S. (1981), The gender revolution and the transition from bisexual horde to patrilocal band: The origins of gender hierarchy. In: *Sexual Meanings,* ed. S. B. Ortner & H. Whitehead. Cambridge: Cambridge University Press, pp. 31–79.

Curtis, R. (1996), The "death of Freud" and the rebirth of free psychoanalytic inquiry. *Psychoanal. Dial.,* 6:563–589.

Cushman, P. (1991), Ideology obscured: Political uses of the self in Daniel Stern's infant. *Amer. Psychol.,* 46:206–219.

Danto, A. C. (2001), Beauty and the beastly. *The Nation,* April 23:25–29.

Davidson, A. I. (1987), How to do the history of psychoanalysis: A reading of Freud's "Three Essays on the Theory of Sexuality." In: *The Trial of Psychoanalysis,* ed. F. Meltzer. Chicago: University of Chicago Press, pp. 39–64.

Davies, J. M. (1994), Love in the afternoon: A relational reconsideration of desire and dread in the countertransference. *Psychoanal. Dial.,* 4:153–170.

——— (1998), Between the disclosure and foreclosure of erotic transference–countertransference: Can psychoanalysis find a place for adult sexuality? *Psychoanal. Dial.,* 8:747–766.

——— (2000), Descending the therapeutic slopes—slippery, slipperier, slipperiest: Commentary on papers by Barbara Pizer and Glen O. Gabbard. *Psychoanal. Dial.,* 10:219–230.

——— & Frawley, M. G. (1992), Dissociative processes and transference–countertransference paradigms in the psychoanalytically oriented treatment of adult survivors of childhood sexual abuse. *Psychoanal. Dial.,* 2:25–36.

————— & ————— (1994), *Treating the Adult Survivor of Childhood Sexual Abuse.* New York: Basic Books.

Dawkins, R. (1976), *The Selfish Gene.* Oxford: Oxford University Press.

Dean, T. (1994), Bodies that mutter. *Pre/Text,* 15:81–117.

de Beauvoir, S. (1949), *The Second Sex,* trans. H. M. Parshley. New York: Vintage.

de Lauretis, T. (1990), Eccentric subjects: Feminist theory and historical consciousness, *Femin. Stud.,* 16:115–151.

————— (1994), *The Practice of Love: Lesbian Sexuality and Perverse Desire.* Bloomington: Indiana University Press.

Delmar, R. (1986), What is feminism? In: *What Is Feminism?* ed. J. Mitchell & A. Oakley. New York: Pantheon, pp. 8–33.

de Saussure, F. (1916), *Course in General Linguistics.* New York: McGraw-Hill, 1985.

Deutsch, H. (1944), *The Psychology of Women, Vols. 1 & 2.* New York: Grune & Stratton.

de Waal, F. & Lanting, F. (1997), *Bonobo: The Forgotten Ape.* Berkeley: University of California Press.

Diamond, S. (1974), *In Search of the Primitive.* New York: Transaction Books.

Dimen, M. (1976), Regional studies and their potential value for the ethnography of modern Greece and Cyprus. *Annals New York Acad. Sci.,* 263:3–9.

————— (1981), Variety is the spice of life. *Heresies,* 3:66–70.

————— (1982), Notes towards the reconstruction of sexuality. *Social Text,* 6:22–30.

————— (1984), Politically correct? Politically incorrect? In: *Pleasure and Danger: Exploring Female Sexuality,* ed. C. S. Vance. London: Routledge & Kegan Paul, pp. 138–148.

————— (1986), *Surviving Sexual Contradictions: A Startling and Different Look at a Day in the Life of a Contemporary Professional Woman.* New York: Macmillan.

————— (1992), Theorizing social reproduction: On the origins of decentered subjectivity. *Genders,* 14:98–125.

————— (1994), Money, love and hate: Contradiction and paradox in psychoanalysis. *Psychoanal. Dial.,* 4:60–100.

————— (1995), Introduction to Symposium on Sexuality/Sexualities. *Psychoanal. Dial.,* 5:157–63.

————— (1998), Polyglot bodies. In: *The Relational Construction of the Body,* ed. F. S. Anderson & L. Aron. Hillsdale, NJ: The Analytic Press, pp. 65–93.

————— (2000), A tale of three selves. In: *Self-Relations in the Psychotherapy Process,* ed. J. C. Muran. Washington, DC: American Psychological Association, pp. 211–218.

————— (2002), The disturbance of sex. In: *Bringing the Plague: Toward a Postmodern Psychoanalysis,* ed. S. Fairfield, L. Layton & C. Stack. New York: Other Press, pp. 295–308.

————— & Goldner, V. (2002), Introduction. In: *Gender in Psychoanalytic Space: Between Clinic and Culture,* ed. M. Dimen & V. Goldner. New York: Other Press, pp. xv–xx.

————— & Harris, A. (2001), Introduction. In: *Storms in Her Head: Freud and the Construction of Hysteria,* ed. M. Dimen & A. Harris. New York: Other Press, 1–30.

————— & Shapiro, S. (n.d.), Trouble between women. Unpublished manuscript.

Dimen-Schein [Dimen], M. (1977), *The Anthropological Imagination.* New York: McGraw-Hill.

Dinnerstein, D. (1976), *The Mermaid and the Minotaur: Sexual Arrangements and Human Malaise.* New York: Harper & Row.

Doane, M. A. (1991), *Femmes Fatales: Feminism, Film Theory, Psychoanalysis.* New York: Routledge.

Domenici, T. (1995), Exploding the myth of sexual psychopathology: A deconstruction of Fairbairn's anti-homosexual theory. In: *Disorienting Sexuality*, ed. T. Domenici & R. Lesser. New York: Routledge, pp. 33–64.

———— & Lesser, R. eds. (1995), *Disorienting Sexuality*. New York: Routledge.

Douglas, M. (1970), *Purity and Danger: An Analysis of the Concepts of Pollution and Taboo*. New York: Penguin.

Dyess, C. & Dean, T. (2000), Gender: The impossibility of meaning. *Psychoanal. Dial.*, 10:735–757.

Eagelton, T. (1996), *The Illusions of Postmodernism*. Oxford, Engl.: Blackwell.

Echols, A. (1987), *Daring to Be Bad*. New York: Routledge & Kegan Paul.

———— (1999), *Scars of Sweet Paradise: The Life and Times of Janis Joplin*. New York: Henry Holt.

Egan, J. (1997), The thin red line. *The New York Times Magazine*, July 27, pp. 21–46.

Ehrenberg, D. (1992), *The Intimate Edge: Extending the Reach of Psychoanalytic Interaction*. New York: Norton.

Ehrenreich, B. (1989), *Fear of Falling: The Inner Life of the Middle Class*. New York: Pantheon.

———— & Ehrenreich, J. (1979), The professional-managerial class. In: *Between Labor and Capital*, ed. P. Walker. Boston: South End Press, pp. 5–45.

Eichenbaum, L. & Orbach, S. (1988). *Between Women*. New York: Penguin.

Eigen, M. (1993), *The Electrified Tightrope*, ed. A. Phillips. Northvale, NJ: Aronson.

Elias, N.(1939), *The Civilizing Process*. New York: Urizen, 1978.

Ellenberger, H. F. (1970), *The Discovery of the Unconscious: The History and Evolution of Dynamic Psychiatry*. New York: Basic Books.

Elliott, A. (1996), *Subject to Ourselves*. Cambridge: Polity Press.

———— & Spezzano, C. (1996), Psychoanalysis at its limits: Navigating the postmodern turn. *Psychoanal. Quart.*, 65:52–83.

el Saadawi, N. (1980), *The Hidden Face of Eve*. London: Zed Books.

Epstein, M. (1995), *Thoughts Without a Thinker*. New York: Basic Books.

Erikson, E. (1950), *Childhood and Society*, 2nd ed. New York: Norton, 1963.

Fairbairn, W. R. D. (1952), *Psychoanalytic Studies of the Personality*. London: Routledge & Kegan Paul.

———— (1954), Observations on the nature of hysterical states. *Brit. J. Med. Psychol.*, 27:105–125.

Fairfield, S. (2001), Analyzing multiplicity: A postmodern perspective on some current psychoanalytic theories of subjectivity. *Psychoanal. Dial.*, 11:221–251.

———— Layton, L. & Stack, C. (2002), Introduction: Culture and couch. In: *Bringing the Plague: Toward a Postmodern Psychoanalysis*, ed. S. Fairfield, L. Layton & C. Stack. New York: Other Press, pp. 1–31.

Faludi, S. (1999), *Stiffed*. New York: Putnam.

Fast, I. (1984), *Gender Identity*. Hillsdale, NJ: The Analytic Press.

Fausto-Sterling, A. (1986), *Myths of Gender: Biological Theories of Women and Men*. New York: Basic Books.

———— (1993), The five sexes: Why male and female are not enough. *The Sciences*, March/April:20–24.

Fedigan, L. M. (1982), *Primate Paradigms: Sex Roles and Social Bonds*. Montreal: Eden Press.

Ferenczi, S. (1911), On obscene words. In: *Contributions to Psycho-analysis*. London: Hogarth Press, 1952, pp. 132–153.

———— (1933), The confusion of tongues between adults and the child. *Contemp. Psychoanal.*, 24:196–206, 1988.

Firestone, S. (1970), *The Dialectic of Sex*. New York: William Morrow.

Flax, J. (1983), Political philosophy and the patriarchal unconscious: A psychoanalytic perspective on epistemology and metaphysics. In: *Discovering Reality*, ed. S. Harding & M. Hintikka. Dordrecht, The Netherlands: D. Reidel, pp. 245–282.

———— (1990), *Thinking Fragments: Psychoanalysis, Feminism, and Postmodernism in the Contemporary West.* Berkeley: University of California Press.

———— (2002), Resisting woman: On feminine difference in the work of Horney, Thompson, and Moulton. *Contemp. Psychoanal.*, 38:257–278.

Fliegel, Z. (1986), Women's development in analytic theory: Six decades of controversy. In: *Psychoanalysis and Women: Contemporary Reappraisals*, ed. J. L. Alpert. Hillsdale, NJ: The Analytic Press, pp. 3–32.

Fogel, G., Lane, F. M. & Liebert, R. S. (1986), *The Psychology of Men.* New York: Basic Books.

Forrester, J. (1992), Freud's female patients/female analysts. In: *Feminism and Psychoanalysis: A Critical Dictionary*, ed. E. Wright. Oxford: Blackwell, pp. 134–139.

Foucault, M. (1965), *Madness and Civilization: A History of Insanity in the Age of Reason*, trans. R. Howard. New York: Vintage.

———— (1966), *The Order of Things.* New York: Vintage, 1994.

———— (1975), *The Birth of the Clinic*, trans. A. M. Sheridan Smith. New York: Vintage.

———— (1976), *The History of Sexuality, Vol. I*, trans. R. Hurley. New York: Vintage, 1980.

———— (1988), The political technologies of individuals. In: *Technologies of the Self: A Seminar with Michel Foucault*, ed. L. Martin, H. Gutman & P. Hutton. Amherst: University of Massachusetts Press, pp. 145–161.

Fourcher, L. A. (1996), The authority of logic and the logic of authority: The import of the Grünbaum debate for psychoanalytically informed psychotherapy. *Psychoanal. Dial.*, 6:515–532.

Freud, S. (1905a), Fragment of an analysis of a case of hysteria. *Standard Edition*, 7:7–122. London: Hogarth Press, 1953.

———— (1905b), Three essays on the theory of sexuality. *Standard Edition*, 7:125–243. London: Hogarth Press, 1953.

———— (1905c), Jokes and their relation to the unconscious. *Standard Edition*, 8:3–248. London: Hogarth Press, 1960.

———— (1908), "Civilized" sexual morality and modern nervousness. *Standard Edition*, 9:181–204. London: Hogarth Press, 1959.

———— (1910), Leonardo da Vinci and a memory of his childhood. *Standard Edition*, 11:59–130. London: Hogarth Press, 1957.

———— (1911), Formulations on the two principles of mental functioning. *Standard Edition*, 12:213–225. London: Hogarth Press, 1958.

———— (1913), Totem and taboo. *Standard Edition*, 13:1–162. London: Hogarth Press, 1955.

———— (1914), Remembering, repeating, and working through (further recommendations on the technique of psychoanalysis). *Standard Edition*, 12:145–156. London: Hogarth Press, 1958.

———— (1915), A case of paranoia running counter to the psycho-analytic theory of the disease. *Standard Edition*, 14:261–270. London: Hogarth Press, 1957.

———— (1920a), Beyond the pleasure principle. *Standard Edition*, 18:7–64. London: Hogarth Press, 1955.

———— (1920b), The psychogenesis of a case of homosexuality in a woman. *Standard Edition*, 18:145–172. London: Hogarth Press, 1955.

———— (1924a), The economic problem of masochism. *Standard Edition*, 19:157–172. London: Hogarth Press, 1961.

———— (1924b), The dissolution of the Oedipus complex. *Standard Edition*, 19:173–181. London: Hogarth Press, 1961.

———— (1925a), Some psychical consequences of the anatomical distinction between the sexes. *Standard Edition*, 19:241-259. London: Hogarth Press, 1961.

———— (1925b), Preface to Aichhorn's *Wayward Youth*. *Standard Edition*, 19:272–275. London: Hogarth Press, 1961.

———— (1927), Fetishism. *Standard Edition*, 22:152–157. London: Hogarth Press, 1957.

———— (1930), Civilization and its discontents. *Standard Edition*, 21:64–146. London: Hogarth Press, 1961.

———— (1931), Female sexuality. *Standard Edition*, 21:221–245. London: Hogarth Press, 1961.

———— (1933), On femininity. In: New introductory lectures. *Standard Edition*, 22:112–134. London: Hogarth Press, 1964.

Friedan, B. 1963. *The Feminine Mystique*. New York: Norton.

Gabbard, G., ed. (1989), *Sexual Exploitation in Professional Relationships*. Washington, DC: American Psychiatric Press.

———— (2000), Consultation from the consultant's perspective. *Psycho-anal. Dial.*, 10:209–218.

Gailey, C. (1988), Evolutionary perspectives on gender hierarchy. In: *Analyzing Gender*, ed. B. Hess & M. Ferree. Newbury Park, CA: Sage, pp. 32–67.

Gallop, J. (1982), *The Daughter's Seduction: Psychoanalysis and Feminism*. Ithaca, NY: Cornell University Press.

———— (1988), *Thinking Through the Body*. New York: Columbia University Press.

Garber, M. (1992), *Vested Interests*. New York: Routledge.

Gay, P. (1988), *Freud: A Life for Our Time*. New York: Norton.

Geertz, C. (1973), *The Interpretation of Cultures*. New York: Basic Books.

Gerson, S. (1996), Neutrality, resistance, and self-disclosure in an intersubjective psychoanalysis. *Psychoanal. Dial.*, 6:623–645.

Ghent, E. (1989), Credo: The dialectics of one-person and two-person psychologies. *Contemp. Psychoanal.*, 25:169–211.

———— (1992), Paradox and process. *Psychoanal. Dial.*, 2:135–159.

Giddens, A. (1992), *The Transformation of Intimacy: Sexuality, Love and Eroticism in Modern Societies*. Cambridge: Polity Press.

Gilligan, C. (1980), In a different voice: Women's conceptions of self and of morality. In: *The Future of Difference*, ed. H. Eisenstein & A. Jardine. New Brunswick, NJ: Rutgers University Press, pp. 274–317.

———— (1982), *In a Different Voice: Psychological Theories and Women's Development*. Cambridge, MA: Harvard University Press.

Gilman, S. (1995), *Freud, Race, and Gender*. Princeton, NJ: Princeton University Press.

Godley, W. (2001), Saving Masud Khan. *London Rev. Books*, February 22:3–7.

Goffman, E. (1961), *Asylums: Essays on the Social Situation of Mental Patients and Other Inmates*. Garden City, NY: Anchor Books.

Goldner, V. (1991), Toward a critical relational theory of gender. *Psychoanal. Dial.*, 1:249–272.

———— (1998), Theorizing gender and sexual subjectivity. Presented at annual meeting of Division of Psychoanalysis (Division 39), American Psychological Association, Boston, April.

———— (2003), Ironic gender, authentic sex. *Studies Gender & Sexual.*, 4:113–139.

———— (n.d.), Violence and victimization: Enactments from the gender wars. Unpublished manuscript.

Gornick, V. & Moran, B. K., eds. (1971), *Woman in Sexist Society: Studies in Power and Powerlessness*. New York: Signet Press.

Gould, S. J. (1977), *Ever Since Darwin*. New York: Norton.

—— (1981), *The Mismeasure of Man*. New York: Norton.

—— (1987), *An Urchin in the Storm: Essays about Books and Ideas*. New York: Norton.

—— (2002), *The Structure of Evolutionary Theory*. Cambridge: Harvard University Press.

Grafton, A. (1997), *The Footnote*. Cambridge, MA: Harvard University Press.

Gramsci, A. (1929–1937), *Selections from the Prison Notebook of Antonio Gramsci*. Ed., trans. Q. Hoare & G. N. Smith. New York: International Publishers, 1971.

Grand, S. (1997), On the gendering of traumatic dissociation: a case of mother-son incest, *Gender & Psychoanal.*, 2:55–79.

Green, A. (1996), Has sexuality anything to do with psychoanalysis? *Internat. J. Psycho-Anal.*, 76:871–883.

—— (1997), Opening remarks to a discussion of sexuality. *Internat. J. Psycho-Anal.*, 77:345–350.

Green, M., ed. (1964), *Interpersonal Psychoanalysis: The Selected Papers of Clara Thompson*. New York: Basic Books.

Greenberg, J. (1993), *Oedipus and Beyond*. Cambridge, MA: Harvard University Press.

—— & Mitchell, S. A. (1983), *Object Relations in Psychoanalytic Theory*. Cambridge, MA: Harvard University Press.

Grosz, E. (1992), Phallus: Feminist implications. In: *Feminism and Psychoanalysis: A Critical Dictionary*, ed. E. Wright. Oxford: Blackwell, pp. 320–323.

—— (1994), *Volatile Bodies*. New York: Routledge.

Hanh, T. N. (1990), The flute of the Buddha: Art, practice, and everyday life. *Inquiring Mind*, 7:1.

Hanisch, C. (1969), The personal is political. In: *Feminist Revolution: An Abridged Edition with Additional Writings*, ed. Redstockings of the Women's Liberation Movement. New York: Random House, 1978, pp. 204–205.

Haraway, D. (1989), *Primate Visions: Gender, Race, and Nature in the World of Modern Science*. New York: Routledge.

Harris, A. (1985), Women, baseball, and words. *PsychCritique*, 1:35–54.

—— (1989), Bringing Artemis to life: A plea for militance and aggression in feminist peace politics. In: *Rocking the Ship of State*, ed. A. Harris & Y. King. Boulder: Westview Press, pp. 93–114.

—— (1991), Gender as contradiction. *Psychoanal. Dial.*, 1:197–220.

—— (1996a), False memory? False memory syndrome? The so-called false memory syndrome? *Psychoanal. Dial.*, 6:155–187.

—— (1996b), The anxiety in ambiguity. *Psychoanal. Dial.*, 6:267–279.

—— (1996c) Editor's statement. *Gender & Psychoanal.*, 1:23–24.

—— (1997), Aggression, envy and ambition: Circulating tensions in women's lives. *Gender & Psychoanal.*, 2:291–326.

—— (2000), Politicized passions: A discussion of Dianne Elise's "Woman and desire: Why women may *not* want to want." *Studies Gender & Sexual.*, 1:147–156.

—— (in press), *Gender as A Soft Assembly*. Hillsdale, NJ: The Analytic Press.

Harris, M. (1968), *The Rise of Anthropological Theory*. New York: Thomas Y. Crowell.

Harris, O. & Young, K. (1981), Engendered structures: Some problems in the analysis of reproduction. In: *The Anthropology of Precapitalist Societies*, ed. J. S. Kahn & J. R. Llobera. London: Macmillan, pp. 109–147.

Harvey, D. (1989), *The Condition of Postmodernity*. Oxford: Oxford University Press.

Haubegger, C. (1997), I'm not fat, I'm Latina. In: *Reconstructing Gender: A Multi-cultural Anthology,* ed. E. Disch. Mountain View, CA: Mayfield, pp. 177–179.

Herdt, G. (1998), *Same Sex, Different Cultures.* New York: Perseus.

Hewlett, S.A. (2002), *Creating a Life: Professional Women and the Quest for Children.* New York: Talk Miramax.

Hoffman, I. Z. (1998), *Ritual and Spontaneity in the Psychoanalytic Process: A Dialectical-Constructivist View.* Hillsdale, NJ: The Analytic Press.

Holquist, M., ed. (1981), *The Dialogic Imagination: Four Essays by M. M. Bakhtin,* trans. C. Emerson & M. Holquist. Austin: University of Texas Press.

Holt, R. (1989), *Freud Reappraised: A Fresh Look at Psychoanalytic Theory.* New York: Guilford Press.

Hoodfar, H. (1997), *Between Marriage and the Market.* Berkeley: University of California Press.

Horney, K. (1923), On the genesis of the castration complex in women. In: *Feminine Psychology,* ed. H. Kelman. New York: Norton, 1967, pp. 37–53.

——— (1926), The flight from womanhood. In: *Feminine Psychology,* ed. H. Kleman. New York: Norton, 1967, pp. 54–70.

——— (1933), The denial of the vagina. In: *Feminine Psychology,* ed. H. Kleman. New York: Norton, 1967, pp. 147–161.

Hrdy, S. B. (1981), *The Woman That Never Evolved.* Cambridge, MA: Harvard University Press.

Hubbard, R. (1999), Body language. Review of *Woman* by N. Angier. *Women's Rev. Books,* 16:14–15.

Irigaray, L. (1985), *This Sex Which Is Not One,* trans. C. Porter with C. Burke. Ithaca, NY: Cornell University Press.

Jackowitz, A. (1984), Anna O/Bertha Pappenheim and me. In: *Between Women,* ed. C. Ascher, L. DeSalvo & S. Ruddick. Boston: Beacon Press, pp. 253–310.

Jacobson, L. (1996), Introduction to symposium on the Grünbaum debate. *Psychoanal. Dial.,* 6:497–502.

Jacoby, R. (1983), *The Repression of Psychoanalysis: Otto Fenichel and the Political Freudians.* Chicago: University of Chicago Press.

Jaggar, A. B. (1983), *Feminist Politics and Human Nature.* Totowa, NJ: Rowman & Allenheld.

——— (1989), Love and knowledge: Emotion and feminist epistemology. In *Gender/Body/Knowledge: Feminist Reconstructions of Being and Knowing,* ed. A. Jaggar & S. Bordo. New Brunswick, NJ: Rutgers University Press, pp. 145–171.

——— & Bordo, S., eds. (1989), *Gender/Body/Knowledge: Feminist Reconstructions of Being and Knowing.* New Brunswick, NJ: Rutgers University Press.

Jakobson, R. (1962), *Selected Writings.* The Hague: Mouton.

Jameson, F. (1991), *Postmodernism, or The Cultural Logic of Late Capitalism.* Durham, NC: Duke University Press.

Jones, E. (1927), Early development of female sexuality. In: *Papers on Psychoanalysis.* Boston, MA: Beacon Press, pp. 438–451.

——— (1953), *The Life and Work of Sigmund Freud, Vol. 2.* New York: Basic Books.

Jordan, J. V., Kaplan, A. G., Miller, J. B., Stiver, I. P. & Surrey, J. L. (1991), *Women's Growth in Connection: Writings from the Stone Center.* New York: Guilford Press.

Josephs, B. (1989), *Psychic Equilibrium and Psychic Change,* ed. M. Feldman & E. B. Spillius. London: Tavistock/Routledge.

Kaplan, L. J. (1991), *Female Perversions.* New York: Anchor Books.

Katz, J. N. (1990), The invention of heterosexuality. *Socialist Rev.,* 20:7–34.

Keller, E. F. (1983), *A Feeling for the Organism: The Life and Work of Barbara McClintock.* New York: Freeman.

———— (1985), *Reflections on Gender and Science*. New Haven, CT: Yale University Press.

———— (1992), *Secrets of Life, Secrets of Death: Essays on Language, Gender and Science*. New York: Routledge.

———— & Moglen, H. (1987), Competition: A problem for academic women. In: *Competition: A Feminist Taboo?* ed. V. Miner & H. Longino. New York: Feminist Press, pp. 21–37.

Kernberg, O. (1976), *Object Relations Theory and Clinical Pychoanalysis*. New York: Aronson, pp. 185–214.

———— (1995), *Love Relations: Pathology and Normality*. New Haven, CT: Yale University Press.

———— (2000), A concerned critique of psychoanalytic education. *Internat. J. Psycho-Anal.*, 81:97–120.

Kestenberg, J. (1968), Outside and inside, male and female. *J. Amer. Psychoanal. Assn.*, 4:454–476.

Khan, M. M. R. (1979), *Alienation in Perversions*. New York: International Universities Press.

Kinsey, A. C. (1948), *Sexual Behavior in the Human Male*. Bloomington: Indiana University Press, 1998.

———— (1953), *Sexual Behavior in the Human Female*. Bloomington: Indiana University Press, 1998.

Kirsner, D. (2001), The future of psychoanlaytic institutes. *Psychoanal. Psychol.*, 18:195–212.

Klein, G. (1961), Freud's two theories of sexuality. In: *Psychology vs. Metapsychology: Psychoanalytic Essays in Memory of George S. Klein*, ed. M. Gill & P. S. Kolzman. New York: International Universities Press, pp. 14–70.

Klein, M. (1928), Early stages of the Oedipus conflict. *Internat. J. Psycho-Anal.*, 9:167–180.

———— (1950), *Contributions to Psycho-Analysis*. London: Hogarth Press.

———— (1981), *The Writings of Melanie Klein, Vol. I: Love, Guilt, and Reparation*, ed. R. E. Money-Kyrle. London: Hogarth Press.

———— Heimann, P., Isaacs, S. & Rivière, J. (1952), *Developments in Psycho-Analysis*. London: Hogarth Press.

———— & Rivière, J. (1964), *Love, Hate, and Reparation*. New York: Norton.

Koedt, A. (1968), The myth of the vaginal orgasm. In: *Radical Feminism*, ed. A. Koedt, E. Levin & A. Rapone. New York: Quadrangle Books, 1970, pp. 198–207.

Kofman, S. (1985), *The Enigma of Woman*, trans. C. Porter. Ithaca, NY: Cornell University Press.

Kohut, H. (1977), *The Restoration of the Self*. New York: International Universities Press.

Kojève, A. (1969), *Introduction to the Reading of Hegel*. New York: Basic Books.

Konner, M. (1985), One gene at a time. *The New York Times Book Review*, October 6, p. 48.

Kovel, J. (1979), Remarks to the Group for a Radical Human Science, New York City, September 9.

———— (1981), *The Age of Desire*. New York: Pantheon.

Kristeva, J. (1982), *Powers of Horror*, trans. L. Roudiez. New York: Columbia University Press.

———— (1983), *Tales of Love*, trans. L. S. Roudiez. New York: Columbia University Press.

Kropotkin, P. (1902), *Mutual Aid: A Factor of Evolution*. London: Penguin Press, 1972.

Kuhn, T. (1972), *The Structure of Scientific Revolutions*. Chicago: University of Chicago Press.

Kulick, D. (1995), Introduction: The sexual life of anthropologists: Erotic subjectivity and ethnographic work. In: *Taboo: Sex, Identity, and Erotic Subjectivity in Anthropological Fieldwork*, ed. D. Kulick & M. Willson. New York: Routledge, pp. 29–51.

—— & Willson, M., eds. (1995), *Taboo: Sex, Identity, and Erotic Subjectivity in Anthropological Fieldwork*. New York: Routledge.

Lacan, J. (1955–1956), *Le séminaire, Livre 3: Les psychoses*. Paris: Seuil.

—— (1958), The meaning of the phallus. In: *Feminine Sexuality: Jacques Lacan and l'école freudienne*, ed. J. Mitchell & J. Rose. New York: Pantheon, 1982, pp. 54–85.

—— (1977), *Écrits*, trans. A. Sheridan. New York: Norton.

Laclau, E. (1988), Metaphor and social antagonisms. In: *Marxism and the Interpretation of Culture*, ed. C. Nelson & L. Grossberg. Urbana: University of Illinois Press, pp. 249–258.

—— & Mouffe, C. (1985), *Hegemony and Socialist Strategy: Towards a Radical Democratic Politics*. London: New Left Books.

Ladas, A. K., Whipple, B. & Perry, J. D. (1983), *The G Spot*. New York: Dell.

Laplanche, J. (1976), *Life and Death in Psychoanalysis*, trans. J. Mehlman. Annapolis, MD: Johns Hopkins University Press.

—— & Pontalis, J.-B. (1967), *The Language of Psycho-Analysis*, trans. D.N. Smith. New York: Norton, 1973.

Laqueur, T. (1990), *Making Sex*. Cambridge, MA: Harvard University Press.

Lattimore, O. (1951), *Inner Asian Frontiers of China*. Irvington-on-Hudson, NY: Capitol.

Leary, K. (1994), Psychoanalytic "problems" and postmodern "solutions." *Psychoanal. Quart.*, 63:433–465.

Lee, R. B. (1979), *The !Kung San: Women, Men, and Work in a Foraging Society*. Cambridge: Cambridge University Press.

Levenson, E. (1994), Beyond countertransference. *Contemp. Psychoanal.*, 30:691–707.

Levine, J. (1991), *My Enemy, My Love: Man-Hating and Ambivalence in the Nineties*. New York: Doubleday.

Lévi-Strauss, C. (1949), *The Elementary Structures of Kinship*. New York: Eyre & Spottiswode, 1969.

Lewontin, R. C. (1991), *Biology as Ideology: The Doctrine of DNA*. New York: Harper Perennial.

—— Rose, S. & Kamin, L. J. (1984), *Not in Our Genes: Biology, Ideology, and Human Nature*. New York: Pantheon.

Lichtenstein, G. (1987), Competition in women's athletics. In: *Competition: A Feminist Taboo?* ed. V. Miner & H. Longino. New York: Feminist Press, pp. 48–56.

Lichtenstein, H. (1961), Identity and sexuality. *J. Amer. Psychoanal. Assn.*, 19:179–260.

Lightfoot-Klein, H. (1989), *Prisoners of Ritual*. New York: Haworth Press.

Lindenbaum, J. (1985), The shattering of an illusion: The problem of competition in lesbian relationships. In: *Competition: A Feminist Taboo?*, ed. V. Miner & H. Longino. New York: Feminist Press, 1987, pp. 195–208.

Lodge, D. (1984), *Small World: An Academic Romance*. New York: Warner.

Longino, H. E. & Miner, V. (1987), A feminist taboo? In: *Competition: A Feminist Taboo?* ed. V. Miner & H. Longino. New York: Feminist Press, pp. 1–7.

Lydon, M. (1969), The Janis Joplin philosophy: Every moment she is what she feels. *The New York Times Magazine*, February 23, pp. 36–52.

Macey, D. (1992), Phallus: Definitions. In: *Feminism and Psychoanalysis: A Critical Dictionary*, ed. E. Wright. Oxford, Engl.: Blackwell, pp. 318–320.

Mahler, M., Pine, F. & Bergman, A. (1975), *The Psychological Birth of the Human Infant: Symbiosis and Individuation*. London: Hutchinson.

Malone, K. R. (1995), Sexuality and the law: A Lacanian examination of date rape. *Psychoanal. Rev.*, 82:745–767.

Marcus, S. (1965), *The Other Victorians*. New York: Basic Books.

——— (1984), *Freud and the Culture of Psychoanalysis*. Boston: Allen & Unwin.

Marcuse, H. (1955), *Eros and Civilization*. Boston: Beacon Press.

Maroda, K. (1994), *The Power of Countertransference*. Northvale, NJ: Aronson.

Marshall, K. (2000), Termination of an "infinite conversation": Reflections on the last days of an analysis. *Psychoanal. Dial.*, 10:931–947.

Marx, K. (1867), *Capital*. Vol. I. New York: International Publishers, 1967.

Massey, C. (1996), The cultural and conceptual dissonance in theoretical practice: Commentary on "The Bilingual Self," *Psychoanal. Dial.*, 6:123–140.

Masters, W. & Johnson, V. (1966), *Human Sexual Response*. Boston: Little, Brown.

Mauss, M. (1936), Techniques of the body. *Econ. & Soc.*, 2:70–88, 1973.

May, R. (1986), Concerning a psychoanalytic view of maleness. *Psychoanal. Rev.*, 73:179–194.

——— (1995), Re-reading Freud on homosexuality. In: *Disorienting Sexuality*, ed. R. Lesser & T. Domenici. New York: Routledge, pp. 153–166.

McDougall, J. (1980), *Plea for a Measure of Abnormality*. New York: International Universities Press.

——— (1985), *Theatres of the Mind: Illusion and Truth on the Psychoanalytic Stage*. New York: Basic Books.

——— (1989), *Theatres of the Body*. New York: Norton.

——— (1995), *The Many Faces of Eros*. New York: Norton.

McGuire, W., ed. (1988), *The Freud/Jung Letters,* trans. R. Manheim & R. F. C. Hull. Cambridge, MA: Harvard University Press.

Mead, M. (1928), *Coming of Age in Samoa*. New York: Dell.

Merleau-Ponty, M. (1962), *The Phenomenology of Perception,* trans. C. Smith. New York: Routledge.

Miller, J. B. (1976), *Toward a New Psychology of Women*. Boston: Beacon Press.

——— (1991), The construction of anger in women and men. In: *Women's Growth in Connection: Writings from the Stone Center*, ed. J. V. Jordan, A. G. Kaplan, J. B. Miller, I. P. Stiver & J. L. Surrey. New York: Guilford Press, pp. 181–196.

Millett, K. (1970), *Sexual Politics*. New York: Simon & Schuster.

Mills, C. W. (1959), *The Sociological Imagination*. Oxford: Oxford University Press.

Miner, V. & Longino, H., ed. (1987), *Competition: A Feminist Taboo?* New York: Feminist Press.

Mitchell, J. (1963), *Women's Estate*. London: Penguin.

——— (1974), *Psychoanalysis and Feminism*. New York: Pantheon.

——— (1982), Introduction—I. In: *Feminine Sexuality: Jacques Lacan and l'école freudienne*, ed. J. Mitchell & J. Rose. New York: Norton, pp. 1–26.

——— (1991), Commentary on Muriel Dimen's "Deconstructing difference: Gender, splitting and transitional space." *Psychoanal. Dial.*, 2:353–358.

——— & J. Rose, eds. (1982), *Feminine Sexuality: Jacques Lacan and l'école freudienne,* trans. J. Rose. New York: Pantheon.

Mitchell, S. A. (1986), The wings of Icarus. In: *Relational Psychoanalysis,* ed. S. A. Mitchell & L. Aron. Hillsdale, NJ: The Analytic Press, 1999, pp. 153–179.

——— (1988), *Relational Concepts in Psychoanalysis: An Integration*. Cambridge, MA: Harvard University Press.

——— (1993), Introduction [to commentaries on Trop and Stolorow. *Psychoanal. Dial.*, 3:623–626.

——— (2000), *Relationality: From Attachment to Intersubjectivity*. Hillsdale, NJ: The Analytic Press.

——— (2002) *Can Love Last?* New York: Norton.

Money, J. (1961), Components of eroticism in man: II. The orgasm and genital somesthesia. *J. Nerv. Mental Dis.*, 132:289–267.

Morgan, L. H. (1870), *Systems of Consanguinity and Affinity of the Human Family*. Washington, DC: Smithsonian Institution.

Morrison, A. (1989) *Shame: The Underside of Narcissism*. Hillsdale, NJ: The Analytic Press.

Mouffe, C. (1988), Hegemony and new political subjects: Toward a new concept of democracy. In: *Marxism and the Interpretation of Culture*, ed. C. Nelson & L. Grossberg. Urbana: University of Illinois Press, pp. 89–101.

Müller, J. (1932), A contribution to the problem of libidinal development of the genital phase in girls. *Internat. J. Psycho-Anal.*, 13:361–368.

Murphy, R. (1971), *The Dialectics of Social Life*. New York: Basic Books.

——— (1987), *The Body Silent*. New York: Holt.

Muse, D. (1987), Higher stakes, meager yields: Competition among black girls. In: *Competition: A Feminist Taboo?* ed. V. Miner & H. Longino. New York: Feminist Press, pp. 152–160.

Newman, K. (1988), *Falling from Grace*. Berkeley: University of California Press, 1999.

O'Connor, N. & Ryan, J. (1994), *Wild Desires and Mistaken Identities: Lesbianism and Psychoanalysis*. New York: Columbia University Press.

Odier, D. (1997), *Tantric Quest*, trans. J. Gladding. Rochester, VT: Inner Traditions.

Ogden, T. (1989), *The Primitive Edge of Experience*. New York: Aronson.

——— (1994), *Subjects of Analysis*. Northvale, NJ: Aronson.

——— (1997), The perverse subject of analysis. *J. Amer. Psychoanal. Assn.*, 44:1121–1145.

O'Neill, E. (1940), The iceman cometh. In: *Best American Plays, Third Series 1945–51*, ed. J. Gassner. New York: Crown, 1952, pp. 95–172.

Ortner, S. (1973), On key symbols. *Amer. Anthropol.*, 75:1338–1346.

——— (1974), Is male to female as nature is to culture? In: *Women, Culture, and Society*, ed. L. Lamphere & M. Rosaldo. Stanford, CA: Stanford University Press.

Perry, D. C. (1989), Procne's song: The task of feminist literary criticism. In: *Gender/Body/Knowledge: Feminist Reconstructions of Being and Knowing*, ed. A. M. Jaggar & S. Bordo. New Brunswick, NJ: Rutgers University Press, pp. 293–308.

Person, E. (1980), Sexuality as the mainstay of identity. *Signs*, 5:605–630.

——— (1986), A psychoanalytic approach. In: *Theories of Sexuality*, ed. J. Geer & W. O'Donohue. New York: Plenum, pp. 385–410.

Phillips, A. (1988), *Winnicott*. Cambridge, MA: Harvard University Press.

Piaget, J. (1970), *Structuralism*, trans. C. Maschler. New York: Harper & Row.

Pizer, B. (2000), The therapist's routine consultations: A necessary window in the treatment frame. *Psychoanal. Dial.*, 10:197–209.

Pizer, S. (1998), *Building Bridges: Negotiation and Paradox in Psychoanalysis*. Hillsdale, NJ: The Analytic Press.

Pollitt, K. (1994), *Reasonable Creatures*. New York: Knopf.

Price, M. (1996), The power of enactment and the enactment of power. Presented at meeting of Division 39, American Psychological Association, April, New York.

Protter, B. (1996), Classical, modern, and postmodern psychoanalysis: Epistemic transformations. *Psychoanal. Dial.*, 6:533–562.

Rabinow, P. (1984) *The Foucault Reader*. New York: Pantheon.

Ragland-Sullivan, E. (1992), The Imaginary. In: *Feminism and Psychoanalysis: A Critical Dictionary*, ed. E. Wright. Oxford: Blackwell, pp. 173–176.

Random House Dictionary of the English Language (1966), New York: Random House.

Rapp, R., Ross, E. & Bridenthal, R. (1979), Examining family history. *Feminist Studies*, 5:181–200.

Reis, B. E. (1999), Thomas Ogden's phenomenological turn. *Psychoanal. Dial.*, 9:371–394.

Renik, O. (1996), The perils of neutrality. *Psychoanal. Quart.*, 65:495–517.

———— ed. (1998), *Knowledge and Authority in the Psychoanalytic Relationship*. Northvale, NJ: Aronson.

Ring, J. (1987), Perfection on the wing. In: *Competition: A Feminist Taboo?* ed. V. Miner & H. Longino. New York: Feminist Press, pp. 57–69.

Rivera, M. (1989), Linking the psychological and the social: Feminism, poststructuralism, and multiple personality. *Dissociation*, 2:24–31.

Rivière, J. (1929), Womanliness as a masquerade. *Internat. J. Psycho-Anal.*, 10:303–313.

———— (1936), On the genesis of psychical conflict in earliest infancy. In: *Developments in Psycho-Analysis*, ed. M. Klein, P. Heimann & S. Isaacs. London: Hogarth Press, 1952, pp. 37–66.

Rorty, R. (1989), *Contingency, Irony, Solidarity*. New York: Cambridge University Press.

Rose, J. (1986), *Sexuality in the Field of Vision*. London: Verso.

———— (1982), Introduction—II. In: *Feminine Sexuality: Jacques Lacan and l'école Freudienne*, ed. J. Mitchell & J. Rose. New York: Norton, pp. 27–58.

Rose, P. (1984), *Parallel Lives*. New York: Random House.

Rosenfeld, H. (1987), *Impasse and Interpretation*. London: Tavistock/Routledge.

Ross, A. (1994), *The Chicago Gangster Theory of Life: Nature's Debt to Society*. London: Verso.

Rubin, G. (1975), The traffic in women: Notes toward the political economy of sex. In: *Toward an Anthropology of Women*, ed. R. R. Reiter. New York: Monthly Review Press, pp. 157–210.

———— (1984), Thinking sex: Notes for a radical theory of the politics of sexuality. In: *Pleasure and Danger: Exploring Female Sexuality*, ed. C. Vance. New York: Routledge, pp. 267–319.

Ruddick, S. (1980), Maternal thinking. *Feminist Studies*, 6:342–367.

Ruse, M. (1992), Darwinism, In: *Keywords in Evolutionary Biology*, ed. E. F. Keller & E. A. Lloyd. Cambridge, MA: Harvard University Press, pp. 74–80.

Sampson, E. E. (1993), Identity politics: Challenges to psychology's understanding. *Amer. Psychol.*, 48:1219–1230.

———— (1996), Establishing embodiment in psychology. *Theory & Psychol.*, 6:601–624.

Sands, S. H. (1997), Self psychology and projective identification—Whither shall they meet? A reply to the editors. *Psychoanal. Dial.*, 7:651–658.

Santner, E. (1996), *My Own Private Germany*. Princeton, NJ: Princeton University Press.

Sartre, J-P. (1959), *Search for a Method*, trans. H. Barnes. New York: Vintage, 1963.

Scarry, E. (1985), *The Body in Pain*. Oxford: Oxford University Press.

Schachtel, E. (1959), *Metamorphosis*. Hillsdale, NJ: The Analytic Press, 2001.

Schafer, R. (1977), Problems in Freud's psychology of women. In: *Female Psychology: Contemporary Psychoanalytic Views*, ed. H. Blum. New York: International Universities Press, pp. 331–360.

Scheman, N. (1993), *Engenderings*. New York: Routledge.

Schor, N. (1981), Female paranoia: The case for psychoanalytic feminist criticism. *Yale French Stud.*, 62:204–219.

Schore, A. (1996), The experience-dependent maturation of a regulatory system in the orbital prefrontal cortex and the origin of developmental pathology. *Devel. & Psychopathol.*, 8:59–87.

Schroeder, P. (1994), Female genital mutilation—A form of child abuse. *New Eng. J. Med.*, 332:739–740.

Schwartz, D. (1993), Heterophilia—The love that dare not speak its aim. *Psychoanal. Dial.*, 3:643–52.

Schwartz, J. (1996), Physics, philosophy, psychoanalysis, and ideology: On engaging with Adolf Grünbaum. *Psychoanal. Dial.*, 6:503–514.

Scott, J. W. (1988), Deconstructing equality-versus-difference: Or, the uses of postconstructionalist theory for feminism. *Feminist Studies*, 14:33–50.

Sedgwick, E. (1990), *Epistemology of the Closet*. Berkeley: University of California Press.

Seeger, P. (1995), Interview: The old left. *The New York Times Magazine*, January 22, p. 13.

Segal, L. (1994), *Straight Sex: The Politics of Pleasure*. London: Virago.

Shainberg, L. (1989), Finding the zone. *The New York Times Magazine*, April 9, p. 34.

Shapiro, S. A. (1996), The embodied analyst in the Victorian consulting room. *Gender & Psychoanal.*, 1:297–322.

———(2002), The history of feminism and interpersonal psychoanalysis. *Contemp. Psychoanal.*, 38:213–256.

Shostak, M. (1981), *Nisa*. New York: Random House.

Simmel, G. (1950), *The Sociology of Georg Simmel*, trans. ed. K. H. Wolff. London: Free Press of Glencoe.

Slavin, M. O. & Kriegman, D. (1992), *The Adaptive Design of the Human Psyche: Psychoanalysis, Evolutionary Biology, and the Therapeutic Process*. New York: Guilford Press.

Small, M. F. (1993), *Female Choices: Sexual Behavior of Female Primates*. Ithaca, NY: Cornell University Press.

Smuts, B. B. (1985), *Sexual Friendship in Baboons*. Chicago: Aldine.

Sontag, S. (1964), *Against Interpretation*. New York: Anchor Books.

Spezzano, C. (1993), *Affect in Psychoanalysis*. Hillsdale, NJ: The Analytic Press.

Spitz, R. (1957), *No and Yes*. New York: International Universities Press.

Spivak, G. C. & Rooney, E. (1994), In a word. Interview. In: *The Essential Difference*, ed. N. Schor & E. Weed. Bloomington: Indiana University Press, pp. 151–184.

Stack, C. (1994), Different voices, different visions: Gender, culture, and moral reasoning. In: *Women of Color in U.S. Society*, ed. M. B. Zinn & B. T. Dill. Philadelphia: Temple University Press, pp. 291–301.

Stein, R. E. (1991), *Psychoanalytic Theories of Affect*. New York: Praeger.

———(1998), The poignant, the excessive and the enigmatic in sexuality. *Internat. J. Psycho-Anal.*, 79:253–267.

———(2000), "False love"—"Why not?" Fragments of an analysis. *Studies Gender & Sexual.*, 1:167–190.

Stern, D. N. (1985), *The Interpersonal World of the Infant: A View from Psychoanalysis and Developmental Psychology*. New York: Basic Books.

Stern, D. B. (1997), *Unformulated Experience: From Dissociation to Imagination in Psychoanalysis*. Hillsdale, NJ: The Analytic Press.

Steward, J. (1955), *The Theory of Multilineal Evolution*. Bloomington: Indiana University Press.

Stoller, R. (1975), *Perversion: The Erotic Form of Hatred*. Washington, DC: American Psychiatric Press.

——— (1979), *Sexual Excitement*. New York: Pantheon.

Suleiman, S. (1990), *Subversive Intent: Gender, Politics, and the Avant-Garde*. Cambridge, MA: Harvard University Press.

Sullivan, H. S. (1953), *The Interpersonal Theory of Psychiatry*, ed. H. S. Perry & M. L. Gawel. New York: Norton.

Suttles, W. (1964), Affinal ties, subsistence, and prestige among the Coast Salish. *Amer. Anthropol.*, 62:296–305.

Sweetnam, A. (1996), The changing contexts of gender: Between fixed and fluid experience. *Psychoanal. Dial.*, 6:437–460.

——— (1999), Sexual sensations and gender experience: The psycho-logical positions and the erotic third. *Psychoanal. Dial.*, 9:437–460.

Swift, J. (1732), *Jonathan Swift: The Complete Poems*, ed. P. Rogers. New York: Penguin, 1983.

Talbot, M. (2002), Girls just want to be mean. *The New York Times Magazine*, February 24, pp. 24, 38.

Tanakh: The Holy Scriptures (1988), *The New JPS Translation According to the Traditional Hebrew Text*. New York: Jewish Publication Society.

Tate, C. (1996), Psychoanalysis as enemy and ally of African Americans. *J. Psychoanal. Culture & Soc.*, 1:53–62.

Tax, M. (1968), *Woman and Her Mind: The Story of Daily Life*. Boston: New England Free Press, 1970.

Thornhill, R. & Palmer, C. T. (2000), *A Natural History of Rape: Biological Bases of Sexual Coercion*. Cambridge, MA: MIT Press.

Tisdale, S. (1994), *Talk Dirty to Me*. New York: Anchor.

——— (1996), Lecture. Open Center, New York.

Toews, J. (1998), Having and being: The evolution of Freud's Oedipus theory as a moral fable. In: *Freud: Conflict and Culture*, ed. M. S. Roth. New York: Knopf.

Toubia, N. (1993), Female circumcision as a public health issue. *New Engl. J. Med.*, 331:712–716.

Traub, V. (1995), The psychomorphology of the clitoris. *Gay/Lesbian/Queer*, 2:81–114.

Trivers, L. (1972), Parental investment and sexual selection. In: *Sexual Selection and the Descent of Man*, ed. B. Campbell. London: Heinemann.

Tylor, E. B. (1889), On a method of investigating the development of institutions: Applied to laws of marriage and descent. *J. Royal Anthropol. Inst.*, 18:245–69.

Vance, C. S. (1991), Anthropology rediscovers sexuality: A theoretical comment. *Soc. Sci. Med.*, 33:875–884.

Walker, A. (1992), *Possessing the Secret of Joy*. New York: Harcourt Brace Jovanovich.

Walley, C. (1997), Searching for "Voices": Feminism, anthropology, and the global debate over female genital operations. *Cur. Anthropol.*, 12:405–438.

Walton, J. (1995), Re-placing race in (white) psychoanalytic discourse: Founding narratives of feminism. *Crit. Inq.*, 21:775–804.

Webster's New World Dictionary of the American Language. (1956). New York: World.

Weinbaum, B. & Bridges, A. (1979), The other side of the paycheck: Monopoly capital and the structure of consumption. In: *Capitalist Patriarchy and the Case for Socialist Feminism*, ed. Z. Eisenstein. New York: Monthly Review Press, pp. 190–205.

Weisstein, N. (1970), *Kinder, küche, kirche* as scientific law: Psychology constructs the female. In: *Sisterhood Is Powerful*, ed. R. Morgan. New York: Random House, pp. 205–220.

Wentworth, H. & Flexner, S., ed. (1967), *Dictionary of American Slang*. New York: Thomas Y. Crowell.

Weston, K. (1991), *Families We Choose: Lesbians, Gays, Kinship*. New York: Columbia University Press.

Whipple, B. & Komisaruk, B. R. (1991), The G-spot, orgasm, and female ejaculation: Are they related? In: *Proceedings: First International Conference on Orgasm*, ed. P. Kohari. Bombay, India: VRP, pp. 227–237.

Willis, E. (1984), Radical feminism and feminist radicalism. In: *The Sixties Without Apology*, ed. S. Sayres, A. Stephanson, S. Aronowitz & F. Jameson. Minneapolis: University of Minnesota Press, pp. 91–118.

Wilner, W. (1998), Sex: An interpersonal view. Colloquium on Sexuality in Psychoanalysis, New York University Postdoctoral Program in Psychotherapy and Psychoanalysis, March 6.

Wilson, E. O. (1977), *Sociobiology*. Cambridge, MA: Harvard University Press.

Winnicott, D. W. (1953), Transitional objects and transitional phenomena. *Internat. J. Psycho-Anal.*, 34:89–97.

———— (1958), Hate in the counter-transference. In: *Collected Papers: Through Paediatrics to Psycho-analysis*. New York: Basic Books, 1975, pp. 194–203.

———— (1960), The theory of the parent–infant relationship. In: *The Maturational Processes and the Facilitating Environment*. New York: International Universities Press, 1965, pp. 37–55.

———— (1969a), Creativity and its origins. In: *Playing and Reality*. New York: Basic Books, 1971, pp. 65–85.

———— (1969b), The use of an object and relating through identification. In: *Playing and Reality*. New York: Basic Books, 1971, pp. 86–94.

———— (1971), *Playing and Reality*. New York: Penguin.

———— (1975), *Collected Papers: Through Paediatrics to Psycho-Analysis*. New York: Basic Books.

Wolstein, B. (1975), Toward the conception of unique individuality. *Contemp. Psychoanal.*, 11:145–160.

Wright, E., ed. (1992), *Feminism and Psychoanalysis: A Critical Dictionary*. Oxford: Blackwell.

Wrye, H. (1998), The embodiment of desire: Relinking the bodymind within the analytic dyad. In: *Relational Perspectives on the Body*, ed. L. Aron & F. S. Anderson. Hillsdale, NJ: The Analytic Press, pp. 97–116.

———— & Welles, J. (1996), *The Narration of Desire: Erotic Transferences and Countertransferences*. Hillsdale, NJ: The Analytic Press.

Wynne-Edwards, V. (1962), *Animal Dispersion in Relation to Social Behavior*. New York: Haffner.

Yanigasako, S. J. & Collier, J. F. (1987), Toward a unified analysis of gender and kinship. In: *Gender and Kinship: Toward a Unified Analysis*, ed. J. F. Collier & S. J. Yanigasako. Stanford, CA: Stanford University Press, pp. 14–52.

Young, I. M. (1990), *Throwing Like a Girl and Other Essays*. Bloomington: Indiana University Press.

Zborowski, M. & Herzog, E. (1952), *Life Is with People: The Jewish Little Town in Eastern Europe*. New York: International Universities Press.

Žižek, S. (1989), *The Sublime Object of Ideology*. London: Verso.

———— (1996), Revisioning Lacanian social criticism: The law and its obscene double. *J. Psychoanal. Cult. & Soc.*, 1:15–25.

Zuk, M. (2002), *Sexual Selections: What We Can and Can't Learn About Sex from Animals*. Berkeley: University of California Press.

Index

317

P30 definition of postmodernism

P48 Do humans _desire_ or procreate?

Chapt 2 Gender as multiplicity not entity.

78 Difference between multiplicity (dissociation) & multiplicity

138 Fecal smell vignette with the transference interp! then must hold shame. (all 3 of K's self obj. transf contained)

142 Symbolic power of Physicality (sex)

160 libido is to sex as hunger is to nutrition

163 Discussion of the meaning of libido

173 admitting to sex oth on pt of then

198 Doesn't know what masc / fem are. Discussion of what gender is

217 → sex: Between _dream_ & waking life Very important

220 The value of liberated desire

274 TRUTH is what is held by Power

282 Whole - obj. rel. is also a moral stand.

282 Discussion of stigmatizing via diagnosis

287 Label of perversion is clinically superfluous.

P10 Dwes on Transitional space

P23 Psa denies Social theory (including Marx)

P 35 similarities among Darwin / Marx / Psa / Postmod.